TE DEUM

Te Deum

The Church and Music

PAUL WESTERMEYER

A Textbook

A Reference

A History

An Essay

FORTRESS PRESS | MINNEAPOLIS

To the students I have been privileged to teach,
from whom I have been privileged to learn.

TE DEUM
The Church and Music
Paul Westermeyer

Copyright © 1998 Augsburg Fortress. All rights reserved. Except for brief quotations in critical articles or reviews, no part of this book may be reproduced in any
manner without prior written permission from the publisher or from the other
copyright holders. Write to: Permissions, Augsburg Fortress, P.O. Box 1209, Minneapolis, MN 55440-1209.

Editors: Norma Aamodt Nelson, Frank Stoldt, Lani Willis
Cover art: *Choir of Angels,* Hans Memling (c. 1433-1494). Netherlandish. Muse-
    um voor Schone Kunsten, Antwerp. Photo copyright © SuperStock, Inc. Used
    by permission.
Cover design: David Meyer
Interior design: Ellen Maly

Library of Congress Cataloguing-in-Publication Data
Westermeyer, Paul, 1940–
Te Deum : the church and music / Paul Westermeyer
p.   cm.
Includes bibliographical reference and index.
ISBN 0-8006-3146-3 (alk. paper)
1. Music--Religious aspects--Christianity. Music in churches.
3. Public worship. 4. Church music—Protestant churches.
I. Title.
BV290.W47   1998
246'.75'09--dc21   98-4062
                                                                              CIP
The paper used in this publication meets the minimum requirements of American
National Standard for Information Sciences—Permanence of Paper for Printed
Materials, ANSI Z329.48-1984. ∞ ™
Printed in the USA.

1-3146   ISBN 0-8006-3146-3
03 02   2 3 4 5 6 7 8 9 10

Table of Contents

REFORMATION CURRENTS

AFTER THE REFORMATION

BEFORE AND AFTER THE FRENCH AND AMERICAN REVOLUTIONS

NOW

Abbreviations

ABD	The Anchor Bible Dictionary
ANF	The Ante-Nicene Fathers
BH	The Baptist Hymnal, 1991
CCL	Corpus Christianorum, Series Latina
CM	Current Musicology
DH	A Dictionary of Hymnology (Julian)
EH82	The [Episcopal] Hymnal 1982, 1985
HC	The Hymnal 1982 Companion (Glover)
HCSR	Hymnology, A Collection of Source Readings (David Music)
IDB	The Interpreter's Dictionary of the Bible
LBW	Lutheran Book of Worship, 1978
LW	Luther's Works
MBE	Music in the Baroque Era (Bukofzer)
MBW	Moravian Book of Worship, 1995
MECL	Music in Early Christian Literature (James McKinnon)
MMA	Music in the Middle Ages (Reese)
MR	Music in the Renaissance (Reese)
NGDAM	New Grove Dictionary of American Music
NGDMI	New Grove Dictionary of Musical Instruments

NGDMM	New Grove Dictionary of Music and Musicians
NPNF	A Select Library of the Nicene and Post-Nicene Fathers of the Christian Church
PG	Patrologiae cursus completus, Series Graeca
PH	The Presbyterian Hymnal, 1990
PL	Patrologiae cursus completus, Series Latina
RL	Rejoice in the Lord, 1985
SL	Dr. Martin Luthers Sämmtliche Schriften (Saint Louis edition)
SRMH	Source Readings in Music History (Oliver Strunk)
UMH	The United Methodist Hymnal, 1989
WA	Dr. Martin Luthers Werke (Weimar Ausgabe)
WEP	Worship of the English Puritans (Davies)
WTE	Worship and Theology in England (Davies)

Introduction

An earlier book, *The Church Musician*,[1] was stimulated by the need to understand the church musician's role. This book was stimulated by the need to understand church music itself. It began before *The Church Musician* and logically precedes it as context, but was put on hold because it and other projects seemed more pressing.

This book began to take shape after I had taught an interdisciplinary undergraduate course about theology and church music at Elmhurst College a number of times. I used many different texts and readings for the class. All were useful in their own ways, but students expressed frustration at the lack of a single satisfactory introduction to the topic. Teachers of similar courses across the country have shared with me the same frustration: they do not have an adequate introductory text.

The course I taught at Elmhurst College was designed for a variety of persons with a variety of backgrounds. Some students had musical training or were music majors; some had virtually no musical background at all. Some were conversant with theological categories; some knew almost nothing about theology. Some were faithful churchgoers from a variety of confessional backgrounds; some had almost no contact with the church whatsoever; a few wanted no such contact, though this topic intrigued them. Some took the course because of an interest; some did it to fulfill a requirement. A successful textbook for this varied group would have to give an introduction to church music, to the musical and theological issues it raises, and to the materials of its study. It would have to be coherent but brief, understandable but not contemptuously simplistic.

[1] Paul Westermeyer, *The Church Musician* (San Francisco: Harper & Row, Publishers, 1988; rev. ed., Minneapolis: Augsburg Fortress, 1997).

After teaching the undergraduate course at Elmhurst for a number of years, I taught a similar one for graduate students enrolled
in both Yale University's Institute of Sacred Music and its Divinity
School, then briefer but comparable ones at Trinity Seminary in
Columbus, Ohio, and the Lutheran School of Theology at Chicago. In each of these instances I again sensed the need for a textbook
that did not exist—a basic interdisciplinary introduction to church
music for a wide variety of students, including but not limited to
future church musicians and pastors. The course I currently teach
at Luther Seminary, and to some extent the one at St. Olaf College
for undergraduates, have heightened my recognition of the need.

Not only the students in college and seminary classes for whom
it was specifically written, but also musicians, pastors, and thought-
ful Christians generally may find what is treated here will help them
either individually or in study groups. It is intended to provide perspective on a topic that is ever-present, often misunderstood, and
upon examination always more complicated than first appearances
suggest. I do not mean to imply that this text or any text will be
complete or a quick fix for the grid of problems that music can raise
in churches, but I hope it introduces the topic, serves as a resource,
provides perspective, contributes to solutions, and makes for
delight in church music.

In February of 1992 the Laidlaw Lectures at Knox College at the
University of Toronto in Canada provided the opportunity to complete initial forms of the chapters on psalmody and the Reformation. The chapter on controversies among the Calvinists about
psalm singing had an earlier form in October of 1994 as the Gheens
Lecture at Southern Baptist Theological Seminary in Louisville, Kentucky, and was later published in *The Hymn*.[2] Several articles I have
written, cited at the beginning of chapter 15, served as the basis for
parts of the last chapters. Other parts were brewing before I taught
the church music course at Elmhurst College, especially in research
in graduate school at the University of Chicago. Everything has been
reworked, most of it written from scratch during a sabbatical in
1996–1997, for which I am grateful to Luther Seminary.

This book seeks to provide a succinct introductory overview to
church music from a historical and theological point of view. It is in
no sense complete. It is limited by constraints I have set on numbers
of pages, what might fit one quarter or semester of study, and what

---

[2] Paul Westermeyer, "The Breach Repair'd," *The Hymn* 47:1 (January 1996):
10–16.

relates especially to the English-speaking West as filtered to the
United States. It assumes teachers would contract or expand it and
does not include detailed musicological, ethnomusicological, sociological, institutional, liturgiological, hymnological, or other similar
considerations. There could be more chapters, and each chapter
could be a whole book. Some things are left out. More thorough
studies are available about many of the topics treated here.

This book bears relations to and lives in partnership with, but is
not the following:

- a text one might use in a music theory class, though it includes
  syntactical musical details
- a text one might use in a class devoted solely to theology,
  though its orientation is theological
- a history or survey of music, such as Karl Gustav Fellerer, *The
  History of Catholic Church Music*,[3] Donald Grout's *A History
  of Western Music*,[4] or Andrew Wilson-Dickson's *The Story of
  Christian Music*,[5] David Hiley's *Western Plainchant*,[6] or
  William Rice's *Concise History of Church Music*,[7] though it
  is organized in a historical way
- a music appreciation text such as Joseph Machlis's *The Enjoyment of Music*[8]
- a text about hymnody, such as Eskew and McElrath's *Sing with
  Understanding*,[9] Millar Patrick's *The Story of the Church's Song*,[10]
  or Reynolds and Price's *A Survey of Christian Hymnody*,[11]
  though hymnody comes into play

---

[3] Karl Gustav Fellerer, trans. Francis A. Brunner, *The History of Catholic
Church Music* (Baltimore: Helicon Press, 1961).

[4] Donald Jay Grout and Claude V. Palisca, *A History of Western Music*, 5th ed.
(New York: W. W. Norton & Company, 1996). Any of the Grout editions or any
standard history of music will illustrate.

[5] Andrew Wilson-Dickson, *The Story of Christian Music* (Minneapolis: Augsburg Fortress, 1996).

[6] David Hiley, *Western Plainchant: A Handbook* (Oxford: Clarendon Press, 1993).

[7] William C. Rice, *A Concise History of Church Music* (Nashville: Abingdon
Press, 1964).

[8] Joseph Machlis, *The Enjoyment of Music*, 4th ed. (New York: W. W. Norton
& Company, 1977). Any of the Machlis editions or any standard music appreciation text will illustrate.

[9] Harry Eskew and Hugh T. McElrath, *Sing with Understanding: An Introduction to Christian Hymnology* 2d rev. ed. (Nashville: Church Street Press, 1995).

[10] Millar Patrick, rev. James Rawlings Sydnor, *The Story of the Church's Song*
(Richmond: John Knox Press, 1962).

[11] William J. Reynolds and Milburn Price, *A Survey of Christian Hymnody*
(Carol Stream: Hope Publishing Company, 1987).

- a history of ideas about the church's art music like Quentin Faulkner's *Wiser Than Despair*[12]
- what might be called a theology of music: Harold Best's *Music through the Eyes of Faith*,[13] Archibald Davison's *Church Music: Illusion and Reality*,[14] Edward Foley's *Ritual Music*[15] (a "liturgical musicology"), Joseph Gelineau's *Voices and Instruments in Christian Worship*,[16] Donald Hustad's *Jubilate II*,[17] two texts by Calvin Johansson,[18] Erik Routley's *Church Music and the Christian Faith*,[19] Miriam Therese Winter's *Why Sing?*,[20] and *Ears to Hear . . . Tongues to Sing: Church Music as Pastoral Theology*, a work in progess by Francis Williamson
- a "practical" manual as in Lawrence and Ferguson's *A Musician's Guide to Church Music*,[21] Lovelace's and Rice's *Music and Worship in the Church*,[22] Dwight Steere's *Music in Protestant Worship*[23]

It bears a similarity to some books that are out of print:
- David Appleby's *History of Church Music*[24]
- Winfred Douglas's *Church Music in History and Practice*[25]

---

[12] Quentin Faulkner, *Wiser Than Despair: The Evolution of Ideas in the Relationship of Music and the Christian Church* (Westport: Greenwood Press, 1996). See p. xii.

[13] Harold M. Best, *Music Through the Eyes of Faith* (New York: Harper, 1993).

[14] Archibald T. Davison, *Church Music: Illusion and Reality* (Cambridge: Harvard University Press, 1960).

[15] Edward Foley, *Ritual Music: Studies in Liturgical Musicology* (Beltsville: The Pastoral Press, 1995).

[16] Joseph Gelineau, *Voices and Instruments in Christian Worship: Principles, Laws, Applications*, trans. Clifford Howell (Collegeville: The Liturgical Press, 1964).

[17] Donald P. Hustad, *Jubilate II: Church Music in Worship and Renewal* (Carol Stream: Hope Publishing Company, 1993).

[18] Calvin M. Johansson, *Discipling Music Ministry* (Peabody: Hendrickson Publishers, 1992); and *Music and Ministry: A Biblical Counterpoint* (Peabody: Hendrickson Publishers, 1984).

[19] Erik Routley, *Church Music and the Christian Faith* (Carol Stream: Agape, 1978).

[20] Miriam Therese Winter, *Why Sing? Toward a Theology of Catholic Church Music* (Washington: The Pastoral Press, 1984).

[21] Joy E. Lawrence and John A. Ferguson, *A Musician's Guide to Church Music* (New York: The Pilgrim Press, 1981).

[22] Austin C. Lovelace and William C. Rice, *Music and Worship in the Church* (New York: Abingdon Press, 1960).

[23] Dwight Steere, *Music in Protestant Worship* (Richmond: John Knox Press, 1960).

[24] David P. Appleby, *History of Church Music* (Chicago: Moody Press, 1965).

[25] Winfred Douglas, rev. Leonard Ellinwood, *Church Music in History and Practice: Studies in the Praise of God* (New York: Charles Scribner's Sons, 1961).

- Charles Etherington's *Protestant Worship Music* [26]
- C. Henry Phillips's *The Singing Church* [27]
- Erik Routley's *The Church and Music* [28]
- Russel N. Squire's *Church Music* [29] and
- Robert Stevenson's *Patterns of Protestant Church Music.* [30]

It also has affinities with Edward Foley's *From Age to Age*, which fortunately is in print, but it does not attempt Foley's continuity and does not cover the additional elements of architecture, books, and vessels. [31]

It threads its way among these approaches as a relatively brief overview [32] of some themes or chapters in the history of church music, a theological essay with the people's song the central concern. It does not avoid the music itself, but I am more concerned about what stands behind the music, reasons for or against it, restrictions placed on it, or what has pushed it one way or another. If you discover something of the church's encounter with music in worship before we came on the scene, my intent will have been realized. The book is designed to raise some of the issues church music raises and to meet the needs I have faced in my classrooms. I hope others will find it useful in their classes as well, flexible enough to be adapted in part or whole by teachers for a wide variety of people from many different backgrounds, with enough suggestions in the footnotes and bibliography for further study in sources that are as accessible as possible.

Though this is conceived as a text and resource book you probably will not find it a dispassionate analysis. I hope not anyway. The topic is more interesting than that, and a survey of details doesn't help learning very much. I have some opinions. I'm not sure I can

---

[26] Charles L. Etherington, *Protestant Worship Music: Its History and Practice* (New York: Holt, Rinehart and Winston, 1962).

[27] C. Henry Phillips, *The Singing Church: An Outline History of the Music Sung by Choir and People* (London: Faber and Faber Ltd., 1945).

[28] Erik Routley, *The Church and Music: An Enquiry into the History, the Nature, and the Scope of Christian Judgment on Music* (London: Gerald Duckworth & Co. Ltd., 1950). The quotation is from p. 9.

[29] Russel N. Squire, *Church Music: Musical and Hymnological Developments in Western Christianity* (St. Louis: The Bethany Press, 1962).

[30] Robert M. Stevenson, *Patterns of Protestant Church Music* (Durham: Duke University Press, 1953).

[31] Edward Foley: *From Age to Age: How Christians Celebrated the Eucharist* (Chicago: Liturgy Training Publications, 1991).

[32] Not brief in the sense of Kenneth W. Osbeck, *The Endless Song: 13 Lessons in Music and Worship of the Church* (Grand Rapids: Kregel Publications, 1987).

hide them, and I'm not sure I want to hide them. There's a narrative here, written from my perspective in my time and place, with no apologies. I'll insert opinions from time to time—not solutions, but opinions. I hope they'll encourage you to grapple with the issues yourself, argue with me and the others we encounter along the way, and figure out what you think. The book is organized historically to keep it disciplined by the data and to provide perspective. I have attempted to be as accurate as possible and am grateful for and of necessity dependent on the work of many scholars and secondary sources. Anyone who wants to can work through the secondary sources to the primary ones and correct what I may have gotten wrong. That is only the first step, however. Meaning behind and beyond the details is the central concern about which I hope I have contributed to some dialogue.

Students have often requested a time line. The one given here is by no means complete. It includes mostly nonmusical entries to set things in context. Musical entries are sprinkled in with broader currents. The skeletal character of the list should allow you to weave in your own specific concerns.

I am deeply indebted to teachers and colleagues across almost four decades with whom I have studied and discussed many of the topics treated here. If I have unconsciously used some of their phrases, that should be read as a tribute, not a slight. I have tried to give credit where it is due and hope I have not missed something.

I owe the library staff at Luther Seminary a strong word of gratitude, especially Terry Dinovo, Bruce Eldevik, and Julie Bickel. Librarians are the salt of the earth, as a group the most gracious and competent people I know. Without them we who teach could not do our jobs. While working on this book I have plagued the three just named with continual requests, sometimes obscure ones, and they have always responded efficiently and cheerfully. I am most appreciative of their knowledge, kindness, and hard work.

Numerous friends and colleagues have graciously read and critiqued initial drafts of various portions of the book: David Cherwien, Susan Cherwien, John Ferguson, Terrence Fretheim, Fred Gaiser, Kenneth Hart, Sarah Henrich, Mark Hillmer, Arland Hultgren, James Limburg, Daniel Simundson, and John Witvliet. I have had conversations and correspondence about it with Gerhard Cartford, Carl Schalk, and May Schwarz. In his characteristic way, Martin Marty read the whole book and made some of the most perceptive and helpful comments, both in details and overall perspective. My friend Francis Williamson, with whom I have had discussions about church music since seminary days, also read the whole manuscript. As usual, he forcefully challenged me with pages of closely reasoned suggestions. The students in my church music class at Luther Seminary the first quarter of the 1997–98 academic year used the book, made corrections, and raised questions from their various perspectives. None of these people bears responsibility for the final text, which is mine, but their suggestions have forced me to rethink and rework things for the better. I am indebted to them all.

The Church Musician was dedicated to the choirs and congregations I have served. This book is dedicated to my students. As the choirs and congregations helped me hammer out the role of the church musician, so my students have helped me search out the nature of church music. To them I am profoundly grateful.

Paul Westermeyer
7 December 1997
Commemoration of Ambrose, Bishop of Milan, 397

OLD TESTAMENT

The Study of Church Music

Analyzing the Terrain

For the average churchgoer, church music is a staple of church life. It is part of most worship services. It may vary widely—from the congregation's hymns, litanies, and responses to large or small choirs of singers with more carefully prepared pieces to instrumental music by organ, piano, guitar, brass, strings, percussion, bells, winds, synthesizers, or whatever. Since church music is so ubiquitous, it is often viewed as a simple matter. Even when it becomes a subject of considerable dispute, as in our day, it is usually viewed as self-evident. To study it, however, is to uncover its complexity.

What makes church music complex is the number of disciplines it calls into play. That makes it all the more interesting, of course, but also suggests its difficulties. To sort out the areas involved, take the words "church music" and consider what they imply.

"Church" brings with it the thought of what the church is engaged in, usually called theology, which reflects on and has implications for music and everything else in its life. Since the central documents of that theology are the Old and New Testaments, biblical study is necessary. There is a history of what the church has done as well as what it has thought, so history is important. Worship has been the focus in the life of the church and the point where music is most directly involved, so liturgical studies must be included. The church has been concerned about education, and music is often tied to that concern, so Christian education cannot be forgotten. Since music is an art, artistic issues are involved. The church has a mission, so evangelism and ethics are present, though they could fit under the broader heading of theology as well. Hymnology, first the study of hymn texts and then the music that clothes those texts, can be included as a separate category, though it could be subsumed under liturgical studies. All the categories could be subdivided—history, for example, into the periods of the Old and New Testaments and then early, medieval, Reformation, and modern church history; theology into branches such as systematic, practical, pastoral, missional, and ethical.

The word "music" in "church music" suggests fewer divisions, but no less complicated ones. The history of music is immediately important with all the actual music composed and used in the church and in the surrounding world. Since the church reaches around the globe by intention and practice, cross-cultural musicological and ethnomusicological studies are called into play. To understand the syntax of music, music theory is involved. Aesthetic considerations cannot be dismissed. As every musician knows, in order to understand what musical activity really is all about, one has to be involved in doing it, which can be called applied music. How music is learned and taught calls music education into the mix.

Obviously what we are dealing with here is profoundly interdisciplinary. No one person has probably ever been, nor ever will be completely and genuinely able to understand and integrate all these fields. Its complexity is part of the reason church music is so often defined in narrow or fragmented terms dependent on the spheres of interest or expertise of the individuals who make the definitions. A comprehensive picture is an impossible ideal; however, it is possible to be open enough to the dimensions of this interdisciplinary discipline to avoid being trapped by our own biases. If we can't know everything about all the possible areas church music involves, a look at some ways the church has approached it at the very least introduces the complexity of the subject.

Church Music in Practice

Church music is not only a discipline to be studied. It is also an ongoing activity practiced week in and week out in churches throughout the world. How one studies and approaches it has practical ramifications. To illustrate the difficulty of defining church music in narrow terms, take this example:

On any given Sunday when a choir is singing an anthem, the anthem obviously has to be chosen. What determines the choice? The choir director is likely to ask several questions. 1) Can the choir sing it? 2) Is the music "good"? 3) Is the text religious? (The third question is sometimes phrased, "Does the text mention Jesus or God?") The first question requires a judgment about applied music and perhaps music education, the second one is aesthetic, and the third implies virtually no theological judgment at all or at best a negative theological one.

The minister or priest who wants a say in the choice of the anthem is likely to have some other concerns. 1) If the church follows historic liturgical patterns, the concern will be for a text that fits the lessons for a given Sunday. 2) If the church is issue-oriented and gearing up for a march related to justice, the clergy is likely to ask for a text that embodies a prophetic call. The request for this text will probably be made very late, sometimes a week or less in advance, because marches for justice cannot always be predetermined or planned. They occur as they occur and demand timely responses. 3) If the minister has a pastoral orientation, something with which the people are familiar may be sought. 4) A minister who thinks the service should entice seekers will desire something with immediate appeal. The clergy may want to replace the choir director and choir with a few singers who have microphones. In the first instance the judgment is liturgical, in the second ethical, in the third potentially pastoral, and in the fourth presumably related to evangelism.

Note that the musician in this instance makes virtually no theological judgment, and the clergy makes no musical judgment. The musician may then accuse the pastor of having no musical understanding, and the pastor is likely to say the musician does not know anything about worship, ethics, people, or evangelism. These configurations can easily change so that the musician accuses the pastor of not knowing anything about worship, for example. However the accusations are made and however correct they may be, both parties are, in the final analysis, wrong because they're playing the game in different ballparks. As long as the frames of reference are so different, there is little hope for discussion and much less hope for any happy issue from these afflictions. The study of church music ought to introduce the dimensions of the topic. It will not solve all the problems, but it does have the advantage of getting the players in the same ballpark.

Why Study Church Music?

The foregoing discussion suggests four reasons for studying church music. One is quite practical. If you are going to be involved in the life of the church either as pastor or musician, or any other capacity in which you will have to make musical decisions, you need to know something about the disciplines related to your decision making.

Another reason is more "theoretical." Study of anything has practical ramifications, though they may not at first be apparent. But one does not have to begin with the practice. Church music can be studied for the same reason a mountain can be climbed—because it's there. What makes church music especially intriguing, perhaps, is the number of areas it involves or impinges upon. People from various backgrounds and disciplines can relate to church music from their own perspectives, as well as learn something about areas they may not normally encounter.

For example, church music is a cultural matter. The music the church uses does not happen in a vacuum. It happens in a specific time and place. The time and place have a history, memory, community, and trajectory that attend them, which at times—like our time—are in various states of upheaval. At other times things may be more calm. The cultural issues involve an enormous range of topics that historians, ethnomusicologists, sociologists, philosophers, and others study in a variety of ways. Church music is worth encountering because, like all interesting fields of study, it challenges and expands the mind. It is worth investigating for purely intrinsic reasons. Or, to say this with a slightly different slant, it's part of the culture and therefore worth knowing about.

There is a third reason to study church music. Consider the following quotation from the very beginning of Martin Marty's *A Short History of Christianity*.

> Historic Christianity has worn many faces. A hymn-sing in a plain Methodist chapel in Iowa and high mass at St. Peter's in Rome; a peasant prayer and an Aquinian system; the percussive affirmation of a tribesman and a choral rendition of the B Minor Mass; the simplicity of a St. Francis and the pomp of a Renaissance pope; the withdrawal of an anchoritic monk and the involvement of a worker-priest or socialist Christian—all are somehow directly related to the Christian faith.[1]

Why begin a book about the history of Christianity with so many musical allusions? Of the ten "faces" of Christianity mentioned, at least five imply music, and the anchoritic monk in a negative way may imply music by the possibility of its absence. Music is often mentioned in a context like this because it provides a symbol for so

---

[1] Martin Marty, *A Short History of Christianity* (New York: The World Publishing Company, 1971, first published 1959), p. 15.

many things. A Methodist hymn-sing, a Calvinist congregation's unison metrical psalm, a Lutheran congregation's chorale, a Roman Catholic choir's Palestrina motet, or an African congregation's percussive sound all are theological and musical embodiments of specific communities. The faith of a community comes to life in its music-making. In music, the faith and life of a people take flesh.

This primacy of identity is why the music of a Christian congregation is a source of such enormous peace or such enormous war, and why some pastors virtually demand certain types of music, and why musicians are so adamant about the music they choose, and why the people want certain hymns. The stakes are high precisely because the musical doing of a people is so potent and so expressive of its being.

To study church music is to attempt to sort things out with some objectivity. This study reveals coherences as the church has struggled with musical matters, to see why a given historical context and theological position may have musical results or why a musical position may have presuppositions and implications not apparent at first glance. One can also see why some theological and musical presuppositions may lead to opposing conclusions, or how unexamined practices may actually oppose what a church believes. This knowledge in and of itself does not necessarily solve problems, but it does provide insights that can help lead to solutions wherever people show willingness to do the solving.

The value of objectivity suggests yet another reason for the study of church music, namely, backing off for a dispassionate view. Music, worship, and theological points of view involve us all at points beyond the rational. They arouse emotions and both conscious and subconscious likes and dislikes, which is true whether we are believers, nonbelievers, pietists, fundamentalists, orthodox, agnostics, or atheists. Nonrational factors are always at work when one deals with issues of this kind.

A student of this topic needs to prepare for this nonrational aspect. None of us will like studying each and every topic under the heading of church music. But our likes and dislikes do not stop the existence of something. Some people react negatively to certain facets, while others react positively. If you are prepared for this dichotomy, the experience can be more helpful than you expect.

A study of this type gives you a chance to back off, suspend emotions and coercive tactics for a period of dispassionate investigation, and give everything a hearing. There is no better way to understand one's own tradition than to see it in the light of what opposes it or raises questions about it. I have often organized church music courses with people taking the roles of different historical figures related in one way or another to church music, then having them discuss their positions in public dialogues with one another. New insights invariably emerge when a mix of people across the centuries—like Miriam, Deborah, David, Amos, Luke, Ambrose, Augustine, Gregory the Great, Guido d'Arezzo, Hildegard of Bingen, Machaut, Palestrina, Calvin, Luther, Bach, Catherine Winkworth, Pius X, Ralph Vaughan Williams, Marian Anderson, Jon Michael Spencer, Carl Schalk, John Rutter, David Cherwien, Gracia Grindal, Marty Haugen, and Handt Hanson—are in the same room together having a discussion.

I have proposed four reasons for studying church music: the practical, the theoretical or intrinsic, sorting out the strands that church music embodies, and backing off for a dispassionate view. The last of these suggests a hazard.

A Hazard

Church music, like theology and the church itself, raises life-and-death questions about the orientation of one's whole existence. We, the finite creature, are dealing here with matters that relate to the infinite creator. The danger in our objective, analytical, dispassionate activity, then, is that we not only study what we do in relation to the creator, but that we subtly shift our stance until we presume to be the creator. We can easily make the fatal mistake of presuming to be God or at least have the capacity to manipulate God. It is a hazard of the theologian and a hazard of anyone who studies matters related to the faith and life of the church.

Maintaining a certain distance to analyze things is obviously necessary, otherwise no study and no understanding would take place. But we are also human beings who worship and sing, who exist in relation to God as God's creatures. One has to be careful therefore not to confuse the kind of thinking necessary to the study of church music with the worship of God itself. The two are not unrelated, of course. One may even generate the other, and our worship should surely be informed by the study we do. But the two are not identifiable and should not be confused.

With those reasons for this book's being, and with that caution, I invite you to the study.

Old Testament

2

Prolegomena

Perspective

Music in modern times tends to be regarded as extrinsic to life—an extra, a commodity, a sophisticated endeavor to which only a few initiates are privy. Its center of gravity is what happens in concerts, concerts of all sorts from folk to rock to country western to high art in concert halls and churches or wherever, but concerts nonetheless. Concerts are like museums. They preserve artifacts, even if the artifacts be from our age. They're sophisticated extras, for people who can afford them. Not everybody goes to them, and many people are quite certain they can do without them.

At the same time music has in some sense become inescapable in the commercial culture all around us. Doesn't that contradict music's extrinsic character in our period? After all, we hear music on the television, at shopping malls, in elevators, on telephone hold lines, in head sets, and in cars and busses. Depending on your perspective, however, all of that is regarded as subliminal, an entertainment we can tune out or turn off, or an annoyance—which brings us back to where we started: music is an extrinsic feature of life we can do without, even though we might not buy so much without its seductive lure.

For primal humanity, however, music was intrinsic to life. As Eric Werner says, "It was an organic part of daily life."[1] It was natural—linked with birth, death, dancing, work, and worship. You didn't go to concerts to get music or hear it through headphones, taking or leaving it at will. You sang it as you put your children to sleep, rowed and worked in the field with others, danced, prayed.

---

[1] E. Werner, "Music," *The Interpreter's Dictionary of the Bible*, ed. George Arthur Buttrick, (New York: Abingdon Press, 1962), hereafter IDB, K–Q, p. 457.

Another way to say it is that music for the ancients was functional. For the people of the Old Testament, which is where the
study of church music begins, Alfred Sendrey says, "The music of
Ancient Israel was, basically, a utilitarian art."[2] In the myth of "the
origin of skills" found in Genesis 4:20–22, Jubal, the first musician,
engages in the "practical" occupation of music alongside the first
smith and cattle-breeder.[3]

That music was functional or utilitarian does not mean it pertained to an arbitrary usefulness with no relation to beauty. It does
not mean artistic elements were absent from music, or that no specially talented musical people existed at the beginnings of human life
and culture. It means rather *organic to* and *characteristic of* human
life. Certainly there have always been those who practiced their craft
and delighted their sisters and brothers[4] by making "controlled variations of sound in the right way."[5] Nor are we totally different from
our ancestors. We still use music in community without a performance mentality attached to it. We dance and pray with music, sing
lullabies to our babies, hum, cry, and whistle. We cannot escape our
humanity at its deepest level, nor can we escape music's connection
with it.

However, our perspective is different, at least superficially. We
need to enter the study of the Old Testament and its music at the
deepest human level, not a more superficial one. Actually we need to
enter the whole study of church music at the deepest human level,
because the music of worship, like worship itself, is one of the most
profound and enduring of human concerns—which leads to the following considerations.

The Story

Jewish feasts or festivals were originally nomadic or agricultural.
The origins of Passover, for example, related to a primitive nomadic

---

[2] Alfred Sendrey, *Music in Ancient Israel* (New York: Philosophical Library,
1969), p. 32; *cf.* p. 61; and Alfred Sendrey and Mildred Norton, *David's Harp: The
Story of Music in Biblical Times* (New York: The New American Library of World
Literature, 1964), p. 108.

[3] Victor H. Matthews, "Music in the Bible," *The Anchor Bible Dictionary,* ed.
David Noel Freedman (New York: Doubleday, 1992), hereafter ABD, 4: K–N,
p. 930. *Cf.* Sendrey, *Music in Ancient Israel*, pp. 60–61

[4] See Sendrey, *Music in Ancient Israel*, p. 32.

[5] This definition of music comes from Augustine's *De Musica*. See W. F. Jackson
Knight, *St. Augustine's De Musica: A Synopsis* (London: The Orthological Institute,
c. 1949), p. 11.

celebration. Just before the spring wandering a lamb was killed. Its blood was sprinkled on the tent posts. A family meal followed. The blood was not considered expiatory, but was thought to have the quality of magic protection.

The rite of protective blood in time was blended with the rite of unleavened bread, which began as an agricultural festival. This celebration seems to have come from the farmer's concern not to mix flour from old and new grain. It was related to seasonal changes and may have originally been a new year's festival.

These two feasts, both originally linked to nature, amalgamated into one. The first was concerned about uncontrollable events, the second with agrarian harmony. Then something new happened. Passover became historicized. After the central Old Testament experience of the exodus from Egypt, Passover recounted and celebrated the deliverance from slavery. The Hebrews began to see that God was active in their history from bondage to freedom, and festivals began to celebrate God's mighty acts.[6] God's power and presence were perceived from creation to the call of Abraham to deliverance from Egypt to the giving of the law to Moses, to prophets, priests, sages, and kings.

Discussing festivals may seem unrelated to our topic, but it has everything to do with music since music is tied so closely to life and especially to its festivals and celebrations of worship. When festivals were related fundamentally to nature, music took on a magic character like the festival itself. When festivals were stripped of magic and celebrated what God does among us in history, music became narrative in character and carried the story of God's mighty acts. Reminiscences of superstition remained like the apotropaic bells on the hem of the priest's garment (Exodus 28:33–35; 39:25–26), and there was apostasy as in the reveling around the golden calf with music (Exodus 32:1–18) or the lure of the followers of Baal for whom music was an incantational magic tool to manipulate God (I Kings 18:26–29); but when they came to know God as active in their history, the fundamental orientation of music was radically changed for the Israelites, along with everything else in their life.

---

[6] See Thierry Maertens, trans. Kathryn Sullivan, *A Feast in Honor of Yahweh* (Notre Dame: Fides Publishers, 1965). The book provides the perspective I'm depending on here, but pp. 69–70, 98–104, and 242 give some summations. See also Aidan Kavanagh, "Jewish Roots of Christian Worship," *The New Dictionary of Sacramental Worship*, ed. Peter E. Fink (Collegeville: The Liturgical Press, 1990), pp. 618–619.

With Miriam and Moses they sang to God the doxological story of their deliverance, "Sing to the Lord, for he has triumphed gloriously; horse and rider he has thrown into the sea" (Exodus 15:20).

Development

If you follow Alfred Sendrey and Mildred Norton and make many suppositions with them, you can trace the development of music in the Old Testament something like this.

> The Hebrew people entered Egypt with an unformed gift for music and "for 400 years submitted this, along with themselves, to the most rigorously organized culture of the antique world." Their years of prosperity and oppression "defined their tribal solidarity 'in a strange land.' . . . By the time the Israelites left Egypt they were a people uniquely given to song."[7]

> Led by Miriam and a choir of women with timbrels, Israel sang and danced to the Lord who "triumphed gloriously" at their rescue from bondage at the Red Sea (Exodus 15:1–21). "Miriam, Deborah, Jephthah's daughter, and the women hailing the young hero David (I Sam. 18:6–7) have become almost archetypes of female musicians."[8] Then, under Samuel, prophetic guilds called Sons of the Prophets, which cultivated the law and music, were formed.[9] From these David learned his musical craft,[10] and the "prototype"[11] of organization was given for music in the temple.

> Music in the temple reached a high level of quality, care, and importance. It was "associated inseparably with the sacrifice . . . [music itself] in effect . . . a form of tonal sacrifice," so that liturgical music was elevated to "an equal plane with all other ritual ceremonies."[12] Without the sacrifice music had no raison d'être.[13] The Levites provided the highest possible musical artistry for the temple under a system of "strict discipline" and "constant rehearsals," replete with rehearsal rooms.[14]

---

[7] Sendrey and Norton, *David's Harp,* p. 4.

[8] Werner, "Music," IDB, K–Q, p. 457.

[9] See Sendrey and Norton, pp. 21–22, and R. Morris Smith, "Church Music as a Part of Our Educational System," *Essays on Church Music,* Series II (n. p.: New York and Buffalo, 1900, 1901), p. 30. For a summary of Smith's article, see Paul Westermeyer, "Church Music at the End of the Nineteenth Century," *Lutheran Quarterly* VIII:1 (Spring 1994): 41–42.

[10] Sendrey and Norton, *David's Harp,* pp. 26–29.

[11] Ibid., p. 39

[12] Ibid.

[13] Werner, "Music," IDB, K–Q, p. 459.

[14] Sendrey and Norton, p. 49.

Training of Levitical boys began in early childhood. After five years of intensive apprenticeship, men were admitted into the temple choir at the age of thirty and left at the age of fifty because their voices would then start to falter.[15] At least twelve choristers were always present in rotations to provide the temple music.[16]

Boys of Levites were admitted to the choir. Wives and daughters of the Levitical choirmasters may also have been choristers,[17] as I Chronicles 15:5–6 implies, though Idelsohn says that "is nowhere traceable."[18] Eventually women were not admitted, however, for two reasons, according to Sendrey and Norton. One was to keep the Hebrew practice free from pagan women's choirs. The other was much less positive, an "antifeminine bias among the priestly caste [which] finally reached such intensity that women were displaced from all ritual functions" and written out of the record.[19]

For "more than ten centuries" the systematic rehearsal work of the Levites [continued] with fanatical zeal."[20] The Levites were supported by the congregation, free of economic concerns.[21] When their payment was embezzled after the rebuilding of the temple, they went on strike (Nehemiah 13:10). Sendrey and Norton regard their action as the first recorded labor dispute in human history.[22]

All the foregoing details may or may not be exactly right.[23] Precisely how the Levites came to be and what they did are matters of debate.[24] The editor of Chronicles may have lived during the Second Temple and "projected the events and practices of his own time on to that of the First Temple."[25] Levites were sometimes poor,[26] the

[15] Ibid., pp. 51–52.

[16] Ibid., p. 49.

[17] Ibid., p. 52.

[18] A. Z. Idelsohn, *Jewish Music in Its Historical Development* (New York: Schocken Books, 1967, first published 1929), p. 16.

[19] Sendrey and Norton, *David's Harp*, p. 185.

[20] Ibid., p. 53.

[21] Ibid., pp. 41–42.

[22] Ibid., p. 183.

[23] For an overview of Temple musicians see Edward Foley, *Foundations of Christian Music: The Music of Pre-Constantinian Christianity* (Bramcote: Grove Books Limited, 1992), pp. 28–30.

[24] See R. Abba, "Priests and Levites," IDB, K–Q, pp. 876–889; Merlin D. Rehm, "Levites and priests," ABD, K–N, pp. 297–310; and Werner, "Jewish music," *The New Grove Dictionary of Music and Musicians* (London: Macmillan Publishers Limited, 1980), hereafter NGDMM, 9, p. 617.

[25] Werner, "Jewish music," NGDMM, 9, p. 617.

[26] See Rehm, "Levites and priests," ABD, K–N, p. 307.

period of Levitical service was not only ages thirty to fifty but varied,[27] music's connection with sacrifice is not a simple matter,[28] the
musical tradition was not static but included "new songs,"[29] and
some of the preceding points that lean on Sendrey and Norton may
exaggerate music's importance. But some sort of remarkable musical
organization and development took place nonetheless. J. S. Bach,
whose glosses on Scripture are always instructive, viewed this organization as the foundation of church music.[30] Whatever and whenever it may have been in its precise details, no matter how simple or
complex, it centered about the characteristic Hebrew form of prayer
and praise, "You are blessed, O God, because you have done. . . ."
This song about God's doing is the focus of the content of church
music and leads to the central importance of the Psalms for the
music of the church. Before we get there, however, we must attend to
some musical details.

Musical Matters

As stated in the introduction, this is not a music theory text. At some
points, nonetheless, almost every text about music has to deal with
some technical theoretical details. We have already come to one of
those points. Even if you have no musical background, read on to
get the overall flavor. Perspective can only be gained by isolating and
organizing the details. If you're a musician, you probably know
about the details and understand their organization well already. If
you're not a musician, you can get the gist of it. Should you be driven to work at it in detail beyond what's given here, ask a music
teacher for help.

[27] See Abba, "Priests and Levites," IDB, K–Q, p. 880.

[28] See Werner, "Music," IDB, K–Q, p. 459.

[29] Ibid., pp. 462–463.

[30] Of I Chronicles 25:1 Bach says, "This chapter is the true foundation of all
God-pleasing church music." And at II Chronicles 5:13 he writes, "With devotion-
al music God is always grace-present." See Howard H. Cox (ed.), *The Calov Bible
of J. S. Bach* (Ann Arbor: UMI Research Press, 1985), pp. 418, 419, and Robin
Leaver, ed., *J. S. Bach and Scripture: Glosses from the Calov Bible Commentary* (St.
Louis: Concordia Publishing House, 1985), pp. 93 and 97. As Joyce Irwin, *Neither
Voice nor Heart Alone: German Lutheran Theology of Music in the Age of the
Baroque* (New York: Peter Lang, 1993), p. 63 indicates, "good music does not come
without expense."

Texture

"Texture" is a technical English musical term that refers to the horizontal and vertical elements of music. Three basic textures can be delineated: *monophony*, a single line of musical pitches in unison, like chant; *polyphony*, two or more independent lines together, like a round where imitation—often associated with polyphony—is employed; and *homophony*, a stack of pitches that move together and generally support a melody, like traditional hymns found in most hymnbooks.

These three types can overlap. When women and men, or children and men, sing the same melody together in unison, for example, actually they are singing in octaves, which is not exactly monophony any more but can be seen as a primitive form of polyphony even though the two voices are not really independent. Monophony can be heterophonic, that is, two versions of the same melody may go along at the same time with differences between the two, for example, one an ornamented version of the other. Polyphony and homophony may be mixed together in various ways.

Tonality, Texture, Composition

Our ears in the West are attuned fundamentally to a homophonic mindset that employs our tonal system of major and minor keys. This generality is true for folk, rock, country western, classical, and virtually any other musical category you may want to isolate. It means, to oversimplify, that each degree of the scale can be numbered; that you can stack a triad (a three-note chord of a third and a fifth, counting from the note itself, with various half-step alterations) on each degree of the scale; that all the tones of the scale will fit into the chords on the first (we label it with the Roman numeral I), fourth (labeled IV), and fifth (labeled V) degrees; that our music gravitates to the pattern I, IV, V, I; and that tonal musical interest for us lies in the ways we "develop" the materials by moving away from I and back home to it. The chief exception is the twelve-tone music of our century, also known as atonal or serial music. Much of the public finds twelve-tone music incomprehensible or offensive. It therefore is not popularly heard.

The ancient world and most of the world, except for the West in a series of developments spanning the last millennium, has not employed homophony or the tonal system that goes with it.[31] For most of the world's history the central musical texture has been monophony, which worked itself out into heterophony and primitive sorts of polyphony.[32] With monophony came two other realities. One is that a modal system with our seven pitches (more about one of these later in the chapter on chant) or a microtonal system (pitches between the half steps of our piano keyboards) or a pentatonic system (five pitches like the black keys of the piano) was employed.[33] The other is that repetition of musical patterns with improvised ornamentation, not musical development as we know it with returns to and modifications of previous themes, characterized ancient music.[34]

Abraham Idelsohn thought the music of the Hebrews was microtonal with twenty-four steps to the octave, but he usually delineated precursors to the modes of Christian chant with seven separate scalar pitches before the first is repeated.[35] Eric Werner spent his life sleuthing out this relationship between Hebrew and Christian tonal syntax.[36] He concluded that three of the modes described in the chapter on chant—the first (Dorian), third (Phrygian), and fifth (Lydian)—are common to all modal systems.[37]

Patterns[38] within the scalar systems just described served as a commonly held musical language. They were basically stepwise (conjunct) motifs woven together in various ways. Each singer improvised on them so that the distinction between composer and performer was not present.[39] Both individual lead singers and the group itself did this improvising, which meant the group's singing could take shape in two ways. One was with everybody singing the

---

[31] This should not be taken to mean that "harmony and polyphony have been a prerogative of the medieval and modern West." As usual, things are more complicated than that, as Curt Sachs, *The Rise of Music in the Ancient World East and West* (New York: W. W. Norton & Company, 1943), p. 48, explains.

[32] See Curt Sachs, *Our Musical Heritage: A Short History of Music* (Englewood Cliffs: Prentice-Hall, 1955), p. 6.

[33] See Sendrey and Norton, *David's Harp*, p. 74.

[34] Sachs, *Our Musical Heritage*, p. 7.

[35] A. Z. Idelsohn, *Jewish Music*, pp. 25–26, 39–91.

[36] Eric Werner, *The Sacred Bridge* (London: Dennis Dobson, 1960), especially chapter 2; Werner, "Music," IDB, K–Q, pp. 464–465; Werner, "Jewish music," NGDMM, 9, pp. 624–625.

[37] Werner, *The Sacred Bridge*, p. 406.

[38] Sometimes patterns are also called modes, which begins to indicate the confusion of terminology here. Each mode was considered to have its own ethos.

[39] Werner, "Music," IDB, K–Q, p. 466.

same notes and rhythms at the same time or close to the same time and with minimal improvisation, as in the congregational song of most Christian churches today. Shorter acclamations like "Amen" characterized this shape. For longer texts everybody might have done the same patterns at different times and in their own ornamented versions, like an orthodox Jewish synagogue today.

The emphasis and interest were on ornamentation. Short notes or tremolos rather than long notes were characteristic. There was no fixed meter, and a free rhythm was used that derived from the text. The only exception to free metrical organization was the music of dance.[40]

Notice two important points here. One is that this music was folk-like in character.[41] It was accessible not only to the initiated, but to everyone. There surely was a rich development that only a trained group could manage and included "newness," as in the music the Levites prepared for the temple, but even that grew out of what the people knew and understood. Second, the transmission was oral.[42] This oral tradition means at least two things we are not so likely to think about. First, it gave the freedom to improvise within a certain context of commonly held patterns. Without the structure of the commonly held patterns the freedom disappears. Second, it precluded any radical break with the past. An oral tradition demands continuity because of its dependence on the corporate memory of the community. Without continuity the memory disappears. Radical innovations are only possible when they can be communicated by written musical notation. Musical notation was not present until the ninth century A.D. and only gradually became precise enough to do something unhooked to memory like twelve-tone music in the twentieth century.

Rhythm and Song

Music starts with rhythm—heartbeat, the pulsation of breath, the rhythmic vibrations themselves that create pitch. Rhythm for the ancient world could have been complicated, more complicated than ours perhaps, as in some forms of drumming. But we must also real-

---

[40] Ibid.

[41] See Edith Gerson-Kiwi, "Jewish music," NGDMM, 9, p. 635.

[42] Suzanne Haïk-Vantoura, trans. Dennis Weber, *The Music of the Bible Revealed* (Berkeley: Bibal Press, 1991) thinks that by means of the cantillation signs she can decipher precisely what the music was.

ize, as Curt Sachs has said, that "music began with singing."[43] Instruments developed after the voice hummed and ululated. Sachs distinguished two forms of expression from this vocal center. One is "*logogenic*, or word-born."[44] The other is *pathogenic*, "much less interested in words, . . . or passion-born." When these two come together and the melodic line itself takes control, Sachs calls the result *melogenic*.[45]

Musical Forms

Singing is not only where music began. Singing is also central to worship. Musical forms for worship are therefore related to verbal ones and to the corporate participation of the people through them.[46] Abraham Idelsohn isolated three such forms.[47] They are variations of the fundamental human pattern of call and response.

One is *responsorial*. The leader sings a line, the people repeat it, the leader sings another line, the people repeat the same line they sang before, the leader sings another line, the people again repeat what they had sung before, etc. That is, the people have the same refrain throughout.

A second pattern is *didactic*, more endemic to the classroom than to worship, though, as we shall see, it has sometimes entered worship as "lining out." Here the leader sings a line, the people repeat it, the leader sings a second line, the people repeat the second line, and so on in the same pattern of people repeating whatever words the leader gives out.

A third pattern is *antiphonal*. A leader or group sings one line, the people sing another one. The leader or group sings a third line, the people a fourth, etc., until the piece is completed. No line, or refrain, need ever be repeated. This type fits worship better than the didactic one, but it is also more demanding than the responsorial type because it means the people need to know the text from memory (or

---

[43] Sachs, *Our Musical Heritage*, p. 4.

[44] Robert A. Skeris, *Chroma Theou: On the Origins and Theological Interpretation of the Musical Imagery Used by the Ecclesiastical Writers of the First Three Centuries, with Special Reference to the Image of Orpheus* (Altötting: Alfred Coppenrath, 1976), p. 159 (and 158), indicates that "Christianity gave a new and fuller dimension" to this term in that its music was "logocentric," which referred ultimately to Christ, the eternal Logos, whose incarnation joined heaven and earth.

[45] Sachs, *Our Musical Heritage*, pp. 4–5.

[46] *Cf.* Werner, "Music," IDB, K–Q, p. 460.

[47] Idelsohn, *Jewish Music*, pp. 20–21.

in modern times have it printed out for them). These reasons explain why the well-known *Shema* could take this shape, and why there are so few biblical references to antiphonal singing.[48] The requirement of knowing the text suggests that the antiphonal type is more likely to presume a choir distinct from the people, while the responsorial type is more inherently congregational.

The Psalms

The Psalms are structured in parallel parts called "stichs." These stichs can be synonymous, antithetical, or synthetic. Synonymous means the two parts say the same thing in different ways, antithetical means they set up a contrast, and synthetic means the second completes or amplifies the first. Massey Shepherd's examples illustrate.[49]

- *Synonymous* (Psalm 27:1)
  The Lord is my light and my salvation;
     whom shall I fear?
  The Lord is the strength of my life;
     of whom shall I be afraid?
- *Antithetical* (Psalm 1:6)
  The Lord knows the way of the just;
     but the way of the wicked will perish.
- *Synthetic* (Psalm 2:6)
  I myself have established my King
     upon Zion, my holy mountain.

The parallel nature of the Psalms is sometimes taken to mean that their structure implies they were sung or should be sung by alternation every half-verse.[50] My experience with congregations and choirs singing the psalms leads me to believe Shepherd is right, that there is no justification for half-verse alternation. It makes for a choppy

---

[48] Ibid., p. 21.

[49] Massey H. Shepherd, Jr., *The Psalms in Christian Worship: A Practical Guide* (Collegeville: The Liturgical Press and Augsburg, 1976), pp. 8–9.

[50] See Elmer F. Krauss, "Psalmody," *Essays on Church Music*, Series I (n. p.: New York and Buffalo, 1898, 1898), p. 76. For a summary, see Paul Westermeyer, "Church Music at the End of the Nineteenth Century," *Lutheran Quarterly* VIII:1 (Spring 1994): 36. See also Sendrey and Norton, *David's Harp*, p. 79; Idelsohn, *Jewish Music*, pp. 20–21; and E. W. Heaton, *Everyday Life in Old Testament Times* (New York: Charles Scribner's Sons, 1956), p. 201.

effect, and it is impossible musically.[51] Kenneth Hart, the director of the graduate program in sacred music at Southern Methodist University's Perkins School of Theology, suggests that the Psalms are rhymed poetry in which ideas, not sounds, are rhymed. Completing the structural rhyme is yet another reason for alternation by verse, not half-verse.

"Musically" here means spoken as well as sung. As soon as you speak a text with a group you have an inherently musical flow or what might be called an elevated form of speech with melodic and rhythmic contours. To preserve any coherent sense of meaning, alternation needs to take place by verse, not half verse. This is true for congregations who speak psalms or for choirs or congregations who sing them. Antiphonal alternation, since it is inherently more choral than congregational, can theoretically be done at the half-verse by choirs alone, but even with practice the choppiness is difficult to overcome. It is preferable to complete the whole musical and verbal—rhymed—thought of the verse with one group rather than to break it up with two groups. It makes much more conversational sense to have one group say something and explain it, then have the other group respond with a new thought and develop it.

The psalm's superscriptions, those comments found at the beginning of some psalms now often given in small or italicized print (perhaps originally subscriptions in the continuous scroll[52]), may well have been at least partly musical instructions. Alfred Sendrey has analyzed them at length.[53] If he is right, they relate to matters such as the melody to be used, choice of instruments, the spirit of the performance, and when or how given psalms would have been used.

Instruments

First came singing, then came instruments—historically.[54] In worship, singing words and the verbal forms they imply also take priority over instruments and instrumental forms—naturally and systematically. The musical practice of the synagogue and the early church demonstrates that you don't even need instruments in wor-

---

[51] Shepherd, *The Psalms in Christian Worship,* pp. 89 and 116 (FN 136).

[52] See Sendrey, *Music in Ancient Israel,* pp. 113–114.

[53] Ibid., pp. 95–159. Proper names and questions of authorship are included (pp. 139–146).

[54] *Cf.* Sendrey and Norton, *David's Harp,* pp. 2–3, and Sendrey, *Music in Ancient Israel,* p. 159.

ship because in these contexts they were not used at all. In the temple, however, instruments were "prominent . . . especially in the rendering of the psalms."[55] They duplicated the monophonic vocal line with slight variations to form heterophony.[56]

The instruments used were related to those of the surrounding countries.[57] Detailed popular and scholarly studies have been made attempting to describe these instruments.[58] All such studies are tentative, in part because most of the instruments were made of wood and "have perished."[59] Here a few allusions will give the flavor.

The *kinnor* is the "modern Hebrew name for the violin" and "the archetypal string instrument of the Bible."[60] It was not bowed as our stringed instruments of the violin or viol family are, but probably was a form of the lyre, plucked with the hand or a plectrum as in all ancient stringed instruments. It was "a general purpose instrument" and "the most important of all the melodic instruments in ancient Israel."[61] The *nevel (nebal)* may have been a "larger, lower-pitched kinnor," perhaps like a lute, though it is more difficult to define.[62] The winds included those used, like a bugle, for signaling and those used in musical compositions. The *shofar* or ram's horn, the silver trumpet, and much later near the time of Christ the *magrepha* were all used for announcements and signaling. The magrepha was a primitive pipe organ, which called priests and

---

[55] Aron Marko Rothmüller, *The Music of the Jews: An Historical Appreciation* (New York: The Beechhurst Press, 1954), p. 56.

[56] See Sendrey, *Music in Ancient Israel*, p. 440.

[57] See Idelsohn, *Jewish Music*, pp. 3–7, and Sendrey and Norton, *David's Harp*, pp. 10–17.

[58] See John Eaton, *The Psalms Come Alive: Capturing the Voice and Art of Israel's Songs* (Downers Grove: InterVarsity Press, 1984), pp. 73–83; Heaton, *Everyday Life in Old Testament Times*, pp. 198–201; Idelsohn, *Jewish Music*, pp. 3–19; Ivor H. Jones, "Musical Instruments," ADB, K–N, pp. 934–939; Rothmüller, *The Music of the Jews*, pp. 24–27, plates between pp. 14 and 15 and pp. 46 and 47; Curt Sachs, *The History of Musical Instruments* (New York: W. W. Norton & Company, Inc., 1940), especially chapter 5; Stanley Sadie, ed., *The New Grove Dictionary of Musical Instruments* (New York: Macmillan Press, 1984); Sendrey, *Music in Ancient Israel*, pp. 262–440; Sendrey and Norton, *David's Harp*, pp. 10–17, 113–131, with illustrations between pp. 132–133; Werner, "Jewish music," NGDMM, 9, pp. 618–623; and Werner, "Musical Instruments," IDB, K–N, pp. 469–476.

[59] Eric Werner, "Jewish music," NGDMM, 9, p. 614.

[60] Jeremy Montagu, "Kinnor," NGDMI, 2, G–O, p. 432.

[61] Ibid., p. 433.

[62] Jones, "Musical Instruments," ABD, 4: K–N, p. 937.

Levites to duty and was so loud you could not hear yourself talk when it sounded.[63] The winds used in musical compositions perhaps included the *uggav* (*ugav, ugab*), though it may have been another stringed instrument.[64] The *halil* or "double pipe"[65] was probably a reed instrument parallel to the Greek *aulos*.[66] It, like the aulos, had sensuous associations and was not so highly regarded for sacred use as the kinnor and nevel.[67] Percussion instruments included shakers, various sorts of cymbals, the *tof* or little drum, and the bells on the hem of the priest's robes.[68]

According to Idelsohn, the temple orchestra near the time of Christ had two to nine nevels, nine to limitless numbers of kinnors, one cymbal, and two to twelve halils.[69] A minimum number of twelve instruments was required.[70] The term "orchestra" may be misleading, because the whole group probably seldom played together at the same time.[71] Small groups or single instruments generally duplicated the vocal line. The temple orchestra was always secondary to the temple chorus.

Having explored these musical and formal details, we move now to the Psalms themselves.

[63] Idelsohn, *Jewish Music,* p. 14.

[64] See Idelsohn, *Jewish Music,* pp. 11–12; Jones, "Musical Instruments," ABD, 4: K–N, pp. 937–938; and Jeremy Montagu, "Ugav," NGDMI, 3, P–Z, pp. 694–695.

[65] Jones, "Musical Instruments," ABD, 4: K–N, p. 936.

[66] Jeremy Montagu, "Halil," NGDMI, G–O, p. 118. For a description of the aulos see James W. McKinnon and Robert Anderson, "Aulos," NGDMI, A–F, pp. 85–87 (virtually the same article in James McKinnon, "Aulos," NGDMM, 1, pp. 699–702).

[67] Idelsohn, *Jewish Music,* pp. 12–13.

[68] Jones, "Musical instruments," ABD, 4: K–N, pp. 935–936.

[69] Idelsohn, *Jewish Music,* pp. 16–17.

[70] Ibid., p. 17.

[71] Heaton, *Everyday Life in Old Testament Times,* p. 201.

3

Psalms

The Importance of the Psalms

The Psalms are the womb of church music.[1] They are not only the hymnal of the Old Testament and the songs of Israel; they are the "voice of the church," as Ambrose said[2] and as one book's title aptly puts it.[3] The church has continually gravitated to the Psalms for the ground of its song. R. E. O. White points out that the first Jewish Christians used the Psalms in their temple and synagogue worship as well as in their private devotion. While such an assertion is probably true though somewhat murky,[4] the rest of the history White points to is clearer: in the third century Tertullian testified to the importance of the Psalms in Christian worship; in the fourth century Chrysostom (actually pseudo-Chrysostom: the passage is probably not by Chrysostom himself[5]) said that in virtually all of the church's worship, David[6] was first and middle and last; in later practice

---

[1] For a quick overview of the shape of the Psalter and psalms, and their relationship to the church's worship, see Massey H. Shepherd, Jr., *The Psalms in Christian Worship* (Collegeville: The Liturgical Press, 1976).

[2] Ambrose, *Explanatio psalmi i*, 9; Jacques Paul Migne, *Patrologiae cursus completus Series Latina* (Paris, 1841ff.), hereafter PL, XIV, 924–925; trans. James McKinnon, *Music in Early Christian Literature* (Cambridge: Cambridge University Press, 1987), hereafter MECL, p. 126.

[3] Andreas Heinz, ed., *Die Psalmen als Stimme der Kirche* (Trier: Paulinus-Verlag, 1982). Eric Werner, *The Sacred Bridge*, p. 128, says "the one book of the Old Testament that came to be the backbone of most liturgies [was] the Psalter."

[4] See chapter 4.

[5] See McKinnon, MECL, p. 90.

[6] Until the nineteenth century (and still in our century as well, though less strongly), the Psalms were assumed to be associated with the king, and King David was taken to be the author of most of them. Therefore the Psalter as a whole was often

monastic parts of the church sang through "the whole Psalter . . . each week;" and in the most popular of all Christian devotional books, *The Imitation of Christ*, Thomas á Kempis (1380–1471) "quotes the psalms more often than the Gospels."[7] Ambrose and Basil are lavish in their praise of the Psalms. Luther worked his hymnody out from the Psalms. Calvinists used the Psalter in metrical versions, with a few additions, as their entire hymnal.

In a book-length summary, John Lamb surveyed the use of the Psalms in Hebrew worship, in the New Testament, in the Eastern and Western churches, and in the Lutheran, Reformed, Anglican, and Scottish churches.[8] Psalms are not only used by different groups of Christians, but employed almost everywhere in the worship of the various groups—from the central service of the Lord's Supper to the baptismal service to the congregational forms of morning and evening prayer to the monastic offices to "free church" worship to the private devotions of the people. It is no accident that commentaries on the Psalms, translations of them, devotional writings based on them, and musical settings of them abound.

A few years ago I punched the keyword "psalms" into the Yale Divinity School Library computer and got an incomplete list of 983 books or musical scores with the word "psalm" in the title. When I gave that number to a class at Luther Seminary a couple years later, a student went to the computer at Luther Seminary's Library and got an incomplete list of 2,199 books on the Psalms. The contemporary "revival" of psalmody in the church's worship is no fluke. Psalmody is in the church's blood and in a constant state of revival. Psalms such as 23, 84, 90, 100, 130, and 150—or at least parts of them—are imbedded in many people's memories. Pastors use them at sickbeds, and at times of reformation and renewal the church has turned to the Psalms again and again.

attributed to him. For a brief summary of this discussion since nineteenth-century criticism, see John H. Eaton, *Kingship and the Psalms* (Trowbridge: JSOT Press, 1986; first published SCM Press, 1976), pp. 1–26.

[7] R. E. O. White, *A Christian Handbook to the Psalms* (Grand Rapids: William B. Eerdmans Publishing, 1984), pp. 3–4. *Cf.* Bernhard W. Anderson, *Out of the Depths* (Philadelphia: Westminster Press, 1983), pp. 15–19. See also the more extended discussion of Samuel Terrien, *The Psalms and Their Meaning for Today* (Indianapolis: The Bobbs-Merrill Company, 1952), pp. vii–xi.

[8] John Alexander Lamb, *The Psalms in Christian Worship* (London: The Faith Press, 1962).

The Psalms may be spoken, but they cry out to be sung. Sung renditions have been their normal character from the beginning.[9] The abundance of music associated with the Psalms creates a spectrum from the simplest to the most complex.[10] At the simplest end are strophic tunes for metrical psalms and psalm tones such as those in the *Lutheran Book of Worship*[11] designed for everyone to sing. At the complex end, complicated musical settings require the most sophisticated forces such as Igor Stravinsky's *Symphony of Psalms* and certain psalm tones such as Anglican chant, which require considerable rehearsal to be done well. Between those two extremes are settings of the Psalms or texts that rely on the Psalms in numerous anthems and motets.

Why Psalms?

Texts

Few would dispute how much the church has used the Psalms, how much music it has generated for them, and how much it has sung them. The question why is complicated and eludes simple answers, but it calls into play concerns that lie at the heart of our study.[12]

In an address to the Hymn Society, Patrick Miller explained that the call in Psalm 150 at the end of the Psalter for everything to praise God is not just a literary device, but an anticipation toward which the whole cosmos is moving. Then he noted that "the answer to the first question of the Westminster Shorter Catechism" defines the "chief purpose of human life in this world" to be glorifying God. "The thing that matters most is" the praise of God.[13] The Psalms and church music are about what matters most.

---

[9] Willi Apel, *Gregorian Chant* (Bloomington: Indiana University Press, 1958), p. 74, notes that all the early Christian writers who mention the Psalms say they were sung.

[10] In James Laster, *Catalogue of Choral Music Arranged in Biblical Order* (Metuchen: The Scarecrow Press, 1983), settings of texts from the entire Bible are listed. More than half of the listings come from the Psalms. (Of the 239 pages of the Catalogue itself, 126 list Psalm texts.) Willi Apel, *Gregorian Chant*, p. 87, points out that the Book of Psalms has been "called the most influential single source of texts in all music history."

[11] *Lutheran Book of Worship* (Minneapolis: Augsburg Publishing House, 1978), hereafter LBW, pp. 290–291.

[12] Cf. Samuel Terrien, *The Psalms and Their Meaning for Today*, pp. xi–xiv.

[13] Patrick D. Miller, Jr., "The Psalms as Praise and Poetry," *The Hymn* 40: 4 (October 1989): 15.

Miller's quote makes it sound as though the Psalms are only about praise. Praise is the Hebrew name for the Psalter[14] and does indeed predominate.[15] But praise, narrowly understood, is not all that is there. Miller also has written about the Psalms' laments.[16] Claus Westermann titled one book, *Praise and Lament in the Psalms*.[17] Walter Brueggemann wrote one book about the Psalms called *Israel's Praise*[18] and another one called *Praying the Psalms*.[19] If you look at the Psalms themselves, you find they not only praise God for steadfast love and faithfulness (Psalm 117), but they also wail out of the depths (Psalms 88 and 130), struggle with God about forsaking us (Psalm 22), project a moral fervor (Psalm 1), plead for justice (Psalm 82), cry for vengeance (Psalms 109 and 137), bask in the grace of God (Psalm 23), savor the Lord's courts (Psalm 84), or contrast the eternity of God with the finitude of humanity (Psalm 90).

In the Psalms we deal with the height and depth of human life, articulated in a most compelling way. We see our struggles against the backdrop of God's goodness and mercy—our struggles with God and God's struggles with us in steadfast love and faithfulness. We view the human drama in its savagery and kindness, in its barbarity and finesse, in the specificity of our daily lives and the cosmic proportions of life, in the call to treat one another justly and with mercy. Mostly we come face to face with God. We bless God because God has done great things for us. The content of the Psalms tells us what we sing about and why it calls forth our song. It tells us why the song is worth singing. It expresses the immensity and power of the song the church has to sing. It also suggests why superficial music simply cannot bear the weight of such a potent and significant song.

---

[14] See Sendrey, *Music in Ancient Israel*, p. 96.

[15] Probably, as Fred Gaiser says, because of the Psalter's eschatological direction. Notes from Fred Gaiser, November, 1996.

[16] Patrick D. Miller, Jr., *Interpreting the Psalms* (Philadelphia: Fortress Press, 1986), pp. 48–64. See also his book-length study of prayer: *They Cried to the Lord: The Form and Theology of Biblical Prayer* (Minneapolis: Fortress Press, 1994).

[17] Claus Westermann, trans. Keith R. Crim and Richard N. Soulen, *Praise and Lament in the Psalms* (Atlanta: John Knox Press, 1981).

[18] Walter Brueggemann, *Israel's Praise* (Philadelphia: Fortress Press, 1988).

[19] Walter Brueggemann, *Praying the Psalms* (Winona: Saint Mary's Press, 1982). Two other books by Walter Brueggemann on the psalms are: *The Message of the Psalms: A Theological Commentary* (Minneapolis: Augsburg Publishing House, 1984), and *The Psalms and the Life of Faith*, ed. Patrick D. Miller (Minneapolis: Fortress Press, 1995).

In a word, if you would see the holy Christian Church painted in living color and shape, comprehended in one little picture, then take up the Psalter. There you have a fine, bright, pure mirror that will show you what Christendom is. Indeed you will find in it also yourself and the true "Know thyself," as well as God himself and all creatures.[20]

Music

But why do we sing at all? What's wrong with speech alone? The texts surely have the meaning just described apart from music. Isn't that enough? Singing a text surely does not alter the content, does it? What more is there?

A number of issues that relate to these questions need to be sorted out. First, let us acknowledge that only our modern world would even think of asking why we sing. As I indicated in the last chapter, primitive peoples did not regard music as the extra that we do.[21] Until prone and Low Mass in the medieval West and parts of especially Zwinglian Protestantism or Quaker worship thereafter, worship was always sung. Even today Jewish synagogues, Eastern Orthodox churches, and many other worshiping communities treat music as intrinsic to their worship.

Once we have asked the question our modern western tendency is to answer it by saying that, before there were microphones, the reason for singing was to amplify the voice so it could be heard better. As Frank Senn has pointed out, singing has inevitably accompanied worship in both large and small spaces, where amplification would be needed and where it would not be needed: amplification is obviously necessary and perhaps tangentially related, but it is not a primary reason for singing in worship.[22]

The real reasons for singing are far more profound. One reason is that singing, like nothing else, *binds together a corporate gathering*. Leaders of nonviolent marches know of and use music's tremendous power. They use music not only because it gives a group a common physical response, but because in the process it also creates a psychosocial unity. Dictators, including Adolf Hitler, have been highly

---

[20] Martin Luther, "Preface to the Psalter," *Luther's Works*, vol. 35 (Philadelphia: Muhlenberg Press, 1960), hereafter LW, p. 257. (I am indebted to Fred Gaiser for steering me to this quotation.)

[21] See E. Werner, "Music," IDB, K–Q, p. 457.

[22] Frank Senn, "The Dialogue Between Liturgy and Music," *The Hymn* 38:2 (April 1987): 25.

aware of music's potentials. They have used music's power for deadly demonic ends, which need to serve as a solemn warning to all of us in the church. If we do not use music well, tyrants will fill the vacuum and use it for devious purposes. But music can be used positively for the common good and for an incredible shalom. People do not think this out logically. They simply yearn to sing when they gather for worship and know how right it is to sing after they have done it. The psalmist, the poet-musician, gives them the voice they yearn for.

Music also *aids the memory*. A text that has been sung will be remembered long after one spoken. This mnemonic capacity of music is related not only to the corporate binding power of music, but to its value over time. Music helps the memory at the moment the worshiping community assembles, and it is one of the primary vehicles for remembering across time, from gathering to gathering, and between gatherings. The sounds of a given hymn, sung weeks or months apart, are ways to remember and live different parts of the story. The sounds of Christmas are different from the sounds of Easter or Pentecost. And sound is part of our individual stories, from birth to death. At old age and death we remember sounds from childhood and youth, which is why it is so important to have sounds we can grow into rather than out of.

Joy inevitably breaks into song. Speech alone cannot carry its hilarity. The physical equipment we use to laugh is the physical equipment we use to sing. From laughter to song is a small step. To praise God, the highest form of joy, is to make music. Song cannot be avoided. The language of joy and praise is the language of song. The repeated *Alleluia*, "Praise Yah,"[23] which frames each of Psalms 146–150 at the end of the Psalter is inherently musical.

The same can be said for *sorrow*, the opposite of joy. Sorrow also inevitably breaks into song. Speech alone cannot carry its moan. The physical equipment we use to cry is also the physical equipment we use to sing. From mourning to song is but a small step. To cry out to God in lament, the deepest form of sorrow, is to make music. The language of sorrow and lament is the language of song. The cry "Miserere" of Psalm 51 is inherently musical.

Music is also the means to *interpret a text*. At one level interpretation gives rise to sing-song formulas like the call of a horse race

---

[23] "Yah" is likely a shortened form of "Yahweh," the Hebrew personal name for "God."

or the call of the auctioneer, which increase in pitch level and melody, in tempo, and in dynamic and rhythmic intensity as the excitement grows. At a much more profound level this gives rise to the cantillation of readings by a Jewish cantor and the ecstatic cries of an African American preacher—which also increase as the excitement grows. In these latter examples the call of God to proclaim and interpret the word is at work. Call-response patterns inevitably arise from this: the call of the cantor and the preacher cannot be imagined without the responses of their congregations. These call-response patterns are inherently musical.[24] They are virtual certainties in any worshiping community, unless, of course, they are artificially blocked.

All the elements we have noted—binding together, memory, joy, lament, and proclamation—find their locus and make sense in the context of a worshiping community. Memory, joy, and lament can, of course, be imagined individually, but apart from a group of persons in the worshiping matrix they quickly lose their meaning, which does not mean that there are no individual singers in worship. Individuals and groups each sing alone, the whole community sings together, and dialogues take place between individuals and the whole community or between groups, depending on the nature of the song to be sung.

The reason this discussion of music relates to the worshiping community is because the Psalms carried by music have been and continue to be related to that community. Artur Weiser says "that the cultus was the native soil from which the psalms sprang."[25] Alfred Sendrey and Mildred Norton say that the "songs of the Psalter . . . are lyrico-religious songs designed for liturgical use."[26] Some scholars may challenge such an assessment, or at least want to emphasize the Psalter as a book of instruction and meditation with its own internal direction and deliberate structure.[27] Such an emphasis need not deny the Psalms' locus in the life of the church at wor-

---

[24] Fred Gaiser points out, leaning on Miller, that the move from prose to poetry to song is a continuum of increasing transcendence, that musical speech is more inherently transcendent than spoken language.

[25] Artur Weiser, *The Psalms: A Commentary* (Philadelphia: The Westminster Press, 1962), p. 24.

[26] Sendrey and Norton, *David's Harp*, p. 62; *cf.* Sendrey, *Music in Ancient Israel*, p. 97.

[27] See, for example, J. Clinton McCann, Jr., *A Theological Introduction to the Book of the Psalms: The Psalms as Torah* (Nashville: Abingdon Press, 1993). Part of the large literature on the Psalms treats the Psalter in this way, and it is not only by

ship. Whatever may be right about the origin of the Psalms is not the point here. The point here is twofold: 1) the community that sings the Psalms and the musicians who lead them invariably locate the Psalms in worship, though they too may use the Psalter in devotional or instructional ways as well; and 2) music is the language of corporate prayer and praise, the language of worship, the language of the Psalms.

World-Making

If music carries and interprets a text, then in another sense, music can be understood to modify a text's content, or, perhaps, more precisely, its context. In *Israel's Praise,*[28] Walter Brueggemann argues that the worship of a people is "world-making," not in the sense that "words and acts in cult . . . form rocks and rivers and minerals," but in the sense that they impose "order, shape, sequence, pattern, and meaning on already existing elements which are disordered and chaotic until acted upon"[29] and in the sense that God has authorized this activity and is known to be present in it.[30]

Music is the cultic language by which this order is imposed.[31] It is the lyrical, imaginative, evocative structural substance to which Brueggemann so eloquently points. But Brueggemann's book has an omission. It points to the clergy's role as "agents in the liturgical drama"[32] and therefore in world-making, and it points to the music itself; but it fails to mention the musician—the chief singer, the cantor, the psalmist—the very person most responsible for the music.

To Brueggemann's discussion[33] one must add the poet-musicians,

biblical scholars. See, for example, Thomas Merton, *Bread in the Wilderness* (Collegeville: The Liturgical Press, 1953). For an array of opinion about the Psalter's origins, generated by Sendrey's musical questions, see Sendrey, *Music in Ancient Israel,* pp. 139–145.

[28] See FN 18 for the citation.

[29] Brueggemann, *Israel's Praise,* p. 52.

[30] Ibid., p. 11.

[31] It's not Brueggemann's point, but has been argued that sound itself "can make order out of chaos." Robert Lawlor, "Geometry at the Service of Prayer: Reflections on Cistercian Mystic Architecture," *Parabola* 3:1 (1978): 18.

[32] Ibid., 7.

[33] I sent Walter Brueggemann a letter that suggested musicians needed to be included in this discussion. He responded (October 16, 1989) very graciously and without disagreement, saying he had to plead ignorance about these things and "ignorance in the scholarly guild about what the musicians were up to in ancient Israel."

the persons who wrote the texts and their music. Someone penned
them, sang them with the people, and gave the people their voice.
That person is "the minstrel to the king," to use Francis
Williamson's phrase, David to Saul and David before God: David is
the psalmist, the chief singer, the normative musician for us church
musicians.[34]

The church's establishments are often nervous about music-making and musicians. The reason is because music and musicians have
to do with a kind of remembering that will not fit categories that can
be easily controlled. The people know better than their establishments, however. Brueggemann explains how primitive and potent
their musical life is.[35] It cannot be controlled by establishments, even
totalitarian ones.[36] The people know that "Israel's [and their] most
powerful praise lives closest to the reality of God's inbreaking
actions"[37] and that the true church musician lives there too. That is
why the church musician—I mean the genuine church musician who
serves the people faithfully, not the musician who happens to be
working in the church or who seeks to impose on it patterns and
practices foreign or contrary to its nature—always lives close to the
people.

Priests and Prophets

Gerhard von Rad said one could not construct "a spiritual
'prophetic' faith" and a "priestly cult religion" from the Old Testament. "The faith of Israel cannot possibly be divided into two
forms of religion which are so completely different and so entirely
foreign to each other."[38] Later he added, "It would be a great mistake to regard the prophets as the spiritual antipodes opposed to the

---

[34] David still today represents the church musician. "The Institute of Sacred
Music Bulletin of Yale University 1995–1997" 91:12 (September 15, 1995): 13,
begins this way. "David, the prototypical representative in the Judeo-Christian
world of the church or synagogue musician, dominates the logo of the Institute of
Sacred Music." A Roman Catholic set of essays on church music begins similarly:
see Robert A. Skeris, Crux et Cithara: Selected Essays on Liturgy and Sacred Music
Translated and Edited on the Occasion of the Seventieth Birthday of Johannes
Overath (Altötting: Alfred Coppenrath, 1983), p. 11.

[35] Brueggemann, Israel's Praise, pp. 84–85.

[36] See Brueggemann, Praying the Psalms, p. 28.

[37] See Brueggemann, Israel's Praise, p. 84.

[38] Gerhard von Rad, Old Testament Theology, vol. I, trans. by D. M. G. Stalker
(New York: Harper & Brothers, 1962), p. 260.

cultic world of the priests. . . . What we witness in the prophets is an attack on abuses."[39]

The faith of Israel may have been an undivided whole, but the Christian church has often divided it into priestly and prophetic pieces. "Catholics" and "Protestants," and "catholics" and "protestants" within each of the larger groups, are the most obvious witness to this division. More "catholic" priests and their communities have identified with the sacrificial system of the temple. They emphasize offering something to God. The direction of the sacrifice is from humanity to God, just like prayer. More "protestant" preachers and their communities identify with the prophets. They emphasize a word from God addressed to humanity.

The divisions are not always neat. People find themselves sometimes identifying with both groups. But communities tend to gravitate one way or the other and to push music and musicians in the direction of their gravitational tendencies. More "priestly" Christian communities identify with the Levites and relate music's reason for being to sacrifice.[40] More "prophetic" Christian communities identify with "Thus says the Lord" and the words of Amos, which smashed all systems and, in the face of injustice, can be seen as obliterating music itself.[41]

Musicians and the song of the Christian church resist these polarities and identify with the psalmists. The psalmists knew about the longing that draws the community together around God in a priestly fashion, as in Psalm 42: "As the deer longs for flowing streams, so longs my soul for you, O God." And they knew about the prophetic cry, which smashes all human community, as in Psalm 68: "Let God arise, let his enemies be scattered; let those who hate him flee before him." But, in Samuel Terrien's words, the psalmists

> offered the pastoral consolations of the priests without neglecting the moral demands of the prophets for righteousness in living. They spoke the harsh word of God's judgment without producing despair, and they conveyed the soothing benefits of religion without inducing indolence or self-arrogance.
>
> . . . the psalms occupy in the Scripture as well as in the church a situation of uniqueness, for they mirror the faith of Israel as a whole, and

---

[39] Ibid., p. 279.

[40] For one of the strongest statements of this relationship see the writings of Robert A. Skeris, especially *Divini Cultus Studium: Studies in the Theology of Worship and of its Music* (Altötting: Alfred Coppenrath, 1990), pp. 16, 20–22, 110.

[41] Amos 5:21–24.

they provide a bridge between moralism which too easily condemns, and sacramentalism, which too easily condones.[42]

The psalmists had a story to tell, a narrative to recount, a ballad to sing—the song of God's rescuing the people. They sang a new song with the people because God has done marvelous things (Psalm 98). The new song is about the victory of this strange king who, unlike all earthly kings, will both reign forever *and* will care for the lowly and the oppressed. The language of this victory celebration is the people's doxological song of joy and praise.

It is tempting to make much too neat distinctions here and—relying on an arbitrary Hegelian formula of thesis, antithesis, and synthesis—drive them back into the Old Testament.[43] That won't work. The Old Testament held the motifs together and not in a Hegelian way. King David as king was priest.[44] The relationship of prophets to the temple is not clear.[45] If the prophetic guilds formed under Samuel provided the model of priestly musical organization for the temple, as Sendrey and Norton suggest, prophetic and priestly distinctions get even more difficult to maintain. David cannot be separated from the priestly Levites because in I Chronicles 1:25 he is designated as the one who appointed them. Prophetic impulses cannot be separated completely from priestly ones. Praise, sacrifice, and proclamation are fused.[46] They form a whole, just as priests, prophets, and psalmists together do. Actually, to make the picture complete, we should add the wisdom literature and its sages.[47]

The point here is not to make easy distinctions, nor to drive them artificially back into the Old Testament, nor to force people into

---

[42] Terrien, *The Psalms and Their Meaning for Today,* pp. 269–270. Cf. Aubrey R. Johnson, *The Cultic Prophet and Israel's Psalmody* (Cardiff: University of Wales Press, 1979), pp. 3ff., and Ambrose, *Explanatio psalmi* I, 7, Jacques Paul Migne, ed., *Patrologiae cursus completus, Series Latina* (Paris, 1841ff.), hereafter PL, XIV, 923; trans. McKinnon, MCEL, p. 126.

[43] As Terrence Fretheim, Fred Gaiser, and Daniel Simundson reminded me.

[44] As Fred Gaiser also reminded me.

[45] See Foley, *Foundations of Christian Music,* pp. 28–30.

[46] See John W. Kleinig, *The Lord's Song: The Basis, Function and Significance of Choral Music in Chronicles* (Sheffield: JSOT Press, 1993), pp. 109 and 145, for example.

[47] For a study that uses these Old Testament motifs through a reconstructed grid from the typology of H. Richard Niebuhr, *Christ and Culture* (New York: Harper Torchbooks, 1956), see Francis Williamson, *Ears to Hear, Tongues to Sing: Church Music as Pastoral Theology.*

arbitrary molds. It is that groups in the church have been tempted to collapse everything into "prophetic" or "priestly" categories. Individuals may find it helpful and freeing to see how they may have been formed by different parts of the church and how psalmists are required for the whole picture. "Protestants" (big or little "p") tend to err on the prophetic side, "catholics" (big or little "c") on the priestly. Since the "prophet" in the pulpit and the "priest" at the table can be seen, they are easily assigned an office—preacher, pastor, minister, clergy, rector, priest. The musician doesn't have to be seen at all to function well because the musician is so closely identified with the song of the people and its nonvisible, temporal character that lodges in the memory once it has sounded. As the history of the church has indicated, the musician, unlike the prophet or priest, can lead the people very well in the midst of them or even behind them. This close identification of the musician with the people has made it difficult to define the office of the musician with the precision of the office of the clergy.

The difficulty of defining the musical office has often been regarded as a liability. Then an attempt at definition forces the musician into "prophetic" or "priestly" molds, which is a mistake. The lack of clarity here is part of the lyrical genius of music and a reminder of the balance needed. It points to the Christian people, their story in song, and their character as pilgrims who never can nail things down too precisely without falling into idolatry. Easy distinctions between prophet and priest cannot be made, but the musician is neither. The singer and leader of the song is different from them, complementary to them, and equally needed.

The Psalms and Christ

It all comes down to this: the Old Testament sings. So does the New. The Christian reads the whole history in the light of Christ, in whom there is song, as I will indicate shortly—which leads to a final comment here. Underneath this whole discussion of the Psalms has been an implicit sense that for Christians they are related to Christ.[48] That theme needs to be made explicit before we consider canticles in the

---

[48] This does no disservice to Jews who use the Psalms in their own (sometimes messianic) way. It simply is the way Christians interpret things, especially the Psalms. We live together best if we acknowledge honestly our own position, fully aware that others may not share it and that we have no business trying to force it on others.

next chapter. It's not a statistical matter, but Massey Shepherd gives
some statistics that lead us to it.

35

The Psalms
and Christ

In the New Testament there are 93 quotations from more than 60 of the
Psalms. Among the sayings of Jesus in the Gospels there are more quo-
tations from the Psalter than from any other book in the Old Testament.
The evangelists added many more. . . .[49]

Not only are the Psalms referred to often in the New Testament,
but they and especially the Royal Psalms[50] have been "applied to
Christ" by Christians.[51] In the word portion of the church's service
of word and table, the Psalms link the Old Testament to the New.
Actually they do even more by providing the context for the other
lessons. The church's gravitational pull to the Psalter at the center of
its music is essentially a christocentric move. Dietrich Bonhoeffer
spoke for the church when he viewed the Psalter as the prayer book
of Christ, which means the one who prays the Psalms is Christ, and
it is in Christ that Christians then pray them.[52] Luther painted with
even broader strokes.

The Psalter ought to be a precious and beloved book, if for no other reason than this: it promises Christ's death and resurrection so clearly—
and pictures his kingdom and the condition and nature of all Christendom—that it might well be called a little Bible. In it is comprehended
most beautifully and briefly everything that is in the entire Bible. It is
really a fine enchiridion or handbook. In fact, I have a notion that the
Holy Spirit wanted to take the trouble himself to compile a short Bible
and book of examples of all Christendom or all saints, so that anyone
who could not read the whole Bible would here have anyway almost
an entire summary of it, comprised in one little book.[53]

[49] Shepherd, *The Psalms in Christian Worship*, p. 32.

[50] Those associated with the king and his sacrifice at Jerusalem, such as 2, 18, 20,
21, 72, 101, 110, 132.

[51] Shepherd, *The Psalms in Christian Worship*, p. 33.

[52] Dietrich Bonhoeffer, *Life Together*, trans. by John W. Doberstein (New York:
Harper & Brothers, 1954), pp. 45–46. Another christological reading of the Psalms
is given by William L. Holladay, *The Psalms through Three Thousand Years: Prayer
Book of a Cloud of Witnesses* (Minneapolis: Fortress Press, 1993), pp. 346ff.

[53] Martin Luther, "Preface to the Psalter," LW, 35, p. 254. (I am indebted to Fred
Gaiser for leading me to this quotation, which I had confused with another.) *Cf.*
James Luther Mays, *Psalms* (Louisville: John Knox Press, 1994), pp. 1–3.

NEW TESTAMENT

4

Canticles

The New Testament

The last chapter, narrowly speaking, was about the Psalms. Broadly speaking it and the chapter before it were about the Old Testament and the issues it raises. Narrowly speaking this chapter is about canticles. Broadly speaking it is about the New Testament and what stems from it, which leads to several introductory comments.

First, like the Old Testament, the New Testament sings. Parallel to the telos of the Psalms in Psalm 150, so the telos of the New Testament in Revelation is jubilant song. The "lyrical quality" of the New Testament leads to a reverberant musical celebration of the whole creation around the throne of the Lamb. (Seeing Revelation on its terms as dream-like, metaphorical, musical, and eschatological frees one from the madness of trying to interpret it literally.)

It is hard to isolate any New Testament current that leads to silence unless Jesus' lack of response to Pilate's question is so interpreted.[1] Jesus drove out the moneychangers in the temple with a fury equal to Amos, but, unlike Amos whose words[2] could be understood (wrongly, I would say) to induce silence, Jesus' action led to the musical laugh of children singing out, "Hosanna to the Son of David."[3] At the darkest moment on the cross, Jesus was reduced not to silence, but to the musical moan of Psalm 22, "My God, my God,

---

[1] Mark 15:5. One could see Jesus' preparation for his ministry in the wilderness (Matthew 4:1–11, Luke 4:1–13, Mark 1:12–13) as silent, but it leads to song. Song in this case, as always, grows out of silence.

[2] Amos 5:23.

[3] Matthew 21:15.

why have you forsaken me?"[4] His healing included giving voice to one who was mute.[5]

Though silence seems virtually absent, there is a New Testament note of restriction on music. It comes in I Corinthians 13:1 where Paul disparaged the noisy gong and the clanging cymbal. Eric Werner says this passage reflects a view held by Pharisaic Judaism in which vocal music was regarded as superior to instrumental,[6] and it can be read as leading to restrictions on musical instruments. But this is a minor note. By and large the New Testament is graciously lyrical and fully embraces the music of God's good creation, reminding one of the morning stars singing at creation[7] and looking forward to the fullness of sound in the consummation to which Revelation points.

Second, the Old Testament materials relate roughly to a 1,500-year time span. The New Testament materials, on the other hand, relate roughly to a 70-year time span. The Old Testament was generated by many events over a millennium and a half, whereas the New Testament was generated by the coming of Christ and its immediate aftermath. The literature of the Old Testament therefore is far more varied and diffuse than that of the New Testament.

The New Testament contains essentially two sorts of documents: 1) letters written to the apostolic churches, and 2) gospels about the person and work of Jesus. Liturgical and other materials are imbedded in these letters and gospels. The gospel of Matthew, for example, may have been developed and used liturgically.[8] The short time span of the New Testament writings should not lead one to conclude therefore that they are all the same or express a uniformity. The four Gospels contain differences, and the letters reveal different parties and positions. Though it gives us a richly compelling texture, the New Testament does not have the historical sweep of literature across the centuries that the Old Testament has.

Third, though the New Testament is graciously lyrical and musical in its message and its being, music as such was not one of its cen-

---

[4] Matthew 27:46.

[5] Matthew 9:33.

[6] Werner, "Music," IDB, K–Q, p. 466.

[7] Job 38:7.

[8] See Arland J. Hultgren, "Liturgy and Literature: The Liturgical Factor in Matthew's Literary and Communicative Art," *Texts and Contexts: Biblical Essays in Their Textual and Situational Contexts: Essays in Honor of Lars Hartman*, ed. Tord Fornberg and David Hellholm (Oslo: Scandinavian University Press, 1995), pp. 659–673.

tral concerns. Further, the distinctions we make between music and speech were foreign to it. As Joseph Gelineau says, "The frontier between singing and speech was far less precise."[9] For both of these reasons it is easy to overlook the musical practice which the New Testament church simply assumed. When friends write letters they do not spell out things they take for granted in their culture and relationships—things, for example, about their families, their friends, their language, the art work on their walls, and the music they sing or hear at concerts or play on their stereo systems. Outsiders or historians who may later encounter the friends' correspondence must supply the givens. The same is true for the New Testament. The writers there did not write what they and their readers assumed. We have to supply the assumptions.

The First Christians

We need to begin then by noting that the first Christians were Jews. If they lived in Jerusalem, they may have continued to attend the Temple, as Acts 2:46 indicates, until it was destroyed in 70 A.D. There a large group of professional instrumentalists and singers from the tribe of Levi led the music. The texts probably included some Psalms and Psalm-like narratives such as the song of Deborah (Judges 5) and the song of Moses (Exodus 15:1–18).[10] The people probably sang some of these well-known texts from memory, refrains from them, and certainly *Alleluias*, but the professional musicians dominated the sacrifices.[11]

Jewish Christians in Jerusalem might have also attended one of the 394 synagogues that were in the city at the time of the Temple's destruction.[12] Outside of Jerusalem, and after 70 A.D., they continued to attend the synagogues. The synagogue may have developed before the Babylonian exile, or at the time of the exile in 587 B.C. when there was no access to the Temple, or after the exile among laity who were attached to weekly courses of priests in Jerusalem. The third instance suggests that some of these lay people

---

[9] J. Gelineau, "Music and Singing in the Liturgy," *The Study of Liturgy*, ed. Cheslyn Jones, Geoffrey Wainwright, and Edward Yarnold (New York: Oxford University Press, 1978), p. 444.

[10] See Foley, *Foundations of Christian Music*, pp. 31–32.

[11] See Edward Foley, *From Age to Age* (Chicago: Liturgy Training Publications, 1991), pp. 9–12, for a good summary.

[12] Eric Werner, *The Sacred Bridge*, p. 2.

attended the Temple sacrifices, while others stayed in their villages, read the Pentateuch, and offered prayers in their synagogues at the times of the sacrifices.[13]

In any case, the synagogue service does not involve sacrifice as the Temple did. It is a lay liturgy, which consists of a series of benedictions, prayers, the reading of the law and the prophets, possibly interspersed with psalmody,[14] and a sermon that may not have been present at first, but evolved out of the readings.[15] This worship practice is what the early Jewish Christians would have been accustomed with, and it "set the pattern" for the Word service "of the primitive Christian community."[16] As indicated in the last chapter, singing was simply assumed in all worship. Lessons and prayers, for example, were intoned, and, as Edward Foley reminds us, "to recite scripture without chant was considered a minor sacrilege."[17] The singing of the synagogue, unlike the Temple, included no instruments except the shofar, which was only used for purposes of signaling. It was the synagogue's practice which the New Testament community adopted in its worship.[18]

Singing was assumed by the New Testament. Jesus and his disciples sang a hymn before they "went out to the Mount of Olives" (Mark 14:26). Once the Christian community was in place after the resurrection, singing characterized it. The daily celebration of the Lord's Supper included song (Acts 2:46–47), Paul and Silas sang in

---

[13] Scholars do not agree about synogogue origins. Joseph Gutman has summarized the research in "The Origin of the Synagogue: The Current State of Research," *The Synagogue: Studies in Origins, Archaeology and Architecture* (New York: KTAV Publishing House, 1975), pp. 72–76. See also Foley, *Foundations of Christian Music*, pp. 37–38. Eric M. Meyers, "Synagogue," ABD, 6: Si–Z, p. 252, says most scholars would place the synagogue's origins in exilic times.

[14] See David Hiley, *Western Plainchant: A Handbook* (Oxford: Clarendon Pres, 1993), pp. 484–485.

[15] For a description of Jewish worship at the time of early Christianity see Eric Werner, *The Sacred Bridge*, pp. 1–16. See also W. O. E. Oesterley, *The Jewish Background of the Christian Liturgy* (Oxford: Clarendon Press, 1925), and Foley, *From Age to Age*, pp. 12–13.

[16] Werner, *The Sacred Bridge*, p. 2.

[17] Foley, *Foundations of Christian Music*, p. 46. This is Eric Werner's assessment of the same well-known talmudic maxim, which Sendrey, *Music in Ancient Israel*, p. 211, quotes: "If one reads the Scripture without a melody or repeats the Mishnah without a tune, of him the Scripture says: 'Wherefore I gave them also statutes that were not good' (Ezekiel 20:25)."

[18] Werner, "Music," IDB, K–Q, p. 466, says the chant and music of the primitive church were practically identical with the customs and traditions of the synagogue.

prison (Acts 16:25), and the parallel texts from Ephesians 5:19 and Colossians 3:16 encouraged the community to give thanks to God in everything through Jesus Christ, addressing one another in psalms, hymns, and spiritual songs, and making melody to the Lord.

Extrabiblical sources also point to the singing of the early Christians. Around 112 A.D. Pliny the Younger, a governor in the province of Bithynia, addressed a letter to the Emperor Trajan asking what he should do with Christians. In his letter he gave a brief description of normal Christian worship, the Lord's Supper, which included hymn singing.[19]

As long as the Christians were Jews, the musical practice of Jewish chant prevailed. But when Gentiles joined the young church, Hellenistic musical thought and practice also came into play. The introduction of Jewish psalmody and its music apparently came to Gentiles as a "revolutionary event."[20] Gentiles were surely singing before that, but not chanting psalms. The result of Jewish and Hellenistic interpenetration eventually led to what we know as Gregorian chant and to the development of Western music. But that comes later.

Worship

Here two prior realities must be detailed, without which the musical developments of the church would have been impossible and not intelligible. The first concerns worship. "The sources for our knowledge of the various aspects of early Christian worship are exceedingly incomplete and fragmentary until the end of the second century A.D., and are difficult if not impossible to synthesize."[21] There is always the danger of reading the earliest period in light of later periods and to assume an easy singularity about the earliest period. But the sources we do have prior to Hippolytus in the early third century (hints in the New Testament, the *Didache*, the correspondence of Pliny, Justin Martyr[22]) all center around the word and the sacraments of baptism and the Lord's Supper.

---

[19] See *A New Eusebius, Documents Illustrative of the History of the Church to A.D. 337*, ed. J. Stevenson (London: S. P. C. K., 1960, first published 1957), p. 13–14. What is here translated "recite by turns a form of words" means "sing a hymn," as translated in McKinnon, MECL, p. 27.

[20] Werner, "Music," IDB, K–Q, p. 468.

[21] D. E. Aune, "Worship, early Christian," ADB, 6: Si–Z, p. 974.

[22] Ibid., pp. 975–978, lays these out clearly.

Early Christian worship may have first been a daily celebration of the Lord's Supper, to which Christians have since given various names such as Eucharist,[23] (holy) communion, or sacrament of the altar, depending on the tradition and its current usage.[24] It became a weekly event, celebrated on Sunday, the day of the resurrection. The Word service, derived from the synagogue, was originally separate from the Lord's Supper. Eventually the two were joined. By the second century this "word and table sequence"[25] set the pattern for the central service of the Christian church, the service of word and supper, which would become known in the West as the Mass. It is the fundamental liturgical context in which the music of the church developed. Since the early church met in homes and ate together, music accompanied their eating at meals, which blended with the sacramental eating.

In addition to the service of word and table, services of prayer spun themselves out around the rhythm of the day. They developed in simpler forms for laypersons at home and eventually in more complex forms for monks as they appeared. Music accompanied these occasions of daily prayer.

Christ

Second, and most importantly, a word needs to be said about the decisive event, the coming of Christ. It is what stands behind both the liturgical and the musical developments.

The person of Christ paradoxically both particularized and universalized everything. It particularized everything in that the whole sweep of salvation history recounted in the Old Testament—from creation to the call of Abraham to deliverance from Egypt to giving the law to prophets, priests, sages, and kings—found its fulfillment in Christ. In Christ the promise to Abraham was fulfilled. In Christ

[23] Aune, "Worship, early Christian," ADB, 6: Si–Z, p. 983, points out that by the early second century *eucharistia* "had become a technical term for . . . the liturgical commemoration of the Lord's Supper."

[24] Werner, *The Sacred Bridge*, xvii, in trying to distinguish between Jewish and Christian worship, points to the essence of the matter when he says, ". . . we must really abandon the long cherished conception of a 'typically Christian' versus a 'typically Jewish' liturgy. There is but *one* principle that can be considered 'Christian' regardless of Church or denomination: the Eucharist. And likewise there is one nucleus around which all Jewish liturgies have evolved: the *Sh'ma'* (Deut. 5:6)."

[25] Foley, *Foundations of Christian Music*, p. 60.

the law was fulfilled. In Christ the Word of God the prophets had spoken no longer came in words, but took actual flesh and lived on earth. In Christ *the* once-for-all sacrifice was offered, which made all other sacrifices obsolete; humanity's offense, projected across an infinite landscape, was set right when the Infinite One did it by the self-offering of the Son of God on the cross. In Christ, the Ruler of the universe conquered even the twin enemies of evil and death and promised a feast around the Lamb of God. All of human history was viewed as being fulfilled in Christ "in the fullness of time."

On the other hand, the person of Christ universalized everything. In Christ the message of lavish grace was not limited to any one group or people. It was for the whole of humanity: Jews, Gentiles, all cultures, slaves, free, male, female, rich, poor, sick, healthy, and so forth.

Canticles

In response to Christ's coming, the church sang canticles. The term "canticles" refers to those texts in the Bible that were sung. In its broadest sense it includes Old Testament as well as New Testament texts. In the strictest sense it refers to texts that are not the Psalms, though sometimes, especially in the Anglican tradition, it is used for some Psalm texts as well, like the *Jubilate* (Psalm 100), *Cantate* (Psalm 98), and *Deus miseratur* (Psalm 67). Sometimes major and lesser canticles are distinguished, the former from the New Testament and the latter from the Old Testament.[26] Often the term is taken, as it is here, to refer to major texts from the New Testament that were sung.

The discussion of the Psalms noted how they sing the story of God's victorious activity. So do Psalm-like sung texts from outside the Psalter such as the songs of Moses in Exodus 15:1–18, and of Miriam in Exodus 15:21, which are about the story of deliverance from Egypt. All these texts essentially say, "Praise the Lord." Why? "Because God has done. . . ." One of the central characteristics of most canticles is that they also tell the story of God's deliverance. This narrative character becomes especially evident in the canticles the New Testament community sang, where everything is particularized and universalized in Christ. Whether these canticles were sung in exactly the form we find them is a matter of conjecture. It

---

[26] See Willi Apel, *Gregorian Chant*, pp. 20–21.

is probably more accurate to speak of "infancy canticles" for the New Testament community itself.[27] They typify the "lyrical quality"[28] of the New Testament. That they became commonplace in the church's worship and called forth innumerable musical settings over the centuries is not surprising. It was virtually inevitable.

Six of these canticles are especially important. Four are the "infancy canticles" themselves, found in the Gospel of Luke. One, or better, a collage, stands for all the canticles in the book of Revelation. The sixth, the Te Deum, comes later and is not technically a canticle in that it does not come from the Bible, but since it is often called a canticle because of its antiquity and usage we will consider it here.[29]

1. Benedictus, Luke 1:68–79

This song of the New Testament community is attributed by Luke to Zechariah, the priest, who was smitten dumb because he did not believe the promise that his son John would be born. After John was born, on the eighth day when he was to be circumcised and named Zechariah after his father, Zechariah wrote that his name was to be "John." Zechariah's tongue was loosed, and he sang the Benedictus.

This canticle, associated with lauds and morning prayer in the East and the West because it includes the phrase "the dawn from on high shall break upon us," is about the particular activity of a gracious God expressed in a specific history. In language like the Psalms it begins by blessing the God of Israel. Why? Because this God visits and redeems the people, saves them from their enemies, sets them free, makes a covenant so the people can worship without fear, gives knowledge of salvation and forgiveness of sins. How? Not in general, but in a particular history with real people: in an oath to Abraham, through the house of David, spoken through the prophets, now preparing the way for the Savior by John the Baptist.

---

[27] Foley, *Foundations of Christian Music*, pp. 56–57.

[28] J. Gelineau, "Music and Singing in the Liturgy," *The Study of Liturgy*, p. 444.

[29] All of these texts except "Worthy Is Christ" from Revelation, which is numerous texts collated in different ways, can be found with commentary in *Praying Together: The English Language Consultation* (Abingdon Press, 1988). Virtually every hymnal has them in some form or other, often in various settings.

2. Magnificat, Luke 1:46–55

The Magnificat is almost universally associated with the evening office of vespers in the West since St. Benedict (c. 480–c. 550). Luke attributed it to Mary, and through Mary it has become the song of the church: in the evening, as lamps are lit, the church waits, like Mary, "for the fulfillment of the word of promise."[30] In the Eastern Church it is used as a morning canticle.[31]

Related to the Song of Hannah in I Samuel 2:1–10, when Hannah bore Samuel, it is one of the most amazing and heavily used canticles of the church. (Samuel Terrien, in a commentary, which includes references to musical settings, explains it well.[32]) Mary begins in the typical Jewish way, "My soul magnifies the Lord." Why? Because, sings Mary, God has regarded my low estate, has done mighty things, has mercy on those who fear this God in all generations, has shown strength, scattered the proud, put down the mighty, exalted the humble, filled the hungry, sent the rich away empty. How? Not in general, but in the promise to Abraham and Abraham's offspring and now to Mary.

It is a revolutionary text, not appreciated by dictators. If anyone thinks biblical and liturgical texts are tame, this one will quickly set the matter straight.

3. Gloria in Excelsis

This "Greater Doxology" (sometimes so-called to distinguish it from the "Lesser Doxology," the Gloria Patri[33]) is an elaborated form of the song Luke attributed to the angels in Luke 2:14 at Jesus' birth. Its authorship and age are unknown. By the fourth century it was associated with morning prayer and "imported from there into the Eucharist" after the Kyries. [34]

Here it becomes clear that the whole history of God's gracious dealing with humanity finds a focus in Christ. Again, in the typical

---

[30] Philip H. Pfatteicher, Carlos Messerli, ed., *Manual on the Liturgy, Lutheran Book of Worship* (Minneapolis: Augsburg Publishing House, 1979), p. 284.

[31] Marilyn Kay Stulken, *Hymnal Companion to the Lutheran Book of Worship* (Philadelphia: Fortress Press, 1981), p. 118.

[32] Samuel Terrien, *The Magnificat: Musicians as Biblical Interpreters* (New York: Paulist Press, 1995).

[33] "Glory to the Father and to the Son and to the Holy Spirit, as it was in the beginning, is now, and will be forever."

[34] Pfatteicher and Messerli, *Manual on the Liturgy*, p. 213.

Hebrew form, it begins by worshiping God, giving God thanks. Why? "For your glory." Where is this glory found? In the only Son of the Father, Jesus Christ, who is the Lamb of God, who takes away the sin of the world, who has mercy on us, who is seated at the right hand of the Father, who is holy, the only Lord, the most high Jesus Christ, with the Holy Spirit in the glory of God the Father.

The whole of history comes to a focus in Christ who is linked inextricably and equally with the Father and the Holy Spirit.

4. *Nunc Dimittis Luke 2:29–32*

This song of the church in Luke 2:29–32 was attributed by Luke to the devout Jew Simeon who, seeing Jesus in the Temple, sang it before he died. As in all these canticles, Simeon stands for the whole church, and the canticle itself sings the Old Testament in a new way. Here pieces of Second Isaiah have been woven together (Isaiah 40:5; 42:6; 46:13; 49:6; 52:10).

The Nunc Dimittis has been used at daily prayers since the fourth century and in the East at vespers. In the Western breviaries it was used at compline. From there it got to evening prayer in the *Book of Common Prayer*, which in turn set the stage for all the Anglican settings of it coupled with those of the Magnificat. In the Lutheran tradition it is often used as a postcommunion canticle.

Again, the focus in Christ is evident. Lord, let me depart in peace, says Simeon on behalf of the church, for I have seen your (God's) salvation in Christ. And now the universalizing note is sounded. This salvation is prepared before all peoples, not only the glory of Israel, but a light to all the nations.

5. *"Worthy is Christ"*

This is not one canticle in the way the others are, but stands as a compilation for the hymns of the early church, which the book of Revelation records.[35] The current Lutheran version is taken from Revelation 5:12, 9, 13; 7:10, 12; 19:4, 6–9.[36] *The [Episcopal] Hym-*

---

[35] These hymns are translated with commentary in Charles Mountain, " 'Glory and Honor and Blessing': The Hymns of the Apocalypse," *The Hymn* 47:1 (January 1996): 41–47.

[36] LBW, pp. 60–61, 81–82, 102. See Pfatteicher and Messerli, *Manual on the Liturgy*, pp. 213 and 372, FN 8.

nal 1982 has *Dignus est* ("Worthy is") from Revelation 4:11, 5:9–10, 13,[37] and the *Common Service Book of the Lutheran Church* had a canticle called *Dignus est Agnus* ("Worthy is the Lamb") drawn from Revelation 5, 15, and 19.[38] Hymns like Isaac Watts' "Come, Let Us Join our Cheerful Songs"[39] and Horatius Bonar's "Blessing and Honor"[40] are metrical versions of these same texts from Revelation.

Here a feast of victory is celebrated. Christ the Lamb, who was slain, reigns. Power, riches, wisdom, strength, honor, blessing, and glory belong to Christ. Therefore, the whole people of God and the whole of creation join in this hymn. The polarities of particularity in Christ, but universality for all are here with the characteristic paradoxes: victory through death; the kingdom breaks in now, but will be known in its fullness at the end of history; and we now have a foretaste of the feast of victory around the Lamb.

6. Te Deum

Of all the western hymns not taken from the Bible, this one is the best known. Though it was composed after the New Testament period like the elaboration of the Gloria in Excelsis, it represents the telos of the New Testament, so it is appropriate to include here. Sometimes ascribed to Ambrose and Augustine at Augustine's baptism, others like Niceta, the Bishop of Remesiana (d. c. 414), have also been considered its author.[41]

Long associated with morning prayer, it is cast into three parts. First, praise to God everlasting includes a "Holy, holy, holy" Sanc-

---

[37] *The [Episcopal] Hymnal 1982* (New York: The Church Hymnal Corporation, 1985), hereafter EH82, #s S261–266. See Raymond Glover, ed., *The Hymnal 1982 Companion* (New York: The Church Hymnal Corporation, 1994), II, p. 194.

[38] *Common Service Book of the Lutheran Church* (Philadelphia: The Board of Publication of the United Lutheran Church in America, 1917), p. 215.

[39] EH82, #374; LBW, #254; *Rejoice in the Lord: A Hymn Companion to the Scriptures* (Grand Rapids: Wm. B. Eerdmans Publishing Company, 1985), hereafter, RL, #571.

[40] LBW, #525; *The Presbyterian Hymnal: Hymns, Psalms, and Spiritual Songs* (Louisville: Westminster/John Knox Press, 1990), hereafter PH, #147; RL, #602; See LindaJo H. McKim, *The Presbyterian Hymnal Companion* (Louisville: Westminster/John Knox Press, 1993), p. 147.

[41] For a lengthy discussion of this "the most famous non-biblical hymn of the Western Church," see John Julian, *A Dictionary of Hymnology* (New York: Dover Publications, Inc., 1957, reprint of 2d rev. ed., 1907), II, pp. 1119–1134.

tus-like section in which apostles, prophets, martyrs, and the whole church praise the Father, Son, and Holy Spirit. Then a christocentric section points to Christ the King of Glory and tells the whole story of Christ: born of a virgin, conquers death, opens the kingdom of heaven, sits at the right hand of the Father, will come to be our judge. It concludes with a prayer to Christ to help us "whom you have redeemed with your blood." The third section was not originally part of the Te Deum and is sometimes omitted. It is a series of versicles from the Psalms: bless us, save us, keep us without sin. [42]

Other New Testament Texts

James McKinnon has assembled other New Testament passages that may relate to the early Christian community's singing.[43] Edward Foley has divided the "emerging Christian song" of the first century into short praise formulae, infancy canticles, God-hymns, christological hymns, psalms, readings, and table prayers.[44] Arland Hultgren has analyzed the liturgical background and use of Kyrie eleison in the gospel of Matthew.[45] Though his concern is not singing, singing is clearly implied. In addition to the canticles of the New Testament and those they have spawned, such as the Te Deum, let me point briefly to a series of doxological and christological formulations that may have been sung, perhaps drawn from the New Testament community at worship. These and similar formulations have remained part of the church's doxological doing and have given rise in some instances to further poetic and musical settings.

1. Philippians 2:6–12

Christ humbled himself, died on the cross, is exalted at God's right hand, so that at the name of Jesus every knee should bow.[46]

---

[42] Pfatteicher and Messerli, *Manual on the Liturgy*, p. 295; *Praying Together*, p. 44.

[43] McKinnon, MECL, pp. 12–17.

[44] Foley, *Foundations of Christian Music*, pp. 54–66.

[45] Hultgren, "Liturgy and Literature," pp. 664–666.

[46] *Cf.* Caroline Noel's "At the Name of Jesus," *The Baptist Hymnal* (Nashville: Convention Press, 1991), hereafter BH, #198; EH82, #435; LBW, #179; *The United Methodist Hymnal* (Nashville: The United Methodist Publishing House, 1989), hereafter UMH, #168; PH, #148; RL, #336; *Worship Third Edition: A Hymnal and Service Book for Roman Catholics* (Chicago: GIA Publications, Inc., 1986), here-

2. *Romans 11:36*

From God and through God and to God are all things. To God be glory forever. Amen.

3. *II Corinthians 11:31*

"The God and Father of the Lord Jesus, who is blest forever, knows that I do not lie."

4. *Philippians 4:20*

"To our God and Father be glory forever and ever. Amen."

5. *I Timothy 1:17*

"To the king of ages, immortal, invisible, the only God, be honor and glory forever and ever. Amen."[47]

Reflections

The coming of Christ required those who were grasped by him to make some judgments. Who was he? What did he do? Those two questions—first about the person and then about the work of Christ—led the church to what it eventually called christology. The church had to figure out who it was, which gave rise to what was eventually called ecclesiology, the theology of the church. The church had to make judgments about Christ in relation to time, which gave rise to what was eventually called eschatology.

These areas are all inextricably concerned with music. Though a sounded response to the christological, ecclesiological, and eschatological ideas seems inevitable for Christians, what shape the sound takes can vary with the theological judgments a community makes. It might be well to pause here, therefore, with a brief series of systematic reflections unrelated to specifically historical considerations. These reflections might suggest possibilities to stimulate you, the reader, to draw out your own implications.

---

after Wor3, #499. Werner IDB, K–Q, p. 467, says this "poetic outburst" was probably not sung and is the "first perceptible deviation from spirit and [parallel] structure of Hebrew poetry."

[47] *Cf.* Walter Smith's "Immortal, Invisible, God Only Wise," BH, #6; EH82, #423; LBW, #526; UMH, #103; PH, #263; RL #7; Wor3, #512.

Who Christ Is

Three options quickly arise when faced with the issue of who Christ is. The first of these says Christ was a human being. He may have been an unusual human being, even one of the greatest or even the greatest who ever lived or will live—a mountaintop of humanity—but he was still essentially human, not divine.

The second option says Christ was God. He may have looked like a human being, but really he was God. In this case the humanity of Christ is diminished or denied, and the deity of Christ is emphasized at the expense of the humanity.

The third option is the one the church settled on, that neither of the first two possibilities does justice to the reality of Christ faced by the world. Instead, it says that Christ was both human and divine. No matter how difficult it may be to say or to comprehend, in him God was present, but he also took on our human nature.

These options have practical ramifications, including musical ones. If you emphasize Christ's humanity at the expense of his divinity, you might choose music that affirms our humanity—music that relates to us who are beings with bodies. If you follow this logic, the music may be rhythmic and perhaps even sensuous. Or it may be the highest possible art.

The second choice, emphasizing Christ's divinity at the expense of his humanity, suggests mystery, what is not bodily, and what stands above the body in contemplation and beyond contemplation. In this case you might choose music that is other-worldly, ethereal, unrelated to our bodies and therefore with a rhythmic pulse governed more by contemplation than by physical movement.

The third option, that Christ is both God and human, comes with an inherent paradoxical tension. The tension of the position might be reflected in music controlled by this paradox. Music that affirms bodily movement and music that lives in an ethereal world of contemplative mystery might be forced to live in an incarnational tension. The theological posture will not logically allow either musical style to exist without the other.

What Christ Did

Four options cover concerns over what Christ did. In the first you have to make the assumption that humanity is not in such bad shape. To use the theological shorthand, the fall is not really radical. All that people need is an example. If they have the right example, they will be able to do what the example shows them to do. Christ is the example, the leader. As *the* human being of all human beings, he shows the way people can indeed follow.

The second option presumes that the fall of humanity is more radical. (It must be understood here that the argument about whether the fall was an actual historical happening or is a statement of the human condition is irrelevant. The existential reality of a broken humanity, even a broken world or universe or cosmos, is the operative issue.) Here the plight of humanity is considered too desperate for just an example. Humanity has to be rescued. The need is for a savior. Christ is viewed as the Savior who takes on the sinful condition of humanity, which is nailed to the cross in his own person, thereby redeeming lost humanity.

The third option, instead of using the images of example and redeemer as the primary ones, chooses to see Christ as conqueror. The fundamental problem here is that the twin enemies of death and evil are at war against us. Their power needs to be broken, and Christ breaks it. Sin and death think that in the cross they will destroy Christ, but they are destroyed instead.

The fourth option is to hold all three together so that Christ is viewed as example, savior, and conqueror.

The logical musical results of Christ as example might lead in two directions. One is to see music essentially related to ethics, especially societal ethical issues. The center of gravity here will fall on the music of protest marches, simple music that a group of marchers can sing and use to stir themselves to action. The other direction is quite different. Since humanity and humanity's reach is affirmed with Christ as the example, one can fasten on high art as humanity's stretch to reach as far as it can. This direction leads to a Renaissance or Enlightenment mentality in which human achievement takes center stage, and it can view Beethoven as a model because he affirms his highest humanity by creating music that stretches beyond him.

In the second option, the cross is critical. Music might therefore reflect the pain of the cross, Christ's suffering, and death. It might emphasize mourning. The scrape of dissonance will characterize such music. The dissonance will be resolved, of course, because the cross did accomplish rescue, but the sting of suffering and the cries of anguish will be heard.

In the third option, victory is critical. Here joy and celebration might characterize the music. The pain will not be avoided because of the necessary battle. Battles are costly and painful, especially one in which the creator of the whole cosmos is involved; but since the outcome is a victory, the emphasis will fall on the eschatological feast and its celebration, which humanity already now can enjoy.

Holding all three in tension means a wide scope in which the music of marches, high art, suffering, and victory are all given place. Few communities manage to hold together the fullness of the theological affirmations much less the fullness of the musical ones.

Ecclesiology

In addition to the christological issues, the presence of a group of people linked in some fashion to Christ forces this group, called church, to determine who they are.

Of the three basic ecclesiological options, the first two could be placed on opposite ends of a spectrum. At one end the church is conceived as the followers of Christ. Christ is the leader, and the church is the group that follows his leading, either in individual actions or in societal actions or both. At the other end of the spectrum the church is conceived as the body of Christ in the world. Here the church is seen as sustained by the sacramental body and blood of Christ given by Christ to Christ's body who are the people baptized into Christ. The ambiguity of imagery is not accidental and itself points to the nature of this position. The third option either takes its place on the spectrum between these two, or embraces both positions and then affirms that each necessitates the other.

Musically, the first of these options can be seen to lead to the music of marches or that of martyr ballads. The second option can be understood to lead to music that celebrates, perhaps more quietly, the mystery of the sacramental presence. Holding the two together or keeping the two in some sort of balance and tension is the third musical result, a much more challenging task.

Eschatology[48]

The community that confesses Christ invariably concludes that some new thing has broken into this world. This new thing can be described variously as the reign of God or a turning from one age,

---

[48] I am indebted to Arland Hultgren for his suggestions of and about this section on eschatology.

one reality, to another. It means that both temporal and transtemporal matters are in play. Reflections here lead to three options.

One is to emphasize the *already* of this new age at the expense of the *not yet,* thereby playing down or even denigrating the creation in which we live called good in Genesis. It might also impel an ethical fervor that turns sour when the reality of *not yet* becomes apparent.

The second is to highlight the *not yet* of the new age at the expense of the *already*, emphasizing that the reign of God will come sometime in the future and thereby dwelling on the misery of this world and its fallen condition. This interpretation might suggest waiting with little or no action. The third is to hold the *already* and the *not yet* in tension—action and waiting, or freedom for ethical action, or celebration with patience, or *not yet* with its presupposition of restoration taking the edge off of denigration and *already* taking the edge off of misery.[49]

Musically the first option might suggest the rhythmic pulse of celebration or accompaniment of active engagement in the world. The second might be more patient and deliberate in its pulse, less active, maybe even mournful because of the wait though perhaps quietly joyful because of the end. The third view holds the musical possibilities in deliberate tension, thereby calling into play a wide palette.

Tensions

These tensions and other ones are inherent in the New Testament, including its song. As Arland Hultgren suggested to me with regard to eschatology, for example, in the Gloria in Excelsis, Christ is at the right hand of God *already*, and there is peace on earth *not yet*. In "Worthy Is Christ" the Lamb has *already* begun his reign, but we join the hymn of creation as people of God still on earth *not yet* in the new age. In the Benedictus God has *already* come to set the people free, but we continue to worship all the days of our lives *not yet* in the totally freed condition. In the Te Deum the reign of Christ is *already* begun, but that Christ will come to be our judge suggests the *not yet* in which we live. In the Magnificat God has *already* cast down the arrogant, but there is *not yet* in the mercy from generation to generation.

That the inherent tensions in the New Testament should lead to tensions in church music should not surprise us. The New Testament

---

[49] For a discussion of this tension in Paul, see Günther Bornkamm, trans. D. M. G. Stalker, *Paul* (New York: Harper & Row, 1969), pp. 196–227.

witnesses to a reality that is *in* but not *of* the world, just like the church, which produced the witness itself and then seeks to live by it. As we shall see in the next chapters, this tension in witness produces musical results: the church *already* sings with one voice, but the *not yet* of diffusion is ever present.

THE FIRST CENTURIES

5

With One Voice

"The Christian Church was born in song."[1] It sang hymns, psalms, and spiritual songs, as the parallel passages in Ephesians 5:18–20 and Colossians 3:16–17 indicate. Singing continued in the postapostolic period, but precisely what it means the church sang is difficult to say because the terms "psalms, hymns, and spiritual songs" probably were general rather than specific.[2] Whatever the terms meant,

---

[1] Ralph Martin, *Worship in the Early Church* (Westwood: Fleming H. Revell Company, 1964), p. 39.

[2] Christian Hannick, "Christian Church, music of the early," NGDMM, 4, p. 363, thinks these "three terms have plerophoric value and are not evidence of different types of chant." Margot Fassler and Peter Jeffrey, "Christian Liturgical Music from the Bible to the Renaissance," *Sacred Sound and Social Change: Liturgical Music in Jewish and Christian Experience*, ed. Lawrence A. Hoffman and Janet R. Walton (Notre Dame: University of Notre Dame Press, 1992), p. 85, regard the terms in the same way, as "loose synonyms used interchangeably" with others. Hannick's article provides an overview of the music of the early church. So does Foley, *Foundations of Christian Music* and Fassler and Jeffrey's, "Christian Liturgical Music," the latter obviously within the context of a larger historical sweep. James McKinnon, *Music in Early Christian Literature* (Cambridge: Cambridge University Press, 1987), pp. 1–11, also surveys the early period. For the remainder of his book McKinnon lays out the writings about music in the period following the New Testament. He brings consistent English translations of this material together in one handy volume along with helpful introductory comments about it. Robert A. Skeris, *Chroma Theou*, also lays out the passages related to musical imagery from the first three centuries in English and the original Greek or Latin, "with a view to illuminating the sources of such imagery, setting fourth its theological content, and estimating its pastoral value as a clear reflection of liturgical adaptation" (p. 17). Two other collections of source readings are Oliver Strunk, *Source Readings in Music History: From Classical Antiquity through the Romantic Era* (New York: W. W. Norton & Company, 1950) and David W. Music, *Hymnology: A Collection of Source Readings* (Lanham: The Scarecrow Press, 1996).

remember the underlying reality to which Joseph Gelineau and Edward Foley pointed in the last chapter, "that worship was lyrical" with no clear distinction between singing and speech, that lessons were cantillated and prayers were intoned.[3] The whole of worship was musical, so that it is difficult to distinguish music as a separate element of worship. To use Foley's apt phrase, music was the "aural aspect" of the church's worship.[4] Or, in Gelineau's words, there was "an intense lyrical quality in the life of the apostolic church, particularly in its liturgical assemblies."[5] As Foley says, ". . . our ability to elaborate worship without music . . . would be completely unintelligible to Christians of the first centuries."[6]

It is not clear just how early one can say with certainty what Christians sang. But out of the musical orb just described the congregation certainly grew to sing psalms,[7] canticles, nonscriptural

---

For a different view on "psalms, hymns, and spiritual songs," see Egon Wellesz, *A History of Byzantine Music and Hymnography* (Oxford: Clarendon University Press, 1961), pp. 33–43. Wellesz thinks the terms cannot be differentiated musically, but are liturgical designations for the chants. "Psalms" means "Psalms and Canticles"; "Hymns" means "Verses, Stanzas and Hymns, Litanies and Processional songs"; and "Spiritual Songs" means "Alleluias, Songs of Praise" (p. 42).

[3] Foley, *From Age to Age*, p. 9. *Cf.* Hannick, "Christian Church, music of the early," NGDMM, 4, p. 366.

[4] Foley, *From Age to Age*, p. 33.

[5] J. Gelineau, "Music and Singing in the Liturgy," *The Study of Liturgy*, ed. Jones et al., p. 444.

[6] Foley, *Foundations of Christian Music*, p. 5. This book begins by exploring how the orality of the early church differs from our environment.

[7] Whether they sang psalms or nonbiblical hymns at first is a matter of dispute. McKinnon, MECL, p. 8, leaves the question open. L. Duchesne, trans. by M. L. McClure, *Christian Worship: Its Origin and Evolution* (London: Society for Promoting Christian Knowledge, 1927), p. 113, says "The chanting of the psalms was from the beginning . . . one of the essential elements of public worship." Willi Apel, *Gregorian Chant*, p. 19 agrees: "In the earliest days of Christian worship the service consisted only of psalm-singing." Edward Foley, "The Cantor in Historical Perspective," *Worship* 56:3 (May 1982): 207, however, points out that "only in the late second and into the third century" is there any clear reference to congregational singing at all. Christian Hannick, "Christian Church, music of the early," NGDMM, 4, p. 366, thinks hymns were used by Christians until the third century, and only then were Old Testament psalms employed in their worship. Justin Martyr (c. 100–c. 165), for example, in his description of the Sunday morning Eucharist, does not mention psalmody (which by itself does not prove anything, of course). See McKinnon, MECL, p. 20.

hymns like the Phos Hilaron,[8] doxological and christological formulations similar to those cited in the last chapter, call-and-response dialogues like the Sursum corda ("Lift up your hearts") between leader and people, and other liturgical pieces like the Trisagion ("Holy God, Holy and Mighty, Holy and Immortal, have mercy on us")[9] and the Sanctus ("Holy, holy holy . . .").[10] Short "ordinary" liturgical chants that could be memorized easily, the Sanctus, for example, we can assume were sung together by the whole community. Psalms—"proper" to given days, longer, and not amenable to memorization—at least from the time of Tertullian at the beginning of the third century were likely sung *responsorially*, that is, with a soloist singing the psalm and the congregation punctuating it with a single repeated verse or an Alleluia. This practice could have moved in several directions—to a *direct* psalmody where the soloist sang everything until the congregation supplied an "Amen" at the end, to a *unison* psalmody where everybody sang the whole psalm, or to *antiphonal* psalmody where the congregation was divided into two choirs who alternated verses with one another. Unison singing could have been early, while the evidence for antiphony comes from the fourth or fifth centuries and is murkier than that for the responsorial type.[11] Different places may well have done different things during the same period. Gregory the Great, for example, says among the Greeks at his time everybody sang the Kyrie eleison, whereas "with us" the clerics were answered by the people.[12]

[8] Known in Robert Bridges' translation as "O Gladsome Light." It can be found in EH, #36; LBW, p. 143 and #279; PH, #549; RL, #623; UMH, #686; Wor3, #12 and #679. For comments about this hymn with the text, see Routley, *A Panorama of Christian Hymnody* (Collegeville: The Liturgical Press, 1979), p. 78. For more detail and a list of English versions see M. Eleanor Irwin, "Phos Hilaron: the Metamorphoses of a Greek Hymn," *The Hymn* 40:2 (April, 1989): 7–12.

[9] For possible origins of this ancient chant, see David Flusser, "Jewish Roots of the Liturgical Trisagion," *Immanuel* 3 (Winter 1973/74): 37–43.

[10] See Fassler and Jeffrey, Hoffman and Walton, eds., *Sacred Sound*, pp. 85–86.

[11] See McKinnon, p. 10; Hannick, pp. 366–367; Gelineau, *The Study*, ed. Jones et al., p. 446; Foley, *Foundations of Christian Music*, p. 81; and Apel, *Gregorian Chant*, p. 185ff.

[12] Gregory the Great, "Letter to Bishop John of Syracuse," in Robert F. Hayburn, *Papal Legislation on Sacred Music, 95 A.D. to 1977 A.D.* (Collegeville: The Liturgical Press, 1979), p. 5.

However diffuse the practice of the early church, it included the ideal of singing "with one voice." Clement (fl. c. 96), bishop of Rome, in what might be a reference to the Sanctus of the Eucharist, said.

> Let us consider the entire multitude of angels, how standing by you they minister to his will. For the Scripture says: "Ten thousand stood by him and a thousand ministered to him and cried out, 'Holy, holy, holy is the Lord of Sabaoth, the whole creation is full of his glory.' (Is.6.3)" Let us, therefore, gathered together in concord by conscience, cry out earnestly to him as if *with one voice*, so that we might come to share in his great and glorious promises.[13]

Ignatius (c. 35–c. 107), bishop of Antioch, put it this way.

> . . . you make up a chorus, so that joined together in harmony [referring to the harmony of Christians, not what we today call musical harmony] and having received the godly strain in unison, you might sing *in one voice* through Christ to the Father, so that he might hear you and recognize you through your good deeds as members of his son. . . ."[14]

Johannes Quasten quotes this passage from Clement of Alexandria (c. 150–c. 215).

> We want to strive so that we, the many, may be brought together into one love, according to the union of the essential unity. As we do good may we similarly pursue unity. . . . The union of many, which the divine harmony has called forth out of a medley of sounds and division, *becomes one symphony*, following the one leader of the choir and teacher, the Word, resting in that same truth and crying out, "Abba, Father."[15]

Quasten takes Clement of Alexandria to mean the early Christians expressed their unity and harmony musically in "one symphony" of unison singing, that they understood unity and harmony as opposites to duality and disharmony and therefore

---

[13] Clement of Rome, *I Corinthians* xxxiv, ed. Jacques Paul Migne, *Patrologiae cursus completus Series Graeca* (Paris, 1857ff.), hereafter PG, I, 275–278; trans. McKinnon, MECL, p. 18. Italics mine.

[14] Ignatius of Antioch, *Ephesians* iv; PG V, 733–736; trans. by McKinnon, MECL, p. 19. For another trans. see Alexander Roberts and James Donaldson, ed., *The Ante-Nicene Fathers* (Grand Rapids: Wm. B. Eerdmans Publishing, 1885ff.), hereafter ANF, I, pp. 50–51.

[15] Clement of Alexandria, *Protrepticus* ix, PG VIII, 199–202; trans. in Johannes Quasten, trans. by Boniface Ramsey, *Music and Worship in Pagan and Christian Antiquity* (Washington: National Association of Pastoral Musicians, 1983), p. 67. Italics mine.

rejected heterophony and polyphony.[16] Some might want to ask whether Clement was referring specifically to music here and then wonder (with Quasten himself) about the musical practice of pagan antiquity into which the church was born, whether it knew harmony or polyphony at all, and what the precise nature of the heterophony of the time may have been. But none of that alters Quasten's fundamental insight. The unison song (actually "a simple polyphony, at the octave"[17] because men, women, and children all sang together) of the early church was more than a musical phenomenon. It was "an image of the unity and harmony of all Christians,"[18] as Clement of Rome and Ignatius of Antioch also indicate. The sense here, as Robert Skeris explains, is actually not so much about performance practice as it is about "the unity of the worshippers themselves and with God in and through Christ, but also with the heavenly liturgy."[19] Or, said in another way, "the Incarnation of Christ the eternal Logos rejoined heaven and earth," and the baptized sang a new song in the Spirit.[20] There's a proleptic reality at work here, an eschatological *already* and *not yet* held in an incarnational tension that is expressed musically.

A striking parallel can be made between these passages about music and one about the Eucharist in the *Didache*. The *Didache* was a paste and scissors compilation from the middle of the second century which included a eucharistic prayer that probably came from the first century. There the church prayed it might be brought together from the ends of the earth as the bread for the Eucharist was baked together into one loaf from wheat that had been scattered over the hills.[21] The music of the early church reflected the same idea as the Eucharist, namely, a group of diverse people from various places joined together into one voice.

---

[16] Quasten, *Music and Worship in Pagan and Christian Antiquity*, pp. 66–72.

[17] Hannick, "Christian Church, music of the early," NGDMM, 4, p. 368.

[18] Quasten, *Music and Worship in Pagan and Christian Antiquity*, p. 67.

[19] Robert A. Skeris, *Chroma Theou*, p. 122. Cf. pp. 176–177.

[20] Ibid., p. 158.

[21] *The Didache*, in "Early Christian Fathers," *The Library of Christian Classics*, vol. I (Philadelphia: The Westminster Press, 1953), p. 175.

Notice the connections between Eucharist, song, life together,[22] and "doing good." These were not conceived as isolated elements, each restricted to a separate and independent existence. They all had to do with the life together of the many made one, and they cohered in the incarnate Word. Musically the unity in Christ was expressed "with one voice."[23] Note also that "with one voice" meant everyone was included in the song—not only men, but women, children, the baptized past and present, everyone.[24] The song took incarnational shape as the participation of the whole body was welcomed. Nobody was excluded.

Context

The early church came singing into a world of real people with real problems to face. It was widely dispersed, with Jewish and Gentile traditions, poor means of communication from place to place, the mission that Paul's conversion propelled, and questions about jurisdiction. The church therefore had to organize itself.[25]

Its youthful vigor produced what are technically known as enthusiasts, among them people called Montanists (followers of Montanus)[26] who came on the scene in the latter half of the second century after the martyrdom of Bishop Polycarp around 155. These people and groups felt they had direct contact with the Holy Spirit. Enthusiasts always were in danger of setting themselves above the

[22] Dietrich Bonhoeffer, trans. John W. Doberstein, *Life Together* (New York: Harper & Brothers, 1954), pp. 59–61, in our century, seems to reflect an insight of the early church in a passage about the spiritual discipline of unison singing in the life together of Christians.

[23] There is also the note that Christ is the leader of the song, in Skeris's view, in place of Orpheus. See Robert A. Skeris, *Chroma Theou*, pp. 83, 96, 125, (131), 146–156, 159.

[24] See Quasten, *Music and Worship in Pagan and Christian Antiquity*, pp. 85 and 88, and Hannick, "Christian Church, music of the early," NGDMM, p. 368.

[25] For a description of organizational matters, see Robert Grant, *Augustus to Constantine: The Thrust of the Christian Movement into the Roman World* (New York: Harper & Row, 1970), pp. 53–74.

[26] For allusions of Montanus to music see Robert A. Skeris, *Chroma Theou*, pp. 35–36.

community as laws unto themselves. The church therefore confronted the necessity of theological and liturgical definition from within.

It also had to define itself against Gnosticism. Gnosticism, represented especially by Valentinus in the latter half of the second century, was a pattern of thought that made itself felt inside and outside the church. It held that matter was evil, God was good, and the two could not get mixed up with one another. God could not have created the world of matter and still remained good, so a whole series of emanations from God had to be posited to get to a "creator" God sufficiently unrelated to Godness to have created physical things. Against this thought of the world, the church pressed the physicality of the incarnation.

A certain Marcion in the second century caused the church considerable pain. He was excommunicated in 144, but established a rival group that was still active in the fourth century. Marcion sounded like a Gnostic, but probably was not. His fundamental point was to reject the Old Testament and to keep as Scripture ten letters of Paul and a version of the Gospel of Luke. He held that the gospel was Love, that Paul understood it, and that what he regarded as the capricious God of Law in the Old Testament had nothing to do with the loving God of Christ in the New Testament. His rejection included the Psalms, of course, which flew in the face of the church's christological use of them.

The early church also faced the stark reality of persecution. In the first centuries of its existence, therefore, it was not apt to gather publicly. It met in private houses until after about 311–313, when edicts of toleration made Christianity legal and safe from persecution. In members' homes it shared "common meals" that were like "ritualized Jewish banquets" or "family-centered meals that still survive today in Jewish homes."[27] Historians have found it virtually impossible to sort out the precise relationship of the Eucharist to these meals. Suffice it to say that there certainly were common elements, overlaps, and mixing. Lamplighting or vespers services at the close of the day were also prayed.[28] The meals "included Scripture read-

[27] Fassler and Jeffrey in Hoffman and Walton, "Christian Liturgical Music," Hoffman and Walton, ed., *Sacred Sound*, pp. 84–85.

[28] One of the earliest hymns we have is the lamplighting hymn, the Phos hilaron, mentioned already.

ing, religious instruction, prayer, and singing,"[29] as Fassler and Jeffrey suggest, and many of the references to music in the early church compare pagan meals, called banquets or symposia, to Christian ones.

After Christianity was legalized, the church found itself divided internally, partly about who Christ was. Arius (c. 250–c. 336), a presbyter in Alexandria who has become known as the archheretic of the church, insisted so strongly on the absolute uniqueness of God that he subordinated the person of Christ. He was a public relations expert who wrote jingles to popular tunes and embodied technical theological detail in these songs, known as *Thalia* or "Banquet."

> The Father is alien to the Son in essence,
> for the Father is without beginning.
> The Unbegun made the Son the beginning
> of things originated.
> When the Son was not the Father was God.[30]

At the Council of Niceae in 325, the church decided Arius's position did not match its experience of Christ. Arianism was rejected though it remained a strong force for a long time. The Council worked out the Nicene Creed and debated other matters such as when to celebrate Easter.

Against Musical Instruments

Music was part of the same real world as persecution, organization, internal and external definition. As the church was to discover, being *in* but not *of* the world was difficult. Music posed problems like everything else. The church in its worship simply adopted the vocal chant of the synagogue, without instruments.[31] By the third and fourth centuries, however, it came to realize that in confronting the pagan culture outside the church's worship, music and music's asso-

---

[29] Fassler and Jeffrey in Hoffman and Walton, "Christian Liturgical Music," Hoffman and Walton, ed., *Sacred Sound*, p. 85.

[30] These translations are from a lecture by Bard Thompson at Lancaster Seminary, Lancaster, Pennsylvania, February 2, 1963.

[31] There are those who think instruments were used both in the synagogue and by the early Christians, but even they concede this was exceptional or restricted to "isolated instances." See Sendrey, *Music in Ancient Israel*, pp. 182–183.

ciations were part of the package it had to confront. The musical part of this confrontation became most obvious in the polemic against musical instruments.

As indicated in the preceding chapter, already in the New Testament one can see evidence of a view that regarded vocal music as superior to instrumental music. Werner points out that this view characterized the Pharisees and was reflected by Paul in his thirteenth chapter of First Corinthians where he disparaged the noisy gong and the clanging cymbal.[32]

In the period following the New Testament, instrumental music was not only regarded as inferior to vocal music, however. It was banned. As Hannick indicates, this move was not all that revolutionary in practice, for instruments were not used in the synagogue, and with the destruction of the Temple in 70 A.D. they obviously disappeared there too.[33] But the vehemence of the objections in the early church is startling. After the high regard for instruments in the Old Testament and the gracious nature of the New Testament—which, in spite of what may be seen as disparaging remarks by Paul in I Corinthians 13, never seems hostile toward instruments—the force of the language that follows the New Testament is striking.

Clement of Alexandria

Clement of Alexandria made the point quite clearly.

> We, however, make use of but one instrument, the word of peace alone by which we honor God, and no longer the ancient psaltery, nor the trumpet, the tympanum and the aulos, as was the custom among those expert in war and those scornful of the fear of God who employed string instruments in their festive gatherings, as if to arouse their remissness of spirit through such rhythms.[34]

Part of the reason for rejecting instruments, as Quasten notes, may have been the concern that the heterophony of instrumental music confounded the idea of unity which unison, or octave, singing

---

[32] Werner, "Music," IDB, K–Q, p. 466.

[33] Christian Hannick, "Christian Church, music of the early," NGDMM, 4, p. 368.

[34] Clement of Alexandria, *Paedagogus* II, iv, PG VIII, 443–444; trans. McKinnon, MECL, p. 33.

expressed.[35] Part of the reason may have been an association of instrumental music with temple priesthood and sacrifice, which were rejected.[36] Part of the reason, as this last quotation from Clement of Alexandria suggests, was the connection of instruments with war. But mostly instruments were suspicious because of their associations with idolatry and immorality. Here's Clement again.

> Let carousing be absent from our rational enjoyment, and also foolish vigils which revel in drunkenness. . . . Let lust, intoxication and irrational passions be far removed from our native choir. . . . The irregular movements of auloi, psalteries, choruses, dances, Egyptian clappers and other such playthings become altogether indecent and uncouth, especially when joined by beating cymbals and tympana and accompanied by the noisy instruments of deception. Such a symposium, it seems to me, becomes nothing but a theatre of drunkenness. . . .
>
> Let the syrinx be assigned to shepherds and the aulos to superstitious men who are obsessed by idolatry. In truth these instruments are to be banished from the sober symposium. . . .[37]

Tertullian

Clement did not stand alone. Tertullian (c. 170–c. 225), a Christian writer whose rigor is symbolized in that he became a Montanist, wrote a pamphlet called "De Spectaculis." Instrumental music was associated with the shows, and Tertullian regarded them as idolatrous[38]—in their origins, titles, superstitions, places, and patrons. The sporting of young men, he said, came from festal days, temples, and objects of religious veneration.[39] Festivals were called Apollo of Ceres, Neptune, Jupiter Latiaris, and Flora.[40] The circus was "chiefly consecrated to the sun."[41] Horseback riding was sacred to Castor

---

[35] Quasten, *Music and Worship in Pagan and Christian Antiquity*, pp. 66–67. McKinnon, MECL, pp. 3–4, makes it clear that an a cappella ideal is not at issue here. Vocal performance and the polemic against instruments were unrelated realities for the early church.

[36] See Foley, *Foundations of Christian Music*, p. 67.

[37] Clement of Alexandria, *Paedagogus* II, iv, PG VIII, 439–440; trans. McKinnon, MECL, p. 32.

[38] Tertullian, "De Spectaculis" IV, *Corpus Christianorum*, Series Latina, hereafter CCL, I (Turnholt, 1954ff.), p. 231; trans. ANF 3, p. 81.

[39] Ibid., V, CCL I, pp. 231–232; trans. ANF 3, p. 81.

[40] Ibid., VI, CCL I, p. 233; trans. ANF 3, p. 82.

[41] Ibid., VIII, CCL I, p. 234; trans. ANF 3, p. 82.

and Pollux.[42] The theatrical exhibitions had a common origin with the circus and resembled each other in their pomp, processions, and "music of pipes and trumpets."[43]

Tertullian had other objections. 1) The shows were a form of lust, the lust of pleasure.[44] 2) The lust of pleasure leads to "keenness of feeling" which leads to "rivalry" which leads to "rage, bitterness, wrath, and grief."[45] In short, the shows produce "spiritual agitation," "strong excitement," and "passionate desire." For Tertullian these are the antithesis of Christian conduct, which in his view is characterized by calmness, gentleness, quietness, and peace.[46] 3) The theater with its licentious speech and immodest gesture is impure.[47] 4) It is cruel. There are blows, kicks, men thrown to wild beasts, and the pleasure of the crowd in another's sufferings.[48]

Basil

Basil the Great (c. 330–370), who came after the Council of Nicaea in 325, was one of the "Cappadocian Fathers." As the bishop of Caesarea he championed the Christian faith with the Nicene formulations against the Arian denial of Christ's divinity. He represents a more temperate approach to music than Tertullian, but not different in essentials from either Clement of Alexandria or Tertullian before the Council of Nicaea. He distinguished between two types of music. One kind befits Christians. It is vocal, and its purpose is to be a kind of honey, which imperceptibly makes the text palatable.

> What did the Holy Spirit do when he saw that the human race was not led easily to virtue, and that due to our penchant for pleasure we give little heed to an upright life? He mixed sweetness of melody with doctrine so that inadvertently we would absorb the benefit of the words through gentleness and ease of hearing, just as clever physicians frequently smear the cup with honey when giving the fastidious some rather bitter medicine to drink. Thus he contrived for us these harmo-

[42] Ibid., IX, CCL I, p. 235; trans. ANF 3, p. 83.
[43] Ibid., X, CCL I, p. 236; trans. ANF 3, p. 83f.
[44] Ibid., XIV, CCL I, pp. 239–240; trans. ANF, 3, p. 85.
[45] Ibid., XV, CCL I, p. 240; trans. ANF 3, p. 86.
[46] Ibid., XV, CCL I, pp. 240–241; trans. ANF 3, p. 86.
[47] Ibid., XVII, CCL I, pp. 242–243; trans. ANF 3, p. 87.
[48] Ibid., XVIII–XIX, CCL I, pp. 243–244; trans. ANF 3, p. 87.

nious psalm tunes, so that those who as children in actual age as well as those who are young in behavior, while appearing only to sing would in reality be training their souls. For not one of these many indifferent people ever leaves church easily retaining in memory some maxim of either the Apostles or Prophets, but they do sing texts of the Psalms at home and circulate them in the marketplace.

> A psalm is tranquility of soul and arbitration of peace; it settles one's tumultuous and seething thoughts. It mollifies the soul's wrath and chastens its recalcitrance. A psalm creates friendships, unites the separated and reconciles those at enmity. Who can still consider one to be a foe with whom one utters the same prayer to God! Thus psalmody provides the greatest of all goods, charity, by devising in its common song a certain bond of unity, and by joining together the people into the concord of a single chorus.[49]

Here the single and unaccompanied voice of the people carries a bond of unity into the marketplace from worship, plus the idea that music helps us swallow the bitter medicine of the texts. Basil also knew of a dissolute music, however. It was connected to the theatrical shows, and instruments were part of it.

> There are towns where the inhabitants, from dawn to eve, feast their eyes on the tricks of innumerable conjurors. They are never tired of hearing dissolute songs which cause impurity to spring up in their souls, and they are often called happy, because they neglect the cares of business and trades useful to life, and pass the time, which is assigned them on this earth, in idleness and pleasure. They do not know that a theatre full of impure sights is, for those who sit there, a common school of vice; that these melodies and meretricious songs insinuate themselves into men's souls, and all who hear them, eager to imitate the notes of [kithara and aulos players], are filled with filthiness.[50]

Chrysostom

John Chrysostom (c. 347–407), one of the early church's most austere and famous preachers, perhaps most forcefully set out in bold relief the two sorts of music that Basil described. It might be help-

---

[49] Basil the Great, *Homiliae in Psalmos*, 1:1–2, PG XXIX, 212; trans. McKinnon, MECL, pp. 65–66.

[50] Basil the Great, *Homiliae in Hexaemoron* IV, 1; PG, XXIX, 77–80; trans. Philip Schaff, ed., *A Select Library of Nicene and Post-Nicene Fathers of the Christian Church*, hereafter NPNF, Second Series (1890ff., republished Grand Rapids: Wm. B. Eerdmans Publishing, 1952–1956) VIII, p. 72.

ful to linger over Chrysostom for a moment to visualize things more clearly. John grew up in a wealthy Christian family in Antioch, attending the law courts and excited by the theater. He was baptized around 372. (Even if one was born into a Christian family, baptism was often delayed, a practice a number of bishops, including Chrysostom, condemned.) From an early age he wanted to become a monk, but his widowed mother (his father died when he was twenty) persuaded him to stay with her until her death. He turned their home into a monastery, and, when she died in 373 or 374, he retreated to the desert as a hermit. After inflicting on himself a lifestyle sufficiently severe to ruin his health, he returned to Antioch in 381. He was made a deacon by Bishop Meletius. Five years later he became a priest under Bishop Flavian who gave him special responsibilities for preaching. He carried out those responsibilities until 398, gaining for himself the reputation "Chrysostom" or "golden-mouthed."

In 398, against his wishes, Chrysostom was made patriarch of Constantinople. (He had once before escaped a bishop's throne in Syria when by a "pious fraud"[51] he successfully engineered a scheme to have his friend Basil taken as bishop.) Continuing his typical lifestyle, he sold the elegant furnishings of the episcopal palace and gave the money to the poor and to hospitals. He stopped episcopal banquets, refused invitations to other banquets, ate simple food by himself, and reduced the formerly elegant episcopal life to the utmost simplicity. Neither did he fail in his preaching to chide the rich on behalf of the poor nor to speak out in his honest but tactless way whenever he felt the need. This gained him the support of the people of Constantinople, but it also provided fodder for Theophilus, the envious patriarch of Alexandria; and it offended the Empress Eudoxia. In 403, therefore, at the Synod of the Oak, presided over and controlled by Theophilus, twenty-nine charges were leveled against Chrysostom. He was banished. The following day, however, a frightened Empress had him recalled. Scarcely two months later, Eudoxia was again offended, and in 404 a second decree of banishment was issued. In 407 enforced walking for three months on the way to Pityus on the east shore of the Black Sea killed him.

---

[51] Philip Schaff, "Prolegomena, The Life and Work of St. John Chrysostom," NPNF, First Series, p. 8.

It's helpful to know Chrysostom's background and austerity so the amusement he opposed can be seen in contrast. At the time of John Chrysostom "the greatest single institution for sport and amusement" for Antioch's citizenry was Daphne.[52] Daphne was a suburban park, eight kilometers from Antioch and sixteen kilometers in circumference, almost as large as Antioch itself. Daphne's principal event was the Olympic games, celebrated every four years. These included prize fights, betting on foot races, boxing, archery contests, horse racing, music, and singing. There were other events like horse races every Sunday and theatrical and dance exhibitions.[53]

When Chrysostom went to Constantinople he found much the same scene he had encountered in Antioch. The difference was proximity: in Antioch Daphne was eight kilometers away. In Constantinople many Daphne-type elements, one of the two theaters and the baths, were near the cathedral. The circus or Hippodrome was so near the cathedral that its clamor could be heard in church. The Hippodrome was the size of the Circus Maximus in Rome. It surpassed any other circus in the world. There bets were made on horses, and actual as well as political battles, sometimes passionate, were fought. By the time of Chrysostom the Hippodrome had become the heart of Constantinople.[54]

Whereas Tertullian attacked the shows for their idolatry, Chrysostom saw the problem as immorality. For him the theater was a source of temptation that ensnared people. The music of the theater matched its impure gait, dress, and gesture, subverting marriage and society. That is why he set the "lascivious" songs of the theater against the "spiritual" psalms of the church.[55]

> Where are they who give themselves to devilish choirs, and harlot's songs, and sit in theatres? For I am ashamed to make mention of them. . . .
>
> But here the grace of the Spirit pours forth a sound, using instead of flute or lyre or pipes, the lips of the saints.[56]

---

[52] Chrysostomus Baur, *John Chrysostom and His Time*, trans. M Gonzaga (Westminster: The Newman Press, 1959), I, p. 38.

[53] See Baur, I, p. 38f.

[54] See Baur, II, p. 22ff.

[55] John Chrysostom, "Exposition of Psalm XLI," PG LV, 157; trans. Strunk, *Source Readings*, p. 68.

[56] John Chrysostom, "Homilies on the Gospel of St. Matthew," Homily LXVIII, 4; PG, LVIII, 644–645; trans. NPNF 10, p. 418.

Chrysostom's quarrel was not with music as such. "God . . . blended melody," he said,

> with prophecy in order that, delighted by the modulation of the chant, all might give forth sacred hymns to Him. For nothing so uplifts the mind, giving it wings and freeing it from earth, releasing it from the chains of the body, affecting it with love of wisdom, and causing it to scorn all things pertaining to this life as modulated melody and the divine chant composed of number.[57]

He went on to speak with appreciation and understanding of lullabies, songs of travelers that ease the journey, and of work songs that "lighten . . . the labor endured in working."[58] Chrysostom's quarrel was with music's associations "Demons congregate," he said, "where there are licentious chants, but where there are spiritual ones there the grace of the Spirit descends."[59]

Like Tertullian, Chrysostom had some other concerns folded into his overriding one of immorality. The savagery and blasphemy of the circus bothered him, and he was especially incensed that the music of the shows cost so much. The result, he said, was that the poor who needed help did not get it.[60] The rich revealed their barbarity and inhumanity.

Alexandria and Antioch

Some twentieth-century Christians may be put off with what appears to be the ungracious stringency in these early writers, but for the moment let us grant the cultural associations of musical instruments with immorality and idolatry in pagan antiquity along with the church's sense that it had to oppose them. This cultural tension does not address the many positive references to musical instruments in the Old Testament. How were those references to be interpreted?

If you followed the Alexandrian practice, the tradition of allegorizing put the solution near at hand. Here's how Clement of Alexandria interpreted Psalm 150.

---

[57] John Chrysostom, "Exposition of Psalm XLI; PG LV, 156; trans. Strunk, *Source Readings*, p. 67.

[58] Ibid., PG, 55, 157; trans. Strunk, *Source Readings*, p. 68.

[59] Ibid.

[60] John Chrysostom, "Homilies on the Gospel of Matthew," LXVI, 3; PG LVIII, 630; trans. NPNF, 10, p. 407.

The Spirit, distinguishing the divine liturgy from this sort of revelry, sings: "Praise him with the sound of the trumpet," and indeed he will raise the dead with the sound of the trumpet. "Praise him on the psaltery," for the tongue is the psaltery of the Lord. "And praise him on the cithara," let the cithara be taken to mean the mouth, played by the Spirit as if by a plectrum. "Praise him with tympanum and chorus" refers to the Church meditating on the resurrection of the flesh in the surrounding membrane. "Praise him on strings and the instrument" refers to our body as an instrument and its sinews as strings from which it derives its harmonious tension, and when strummed gives off human notes. "Praise him on the clangorous cymbals" speaks of the tongue as the cymbals of the mouth which sounds as the lips are moved.[61]

If you followed the more literal school of Antioch, you might, like John Chrysostom, explain the former use of instruments as a concession to weakness.

Some also take the meaning of these instruments allegorically and say that the tympanum calls for the death of the flesh and that the psaltery looks to heaven. . . . But I would say this: that in ancient times, they were thus led by these instruments due to the slowness of their understanding, and were gradually drawn away from idolatry. Accordingly, just as he allowed sacrifices, so too did he permit instruments, making concession to their weakness.[62]

Possible Exceptions

The writings of the early church, then, consistently condemn instruments and with them hand-clapping and dance. Is it possible, however, that there were exceptions to these prohibitions? As Quasten suggests, theory and practice are not always synonymous, and "every legal determination[63] presupposes the existence of diverse

---

[61] Clement of Alexandria, *Paedagogus* II, iv, PG VIII, 441–442; trans. McKinnon, MECL, pp. 32–33. *Cf.* Athanasius in Robert A. Skeris, *Chroma Theou*, p. 101.

[62] John Chrysostom, In psalmum CXLIX, 2; PG LV, 494; trans. McKinnon, MECL p. 83. See McKinnon, MECL, pp. 6–7.

[63] The polemic against instruments also occurred in legislation, for example, in the Canons of Basil, Canon 74; trans. by McKinnon, MECL, p. 120. See also James McKinnon, "The Meaning of the Patristic Polemic Against Musical Instruments," *Current Musicology* (hereafter CM) 1 (1965): 69. McKinnon points out that "there was a widespread legal tradition that denied baptism to aulos and kithara players unless they renounced their trade, and a fourth-century Alexandrian law set excommunication as the penalty for a cantor who learned to play the kithara."

possibilities which prove its necessity."[64] He suggests that the cithara may have been used in the earliest Christian assemblies,[65] and it is possible that later a deacon named Ephraem of Syrus (c. 306–373) used the cithara (or kinnor).[66] Hannick thinks any references to such usages in worship were metaphorical and that the prohibition against instruments was complete except perhaps for some family festivals or paraliturgical ceremonies.[67] McKinnon has conclusively demonstrated the same thing. He says Clement of Alexandria's "apparent toleration for the lyre and the kithara" is the "only genuine exception."[68] Otherwise the passages against instruments always refer to "the banquet, the theater, or the festivities accompanying a marriage, but . . . never the liturgy."[69] One has to assume Hannick and McKinnon are correct, that in the liturgy the church adopted the practice of the synagogue without instruments, which is to say the question of their use never arose there, and that whatever minor exceptions may have existed to the ban on instruments took place outside the liturgy.[70]

As to dancing and hand-clapping in worship, the Ethiopian and Coptic churches apparently practiced them from their beginnings.[71] They were able to ground their rhythm and ecstasy in the word the way the rest of the church at the time could not, but their practice was exceptional and only later would become more normative for other orthodox Christians. Such activities at the time were usually "relegated to the communities on the fringe of the official Church, the heretics and gnostics."[72] Clement of Alexandria opposed chromatic modes, whatever that may have meant.[73] The song of the

---

[64] Quasten, *Music and Worship in Pagan and Christian Antiquity*, p. 72.

[65] Ibid., pp. 72–74.

[66] See McKinnon, MECL, p. 93ff–95.

[67] Hannick, "Christian Church, music of the early," NGDMM, 4, p. 368.

[68] McKinnon, "The Meaning," CM, pp. 70–71.

[69] Ibid., p. 71. See also James McKinnon, "The Church Fathers and Musical Instruments" (Columbia University Ph.D. dissertation, 1965), p. 2.

[70] See McKinnon, "The Meaning," CM, pp. 72–74, and McKinnon, "The Church Fathers," pp. 260–264. Cf. Robert A. Skeris, *Chroma Theou*, p. 70.

[71] See McKinnon, "The Church Fathers," p. 261, FN 1.

[72] See Hannick, "Christian Church, music of the early," NGDMM, 4, p. 369, and Quasten, *Music and Worship in Pagan and Christian Antiquity*, p. 98.

[73] Clement of Alexandria, *Paedagogus* II; PG VIII, 445–446; McKinnon, MCEL, p. 34. See Foley, *Foundations of Christian Music*, p. 83.

church generally was not called "musica" but "psalms and hymns" which indicated a unique performance practice that did not require or use dancing, instruments, or regular meter.[74] "Rhythm," says Hannick, "had little place in the liturgy,"[75] and there probably was "an intrinsic relationship between the absence of metre and of instruments."[76] The overall theory and practice of unaccompanied, monophonic (octave), and nonmetric singing were characteristics of the worship of the early church. Whatever exceptions there may have been were truly exceptional and not related to worship.[77]

The ideal of singing with one voice hovered over the church's song, but the actuality of diffusion was never far away. The next chapter indicates how.[78]

[74] McKinnon, "The Meaning," CM: 70–71.

[75] Hannick, "Christian Church, music of the early," NGDMM, 4, p. 364.

[76] McKinnon, "The Church Fathers," p. 264.

[77] The Oxyrhynchos Papyrus with a hymn from the end of the third century is "an isolated attempt to record a melody" copied "for private use" and cannot be regarded as "typical of early Christian music." Hannick, NGDMM 4, pp. 367–368.

[78] My friend Francis Williamson is fairly critical of the way I have treated the Bible and the early church. His critique has to do with 1) not making clear enough that both Christians and Jews responded in their worship to the destruction of the Temple and giving the faulty impression that synagogue worship was more established than it was, 2) not indicating that Jews and Christians enfleshed in sound some common settings of the Psalms which are remembered—no matter how fragmentarily—in the synagogue's chant and the church's chant, a remarkable musicological reality in view of the lack of any memory at all of the music of Greece and Rome, 3) not expressing sufficient wonder at how the relatively obscure non-Greek tradition of psalm-singing continued to be practiced by Christians as part of their evangelical movement that reached out to many cultures, 4) implying that the rejection of instruments by the early Christians was more important than it was, that in the overall scheme of things it is not such a big issue, and 5) most importantly, not making it clear enough that one of the ways the Christian community responded to the Christ event was in sound—sung word—which means church music is not a derivative or tangential discipline but a central realm of theological discourse. The nature of the sung word varied in at least the five ways H. Richard Niebuhr isolates in *Christ and Culture* (New York: Harper Torchbooks, 1956), but that only increases the importance of the theological discourse music requires. I'm not sure I'm as guilty as Williamson suggests. I think I agree with the substance of what he wants to say, but, as usual, he and I get at that in different ways. Read his book, *Ears to Hear, Tongues to Sing*, as a corrective to mine—and mine as a corrective to his.

6

Diffusion

The Exclusion of Women

The church was to discover not only that it had to confront music externally in the environment around it, but that internally singing with one voice was also an elusive ideal. The way the two Clements and Ignatius spoke of striving for such an ideal suggests its actuality was always in some sense broken, but when the church began to exclude women from singing the brokenness became more obvious and the actuality more elusive.

If Quasten is right, the exclusion of women happened in this manner.[1] In the beginning, as noted earlier, women joined the liturgical singing "with one voice" with everybody else. For the first two centuries the church welcomed women's presence and participation at worship. It did not have choirs of women as in the pagan cults. After the middle of the third century, however, Paul of Samosata, the heretical bishop of Antioch who "forbade 'psalms . . . addressed to our Lord Jesus Christ,' "[2] and other heretics, such as Bardesanes, organized choirs of women separate from the congregation "to perform the singing at the liturgy."[3] Eusebius of Caesarea (c. 260–c. 340) seems to indicate Paul trained the women to sing *to him!*[4] In response to

---

[1] Quasten, *Music and Worship in Pagan and Christian Antiquity*, p. 85. For the full description see pp. 75–87.

[2] Jaroslav Pelikan, *The Christian Tradition: A History of the Development of Doctrine* (Chicago: The University of Chicago Press, 1971), I, p. 176. For the quotes from Eusebius, see his *Ecclesiastical History* V, XXVIII; PG XX, 511–514; and VII, XXX; PG XX, 713–714; McKinnon, MCEL, p. 99.

[3] Quasten, *Music and Worship in Pagan and Christian Antiquity*, p. 85. Cf. McKinnon, MECL, p. 92.

[4] Eusebius, *Ecclesiastical History* VII, XXX; PG XX, 713–714; trans. McKinnon, MECL, p. 99.

these attractions of heretical groups, the orthodox, maybe especially Ephraem of Syrus who himself wrote many hymns, organized choirs of virgins and boys.[5] (Ephraem is the deacon who may have used the cithara.[6]) Others in the church opposed the development of choirs of women and gradually became more harsh in their opposition. The result was to shut women out of the congregation's singing altogether.[7]

Ambrose was not happy with this development. He went on at length about how "gratifying for all ages and fitting for both sexes" it is to sing psalms.[8] Ambrose represented the ancient practice, but Isidore of Pelusium (d. c. 435), a priest and letter writer, unfortunately illustrates the position the church was more and more to take. He thought it was necessary to stop women from singing in church.[9] As often happens, Isidore moved the argument beyond its initial historical contingencies. He related women's singing to moral laxity and the rousing of passion as in the music of the theater. So he tied the singing of women in church to their "loitering in the city."

Choirs and Cantors

Just as there were no choirs of women in the first centuries of the church's history, so there were no choirs of boys either. There were no choirs of any sort. Persecution and meeting in houses were not likely to generate choirs, and the ideal of "with one voice" led the early church to regard the whole congregation as the choir.

The first mention of boy choirs, apart from Ephraem, comes in the diaries of Egeria (sometimes spelled Etheria), a Christian woman who made a pilgrimage to Jerusalem and recorded its liturgy at the end of the fourth or beginning of the fifth century.[10] As boy choirs

---

[5] Werner, *The Sacred Bridge*, p. 218; McKinnon, MECL, p. 92.

[6] Werner, *The Sacred Bridge*, p. 218.

[7] *Cf.* Faulkner, Quentin. *Wiser Than Despair*, p. 58.

[8] Ambrose, *Explanatio psalmi i*, 9; PL XIV, 925; trans. McKinnon, MECL, p. 126.

[9] Isidore of Pelusium, *Epistle I*, 90; PG LXXVIII, 243–246; McKinnon, MECL, p. 61.

[10] See Quasten, *Music and Worship in Pagan and Christian Antiquity*, p. 89, and Hannick, p. 369. For a brief description of Egeria and selections from her diaries, see McKinnon, MECL, pp. 111–117.

developed, they "eventually relieved the cantor of his position"[11] and are "very closely linked with the employment of boys as lectors in the church."[12]

Now we turn to cantors. If a congregation (or any group) is to sing, someone has to lead it. Call-response patterns between clergy and people can happen without a congregational leader, but even then a "prompter" is helpful. For a freestanding piece such as a hymn, a leader is needed if only to sing the first pitch and establish a pulse. "Only" may be the wrong word here, for pitch and pulse are critical to a community's song. I use "only" to indicate that communal musical leadership does not have to be defined as we tend to define it, namely, a conductor standing before a choir and conducting throughout. Edward Foley points out that the lack of choirs meant that throughout the second and third centuries the church had "no separate liturgical musician." The whole of worship was musical and belonged to the entire assembly.[13] Someone, however, hidden in the assembly perhaps, or a reader who sang the lessons or psalmody, surely served to help set the singing in motion. That person, the "cantor," was so closely identified with the community at the beginning of the church's existence that she or he was anonymous[14] and only gradually comes into view in the fourth century. The references to cantors from the fourth century on provide glimpses into church life that church musicians will find familiar. Here is a list of such references with a few chuckles buried within to lighten the list's tedium.

- The collection called the Canons of Laodicea from the latter half of the fourth century, in McKinnon's words, "perhaps for the first time . . . (1) specifies the cantor as a 'canonical' office, (2) mentions that he sings from the ambo; and (3) that he uses some sort of liturgical text."[15]
- The same Canons group cantors with presbyters, deacons, subdeacons, readers, exorcists, porters, and ascetics, and enjoin them all from entering a tavern.[16]

---

[11] Quasten, *Music and Worship in Pagan and Christian Antiquity*, p. 89.

[12] Ibid., p. 90.

[13] Foley, *From Age to Age*, p. 33.

[14] See Edward Foley, "The Cantor in Historical Perspective," *Worship* 56:3 (May 1982): 194–213.

[15] Canons of Laodicea, Canon 15; trans. McKinnon, MECL, p. 119.

[16] Ibid., Canon 24.

- Pseudo-Ignatius from the same period includes cantors among the people he greets.[17]
- In the earliest reference to psalmody at communion, Cyril of Jerusalem (c. 315–386) mentions the "singer."[18]
- Ambrose (c. 340–397) distinguishes between lectors and the one who sings the psalm,[19] and includes cantors among the "others" who wrongly add "Lord" to the text of Luke 23:46, "Into your hands I commend my spirit."[20]
- Jerome (341–420), the translator of the *Vulgate* Bible, warns against cantors who wave their hair with curling irons (!),[21] and he wants to be sure the words and not the voice of the singer "give pleasure."[22]
- Socrates (c. 380–450) says that in Alexandria catechumens or the faithful may be readers and cantors, but elsewhere "only the faithful" are promoted to "this office."[23] McKinnon notes the use of the word "prompters" in this connection.[24]
- Sozomen in the fifth century names Marcian (not Marcion) who was martyred around 350 as a cantor and reader.[25]

As is usual for the church's life and especially its music and its musical office, the picture here is not of a common practice everywhere. Cantors were and weren't the same as lectors. In Alexandria they could be catechumens, elsewhere only the faithful. Some of them apparently added words that weren't in the text, and leaders sought to clarify where and what they sang. Choirs began to take the positions of cantors. And some cantors curled their hair!

---

[17] Pseudo-Ignatius, *Antiochenes* XII; PG V, 907–908; trans. McKinnon, MECL, p. 19.

[18] Cyril of Jerusalem, *Mystagogical Catechesis* V, 20; PG XXXIII, 1123–1124; trans. McKinnon, MECL, p. 77.

[19] Ambrose, *De officiis*, XLIV, 215; PL XVI, 87; trans. by McKinnon, MECL, p. 132.

[20] Ambrose, *De interpellatione Job et David* VI, 23–24; PL XIV, 821; trans. McKinnon, MECL, p. 129.

[21] Jerome, Epistle LII, *Ad Nepotianum* 5; PL XXII, 532; trans. by McKinnon, MECL, p. 141.

[22] Jerome, *Commentarium in epistulam ad Ephesios* III, V, 19; PL XXVI, 562; trans. by McKinnon, MECL, p. 145.

[23] Socrates, *Ecclesiastical History* V, xxii; PG LXVII, 635–638; trans. by McKinnon, MECL, p. 101.

[24] McKinnon, MECL, p. 101.

[25] Sozomen, *Ecclesiastical History* IV, iii; PG LXVII, 1113–1115; trans. by McKinnon, MECL, p. 103.

But there was music, and there were those who led it, in an increasingly diffuse way. A number of reflections may help to order the diffusion. To those we turn with Ambrose, Pambo, and Augustine to lead us.

Questions

Having granted the associations of music with immorality and idolatry in the postapostolic world, questions about the church's response still remain. One of them is what McKinnon calls "the most acute sensitivity" to "sexual morality in particular," which he suggests "is not an altogether attractive trait."[26] It does not easily square with the broader biblical concern for justice and the biblical affirmation of the goodness of the body. A concern for the poor is not absent from these early writers—witness Chrysostom—nor are concerns for treating people well, not cruelly, as in the spectacles. But biblical-type affirmations of the goodness of the bodily creation are hard to find.

We may ask in this connection to what extent classical Greek rather than biblical perspectives have consciously or unconsciously determined the posture of the early church.[27] The persistent references to things being in moderation, for example; the moderation of Christian meals versus the frenzy of pagan banquets and the spectacles; the importance of the sung word versus a purely instrumental art; given a preference, the choice of stringed instruments[28] and their association with singing; the connection of the mind with moderation, order, and voice versus the connection of the flesh with pleasure, disorder, and instruments (especially of the wind variety) all are Greek, not specifically Christian, in origin. Even granting the backdrop of the idolatry and brutality of the spectacles and the immorality associated with actors and the theater, nonetheless a Greek perspective seems to have been as powerful a control as the New Testament in how the church confronted music and musical instruments.

[26] McKinnon, MECL, p. 3.

[27] Cf. Egon Wellesz, A History of Byzantine Music and Hymnography (Oxford: The Clarendon Press, 1961), p. 96.

[28] Gustave Reese, Music in the Middle Ages (New York: W. W. Norton & Company, 1940), p. 61, observes of Clement of Alexandria, for example, that "while he tolerated the lyra and kithara . . . he disapproved of most other instruments." And we have seen the possibility that if any instrument was used in Christian assemblies, which is very doubtful, it was the cithara (kithara).

Having said that, however, the embrace of sound—the "lyrical quality"—of apostolic and postapostolic worship did indeed point to what was central, namely, the incarnate Word of God and embodied sound in sung words about the Word. No matter how acculturated or enculturated the church may have been, its center was certainly clear. From this center three musical postures emerged. They can be identified with the sound of Ambrose, the silence of Pambo, and the strictures of Augustine. Somewhat similar postures will recur in the sixteenth century, articulated then in considerably more detail.

Ambrose and Sound

Ambrose (c. 340–397) was born on the Moselle River in Trier, the oldest city in what is now Germany, to a ruling Roman family. His father was the pretorian prefect of the Gauls. When his father died, his mother moved to Rome where Ambrose and his brother went to school. He left Rome in 365, practiced law, and around 370 was made governor of Aemilia Liguria with his office in Milan. In 374 Auxentius, the bishop of Milan who was an Arian, died. The people, including both the Arians and the Orthodox in a surprisingly agreeable move, wanted Ambrose for their bishop, though he was only a catechumen at the time. With some reluctance he accepted, in short order was baptized and ordained, then spent the rest of his life as bishop of Milan. He gave part of his property to the church, adopted simple clothes, cultivated prayer especially at night and fasting especially in Lent; defended the church against paganism and Arianism; and devoted himself to study, writing, preaching, the discipline of the clergy, care for the poor and oppressed, and instruction for catechumens—Augustine, one of his admirers, among them.

Ambrose was a "public figure . . . unlike Augustine, the philosopher, or Jerome, the scholar."[29] His administrative skill and "inaccessibility"[30] as a person may make him seem a curious figure for our consideration, but he is also known as the "father of church song." He composed hymn texts that are still sung and can be found in most standard hymnals. He has sometimes been credited with

---

[29] James W. McKinnon, "Ambrose," NGDMM 1, p. 314.

[30] Neil B. McLynn, *Ambrose of Milan* (Berkeley: University of California Press, 1994), p. xvi.

introducing antiphonal chant to the Latin church and composing the
Te Deum. Milanese or Ambrosian chant is named for him—parallel to Roman or Gregorian chant for Gregory the Great. He is perhaps most popularly known among hymnologists for the incident in
386 when Justina, the mother of the boy emperor Valentinian, tried
to impose Arianism on Milan by taking over a basilica for Arian
worship. Ambrose and the catholic faithful staged a sit-in at the
basilica, surrounded by Justina's soldiers. Augustine says that while
they were there "the singing of hymns and psalms in the manner of
the eastern parts [of the church] was established to keep the people
from wasting away through the weariness of sorrow."[31]

Ambrose clearly wrote hymns. To what extent these other matters can be attributed to him, even whether he was responsible for
initiating the singing at the basilican sit-in, is not clear.[32] That the
tradition has assigned such musical significance to him is not accidental, however, and it should probably not be taken as lightly as we
in the twentieth century are apt to take such things.[33] However, it is
not the point I want to make here. The point here is that, though
he adopted the position of the early church about instruments,[34]
Ambrose nonetheless affirmed the sound of music. He not only was
lavish in his praise of psalmody, as already indicated, but he
delighted in the sound of music as the following quotation illustrates. Ambrose speaks here of the sea as a monastic sanctuary and
uses it as a musical metaphor.

> The sea, then, is a sanctuary for temperance, a training ground for con-
> tinence, a retreat for austerity, a secure harbor, peace on earth, and
> sobriety in this world. It is moreover an inducement to devotion for
> these faithful and pious men, that as their psalmody vies with the sound
> of softly lapping waves, the islands applaud with a gentle chorus of
> blessed undulations, and resound with the hymns of the saints. How
> could I grasp the beauty of the sea in its entirety as viewed by its Cre-
> ator? Why say more? What is that harmony of the waves other than the
> harmony of the people? Hence the Church is frequently and appropri-
> ately compared to the sea, first, because all its entrances are flooded by

---

[31] Augustine, *Confessions* IX, VI; CCL XXVII, p. 141; Music, *Hymnology: A Collection of Source Readings*, pp. 10–11. See Ambrose's description, *Letter XX*, 24; PL XVI, 1001; trans., Music, *Hymnology: A Collection of Source Readings*, p. 9.

[32] See McKinnon, "Ambrose," NGDMM 1, p. 314.

[33] See the next chapter for more about the musical attributions made to Ambrose.

[34] See, for example, Ambrose, *Sermo contra Auxentium de basilicis tradendis* XXXIV, PL XVI, 1017–1018; trans., McKinnon, MECL, pp. 132–133.

the incoming tide of people, and then because it hums with the prayer of entire people like the washing of waves, and resounds with the singing of psalm responses like the crashing of breakers.[35]

Pambo and Silence

Not all of the early writers took Ambrose's position. Some, like Hilary of Potiers (c. 315–367) and Niceta of Remesiana (d. c. 414), *did* agree with him. Hilary, the "earliest composer of hymns in the West,"[36] spoke approvingly (though idiosyncratically) of the musical expansions of the "alleluia" called the jubilus.[37] Niceta, one of those who is credited with possibly writing the Te Deum, argued that "singing in the heart" (Ephesians 5:19) meant making actual sounds.[38] He fleshed out this idea with some notions about what the sound of congregational singing with one voice might be—not dragged out, without single voices sticking out, and each singer integrated into the whole.[39] That he had to argue such a case means some people thought singing in the heart meant *not* making actual sounds.

Athanasius (c. 296–373), bishop of Alexandria, did not stop the music altogether, but he was nervous about it. He worried that the music of the psalms might "tickle the aesthetic palate,"[40] and he required the singer of the psalm to make the singing as close as possible to speech.[41] Athanasius saw two reasons for singing psalms, to express love to God with power and because of its unifying effect.[42] The music itself was to be hidden.

Now we have come upon some inherent contradictions. If there is to be the sound of song, no matter how simple and even if it is worship's "aural aspect," to use Foley's wonderful phrase again, someone nonetheless has to be concerned about musical details like

---

[35] Ambrose, *Hexaemoron* III,V, 23; PL XIV, 165; McKinnon, MECL, p. 130.

[36] McKinnon, MECL, p. 121.

[37] Hilary of Potiers, *Tractatus in psalmum* LXV,3, PL IX, 425; trans. McKinnon, MECL, p. 124.

[38] Niceta of Remesiana, *De utilitate hymnorum* 2; McKinnon, MECL, p. 134.

[39] Ibid., 13; p. 138.

[40] A religious of C.S.M.V., *St. Athanasius on the Psalms* (London: A. R. Mowbray & Co., Limited, 1949), p. 35.

[41] Augustine, *Confessions* X, xxxiii, 50; PL XXXII, 800; McKinnon, MECL, p. 155.

[42] A religious, *St. Athanasius on the Psalms*, pp. 35 and 37. *Cf.* Athanasius, *Epistola ad Marcellinum* 29; PG XXVII, 42.

melody, rhythm, and phrasing. Working out this concern forces one to stare at the music, a dangerous activity if one is nervous about it. We are dealing in this early period with an oral and mnemonic tradition, so the "composer" might have been hidden in obscurity. Even so, and even given the communal memory with its teaching power, the music still had to be learned and in part improvised from commonly held formulas. Though our distinction between composer and performer(s) did not pertain, some concentrating on the music was inevitable. The issue is even deeper than the technical details the composer/performer(s) have to be concerned about, however. A piece of music—no matter how simple and with or without text— has its own form, generates its own interest, appeals to human beings at a nonrational level, and creates its own pleasure. If one is nervous about music, trouble is afoot with even the simplest musical sounds.

The obvious solution to this dilemma is to reject music completely, to substitute silence for sound. An incident and some words attributed to an Egyptian abbot named Pambo represent this solution. Pambo, so it is said, sent a disciple to Alexandria where he spent sixteen days in the church of the Apostle Mark and observed the liturgy. When he returned, Pambo saw that he was upset and asked him why. He responded by saying, "Father, we spend our days here serenely and we sing neither canons nor *troparia*. But when I came to Alexandria I saw the choirs in the church and how they sing, and I became very sad that we do not sing canons and *troparia*."[43] Pambo then is reported to have exclaimed,

> Woe to us, my son! The days have come when monks turn away from the enduring nourishment which the Holy Spirit gives them and surrender themselves to singing. What kind of contrition is that? How can tears come from the singing of *troparia*? How can a monk possess contrition if he stays in the church or in his cell and raises his voice like the lowing of cattle?[44]

Pambo and this text are elusive. Gustav Reese identifies Pambo as living from c. 317 to 367.[45] Quasten thinks he died between 385 and 390, but presumes this text represents developments that occurred later than the fourth century.[46] McKinnon says "this anecdote is

---

[43] Quasten, *Music and Worship in Pagan and Christian Antiquity*, p. 95.

[44] Ibid.

[45] Gustave Reese, *Music in the Middle Ages* (New York: W. W. Norton & Company, 1940), p. 66.

[46] Quasten, *Music and Worship in Pagan and Christian Antiquity*, p. 94–95.

apocryphal," probably comes from the sixth century, and that "there is nothing like it in the authentic sayings of Pambo or any of his fourth-century colleagues."[47] Perhaps Pambo never did or said any of this. It probably *is* later than the fourth century. I leave it to others to figure out when and where it comes from. I cite it because of what it represents—silence.

Such a posture was certainly a minority, both for the church as a whole and for monastic communities as well. Christians, it seems, will not be silenced. They invariably sing. And they clearly did so in the first centuries of the church's history. However, among some an argument for not singing took the nervous concerns about music to their logical conclusion—silence. This tendency toward silence was late, probably not until the end of the fourth or the beginning of the fifth century at the earliest, but it did emerge.

Augustine and Restrictions

Augustine (354–430) stood between Ambrose and the position ascribed to Pambo. He embraced the use of music, but restricted it.

One of the most important thinkers in the history of the Christian church, Augustine was born in Thagaste in North Africa, now Souk Ahras in Algeria. His father was a pagan, his mother a Christian named Monica. In 371 he went to the University of Carthage, one of the great cities of the ancient world on the North African peninsula near what is now Tunis in Tunisia. An unbaptized catechumen, he presently lost whatever Christian faith he had. He studied rhetoric and became a liberal arts professor at Thagaste, Madaura, and Carthage, went to Rome, and in 384 came to Milan as a professor of rhetoric. Under the influence of Ambrose and his preaching, Augustine left the academy, retreated to Cassiciacum near Milan, and at the Easter Vigil of 387 was baptized by Ambrose. He returned to his native Thagaste in 388 and formed a kind of monastic community with friends. In 391 he visited Hippo, now the city of Annaba on the north African coast of the Mediterranean Sea. The people there called for his ordination, and the aged bishop Valerius complied. In 396 Valerius died. Augustine became bishop of Hippo until his death in 430 when vandals were attacking the city.

---

[47] McKinnon, MECL, p. 9.

[48] PL, XXXII, 1081–1194. For a literal translation see Robert Catesby Taliaferro, "On Music (*De musica*)," *The Fathers of the Church* (New York: Cima Publishing

In 387, just before he was baptized, Augustine began a book called *De Musica*.[48] He finished it in 391. As Erik Routley says, this work "is an application of Christian theology, not to the use of music in the church, but to the science of music itself."[49] It lies therefore at the edge of our purview, but deserves mention because it provides background for understanding Augustine's thought and gives his wonderful definition of music: *ars bene modulandi*, "how to make controlled variations of sound in the right way."[50] A complicated work in six books, with six more contemplated, it is about "*sounds* as opposed to words," which encompasses poetry as well as music.[51]

Sounds delighted Augustine—"the chanting of the Psalms, songs at harvest time, and, most delightful of all, the entrancing speech" of the people around him in "the melodious rhythms and high sentiments of a good poem."[52] In the first five books of *De Musica* he reflected on the details and syntax of the organized sound of music and poetry. Then, in the sixth book, theological reflections came into play. There Augustine, with a Platonic mindset, saw something more meritorious and free behind the actual sound of music, namely, silent music.[53] Augustine can be understood to view the music that we hear as an imitation of a spiritual model; music as sounding form comes from the music of silence.[54]

When it came to reflecting on the actual "use of music in church," Augustine adopted the position of his time in his typically and massively reflective way. He was more sensitive to sound than Ambrose, but also more wary of it. His wariness led him to consider the silence ascribed to Pambo (quite a different thing from the Platonic notion of silent music and Platonic Ideal Forms) and

Co., Inc., 1947), hereafter FC, II, pp. 153–379. For a synopsis see W. F. Jackson Knight, *St. Augustine's De Musica: A Synopsis* (London: The Orthological Institute, c. 1949).

[49] Erik Routley, *The Church and Music* (London: Gerald Duckworth & Co. Ltd., 1950), p. 56.

[50] Knight, *St. Augustine's De Musica*, p. 11.

[51] Ibid.

[52] Peter Brown, *Augustine of Hippo* (Berkeley: University of California Press, 1969), pp. 35–36.

[53] Augustine, *De musica* VI, xvi; PL XXXII, 1189–1191.

[54] See Henri Davenson [pseudonym for Henri Irénée Marrou], *Traité de la Musique selon l'Esprit de Saint Augustin* (Neuchatel: Les Cahiers du Rhône, 1942) pp. 17ff. Cf. Donald Walhout, "Augustine on the Transcendent in Music," *Philosophy and Theology* 3:3 (Spring, 1989): 285.

Athanasius's attempt to make music as much like speech as possible; but he couldn't quite make either of those moves. He vacillated between the value of music and its danger, arguing finally that music in church is permitted, with this restriction: the meaning of the words and not the singing has to be paramount. His famous passage from the *Confessions*, written about 397 after he had become bishop, explains his position. It deserves to conclude this chapter and to be quoted at length. Augustine is talking about the senses, has just discussed the delight of smell, and now comes to hearing and sound.

> I used to be much more fascinated by the pleasures of sound than the pleasures of smell. I was enthralled by them, but you [God] broke my bonds and set me free. I admit that I still find some enjoyment in the music of hymns, which are alive with your praises, when I hear them sung by well-trained, melodious voices, but I do not enjoy it so much that I cannot tear myself away. I can leave it when I wish. But if I am not to turn a deaf ear to music, which is the setting for the words which give it life, I must allow it a position of some honor in my heart, and I find it difficult to assign it to its proper place. For sometimes I feel I treat it with more honor than it deserves. I realize that when they are sung, these sacred words stir my mind to greater religious fervor and kindle in me a more ardent flame of piety than they would if they were not sung; and I also know that there are particular modes in song and in the voice, corresponding to my various emotions and able to stimulate them because of the mysterious relationship between the two. But I ought not to allow my mind to be paralyzed by the gratification of my senses, which often leads it astray. For the senses are not content to take second place. Simply because I allow them their due, as adjuncts to reason, they attempt to take precedence and forge ahead of it, with the result that I sometimes sin in this way but am not aware of it until later.
>
> Sometimes, too, from over-anxiety to avoid this particular trap I make the mistake of being too strict. When this happens, I have no wish but to exclude from my ears, and from the ears of the church as well, all the melody of those lovely chants to which the Psalms of David are habitually sung; and it seems safer to me to follow the precepts which I remember often having heard ascribed to Athanasius who used to oblige the lectors to recite the psalms with such slight modulation of the voice that they seemed to be speaking rather than chanting. But when I remember the tears that I shed on hearing the songs of the Church in the early days, soon after I had recovered my faith, and when I realize that nowadays it is not the singing that moves me but the meaning of the words when they are sung in a clear voice to the most appropriate tune, I again acknowledge the great value of this practice. So I waver

between the danger that lies in gratifying the senses and the benefits
which, as I know from experience, can accrue from singing. Without
committing myself to an irrevocable opinion, I am inclined to approve
of the custom of singing in church, in order that by indulging the ears
weaker spirits may be inspired with feelings of devotion. Yet when I find
the singing itself more moving than the truth which it conveys, I confess
that this is a grievous sin, and at those times I would prefer not to hear
the singer. [55]

[55] Augustine, *Confessions* X, xxxiii, 49–50; PL XXXII, 799–800; trans. R. S.
Pine-Coffin, Augustine of Hippo, *Confessions* (Hammondsworth: Penguin Classics,
1961), pp. 238–239; for another translation, see McKinnon, MECL, pp. 154–155.

BEFORE AND AFTER CHARLEMAGNE

7

Chant

As we have seen, the apostolic and postapostolic church in its worship adapted the unaccompanied congregational song of the synagogue. By the fourth century, when Latin had replaced Greek as the language of worship in Rome, "there were distinct families of Eastern and Western (Latin) rites, each local rite having its own liturgy and music."[1] What we know today as chant, also called plainchant or plainsong, is the result of this continuing development. "Gregorian chant," though the term is sometimes popularly used as a synecdoche for the whole repertoire of plainchant, is more accurately one subset.[2] Chant, to use Willi Apel's definition, is "the generic designation for a body of religious music, such as Hindu chant, Jewish chant, Byzantine chant, Russian chant, etc."[3] It is "purely melodic," without harmony or counterpoint or accompaniment, and "exclusively vocal" like folksong, but usually without strict meter.[4] The shorthand for this texture is monophonic vocal unison, though, as we have seen, when women and men—or children and men—sing together, "in unison" turns out to mean "in octaves."

[1] Kenneth Levy, "Plainchant," NGDMM, 14, p. 800. Kenneth Levy and John A. Emerson, "Plainchant," NGDMM 14, pp. 800–844 is a good overview of chant and leads the reader into numerous other more specific articles in NGDMM. Substantial bibliographies, which are appended to all of these articles, provide the literature for further study and research. For a huge summary of chant with an equally daunting bibliography, see David Hiley, *Western Plainchant: A Handbook* (Oxford: Clarendon Pres, 1993).

[2] For clear definitions and distinctions see Willi Apel, *Gregorian Chant* (Bloomington: Indiana University Press, 1958), pp. 3–5.

[3] Apel, *Gregorian Chant*, pp. 3–4.

[4] Ibid., p. 4.

Studying Christian chant is difficult. Sources are often fragmentary or absent. Since chant is preeminently oral,[5] to what extent the oral tradition has or has not been continued, influenced, or modified is always a puzzle.[6] Recordings are obviously not available for us to hear what was done centuries ago. Musical notation was not present before the ninth century.[7] Even when notation is present, as musicians know, it does not communicate everything. What further complicates matters is that the least-known chants, the ones that had "the greatest danger of disappearing," were notated first, "while the best-known or simplest chants" were notated last.[8] This tendency means that the congregational parts best-known in an oral tradition are the ones that may be most elusive for us because they were the last to be written down, if written down at all.[9]

Some things can be said, however. From the common materials of the first four centuries, the repertoires of Eastern and Western chant developed.[10] The "chief representative of the Eastern liturgies is the Greek rite of Constantinople," which, by the thirteenth century, had a full repertoire of notated Byzantine chant parallel to the Latin Gregorian chant of the same period.[11] The music of other Eastern rites—Syrian, Coptic, Georgian, Armenian, Ethiopian, Slavonic, Russian—has to be studied from more fragmentary sources and "modern practice."[12] In the West, Old Roman, Gallican, and Mozarabic chant can be distinguished as separate from but also involved in complicated relationships with Gregorian chant. Milanese or Ambrosian chant "is the oldest western repertory of liturgical music to have survived in parallel to the Gregorian repertory."[13]

[5] Levy, "Plainchant," NGDMM 14, p. 804.

[6] The work of A. Z. Idelsohn, who studied Jewish chant chiefly in Yemen where it presumably had been isolated from before the destruction of the second Temple in 70 A.D. and then drew conclusions about relationships to later Jewish and Christian chant, is perhaps the best illustration of this issue. (Apel, *Gregorian Chant*, pp. 34–35, regards Idelsohn's work positively. The link between Jewish and Christian chant defines Eric Werner's work as the subtitle of *The Sacred Bridge* indicates, "The Interdependence of Liturgy and Music in Synagogue and Church during the First Millennium.")

[7] Levy and Emerson, "Plainchant," NGDMM 14, pp. 800 and 807–808.

[8] Ibid., pp. 801–802. See also Kenneth Levy, "Byzantine rite, music of the," NGDMM, 3, p. 555.

[9] See Kenneth Levy, "Byzantine rite, music of the," NGDMM 3, p. 560.

[10] See Apel, *Gregorian Chant*, p. 37.

[11] Levy, "Plainchant," NGDMM 14, p. 801.

[12] Ibid.

[13] Giacomo Bonifacio Baroffio, "Ambrosian [Milanese] rite, music of the," NGDMM 1, p. 314. Carl Parrish, *A Treasury of Early Music* (New York; W. W.

We need to come back again to some fairly technical musical details. If you know something about music, the following may be no problem. If you have no musical background, it may be more difficult. Again, if you need help, ask a music teacher. This section on modes and the next section on rhythm will give a brief but necessary sketch of some technical musical matters, which will at the very least provide a sense of the syntax of chant. I'll say something about the broader significance of this at the end of the section on rhythm.

Byzantine and Gregorian chant both employ a system of eight modes, called *oktoechos* (okto, eight; echos, mode) for Byzantine chant.[14] The pitches of chant melodies gravitate to a home, called a "final," which is either D, E, F, or G when one employs only the white keys of the piano. The final doesn't have to be on those absolute pitches. It can be moved up or down so long as the range is singable. Consistent relationships of half and whole steps are at issue here, not specific notes of the keyboard. The numbering differs, but in the West the modes are numbered I, III, V, and VII in their *authentic* forms. Their *plagal* forms are II, IV, VI, VIII. In the West the authentic forms are sometimes called Dorian, Phrygian, Lydian, and Mixolydian; the plagal forms Hypodorian, Hypophrygian, Hypolydian, and Hypomixolydian. "Authentic" and "plagal" refer to range or *ambitus*. Authentic modes extend from their final up to the next octave. Plagal modes start a fourth lower than the finals and extend a fifth higher.

Both repertoires employ psalm tones,[15] which are formulas for singing psalms.[16] At the center of a psalm tone is a reciting note.

Norton & Company, 1958), pp. 3–19, give examples of Ambrosian, Gallican, Mozarabic, and Gregorian chant. For a descriptive overview, see Robert F. Hayburn, "The Printed Editions of the Chant Books and Their Effect on the Gregorian Tradition," *Cum Angelis Canere: Essays on Sacred Music and Pastoral Liturgy in Honour of Richard J. Schuler*, ed. Robert A. Skeris (St. Paul: Catholic Church Music Associates, 1990), pp. 93–97.

[14] For a description of Byzantine modes and theory, see Levy, 3, "Byzantine rite, music of the," pp. 555–556 and 562. For more complex discussions that give the state of his research in 1977, see Oliver Strunk, *Essays on Music in the Byzantine World* (New York: W. W. Norton & Company, Inc., 1977), especially pp. 3–39.

[15] Strunk, *Essays on Music in the Byzantine World*, p. 39, thought these psalm tones predate Christianity and represent the practice of the synagogue, so that their history runs from the ancient synagogue to the Byzantine tradition as the central early Christian one to its dispersal in the churches of the East and West.

[16] These formulas are called into being at any time you want to sing a text that

Authentic modes have a different reciting note from the plagal ones, called a *dominant*. The authentic dominant is generally a fifth above the final, the plagal dominant a third above it.

The system I have just explained was probably first investigated and classified at the time of Alcuin (735–804) under Charlemagne.[17] It helps to make sense of the relationships of pitches. However, when applied to the actual music itself it is not quite so neat as any description of it might imply.[18] Nor is it only related to chant. The modes also characterize folksong, the Lydian mode perhaps at one time the characteristic "European peasant scale par excellence."[19]

Modes are "pre-tonal," that is, they antedate our system of major and minor keys. They are by no means obsolete, however. They are still employed in chant and folk song,[20] some composers use them,[21] and good jazz musicians practice them with major and minor scales until they are habitual. Though anachronistic, it may be helpful to think of the modes by way of our major and minor keys. Dorian (Mode I) is the minor scale with the sixth degree raised a half step, Phrygian (Mode III) is minor with the second degree lowered a half step, Lydian (Mode V) is major with the fourth degree raised a half step, and Mixolydian (Mode VII) is major with the seventh degree lowered a half step.

Rhythm

Music is not only constructed by relationships of pitches. It has another critical component—pulse, or rhythm. Though today we

will not fit a regular strophic structure with the same number of syllables per line and lines per stanza, stanza after stanza. You can sing any text to a psalm tone— the newspaper, a novel, a weather report, or even a phone book—so long as you "point" it. "Pointing" means indicating where cadences come.

[17] Apel, *Gregorian Chant*, p. 134.

[18] For a brief description of the Byzantine system, see Levy, "Byzantine rite, music of the," NGDMM 3, pp. 555–556. For a longer description of the Gregorian system, which clarifies ambiguities of practical application, see Apel, *Gregorian Chant*, chapter 3, especially pp. 133–137 and 140–178.

[19] A. L. Lloyd, *Folk Song in England* (New York: International Publishers, 1967), p. 41. (See also pp. 40 , 45, 174.)

[20] See Cecil J. Sharp, rev. Maud Karpeles, *English Folk Song: Some Conclusions* (London: Mercury Books, 1965), pp. 47–91.

[21] Peter Tanner's *Sonata for Marimba*, for example, uses the Mixolydian and Dorian modes in the first movement, the Lydian in the second, and the Phrygian in the third.

usually hear chant performed in a way that derives from the methods of the monks at Solesmes in the last century, whether that is what chant sounded like earlier is open to question. Rhythm is perhaps the least clear element of chant.

Both Gustave Reese and Willi Apel organize the proposals regarding the rhythmic organization of chant into three groups. Apel calls the first two groups equalists because they agree that one basic time value was assigned to all the notes. The third group is called mensuralists (mensural, pertaining to measure). Its advocates think different notes got different time values.[22]

Joseph Pothier (1835–1932), a French priest and scholar who became a monk at Solesmes in 1860, is the central figure for group one. Reese calls this group accentualists. Apel highlights "free rhythm" or "free oratoric rhythm." As Reese explains it, the logic here goes like this. When Gregorian chant was in the process of being formed in the fifth century, the pronunciation of Greek and Latin changed from syllables of longs and shorts to syllables of equal length. An accent or stress of weight rather than an agogic stress of length then became the rhythmic element. Chant, says this group, took over the verbal equality of syllables and stresses of weight, making these factors the controlling ones in the music.

Group two is headed by André Mocquereau (1849–1930), another French priest and scholar who became a monk at Solesmes in 1877, seventeen years after Pothier. Mocquereau developed the Solesmes system of "free musical rhythm." He agreed with Pothier about the equal duration of the notes, but disagreed about the verbal accent as the control. Rhythm for him was fundamentally a musical, not a textual matter. In his system the notes go along equally in irregular clusters of twos and threes. An ictus is an important factor in this progression. It is typically described in a somewhat obscure way as "a 'dip' of the voice, an alighting place sought by the rhythm at intervals of every two or three notes in order to renew or sustain its flight until it reaches its final resting place."[23] Reese wonders what perceptible form this ictus actually takes, and Apel sees no historical foundation for the whole theory, calling it a "mixture of historical exactitude and ingenious

---

[22] See Reese, *Music in the Middle Ages*, pp. 140–148 and Apel, *Gregorian Chant*, pp. 126–132. The following discussion relies on these two sources.

[23] Reese, *Music in the Middle Ages*, p. 142, quoting Gregory Suñol, *Els Cants del Romeus*.

fancy[!]"[24] However, as Apel also notes, the Solesmes perspective has been "universally adopted in the churches [and] also has found ardent admirers elsewhere."[25] Musicians have discovered it not only counters mechanical "time-beating," but can produce sensuously beautiful tissues of sound.

The last group, the mensuralists, agree on some form of longs and shorts in irregularly grouped measures, though they have no common metrical solution. Apel comments on and gives examples of the "appallingly different results they have arrived at."[26] Sometimes this general perspective is tied to the idea that the advent of organum, with the addition of one or more parts to the original chant melody, ironed out the longs and shorts into equal notes.[27] Curt Sachs thinks such an idea is untenable.[28] McKinnon suggests that "evidence for measured chant begins to appear only" in the tenth century.[29]

This rhythmic debate, though grounded in scholarly rigor, is not an arid affair without presuppositions and implications. Without setting the following in stone, gently ponder some issues like the ones raised at the ends of the chapters on the Psalms and the canticles. Does the Solesmes position point to what might be called a priestly perspective that accents the approach of humanity toward God? It appeals not to the prophetic Hebrew currents that emphasize God's address to humanity, but to more priestly Greek and Roman ones.[30] Solesmes sees music as God's gift in the sense that humanity might express the complex human feelings, which well up in the heart, and "which words, because they are too material and concrete, are unable to translate."[31] For Solesmes we are dealing with "something of an inward nature, of which the *spirit alone* could grasp the structure."[32] Rhythm is defined as "quite clearly an act of the mind,"[33] so more physical things like weak and strong

---

[24] Apel, *Gregorian Chant*, p. 128. *Cf.* McKinnon, "The Church Fathers," p. 267.

[25] Apel, *Gregorian Chant*, p. 128.

[26] Ibid., p. 129.

[27] Reese, *Music in the Middle Ages*, p. 144. (See pp. 253 and 125–126, which complicate the dating.)

[28] Curt Sachs, *Rhythm and Tempo: A Study in Music History* (New York: W. W. Norton & Company, Inc., 1953), p. 154.

[29] McKinnon, "The Church Fathers," p. 266.

[30] Joseph Gajard, *The Solesmes Method: Its Fundamental Principles and Practical Rules of Interpretation* (Collegeville: The Liturgical Press, 1960), pp. 24–25.

[31] Ibid., p. 30.

[32] Ibid., p. 27. (Italics are in the original.)

[33] Ibid., p. 26.

beats are eschewed in favor of a kind of movement that relates to impetus and rest.[34] The seemingly obscure comments about the ictus are difficult precisely because they are controlled by what lies beyond human sound and comprehension. Consequently, the Solesmes method always results in sounds that recede into silence. A teleological tug pulls the musical line to the silence of pure love. This is not just the silent music of the Platonic model, which we saw in Augustine, or the reminiscence of the soul, which Henri Davenson describes,[35] but eschatological fulfillment.[36] In Joseph Gelineau's words,

> Music can never reveal to us the whole of its mystery until it has become silent and no more sounds reach our ears. For the praise of heaven, pure love, will have no further need for the art of sound.[37]

A prophetic punch at the beginning of the line, which we will get later in Lutheran rhythmic chorales, is a quite different thing, as are comments I've heard from the Lutheran theologian Walter Bouman, who regards the praise of heaven not as silence but as jubilant song. The rhythm of the Genevan Psalter, which we will also encounter later, is still another thing. It has a more sensuous pull than the Lutheran rhythmic punch, but the pull is in a regular beat rather than the nonmetrical Benedictine scheme. Is it surprising that a Lutheran community controlled by prophetic motifs might find a Solesmes chant or Genevan tune something foreign, or that a Benedictine community controlled by priestly motifs might find a Lutheran chorale or Genevan psalm tune something foreign? Is it surprising that Lutherans or Presbyterians or some ethnic groups like African American congregations cannot imagine worship without music—at

---

[34] Ibid., p. 27.

[35] Davenson, *Traité de la Musique*, p. 186.

[36] See Francis Williamson, "The Lord's Song and the Ministry of the Church" (dissertation, New York: Union Theological Seminary, 1967), p. 261. I analyzed some of this in an independent study with James M. Gustafson, "Theology and Cultic Song in Twentieth Century Roman Catholic Thought and Practice" (unpublished, 1973).

[37] Joseph Gelineau, *Voices and Instruments in Christian Worship: Principles, Laws, Applications* (Collegeville: The Liturgical Press, 1964), p. 27. Thomas Merton, in *Bread in the Wilderness*, makes similar comments. "For there is only one language spoken in the City of God. That language is charity. Those who speak it best, speak it in silence" (p. 160). "The Psalter only truly begins to speak and sing within us when we have been led by God and lifted up by Him, and have ascended into its silences" (p. 160). "The Liturgy of Heaven is a most perfect harmony which, like the music of the spheres, sees song transfigured into silence" (p. 161).

the very least one hymn and usually much more, whereas silence hovers over and seems perfectly natural to some Roman Catholic and Episcopal congregations?[38]

Can similar considerations be applied to melodic materials? Is the apparent predilection of Milanese and Mozarabic chant for melodic leaps rather than the more stepwise motion of Gregorian chant an illustration of a more prophetic rather than a priestly presupposition?[39] No easy answers are possible here, for connections between cognitive meaning and musical syntax are notoriously dangerous to make. Further, one has to take into account a rich mosaic of issues, like sacramental theology where, for example, Ambrose was more realistic than Augustine.

Perhaps we can conclude, however, that different theological and musical approaches not only characterize nineteenth- and twentieth-century thought and practice, but that one of the reasons the historical materials can give such varied results is not only because they are fragmentary, but because different approaches have been embodied in actual sound, however complex this relationship may be.[40] Different times and places or even different places at the same time may have done different musical things,[41] which consciously or unconsciously presumed varying theological perspectives. Such a conclusion suggests that our tendency to see a given period or the church or its chant as single monolithic entities needs to be modified toward a reality that is much richer and more complex than we may think.

[38] Thomas Day, *Why Catholics Can't Sing: The Culture of Catholicism and the Triumph of Bad Taste* (New York: Crossroad,1991) can be easily celebrated or attacked, depending on your position. What is usually avoided when it is discussed, however, is the possibility that silence understood positively hovers over parts of the catholic cultus and that asking for a vigorous song in such a context will not fit. Further, the "limitations of history"—like the persecution of Irish Christians to which Richard Schuler points (Day too gives the Irish background)—create not a theological but a historical contingency. See Richard J. Schuler, "The Congregation: Its Possibilities and Limitations in Singing," *Cum Angelis Canere*, p. 327.

[39] See Baroffio, "Ambrosian [Milanese] rite, music of the," NGDMM 1, p. 315.

[40] This embodiment in sound is central to the point Williamson makes in "The Lord's Song."

[41] As Hiley, *Western Plainchant*, p. 385, suggests.

Melodic Style and Musical Forms

101

Melodic
Style and
Musical
Forms

Chant moves from one note per syllable, to up to fifteen notes per syllable, to as many as several hundred notes per syllable. These three groupings of melodic style are classified as syllabic, neumatic, and melismatic.

Three basic musical forms are often delineated. One has reciting notes and includes monotonic recitation of lessons, prayers, blessings as well as psalm tones with more clearly defined intonations and cadences. A second group is repetitive. It can be divided into litanies that repeat phrases, like the Kyrie and Agnus Dei, and strophic forms like hymns. A third group covers everything else and is usually called free, but the term has to be used with discrimination because pieces with internal repetitions, formulaic structures, and genuinely through-composed characteristics all get included here.[42]

Hymns in the East

In contrast to the West where psalmody flourished over hymnody, in the East hymnody flourished over psalmody. Christian Hannick thinks "the worship of the first generations of Christians was centered on hymns."[43] The Gnostics wrote hymns, and Arius created rhymes to popularize his position. Orthodox hymnwriters like Ephraem and Hilary of Potiers responded, and Ambrose took the "decisive step by which Latin hymnody left the stage of infancy to enter that of early maturity as well as artistic culmination."[44] But, at just the same time as Ambrose, the Council of Laodicea banned hymns with an effective edict,[45] which meant that "for many centuries . . . hymns did not attain a liturgical status in the Western church."[46]

Hymns, however, formed a large part of the Byzantine repertoire. Levy opines that 60,000 hymn incipits are published, thousands more are unpublished, and tens of thousands more have disappeared in controversies such as the iconoclastic one that afflicted the East-

[42] See Emerson, "Plainchant," NGDMM 14, pp. 808–809.
[43] Hannick, "Christian Church, music of the early," NGDMM 4, p. 366.
[44] Apel, *Gregorian Chant*, p. 422.
[45] For the text see McKinnon, MECL, p. 119.
[46] Apel, *Gregorian Chant*, pp. 422–423.

ern church from 726 to 843.[47] Both syllabic settings for congregational use like the Phos hilaron[48] with music that was familiar and not written down, as well as more complex cycles of florid settings for soloists and choirs characterize this repertoire of hymns, called troparion, kontakion, kanon, sticheron, and hypakoe.[49] It was not until John Mason Neale translated some of this into Western forms in the nineteenth century that it became available to the Western church.

Ambrose and Gregory

As Ambrosian chant is named for Ambrose, so Gregorian chant is named for Gregory the Great (c. 540–604, pope from 590). Ambrose's association with the formation of Milanese chant and his composition of the Te Deum have generally been denied by modern scholarship.[50] Gregory has sometimes been credited with virtually inventing the Gregorian melodies. The medieval period pictured him with the Holy Spirit as a dove dictating melodies into his ear.[51] Modern scholarship has found Gregory's authorship or even his overseeing a group of composers to be untenable.

Ambrose is sometimes credited with "inventing" the authentic modes and Gregory with "adding" the plagal ones. Here too, as Apel says, "There is not the least bit of evidence to support this story, nor even to make it appear probable or possible."[52]

Clearly, however, Gregory or his staff organized the liturgical and musical materials he inherited, probably ordering them according to the liturgical year.[53] In that sense he can be considered the "father

---

[47] Levy, "Byzantine rite, music of the," NGDMM 3, p. 557. For insights into the Iconoclastic Controversy, especially up to the Second Council of Niceae in 787, but also into iconography more generally, see Jaroslav Pelikan, *Imago Dei: The Byzantine Apologia for Icons* (Princeton: Princeton University Press, 1990).

[48] See chapter 5.

[49] See Levy, "Byzantine rite, music of the," NGDMM 3, pp. 557–559 for descriptions.

[50] See James W. McKinnon, "Ambrose," NGDMM 1, p. 314.

[51] One of these representations, from the Hartker Antiphoner of the tenth or eleventh century, is given in Emerson, "Plainchant," NGDMM 14, p. 805. Another, from a sixteenth century Breviary, can be seen in Romain Goldron, *Byzantine and Medieval Music* (n. p.: H. S. Stuttman Company, Inc., 1968), p. 25.

[52] Apel, *Gregorian Chant*, p. 134.

[53] *Cf.* Robert F. Hayburn, "The Printed Editions of the Chant Books and Their Effect on the Gregorian Tradition," *Cum Angelis Canere*, p. 93.

of chant."[54] So too Ambrose apparently did liturgical and musical organizing in Milan.[55] That organizing, his hymnwriting, and his support of the congregation's singing suggest why he is considered the "father of church song."[56] While some of the details ascribed to Ambrose and Gregory may be wrong, the importance the church has attached to them for its music is probably not misplaced.

Worship

That Ambrose's and Gregory's liturgical and musical organizing would be regarded by the church as of musical importance testifies to the close tie the melodies of chant have to their texts over time, and again highlights the critical importance of worship. The only way any of the musical developments make sense is in connection with the worship of the church, which took shape in two cycles. One was the normal Sunday (sometimes daily) Eucharist, which came to be called the "Mass" in the West.[57] The other was daily prayer, which came to be called the "Daily Office."[58] The two daily offices when the laity can gather before and after work are morning prayer and evening prayer, called "cathedral offices." The monastic cycle consists of eight offices throughout the day: matins, lauds, prime, terce, sext, none, vespers, compline. Prime through none are called the "little hours," prime being the first hour of the day at 6 A.M. with each of the next three coming at three hour intervals. The way these two cycles were fashioned across the seasons of the liturgical year

[54] See Apel, *Gregorian Chant*, pp. 48–50, 57, 61–62, and Hayburn, *Papal Legislation on Sacred Music*, pp. 3–4.

[55] Roy Jesson, "Ambrosian Chant," in Apel, *Gregorian Chant*, p. 465.

[56] There are other "fathers of church song" identified with specific national or ethnic groupings. For example, a large memorial cross in Whitby (a city in northern England where the famous Synod of Whitby in 664 chose the Roman customs and dating of Easter over the Celtic ones) remembers Caedmon, "the father of English sacred song [who] fell asleep hard by 680." On the reverse side of the monument is the first hymn Caedmon sang, reputedly at an advanced age, when the Abbess Hilda (who presided over the sisters and brothers at the Whitby Abbey) invited him to change his secular habit to that of a monk.

[57] For the Mass texts of one Sunday, Septuagesima, with chant, see Claude V. Palisca, ed., *Norton Anthology of Western Music*, Second Edition, Volume I (New York: W. W. Norton & Company, 1988), pp. 4–17.

[58] For the Office texts for Second Vespers, Nativity of our Lord, with chant, see ibid., pp. 18–29.

is also important. It includes what could be considered a third cycle that commemorates "saints." Finally, in both the Mass and the Offices a distinction is made between what ordinarily happens at each service and what happens only on certain days of the year. The former is called the "ordinary," the latter the "propers," creating the whole structure of the liturgical books.[59]

To understand the texts, one starts with Apel's assertion that "nearly all the chants of the Gregorian repertory have a psalmodic background."[60]

- The psalmodic influence is most obvious in the monastic Offices where the entire psalter is traversed each week.
- The antiphons, responsories, hymns, and canticles of the Offices, though they may exude a flavor derived from the psalms, are not so precisely psalmodic.
- The ordinary of the Mass—Kyrie, Gloria, Credo, Sanctus, and Agnus Dei—are likewise derived from essentially non-psalmodic sources. The Kyrie comes from a litany.[61] The Gloria in Excelsis is an expansion of Luke 2:14 modeled on the Psalms and canticles.[62] The creed's use at worship was at first baptismal, which explains the formation of the Apostles' Creed, but the christological controversies of the first centuries led to the introduction of the Nicene Creed from the Council of Niceae (325) into the Eucharist.[63] The Sanctus comes from Isaiah 6:3,[64] the Agnus Dei from John 1:29 and its use in the Gloria.[65]
- The proper introit, gradual, offertory, and communion verses for the Mass were originally full psalms that were cut down to single verses with antiphons.

There is a critical distinction here between the gradual and the other proper psalm verses. As Apel helpfully explains, the introit, offertory, and communion chants accompany liturgical actions, whereas the graduals—and with them the Alleluias and respon-

---

[59] Apel, *Gregorian Chant*, pp. 6–32. See also Hiley, *Western Plainchant*, pp. 1–45, 287–339.

[60] Apel, *Gregorian Chant*, p. 87.

[61] See Cheslyn Jones, Geoffrey Wainwright, Edward Yarnold, ed., *The Study of Liturgy* (New York: Oxford University Press, 1978), pp. 182–183.

[62] Ibid., p. 183

[63] Ibid., p. 187.

[64] Ibid., p. 191 and 195.

[65] Ibid., p. 234, for its introduction into the Mass.

sories—are related to the reading of lessons.[66] The gradual, which is named for the *gradus* or ambo from where it was sung, came between the first two lessons, the Old Testament and epistle. When the Old Testament lesson was dropped the gradual was moved between the epistle and gospel. That is, the graduals are intrinsic to the readings at the Eucharist in a way that the action chants are not. Their importance is clear in the music itself. The lesson chants are responsorial and "highly melismatic," while the action chants are antiphonal and "employ a relatively simpler style."[67]

Liturgical Books

A complete discussion of the books in which the liturgical materials were recorded is beyond our scope. What needs to be remembered is that originally there was no Bible, hymnal, worship book,[68] nor service folders as we know those items today. Printing presses and copy machines were not available for making multiple duplicates. As always, but early on more obviously than at later times, there was first of all a community that worshiped with the requisite liturgical materials. As to the Bible, there has never been complete agreement about the "canon," that is, the rule or standard, of books used for reading in worship, but essentially it was defined for the Old Testament by rabbis at Jamnia in 90 and described for the New Testament by Athanasius in a letter he wrote in 367.

For use in worship at the Eucharist *sacramentaries* developed, which contained parts for the presider, *graduals* the musical parts for the choir, and *lectionaries* the scripture readings or lists of readings. After the tenth century the *missale* took the place of these three books as the Mass turned more and more into a private act of a single priest. For the Offices the psalter, *antiphonaries,* and hymnals found their place in the *breviary.* (Much of the choir's materials from these sources was gathered together in 1896 into the *Liber usualis,* the "usual book.") The *Ordines Romani* contain rubrics for and descriptions of the liturgy, originally at Rome.[69]

---

[66] Apel, *Gregorian Chant,* p. 189.

[67] Ibid. See also Helmut Hucke, "Gradual," NGDMM 7, p. 599.

[68] Either as part of the hymnal such as the *Lutheran Book of Worship* or Roman Catholic *Worship Third Edition,* or under a separate cover such as the Episcopal *Book of Common Prayer* or the Presbyterian *Book of Common Worship.*

[69] See D. M. Hope, "Liturgical Books," *The Study of Liturgy,* pp. 65–69, and

The origin of Gregorian chant as we know it is disputed, but in something similar to its present form it probably can be traced back to around 800.[70] It is the fusion of Roman and Frankish elements Pepin and Charlemagne brought about when, for political reasons, they sought to strengthen their relationship with Rome by imposing the Roman usage into the Frankish empire. This attempt met resistance and caused confusion.[71]

The resistance and confusion had the effect of musical fusion, and the complexity that resulted required a choir, which excluded the people from the singing they had been doing. This exclusion can be detailed as follows.

1. The Gregorian repertoire is formed of layers. The oldest layer of perhaps 650 melodies was formed over a long period up to 750.[72] It may have been syllabic and simpler by comparison with what was later and more melismatic, but whether or not it was syllabic it certainly grew out of a congregational base.[73] In the ninth century a layer of new forms and styles "appeared quite suddenly."[74] This new layer included more complex introits, graduals, and tracts.[75]

2. It also included tropes and sequences. Tropes are interpolations of texts or music, or music and texts, into pre-existent chants. Troping may have begun in the ninth century or earlier.[76] It was done not only to propers such as the introit[77] or the offertory, but also to the

Apel, *Gregorian Chant*, pp. 15–16 and 51–56 for more precision, detail, and additional resources for study.

[70] Apel, *Gregorian Chant*, p. 76.

[71] Ibid., pp. 78–83. See also Levy, "Plainchant," NGDMM 14, p. 801; Reese, *Music in the Middle Ages*, pp. 122–123; and Paul Henry Lang, *Music in Western Civilization*, (New York: W. W. Norton & Company, 1941), p. 67.

[72] Levy, "Plainchant," NGDMM 14, pp. 806 and 813. *Cf.* Robert F. Hayburn, "The Printed Editions of the Chant Books and Their Effect on the Gregorian Tradition," *Cum Angelis Canere*, p. 92.

[73] See Apel, *Gregorian Chant*, pp. 507–508. Apel quotes this "categorical statement" by F. A. Gevaert: "Le chant syllabique est antérieur au chant mélismatique." Emerson, "Plainchant," NGDMM 14, p. 808, disagrees.

[74] Levy, "Plainchant," NGDMM 14, pp. 806 and 813.

[75] Apel, *Gregorian Chant*, pp. 82–83.

[76] Ibid., p. 430.

[77] The trope *Quem quaeritis in praesepe* before the Introit on Christmas day is easily accessible in Palisca, ed., *Norton Anthology of Western Music*, pp. 32–33.

ordinary: the Kyrie, the Gloria in Excelsis, the Sanctus, and the Agnus Dei. Choirs were required for these more complex chants.[78]

Most of us have been taught that sequences began as tropes on the *jubilus* of the Alleluia, then were lopped off and developed as independent compositions. Some scholars think this theory "needs to be abandoned."[79] In any event, the composition of sequences started around 850 and reached its peak in the twelfth century with Adam of St. Victor (d. 1177 or 1192). Sequences continued to be written and used profusely until they cluttered up the Mass to such an extent that the Council of Trent in the sixteenth century (1545–1563) suppressed all but four of them: *Victimae paschali laudes* for Easter,[80] *Veni sancte Spiritus* for Pentecost, *Lauda Sion* for Corpus Christi, and the *Dies Irae* for the Requiem.[81]

3. Though the Schola Cantorum, literally the "school of singers" by which is meant the choir at Rome, may have been formed before Gregory the Great, it was reorganized and given new impetus by him.[82] In the Carolingian period scholas at other places like Metz and Soissons became famous.[83]

4. The language of the Roman liturgy imposed by Pepin and Charlemagne was Latin, which the Frankish people did not know.

5. More complex music than chant began to develop. It was an early form of polyphony called organum.[84]

The result of all this was to devalue the congregation's singing and to accentuate the choir's. The oldest layer of simpler music was congregational and developed over a long period the way folk forms always do. The newer material, which came suddenly, was more complex and foreign to the congregation in both language and music. It could not be easily assimilated except by professionals.

[78] See Ruth Steiner, "Trope," NGDMM 19, pp. 172–187, a fine overview, with examples. See also Emerson, "Plainchant," NGDMM 14, pp. 813–816, and Apel, *Gregorian Chant*, pp. 429–442.

[79] Richard L. Crocker, "Sequence," NGDMM 17, p. 148.

[80] This sequence with music is easily accessible in Palisca, ed., *Norton Anthology of Western Music*, pp. 30–31.

[81] For more about Sequences see Richard L. Crocker and John Caldwell, "Sequence," NGDMM 17, pp. 141–156; Steiner, "Trope," NGDMM 19, pp. 172–173; John A. Emerson, "Plainchant," NGDMM 14, p. 816; and Apel, *Gregorian Chant*, pp. 442–464,

[82] See Emerson, "Plainchant," NGDMM 14, p. 811, and Reese, *Music in the Middle Ages*, p. 121.

[83] Lang, *Music in Western Civilization*, p. 67.

[84] See the next chapter.

Congregational parts of the Mass were therefore assigned to choirs.[85]

This move toward choirs should not be taken to mean that the congregation's singing disappeared suddenly in the ninth century. Charlemagne himself

ordered the people to sing the Gloria Patri after each psalm. Kyrie eleison and Christe eleison were alternated between the men and women, and the writers of the period record the efforts of the clergy to cultivate the singing of the people. Monsignor Anglès has pointed out that "no matter what is said to the contrary, the Church never ceased encouraging singing by the people, both in and out of church." The faithful sang in religious processions, at vigils for the feasts of martyrs, for burial rogation days, translation of holy relics, and many other ecclesiastical occasions. Thus alongside of the marvellous growth of the *scholae cantorum*, the flowering of the great artistic treasures of Gregorian chant, the elaboration of papal, episcopal and monastic rites, the singing of the people continued in all parts of the West in the Celtic, Mozarabic, and Gallican forms of the Latin liturgy as well as in the parochial churches of Italy.[86]

Nonetheless, a slow process was at work over many centuries. Perhaps as early as the fourth century,[87] perhaps after the second half of the fifth century,[88] the gradual psalm was taken over by a trained choir. A choir not only took over the verses which probably had always been done by a cantor or choir anyway, but the congregational responses or refrains were removed as well. Nonmusical realities also militated against the church's song long before Charlemagne's political ones. Barbarian invasions, for example, did not make the continuity of church life—instruction, worship, singing—an easy matter.

These developments did not silence the congregation's song suddenly *or* completely. Christians will not be stopped from singing even when wars and pestilence come or when leaders do not encourage it. Foley says that "at no time in the history of the church was the song of the people completely ignored." Richard Schuler has demonstrated that the "singing of the people is as old as the Church

[85] Lang, *Music in Western Civilization*, p. 72.

[86] Richard J. Schuler, "The Congregation: Its Possibilities and Limitations in Singing," *Cum Angelis Canere*, p. 321.

[87] Apel, *Gregorian Chant*, p. 181.

[88] Hucke, "Gradual," NGDMM 7, p. 599.

and . . . has persisted through the centuries."[89] Nevertheless, in the Middle Ages the people as a whole, not just women but everyone in the congregation, were eventually excluded from singing at the Eucharist.[90] Even there, however, the inertia of the people's singing was hard to break. The Sanctus, the congregational part of the eucharistic liturgy, which is most integral to it,[91] "was considered a chant of the people as late as the twelfth century."[92]

Concluding Reflection

By the time we get to the Carolingian period two tendencies in the church's music are clear. One is toward the people's song as in the first several centuries, the other toward the finest possible musical art of choirs from the fourth or fifth centuries on, when persecution was no longer present. Both inevitably grow out of the New Testament and its message. A critical aspect of musical health in the church has to do with holding these tendencies in an incarnational tension so that they feed and discipline one another rather than dissipate into separate pieces. The history of the gradual illustrates the tension's coming apart.

The graduals moved chant to an artistic musical level[93] and in so doing pointed to the church's best instincts: at the very center of the word portion of the Eucharist, in an integral and interpretive connection with the scriptural readings themselves, the highest human craft in choral art was spawned. Yet the church's best instincts were also to make an inherently congregational response an integral part of this chant. When in the fourth or fifth century the choir started to take over the congregation's participation and followed its own path without the discipline of the congregation's role, the tension was lost.[94] Events in the ninth century silenced the congregation even

---

[89] Richard J. Schuler, "The Congregation: Its Possibilities and Limitations in Singing," *Cum Angelis Canere*, pp. 314.

[90] Foley, *From Age to Age*, p. 102.

[91] Apel, *Gregorian Chant*, p. 25.

[92] Foley, *From Age to Age*, p. 102. *Cf.* p. 75.

[93] Hucke, "Gradual," NGDMM 7, p. 599.

[94] *Cf.* Richard J. Schuler, "The Congregation: Its Possibilities and Limitations in Singing," *Cum Angelis Canere*, p. 324.

more, with perhaps the Sanctus alone persisting among the people until the twelfth or thirteenth century. The congregation lost its musical office in worship. A healthy tension came apart. One might say that the tendencies were to deny Christ's humanity, let high art prevail at the expense of folk art, and turn beauty into idolatry.[95] Though further qualifications need to be made in the next chapter, the people lost their birthright.

[95] For thoughts on the relationship of the beautiful and the holy via Nietzsche and Bach, see Jaroslav Pelikan, *Fools for Christ: Essays on the True, the Good, and the Beautiful* (Philadelphia: Muhlenberg Press, 1955), pp. 118–172. For further descriptions of this complexity, see Frank Burch Brown, *Religious Aesthetics: A Theological Study of Making and Meaning* (Princeton: Princeton University Press, 1989).

8

Choirs and Thought

From Organum to Renaissance Polyphony

While the people were being denied their part at worship, a remarkable development in choral music was simultaneously taking their place. It progressed from chant to organum to Renaissance polyphony.

Organum

"Organum"[1] is the name given to the earliest kind of polyphonic music, namely, singing in parallel fifths or fourths. It can be seen as a logical development of whatever parallel singing may have taken place earlier and the use of a drone.[2]

Organum can also be seen as a logical development of unison singing itself, derived from the natural physical phenomena of music. When you play or sing any pitch, you set into vibration a series of pitches that sound above the pitch you initiate. (The relative loudness of certain of the harmonics or partials in this series creates what we hear as different tone colors or timbres. In the lower or chalumeau register of the clarinet, for example, the strength of the odd-numbered partials gives the instrument what is sometimes characterized as a "hollow" tone color.) You can check this out if you hold down the sustaining pedal of a piano, strike one note while continuing to hold the pedal, and let the note gradually die away; a

---

[1] For a discussion of this term see Fritz Reckow, "Organum," NGDMM 13, pp. 796–797. For the broader historical sweep see Fritz Reckow and Rudolf Flotzinger, "Organum," NGDMM 13, pp. 796–808. For an extensive bibliography see Norman E. Smith, "Organum and Discant: bibliography," NGDMM 13, pp. 808–819.

[2] Reckow, "Organum," NGDMM 13, p. 798.

lower note will work better than a higher one. If you listen carefully, as the note dies out you'll hear at least one and maybe more than one pitch above the one you play. What you hear is a tiny slice of a long stack of pitches known as the harmonic series.

Any horizontal succession of pitches, a melody, is therefore already a parallel progression of a vertical stack of pitches, each melodic note having its own harmonic series. The first two notes of each series form an octave, the second two a fifth, the third two a fourth. We have already encountered women and children singing together with men in parallel octaves. Singing in octaves uses the first two pitches of the natural harmonic series. Organum pushes this one or two steps farther, to singing in fifths or fourths—that is, to the fifth, which is the second interval in the harmonic series or its inversion,[3] a fourth, which is the third interval. David Cherwien calls organum "another way of singing in unison."[4]

Organum was constructed by several methods.[5] One, in the ninth and tenth centuries, was to add a parallel voice a fifth above or a fourth below an original chant melody.[6] A second and later development was to insert a newly composed trope into a preexisting chant. For example, between the first and last phrases of the Agnus Dei (that is, between "Agnus Dei, qui tollis peccata mundi,"[7] and "miserere nobis"[8]), a new text with new music might be composed,

---

[3] An inversion of any interval is formed when you move one of the notes an octave across the other note. For example, if you have middle c¹ on the keyboard with the g¹ above it and you move the g¹ an octave toward and therefore across c¹, you will wind up with the g below middle c¹ and middle c¹. The original fifth will have been "inverted" into a fourth. The total numerical value of inversions is 9: fifths become fourths (5 + 4 = 9), fourths become fifths (4 + 5 = 9), sixths become thirds (6 + 3 = 9), seconds become sevenths (2 + 7 = 9). (Musicians will also know that perfect intervals (unisons, fourths, fifths, and octaves) remain perfect, major and minor intervals (seconds, thirds, sixths, sevenths) become their opposite (major to minor, minor to major), and augmented (half steps more than perfect and major intervals) and diminished (half steps less than perfect and minor intervals) also switch places: a P4 becomes a P5, a m6 becomes a M3, an A4 becomes a d5, etc.)

[4] David M. Cherwien, *Let the People Sing!* (St. Louis: Concordia Publishing House, 1997), p. 118.

[5] These methods and the music that followed organum can be seen very clearly (and heard on the accompanying recordings) in an older though still helpful book: Carl Parrish and John F. Ohl, *Masterpieces of Music Before 1750* (New York; W. W. Norton & Company, 1951).

[6] Ibid., p. 17. See also Palisca, ed., *Norton Anthology of Western Music*, p. 43.

[7] "Lamb of God, who takes away the sins of the world,"

[8] "have mercy on us."

the music consisting of two voices, which flowed freely around the
gravitational pull of what were considered the consonant intervals—
unisons, octaves, and fifths.[9] A third way of constructing organum
was associated with the abbey of St. Martial in southern France, one
of the few Cluniac houses that cultivated organum,[10] during the first
half of the twelfth century. In it the notes of the original chant were
elongated, and then a second freely flowing melismatic voice was
added above the long-note pillars.[11] Again the notes flowed around
the gravitational pull of the open sounds of unisons, fifths, and
octaves. A fourth type was associated with the cathedral of Notre
Dame in Paris after the middle of the twelfth century with the work
of Léonin (fl. 1160–1180)[12] and Pérotin (fl. c. 1200).[13] Here again
the notes of the original chant were elongated, sometimes greatly
elongated. Above them two voices gravitated to the open conso-
nances, this time employing regularly recurring patterns of long and
short note values in what are called rhythmic modes. The long note
was equal to two short notes, giving rise to patterns similar to poetic
feet.[14]

113

From
Organum
to Renais-
sance
Polyphony

Renaissance Polyphony

Around 1322 Philippe de Vitry (1291–1361)—a French composer,
musical theorist, and bishop with a keen intellect—wrote a book
called *Ars Nova*. His title, *Ars Nova,* has since been applied to music
of the fourteenth century to distinguish it from the music of Léonin
and Pérotin in the Notre Dame period, which came to be called the
"Ars Antiqua." This terminology is obviously a retrospective judgment by the "new art" people in the fourteenth century, which later
periods have continued to use. No period calls itself "old art!" Nor
is there eternal significance to such designations. For us both the Ars
Antiqua and the Ars Nova are old, and sometimes what is "old" has
been used to create what is new—as in "neo-Classic" music of the
twentieth century, which went behind the nineteenth century to the
eighteenth or earlier for its inspiration.

[9] See Parrish and Ohl, *Masterpieces*, p. 19, for an example.
[10] See Michael Huglo, "Cluniac monks," NGDMM 4, p. 504.
[11] Ibid., p. 21.
[12] See Ian D. Brent, "Léonin," NGDMM 10, pp. 676–677.
[13] See Ian D. Brent, "Pérotin," NGDMM 14 pp. 540–543.
[14] See Ian D. Brent, "Rhythmic modes," NGDMM 15, pp. 824–825. For the
music of Pérotin see Parrish and Ohl, pp. 24–25; for Léonin and Pérotin, Palisca, ed.,
Norton Anthology of Western Music, pp. 47–65.

The Ars Nova is an apt title, however, in that the fourteenth century does move beyond organum toward Renaissance polyphony
where individual lines became increasingly independent of one
another. The music of Guillaume de Machaut (c. 1300–1377)—the
most important composer of the Ars Nova, not only in the number
of his compositions, but also in their masterful quality—gets closer
to what twentieth century ears find more familiar,[15] though the fourteenth century is still ancient for us. The so-called Landini cadence,
for example, named for the composer Francesco Landini
(1325–1397), is characteristic of the Ars Nova.[16] It sounds medieval.
One voice moves with the scale degrees 7 to 6 to 8, while the other
voice moves in contrary motion 2 to 1.[17]

Guillaume Dufay (1400–1474), the leading composer of the
next century, illustrates several fifteenth-century characteristics.
1) Musical settings of the ordinary of the Mass began to be important parts of composers' work. 2) These settings tended to be unified. At first a couple pieces of the ordinary, like the Sanctus and
Agnus Dei, were paired. Then all five sections (Kyrie, Gloria,
Credo, Sanctus, Agnus Dei) were unified by some musical means
to make complete "cyclic" masses. 3) At least by the thirteenth-
century secular tunes, and sometimes vernacular secular texts as
well, were "inserted into the music of the Church."[18] Dufay used
one of the most popular of these secular tunes, "Se la face ay pale"
for one of his masses.[19]

Johannes Ockeghem (c. 1410–1497), another skillful fifteenth-
century composer, wrote complex imitative music that still sounds
very musical, though there are carefully worked out mathematical
relationships hidden in it.[20] Josquin Desprez (c. 1440–1521), a
singer in the Milan Cathedral and a member of the Papal Chapel,

[15] See Parrish and Ohl, *Masterpieces*, pp. 38–39, and Palisca, ed., *Norton
Anthology of Western Music*, pp. 87–91, for an *Agnus Dei* by Machaut.

[16] See David Fallows, "Landini cadence," NGDMM 10, p. 434.

[17] For Landini cadences in Landini see Parrish and Ohl, *Masterpieces*, pp. 40–42,
and Palisca, ed., *Norton Anthology of Western Music*, pp. 81–82. A Landini cadence
in the next century, in Dufay, can be spotted quickly in Parrish and Ohl, *Masterpieces*, p. 45, second system, second to third measures.

[18] Hayburn, *Papal Legislation on Sacred Music*, p. 17.

[19] Ibid., 43–47. Also see Charles Hamm, "Dufay, Guillaume," NGDMM 5, p.
678. For further musical examples of Dufay, see Palisca, ed., *Norton Anthology of
Western Music*, pp. 104–112.

[20] See Parrish and Ohl, *Masterpieces*, pp. 53–54.

was the most important late fifteenth-century composer[21] and Luther's favorite one. He moves us to sixteenth-century polyphony and the eve of the Reformation. His compositions, said Luther, "flow freely, gently, and cheerfully, are not forced or cramped by rules, and are like the song of the finch."[22] What Luther meant was that Josquin knew the compositional craft and its "rules" so well that he was able to use them to fashion the finest music: "Josquin is a master of the notes, which must express what he desires; on the other hand, other choral composers must do what the notes dictate."[23]

115

From
Organum
to Renais-
sance
Polyphony

Composers and Choirs

This brief sketch of musical developments from the ninth to the sixteenth centuries, which can be fleshed out with further details and examples from standard music history and music appreciation textbooks as well as numerous recordings, is sufficient to indicate that the church musician became the composer of marvelous choral music for choirs. The Old Testament figures of Miriam and David, and the hidden and then less hidden cantors in the church's early history, point to the church musician's role in connection with the people. Even the professional Levites in the Old Testament have to be seen in some relation to the people and their responses. By the sixteenth century of our era, however, compositions for choirs took the place of the people's participation. Church music became the music of choirs. The people could listen to this treasury and probably in many cases were deeply appreciative of it, but no comparable concern was exerted for their active musical participation. They listened and watched as choirs sang for them.

[21] For an Ave Maria of Josquin, see Parrish and Ohl, *Masterpieces*, pp. 60–62. For two other motets by Josquin, see Palisca, ed., *Norton Anthology of Western Music*, pp. 113–129.

[22] *Luther's Works* (Philadelphia: Muhlenberg Press, 1960ff.) 54, "Table Talk," p. 130 (hereafter LW).

[23] Translation by Walter Buszin, *Luther on Music* (Saint Paul: North Central Publishing Company, 1958), p. 13, from Johann Mathesius, *Dr. Martin Luthers Leben* (St. Louis: Druckerei des Lutherischen Concordia-Verlags, 1883), p. 227f. [Also cited by Carl Schalk, *Luther on Music: Paradigms of Praise* (St. Louis: Concordia Publishing House, 1988, p. 21.]

Thought over Sound, Why over How

As will become clear in the next chapter, the apparent lack of the people's participation is not quite so simple as I have just suggested, but a medieval mindset did support it.

Musical Speculation

We are likely to view medieval music the way we view music generally in our period, from the standpoint of how it sounded. That is, for us music means that the actual sounds of music are always in the foreground. In order to understand a dominant, perhaps *the* dominant medieval mindset—at least what we know most about from the medieval period (see the next chapter for some other likely medieval perspectives)—we have to rethink what for us is the norm.

Remember back to Chrysostom and his comment about "the divine chant composed of number."[24] Already in the early church Chrysostom was referring to number symbolism.[25] Quentin Faulkner sees it as one of four pieces that were developed into a medieval speculative musical system. The other three were cosmic harmony, the doctrine of ethos, and music as a science.[26] The four formed a unit, which, at the risk of grave oversimplification, can be described in the following manner.[27]

Boethius (c. 480–c. 524), an erudite Roman writer and philosopher, wrote an influential book—called *De Musica* like Augustine's—that provides an entry into the medieval mindset. Boethius identified three kinds of music: *musica mundana*,[28] the music of the spheres; *musica humana*, the music of the human body and soul; and *musica instrumentalis*,[29] the actual musical sounds we hear. The

---

[24] See chapter 5 and John Chrysostom, "Exposition of Psalm XLI; PG LV, 156; trans. Strunk, *Source Readings*, p. 67.

[25] See Faulkner, *Wiser Than Despair*, p. 109–111.

[26] Ibid., p. 93.

[27] See ibid., pp. 93–133; Calvin Bower, "Boethius, Anicius Manlius Severinus," NBDMM 2, pp. 844–845; Edgar De Bruyne, trans., Eileen B. Hennessy, *The Esthetics of the Middle Ages* (New York: Frederick Ungar, Publishing Co., 1969), pp. 48–55, 149, 190–197; and Routley, *The Church and Music*, pp. 81–82, 87, 235–236.

[28] *Mundana* comes from *mundus* meaning "world." The sense here is not "mundane" as in common or banal, but what pertains to the world understood as cosmos from the Greek, namely, the whole orderly universe or the world of heavens and heavenly bodies as a harmonious system.

[29] All sounding music of voices and instruments is encompassed here.

central reality was the first category, the music of the spheres. John
Milton's poem in the seventeenth century, "Ring out, ye crystal
spheres," was still dependent on this cosmology of music.[30] The
music we actually hear was conceived to be but a dim reflection of
the music made by cosmic spheres spinning within spheres.[31]
Human beings could, it was thought, access this real music by mathematical calculations, which is why music in the medieval period
was set with arithmetic, geometry, and astronomy in the category
of the quadrivium's advanced mathematical "arts."[32] Music was
related to the natural phenomena of vibrations and numerical ratios
of intervals in the harmonic series to which I referred earlier and
which Pythagoras was credited for figuring out.[33] Numbers were
important not only for quantifying the proportions of vibrating bodies, but also for their symbolic significance: 3, the perfect number,
related to the Trinity; 4 represented the elements, directions, seasons;
7 stood for the days of the week, the tones of the scale, the graces
of the Holy Spirit.[34] Following Plato, ethical realities were built into
this system. Some modes were seen to lead to disharmony, frenzy,
and degeneracy. Other modes were seen to lead to calmness, harmony, and building up the individual and the community. *Musica
humana* was to imitate *musica mundana,* and once a good musical
tradition was established innovation signaled decay of the individual
and the whole body politic. The wrong kind or even too much music
enfeebled rather than ennobled humanity.[35] This was all obviously
Greek in origin, processed in the medieval period through a Christian filter in which the creator of this amazing musical universe was
God revealed in Christ.[36]

[30] See Faulkner, *Wiser Than Despair*, p. 98.

[31] Whether this music actually sounded was a "running argument." See Faulkner,
Wiser Than Despair, pp. 95–96.

[32] The elementary studies in the Trivium were grammar, dialectic, and rhetoric.
Together the Trivium and Quadrivium made up the seven liberal arts, after which
one was qualified to study theology.

[33] See Faulkner, *Wiser Than Despair*, pp. 32–33.

[34] See Faulkner, *Wiser Than Despair*, p. 110, and Vincent Foster Hopper,
*Medieval Number Symbolism: Its Sources, Meaning, and Influence on Thought and
Expression* (New York: Cooper Square Publishers, Inc., 1969).

[35] See Faulkner, *Wiser Than Despair*, pp. 36–47, and the quotation from
Boethius in Routley, *The Church and Music*, pp. 235–236.

[36] Faulkner, *Wiser Than Despair*, p. 93.

The Musical Philosopher

This way of thinking may seem curious to us, and insignificant as well. It had enormous implications, however. It meant the true musician was the *musicus* or "musical philosopher who understood the 'why' of music."[37] The "cantor," the singer or player who understood the "how" of music, was inferior to the musicus, even if the musicus was also a skillful composer or able performer. Skill as a composer was not regarded as highly as knowledge of music.[38] The composer was an artisan, a craftsperson, not the independent artist we conceive of. Music itself was not regarded as an art, performance and performance standards were not as important as they are among us, and "'art for art's sake' was inconceivable."[39] The theory of music and its actual practice were two separate things, related and not related.[40] One could speculate on meter abstractly, for example, without those speculations having any effect on the meter of the chant itself.[41]

Lest this mindset still seem insignificant, consider its practical effect. 1) It meant the church musician was farther away from the people than the composer of music for choirs. In a sense the church musician was not even the composer. The church musician became the philosopher who did not actually have to make music at all. 2) As this mindset led to a highly developed musical and "spiritual" art, it further shut out the people's song. An elite group had the secret of music's composition and performance. The complex choral polyphony that developed could be, and certainly was, appreciated by those who did not understand it. But it was not meant for listening as much as for singing by the inside group. As Faulkner says, "to appreciate the complex polyphony fully, one needs to know it thoroughly, and best of all, to sing it."[42] 3) Actually those who were in the know progressed beyond the delight of polyphonic sounds toward a mystical experience. This experience pushed from the peripheral *musica instrumentalis* we hear back to the more central musica mundana of the universe. After the initial pleasure of the surface sounds came attention to the formal structure of the music, which was heard first as confused mathematics. Then abandonment to intelligent listening plunged one into the world of mystery—the laws of harmony, primary proportions, eternal numbers. Finally the

[37] Ibid., pp. 108–109.
[38] Ibid.
[39] Ibid., p. 109.
[40] See Faulkner, *Wiser Than Despair*, pp. 113–133.
[41] See McKinnon, "The Church Fathers," p. 265.
[42] Ibid., p. 109

Christian ascended still higher, from numbers to Unity and mystical ecstasy.[43] This spiritual discipline—a very priestly one, to be sure—gives the lie to notions that Christians have never developed any "spiritualities," but it also indicates their inherent elitist danger: peasants—musical or otherwise—were not able to participate.

Knowledge and Emotion

The foregoing logic suggests that music was tied to knowledge and intellect, not to emotions, for many people in the medieval period. Such a perspective may be even harder for us to understand than the primacy of universal "sound" not heard by human ears. We tend to reverse this medieval view. We are apt to relate music only to emotions and to erase the intellect, whereas the medieval view we have been reviewing was likely to relate music only to the intellect and to erase the emotions.

Our notion that music "embodies, expresses, and excites human emotion, feeling, passion" was not characteristic until the Enlightenment and beyond.[44] Before that music, and especially the church's music, was more likely to be related to an ennobling of the spirit in which emotions were restrained and best kept at an interior level, not to be made outwardly perceptible.[45] Quentin Faulkner sees Josquin as "initiating the innovation [that music] consciously sought to express the emotion of the words."[46] It does not mean, however, that Josquin fits our post-Enlightenment perspective or anything like it. His "compositions (like J. S. Bach's)," says Faulkner, "mark one of those remarkable moments when intellect and emotion find a perfect equilibrium."[47] But it does signal new currents at work in the fifteenth century.[48]

Instruments

As we will see in Luther, one of those new currents regarded sound in its own right. With it came the use of instruments in their own

[43] See De Bruyne, *The Esthetics of the Middle Ages*, pp. 192–197.

[44] See Faulkner, *Wiser Than Despair*, pp. 172–173.

[45] Ibid., pp. 104–105, 124.

[46] Ibid., p. 156.

[47] Ibid.

[48] For a related discussion of different views of word painting in chant, see William Peter Mahrt, "Word-Painting and Formulaic Chant," *Cum Angelis Canere*, pp. 113–144.

right, independent of the voice. Though the Eastern church and places such as the Sistine Chapel in the West continued to use only voices in their worship, instruments eventually became normative for most Western Christian communities, reversing the position of the early church.

Precisely when instruments began to be used in Christian worship remains unclear. If Edmund Bowles and James McKinnon are right, the organ was the first instrument to appear. It was introduced about 1000 to 1300 and only gradually became universal.[49] Several factors made it acceptable: it had no "history of association with immorality and ignorance," was "admirably suited" for teaching musical and mathematical calculations because the dimensions of pipes matched the numerical ratios of pitches,[50] and had a long allegorical and literary tradition attached to it,[51] not to mention its practical capacity to fill large spaces with sound produced with breath through pipes as in the voice. Many early references to the organ do not refer to its actual use in worship at all. It related first not to sound itself, but to the more essential universal essence of sound behind sound, though, curiously enough, its actual use in worship may well have coincided with the coming of measured chant.[52] When it was introduced into worship, it was not used to double voices or accompany them as we so often use it. In the Notre Dame school it played the original chant tune as singers sang the other two parts. In the fifteenth and early sixteenth centuries it played before the singers, after them, or in alternation with them "as a substitute for the singing."[53]

The trumpet may have been introduced into worship in the fifteenth century,[54] though other instruments might have been used as early as the twelfth century.[55] Instruments other than the organ were certainly in use during the Renaissance,[56] possibly at first to duplicate the voices. In the festive works of those such as Giovanni Gabrieli (c. 1553–1612) at St. Mark's in Venice, virtuosic instrumental ensembles were set in independent counterpoint with vocal choirs.

[49] McKinnon, "The Church Fathers," p. 269.
[50] Ibid., p. 276.
[51] Ibid., p. 275.
[52] Ibid., p. 267.
[53] Ibid., p. 280.
[54] Ibid., p. 269.
[55] See Hayburn, *Papal Legislation on Sacred Music*, p. 19.
[56] Faulkner, *Wiser Than Despair*, p. 157.

9

Life and Song

Perspective

In spite of the colorful musical progression toward choirs in balconies at St. Mark's in Venice, it has nonetheless been easy and not uncommon in some Protestant circles to interpret the history of the Christian church from the time of Gregory the Great or so to the time of the Reformation as a great apostasy in which the people were shut out of worship, a gray period of lifeless dullness was ushered in, and music was one of the marks of the church's "fall."[1] In such a view the medieval church completely lost the people's participation, and all the Reformers recovered it. Both halves of that assertion are inaccurate, but it and its presuppositions have led to jumps in Protestant teaching from Gregory the Great or even earlier all the way to the Reformation as if nothing intervened—at least nothing alive and worthy of study or consideration.[2] Among Roman Catholic students I have found that the Protestant sense of medieval apostasy and the importance of the Reformation are not present, but everything prior to the Renaissance or even later often gets glazed

---

[1] This view is still expressed among us, but it is not new. It may have been Andreas Karlstadt's position in the sixteenth century. See the next chapter, Charles Garside, Jr., *Zwingli and the Arts* (New Haven and London: Yale University Press, 1966), pp. 28–33, 54, and John K. Harms, "Music of the Radical Reformation II," *Church Music* (78/1): 19–21.

[2] In the nineteenth century one popular version of German Reformed history said Polycarp founded a mission at Lugdunum in Gaul. In 177 persecution caused refugees from that church to flee to the Alps "where in the sixteenth century their descendants established the Reformed Church." Another version said the descendants "reappeared first in the twelfth century as followers of Peter Waldo, and thus the Reformed Church was really neo-Waldensian." Bard Thompson, "The Catechism and the Mercersburg Theology," *Essays on the Heidelberg Catechism* (Philadelphia: United Church Press, 1963), pp. 58–59.

over with exactly the same lifeless blur that Protestants perceive. There are antecedents for such a view among Renaissance humanists who regarded the period from the Vandal conquest of North Africa in 476 to the fall of Constantinople in 1453 as the "Dark Ages." If you agree, you have to dismiss the contents of this chapter and the last one out of hand.

The obvious needs to be stated, however: people in the periods we call dark or medieval were not phantoms, even if they sometimes felt surrounded by ghosts. People with flesh and blood lived then and did things we do. That included disagreeing, singing, having babies, betraying each other, keeping faith with each other, having fun, being disappointed, getting hot in the summer and cold in the winter, facing sickness, working, eating, bleeding, dying, being baptized into Christ's body the church, and participating in worship as best they could—the same as we participate as well as we can given the limitations of our period in history.

At central points, the people's musical office in worship had been removed. The ordinary of the Mass was taken over by choirs, the people's response in propers like the gradual Psalm had been curtailed, morning and evening prayer beyond the family had become solely choral or monastic, and a mindset that viewed music's essence as something not heard further lessened the importance of the people's singing.

The larger context did not encourage participation either. 1) Low Mass developed in which individual priests *said* Mass. Neither choir, music, nor a congregation were required, though a congregation could be present doing its own devotions. Only a server assisted the priest. 2) The importance of seeing the elevation of the elements at the Mass along with the devaluation of the people's singing may be interpreted to signal for the congregation the importance of sight over sound. 3) The bread and wine in the Lord's Supper came to be perceived as holy in the sense of scary.[3] Between the twelfth and fourteenth centuries the wine was more and more denied to the people because of the danger of spilling it. People's fear stopped them from receiving communion so that at the Fourth Lateran Council in 1215 a rule was made that they had to commune at least once a year.[4] Christ was turned into a remote judge, and Mary virtually became a mediator in Christ's stead.

[3] For a description of the medieval terror of the holy, see Roland Bainton, *Here I Stand: A Life of Martin Luther* (New York: Abingdon Press, 1950), pp. 39–44.

[4] For a quick survey of these last two developments with bibliographies, see John M. Huels, "Communion Under Both Kinds," *The New Dictionary of Sacramental*

Healthy musical participation in worship by the congregation was in trouble, but faithful Christians were still not lifeless sticks. What was denied at one place surfaced in another, people still sang actual music, and they participated in worship.

Prone

In the early church intercessory prayers of the faithful initiated the eucharistic half of the Sunday service. In the sixth century these prayers were moved to a litany with Kyries at the beginning of the word half of the service as part of the gathering rite. About a century later this litany was abandoned so that intercession was now absent from the Mass altogether.[5] Preaching also was in remission.

In the ninth-century Frankish realms under Charlemagne a pastoral concern to revitalize worship led to an insistence on preaching, preaching that was to be understood by the people and that was to happen every Sunday in every church. As a result a vernacular preaching, praying, and teaching office called "prone" was inserted into the Mass right after the gospel. It probably began (or possibly ended) with a sermon and included a bidding prayer, the Lord's Prayer in the vernacular, the Ave Maria, the Apostles' Creed, the Ten Commandments, a general confession of sins with absolution (here is the origin of the confession of sins in corporate worship), and church notices about events such as marriages and special celebrations.[6]

Denied their rightful participation in the Mass itself, the people partially found it in prone. Did they sing any or all of prone? Did they sing responses like Kyries in the bidding prayer? Did they sing the Lord's Prayer, the *Ave Maria?* Additional "hymns" perhaps? Were Germanic acclamations from a category called *Ruf* ("cry," "shout") that are traceable to the ninth century used at the end of the sermon or at the end of the Mass itself?[7] Were more developed

---

Worship, ed. Peter E. Fink (Collegeville: The Liturgical Press, 1990), pp. 240–241, and Frank C. Senn, "Communion, Frequency of Reception of," *The New Dictionary of Sacramental Worship*, ed. Peter E. Fink (Collegeville: The Liturgical Press, 1990), pp. 241–245.

[5] See E. C. Whitaker, "Bidding Prayer," in J. G. Davies, *The New Westminster Dictionary of Liturgy and Worship* (Philadelphia: The Westminster Press, 1986), pp. 91–92.

[6] From a lecture by Bard Thompson, Lancaster Seminary, Lancaster, Pennsylvania, November 9, 1962.

[7] See David Fallows, "Ruf," NGDMM 16, p. 318.

Leisen,[8] so-called because "each stanza ended with some version of
the phrase 'Kyrie *eleis*on,' " used in the bidding prayers as well as on
pilgrimages or to and from work?[9] Prone did not receive its final
form until the twelfth century, so there was ample time for precursors to the Leisen and cantios we know about to develop and to be
used. I have no evidence and can only speculate based on people's
inherent need to sing when they participate vocally in worship.

Even if the people only spoke their parts in prone, their corporate
speaking was itself participatory and proto-musical, as is ours. Further, the people were not simply spectators at the rest of the Mass.
They hummed along and took pieces of chant into their singing during their life throughout the week.[10] The presence of so many Latin
lines in macaronic carols itself indicates an interplay at work
between Latin and the vernacular.[11] People also responded and
reacted to what they heard at worship. The last comment can best
be explored in connection with some disputes.

Opposition

The musical developments in relation to worship, from chant to
organum to Renaissance polyphony, did not proceed smoothly.
Some people opposed them. We know especially about such opposition in the Ars Antiqua and the Ars Nova. For example, in
response to musical developments of the Ars Antiqua, John of Salisbury (1120–1180), bishop of Chartres, said this.

> Bad taste has, however, degraded even religious worship, bringing into
> the presence of God, into the recesses of the sanctuary a kind of luxu-
> rious and lascivious singing, full of ostentation, which with female mod-
> ulation[12] astonishes and enervates the souls of the hearers. When you
> hear the soft harmonies of the various singers, some taking high and
> others low parts, some singing in advance, some following in the rear,

---

[8] See David Fallows, "Leise," NGDMM 10, p. 642.

[9] Carl Schalk, "German Church Song," *The Hymnal 1982 Companion* (New
York: The Church Hymnal Corporation, 1990): I, p. 289.

[10] See John Stevens, "Carol," NGDMM 3, p. 804.

[11] See Richard Leighton Greene, *The Early English Carols* (Oxford: Clarendon
Press, 1977), chapter III, pp. lxxxi–cxvii.

[12] We are likely to read comments like this as sexist. We may be right, but it is
possible that we are blind to the possibility that they are just the reverse, that their
intent is to protect us—men and women—from using music as a manipulative tool.
Cf. Paul Westermeyer, "Church Music at the End of the Twentieth Century,"
Lutheran Quarterly VIII:2 (Summer 1994): 202–203.

others with pauses and interludes, you would think yourself listening to a concert of sirens rather than men, and wonder at the powers of the voices, which the nightingale or the mockingbird, or whatever is most tuneful among birds, could not equal. Such is the facility of running up and down the scale; so wonderful the shortening or multiplying of notes, the repetition of the phrases, or their emphatic utterance: the treble and shrill notes are so mingled with the tenor and bass, that the ears lost their power of judging.[13]

Aelred (1109–1166), a Cistercian abbot, described the same kinds of things John of Salisbury did, adding other offenses—sounds like the "whinnying of a horse" and "theatrical gestures." Then he said this:

In the meantime the people stand in fear and astonishment listening to the sound of the bellows, the crash of cymbals, and the tuning of flutes; but when they see the lascivious gesticulations of the singers, and hear the meretricious alternations and shakings of the voices, they cannot restrain their laughter, and you would think they had come not to prayer, but to a spectacle, not to an oratory, but to a theatre. There is no fear for that fearful Majesty in Whose presence they stand; no reverence for the mystic Crib at which they minister; where Christ is mystically wrapped in swaddling clothes; where heavens are opened; where angels are assisting; where earth and heaven are joined together, and men associated with blessed spirits.

Thus what the holy Fathers instituted, that the weak might be excited to piety, is made to serve unlawful pleasure; for sound is not to be preferred to sense, but combined with sense, so as to help to greater fervor.[14]

While John of Salisbury and Aelred had qualms about the Ars Antiqua and its inroads into worship, a few centuries later someone named Jacob of Liége, a contemporary of Philippe de Vitry, defended the Ars Antiqua and attacked the Ars Nova, suggesting that "even laymen were better pleased with the ancient notes and the ancient manner than with the new."[15] At about the same time (1324–1325), John XXII (1229–1334, pope from 1316) promulgated a papal bull, which expressed concerns about the Ars Nova's music in worship: violence done to the words; new musical techniques like hockets (musical hiccups in the thirteenth and fourteenth centuries); great

---

[13] Hayburn, *Papal Legislation on Sacred Music*, p. 18.

[14] Ibid., p. 19.

[15] Jacob of Liége, *Speculum musicae* in Strunk, *Source Readings*, p. 189. A lengthy section of *Speculum musicae* is given, pp. 180–190.

numbers of notes; intoxication of the ear without satisfying it; dramatic gestures without devotion; lack of what he regarded as appropriate to worship—modesty, gravity, calm, and peaceful character.[16]

Several things about these comments deserve notice. First, they indicate that the people did not stand around like lifeless mummies. They were the church who reacted and laughed at what seemed out of place. Some comments by Erik Routley serve to set these reactions in a broader context. For medieval people worship was "mixed up" with life in a way that our more "uniformly regular" Sunday observances are not, he said. Participation stretched across a year of "feasts and commemorations," presumed not only Sunday but a daily system around Sunday whether everyone always went every day or not, was "lit up" by "flashes of colour" at Mass and at irregular intervals of various feasts, and appealed to all the senses. If people did not sing at Mass, they saw the architecture, art, and pageantry, and smelled the incense in their cathedrals, then sang a carol on the way home. Whether all this made perfectly logical sense in a neat and rational package of "mind to mind" communication was not at issue as it may be for us, and participation was not reduced to the one single thing that many post-Reformation people reduce it to, namely, hymn singing.[17]

Second, medieval people were not always neglected or treated badly by their leaders. A concern for the people and their reactions was present. It is especially evident in Aelred's remarks.

Third, we in our period are primed to regard these sorts of comments as coming from fuddy-duddies who simply opposed change. Jacob of Liége may fit that description, but he was concerned mainly about music and not about worship. The other three can't be pigeonholed so easily and were concerned about worship. If we read far enough, the quotation from John of Salisbury continues with high praise for music and its relation to the rest of life.

> When this goes to excess it is more fitted to excite lust than devotion; but if it is kept within the limits of moderation, it drives away care from the soul and the solicitudes of life, confers joy and peace and exultation in God, and transports the soul to the society of angels. . . .

> See that what you sing with your mouth you believe with your heart, and that what you believe with your heart you obey in your works.[18]

---

[16] Hayburn, *Papal Legislation on Sacred Music*, pp. 20–22.

[17] Erik Routley, *The English Carol* (New York: Oxford University Press, 1959), pp. 113–116.

[18] Hayburn, *Papal Legislation on Sacred Music*, p. 18.

Similarly, Aelred cites Augustine and worries that the pleasure of—or astonishment at!—sound got in the way of meaning. John XXII was more legalistic in prohibiting what he regarded as musical excesses, but even he permitted "the occasional use"—principally on solemn feasts at Mass and at Divine Office—of Ars Nova techniques provided the chant melodies remained intact and the "harmonies are in the spirit and character of the melodies themselves."[19]

Fourth, with little modification of detail, these comments could sound like those in any period of the church's history from the early church to the present. That is because the church by its very nature is forever forced to ask how to enter and serve the marketplace without becoming the marketplace. Mixed in with this tension have come all sorts of internal churchly squabbles about music and other things, sometimes between clergy and musicians, but between clergy and clergy or musicians and musicians or faithful members of the church as well.

In the fourteenth century some of the players in this ongoing saga were "Golliards and wandering singers [who] sang in the market place and the church." They "gained a monopoly over new compositions . . . under the pretext of singing motets of better quality." With their polyphony came "a thousand declamations," both justified and unjustified as usual, against the "clergy, prelates, and papacy."[20] That specific episode has to be seen in the context of a long history where the golliard or jongleur was a successor to the Roman *mimus*. Both were regarded as actors and instrumentalists whose morals were open to serious question and who were denied the sacraments. By the sixteenth century, however, this "buffoon and semi-outlaw" had become "a more or less respectable lay professional."[21]

Fifth, the issues here involve not only the marketplace, but the nature of love. Now the close relatives of the jongleur, the troubadours and trouvères, come into view. If the jongleur was an itinerant musician, the troubadours and trouvères were well-educated twelfth- and thirteenth-century French poet-musicians often associated with courtly society. They constructed sophisticated pieces about the ideal of refined love, "a great imaginative and spiritual

[19] Ibid., p. 21.
[20] Ibid., pp. 21–22.
[21] McKinnon, "The Church Fathers," p. 268.

superstructure built on the foundation of sexual attraction."[22] One possible suggestion for the origin of their work is that it derives from liturgical and paraliturgical sources.[23] Music was integral to it and bears complex melodic and rhythmic relationships to chant.[24] Folquet de Marseille said, "A verse without music is a mill without water."[25] As to poetic content, the ideal of refined love may be connected to a Christian idea of love,[26] which immediately suggests the complex interplay between eros and agape described by Anders Nygren in his classic study.[27]

In the Midst of Earthly Life

Sixth, as has just been implied, none of the musical developments happened in a vacuum. Not only were people alive in the Middle Ages, but, as always, they lived in the midst of nature, seasons, systems, historical inertias, and high-level societal currents. A full-scale survey of these is well beyond the scope of this book, but let the following be suggestive and provide fodder for independent study projects.

- Toward the end of the ninth century or beginning of the tenth, when the people were being excluded from all liturgical singing at the Mass, medieval church dramas began[28] and served as substitutes for the loss.

- In the tenth century the sound of organum came within the frame of Romanesque architecture and its barrel vaults.

- Musicians, like everyone else, were not unrelated to ethical concerns. In 1028, Guido d'Arezzo demonstrated staff notation. Three years later he agitated against the simony of kings and said that lay investiture of bishops was heresy.

---

[22] John Stevens, Theodore Karp, "Troubadours, trouvères," NGDMM, 19, p. 190.

[23] See ibid., p. 190–191, for an overview of hypotheses and their authors.

[24] Ibid., pp. 197–206.

[25] Ibid., p. 196.

[26] Ibid., p. 191.

[27] Anders Nygren, trans., Philip S. Watson, *Agape and Eros* (London: S.P.C.K., 1953). I am indebted to Francis Williamson for reminding me to include this.

[28] See W. L. Smoldon, "Liturgical Drama," *Early Medieval Music up to 1300*, ed. Dom Anselm Hughes (London: Oxford University Press, 1961), pp. 174–219, and Giulio Cattin, trans., Steven Botterill, *Music of the Middle Ages I* (Cambridge University Press, 1984), pp. 120–127.

- The sound of the Ars Antiqua and what followed was set in the context of Gothic architecture with its upward reach and flying buttresses.
- Sailing all around the church at the end of the twelfth century were pungent satires on the corruption and avarice of the papacy.
- In 1209 Francis (1182–1226) founded the Franciscans, and in the summer of 1225—hot, ill, temporarily blind, surrounded by field mice in a hut—he wrote his Canticle of the Sun, sometimes translated "All Creatures of Our God and King."[29] Thomas Aquinas (1275–1274) did his massive theological synthesizing in the same century and also wrote some hymns— *Pange lingua* ("Of the Glorious Body Telling"),[30] *Adoro te devote* ("Thee We Adore").[31]
- The fourteenth century experienced the high art of the Ars Nova and the terror of the Great Plague (the "Black Death"). From 1347 until 1350 one quarter of Europe's population died.
- The fourteenth century was also treated to the "Babylonian Captivity" of the popes at Avignon. John XXII was one of the Avignon popes. The influence of his papal bull was probably limited by his place of residence.[32]
- During the lifetimes of Dufay, Ockeghem, and Josquin, Constantinople fell (1453) and Luther was born (1483).

Monasticism

Cluny and Cîteaux

When one leaps from the first several centuries of the church directly to the Reformation, monasticism is likely to be viewed as a monolithic blur of the "dark" ages in which all monks thought and did the same things behind closed doors. Monks did not all do the same things. Their differences have not been unlike the church's more public disagreements, and they too help us understand the nature of the church's worship and music. The perspectives of the monks at Cluny and Cîteaux in some ways prefigure the Reformation.

---

[29] LBW, #527.
[30] LBW, #120.
[31] LBW, #199.
[32] See Hayburn, *Papal Legislation on Sacred Music*, p. 22.

In 910 William III, Duke of Aquitane called the "Pious," founded a Benedictine monastery at Cluny. The first abbots, especially Abbot Odo (927–942),[33] set in motion a liturgical practice that became well-known. Cluny sought a strict Benedictine observance and a cultivation of the spiritual life. It meant lavish and lengthy liturgical celebrations[34] of the Divine Office and the Mass, in three splendid churches with elaborate processions.[35] The visual was important.

A little more than a century and a half after Cluny's founding, a group of hermits followed Robert and settled at Molesme in 1075. New recruits came easily, but in 1098 the more rigorous monks set out for a remote spot in Cîteaux just south of Dijon. These Cistercians, or White Monks (because of their white habit),[36] "chose a life of silence and seclusion in exact observance of the Rule of St. Benedict."[37] In 1112 Bernard joined them with "30 young friends and relatives,"[38] and two years later his abbot asked him to establish another monastery. Bernard chose Clairvaux where he became abbot in 1118.

Bernard of Clairvaux (1090–1153) is best-known among us for "O Sacred Head, Now Wounded"[39] and *Jesu dulcis memoria* from which several hymns such as "Jesus, the Very Thought of You"[40] are derived. In his time, however, he was regarded as an honest but austere monk whom we today would probably call an influential power broker. Among other things, he had a hand in papal elections, preached the ill-fated Second Crusade, and disagreed with Cluny.[41]

---

[33] Odo of Cluny may have been the writer of a piece on the theory of music, called *Enchiridion musices* or *Dialogus de musica*, which can be found in Strunk, *Source Readings*, pp. 103–116, though his authorship is in doubt. See Michael Huglo, "Odo," NGDMM 13, p. 503.

[34] I have read somewhere and know not where, that Cluny may be the first instance of all group, not solo and group, recitation of verses.

[35] See Michael Huglo, "Cluniac monks," NGDMM 4, pp. 502–503.

[36] Modern-day Trappist monks such as Thomas Merton are Cistercians.

[37] Mary Berry, "Cistercian monks," NGDMM 4, pp. 411–412.

[38] Ibid., p. 412.

[39] LBW, #s 116, 117.

[40] LBW, #316.

[41] He also warred against Abelard (1079–1142), though, from our perspective, Abelard's hymn, "Oh, What Their Joy" (LBW, #337) may feel much the same as a hymn of Bernard—which should put our disputes in perspective and teach us humility.

Bernard and the Cistercians had a different spiritual vision from Cluny. They wanted to suppress the visual for the sake of the acoustic. Worship therefore was shorter and less elaborate. Though they apparently even avoided rhymed hymns as too lavish, they nonetheless anticipated some Reformation themes by valuing sound over sight and the word over ceremonial. Walls were whitewashed; ". . . painting, sculpture and furnishing—and even the image of the crucifix—were forbidden."[42] However, as Robert Lawlor reports, in the twelfth-century Cistercian Abbey near Le Thoronet,[43] "even a pin dropped at the end of the nave some 40 meters away, generates a full range of harmonic overtones."[44] The simple stone vault is "the perfect acoustical volume to enhance the human voice."[45] For Bernard the building of churches was "geometry in the service of prayer," so that there was "no decoration; only proportion"[46]— which meant that the geometric proportions of the building were the same proportions as the ratios of the first notes in the harmonic series.[47] ". . . [H]earing is superior to vision," said Bernard, and "will restore vision to us."[48]

A disciplined common life of silence heightened the sound of worship even more. Cistercian monks drained swamps, cleared forests, terraced hillsides.[49] At Le Thoronet they grew wheat and olives, ate one meatless meal each day, worked for five hours, studied for four, slept from 7 P.M. until 11 P.M. when they arose for worship, then slept again until 3 A.M. when their day began anew. They lived in silence except at four-hour intervals when they assembled in the abbey to sing at worship.[50]

[42] Robert Lawlor, "Geometry at the Service of Prayer: Reflections on Cistercian Mystic Architecture," *Parabola* 3:1 (1978): 16.

[43] ". . . five hundred small, mystical communities were established [at Bernard's direction and example], with abbey churches all following a nearly identical plan and uniform technique of execution." Ibid., p. 15.

[44] Ibid., p. 12.

[45] Ibid., p. 13. The space also is friendly to small solo instruments such as the flute, but not so amenable to large instruments such as pianos or organs. See pp. 12–13.

[46] Ibid., p. 17.

[47] Ibid., p. 13.

[48] Ibid., p. 16.

[49] Ibid.

[50] Ibid., p. 17. For much of this material on the Cistercians I am indebted to a lecture of Nathan Mitchell at Valparaiso University, Valparaiso, Indiana, February 2, 1982. In more recent correspondence with Mitchell, he pointed me to the article by Robert Lawlor, which I have been citing.

One does not have to agree with Bernard and the Cistercians in all particulars nor be a monk to notice that architecture is related not only to sacred visual space, but to sacred aural space as well—for monastic chapels, large cathedrals, or small churches.[51]

Hildegard of Bingen

The Cluniac and Cistercian disagreements should not lead to the conclusion that monasteries were simply places for disputes. Disagreements were part of life, as always, but monastic life included immense learning and creativity as well. The liturgical books with illuminated manuscripts we marvel at today were part of this life, as were the works of poets and musicians. Let Hildegard of Bingen (1098–1179) represent them here.

In the middle of the twelfth century, between 1147 and 1150, Hildegard founded a monastery at Rupertsberg near Bingen, and fifteen years later founded a sister house on the other side of the Rhine near Rüdesheim. Well-known for her visions, like Bernard she too was deeply involved in the worldly decisions of popes, bishops, clergy, kings, and monks. In addition to her biographical, historical, and medical works, she wrote poetry and music, which has of late enjoyed a notable revival. Her hymns, sequences, and antiphons were obviously related to the liturgical practice of the times, but as a whole her work is idiosyncratic, complex, and not based on chant.[52] Hildegard is another indication that the period prior to the Renaissance was not just an easily understood monolith.

Outside and Around Worship

Early in this century, when Béla Bartók (1881–1945), Hungary's greatest composer, began making trips to collect, record, and ana-

---

[51] There are implications here about the possibilities technology has given us for the amplification of sound. Amplification is important in all sorts of ways for our music in and out of the church, but it cannot be assumed to "fix" everything. A worshiping congregation that gathers for word, sacrament, and prayer is essentially an acoustical phenomenon, which is why some church musicians who love and use musical amplification in much of their work do not employ it to lead congregational song. It is also why a bad acoustical space cannot be repaired with amplification, at least not for the congregation's singing.

[52] For a brief overview with examples and a bibliography, see Ian D. Bent, "Hildegard of Bingen," NGDMM 8, pp. 553–556.

lyze Hungarian folksong, he discovered a medieval culture. Here's how A. L. Lloyd described the experience.

> Bartók felt himself back in the Middle Ages . . . no railways, often no roads, pack-horses everywhere, settlements occupied entirely by illiterates, men who have never moved out of their birthplace except perhaps for a military service or appearance at a court of law, a world where every object of daily use was made in the home, and people lived on what they themselves grew, made their clothes and blankets from wool they had shorn, spun and woven, carved their own chairs and beds, hardly used money at all, and had only the frailest contact with the commerce and arts of the towns. He discovered there a submerged world of vigorous music essentially different in many respects from music of learned origin [which he designated] folk music.[53]

If you piece that description together with the one Routley provided earlier about worship in all its color being mixed in with life in the Middle Ages, then add to it another of Routley's observations, that along with the terrors and famines and tortures of medieval life there was an incongruous "world-affirming" spirit,[54] you get something of our context here.

People's "folk song" was part of the context. As Faulkner says, we know next to nothing about it.[55] Possible insights into it have been suggested by A. L. Lloyd. He posited a change in folk song from "collective clan culture" toward feudalism, presumably beginning with the breakup of the Carolingian empire in the ninth century or at different times in different places before or after that.[56] He posited another change when "absolute feudalism began to crack" until "by the end of the fourteenth century, serfdom had practically disappeared" and "the majority of commoners were free peasant small-holders."[57] Then, he said, when John Nameless rose up in peasant insurrections, "the free rambling tunes took on clearer, more formal shape; the bare wintry themes of the Dark Ages began to blossom; though under the blossom the boughs remained the same."[58] What are the boughs and blossoms? Lloyd suggested that

[53] Lloyd, *Folk Song in England*, p. 13. For some of Bartók's thoughts, see Béla Bartók, "The Influence of Peasant Music on Modern Music," trans. Eva Hajnal-Konyi, *Contemporary Composers on Contemporary Music*, ed. Elliot Schwartz and Barney Childs (New York: Holt, Rinehart and Winston, 1967), pp. 73–79.

[54] Routley, *The English Carol*, p. 79.

[55] Faulkner, *Wiser Than Despair*, p. 71.

[56] Lloyd, *Folk Song in England*, p. 55.

[57] Ibid., p. 92.

[58] Ibid.

"the most ancient repertory consisted in the main of a few melody formulas endlessly varied, sung collectively, often in shanty-style with choral refrains . . . constructed on a descending slope."[59] This core developed slowly and laboriously to "solo song, strophic, arch-shaped, regular in rhythm . . . the kind of folk song we are most familiar with now."[60]

Lloyd's sketch is as plausible as any. Let us append comments about two specific forms, adding them to the Ruf and Leisen already mentioned.

Cantios

In the fourteenth, fifteenth, and sixteenth centuries Latin devotional songs called cantios were popular. They may have developed from liturgical roots in the twelfth century and may have been sung at vespers or in processions or for private devotions. They would seem to have been related to monastic life, but they were also picked up by the followers of the early reformer named John Hus (1369–1415).[61]

Carols

Carols seem closer to the folk. They have sometimes been viewed as an invention of the fifteenth century, symbolizing a break through the oppressive puritanism of the medieval period or even earlier. This view would say that finally the people threw off their shackles and sang.[62] Shutting the people out of their song at worship and unfortunate puritanical constraints—along with quite legitimate ethical concerns for life's wholeness and shalom—are part of the church's history, so one can make a case for such an interpretation. R. L. Greene, in his classic study on carols, for example, has highlighted the church's sometimes pointed duel against carols and carol singing from the eighth through the sixteenth centuries.[63] Carol

---

[59] Ibid., p. 56.

[60] Ibid.

[61] John A. Emerson, "Plainchant," NGDMM 14, pp. 817–818.

[62] See Percy Dearmer, "Preface," *The Oxford Book of Carols* (London: Oxford University Press, 1964, first published 1928), p. vi.

[63] Richard Leighton Greene, *The Early English Carols* (Oxford: Clarendon Press, 1977, 2d ed., revised and enlarged), pp. xxiv, lxxiii–lxxiv, cxl. This included clergy troubled by outbreaks of popular rejoicing at Christmas, p. clvii.

singing in churches is recent. Its "present vogue . . . goes back no further" than the 1870s.[64] But the implicit suggestion that the good
news of the New Testament was subverted and repressed for centuries in such a way that puritanical oppression itself became the
engine of the gospel's attraction defies comprehension. The reality
is considerably more complex.[65]

Even careful study has not isolated precisely when and how carols developed or how they were used, however. They were the popular musical form of the fifteenth century in England,[66] but sources
in the preceding centuries are sparse and origins "not fully
known."[67] Carols also make neat lines of demarcation between folk,
popular, and art music a scholarly abstraction or the occasion for
grinding axes by those who eschew scholarship. A. L. Lloyd's comment that both folk music and art music are related to life as "varied
blossoms from the same stock"[68] and that "the traffic between the
arts of different social classes proceeds in both directions"[69] are
helpful reminders in the study of all music, but perhaps especially
of carols.

Like hymns, the definition of carols is broad, especially since
1550. Two characteristics are worthy of note, however, and were
abundantly clear before 1550.[70] One is that they tend to be strophic
with refrains called "burdens" between the stanzas.[71] Greene's definition of a carol is "a song on any subject, composed of uniform
stanzas and provided with a burden."[72] Carols are fundamentally a
participatory responsorial or call-and-response form, a form that
gives the people refrains they can easily learn without the need for
printed materials. The people sing the refrain in answer to lengthier

[64] Richard R. Terry, ed., *A Medieval Carol Book* (London: Burns Oates & Washbourne Ltd., 1931), p. ii.

[65] As is suggested by Hugh Keyte and Andrew Parrott, "Introduction," *The New
Oxford Book of Carols* (Oxford: Oxford University Press, 1992), pp. xiv–xvii, and
John Stevens, "Carol," NGDMM 3, pp. 802–811.

[66] Manfred F. Bukofzer, "Popular and Secular Music in England (to c. 1470),"
*The New Oxford History of Music, Volume III, The Ars Nova and the Renaissance,
1300–1540*, ed. Anselm Hughes and Gerald Abraham (Oxford: Oxford University
Press, 1986, first published 1960), p. 121.

[67] Ibid., p. 119.

[68] Lloyd, *Folk Song in England*, p. 17.

[69] Ibid., p. 54.

[70] Greene, *The Early English Carols*, pp. xi–xxxviii.

[71] Stevens, "Carol," NGDMM 3, p. 802.

[72] Greene, *The Early English Carols*, p. xxxiif.

and more complex stanzas a soloist or solo group can sing. After enough hearing, of course, the people can join in on the stanzas as well so that the call-and-response pattern gets blurred, but the form itself suggests the more primal performance practice.

Second, carols grow out of movement, dance. "They are in direct descent from the vocally accompanied dance, the carole."[73] Dance and movement suggest processions. It is no surprise that John Stevens, in his classic collection of medieval carols, describes carols as "processional music . . . written as 'popular litanies' for use in ecclesiastical processions, but any procession, civic or courtly, provided a suitable setting."[74] Erik Routley implies the same thing.[75] Greene, however, whom both Stevens and Routley cite with deep respect and appreciation, says not only that caroling in its origins was associated with the reverse of sanctity,[76] but asserts categorically that carols were not used in processions.[77]

Whether carols were used in processions or not, the broader scope of their associations with worship needs to be noted. In spite of their less than sanctified bawdy and even pagan origins, carols were gradually associated with Christianity until five out of every seven of them treated Christian subjects.[78] This change happened not only naturally, but partially because "sacred" carols were consciously written to displace the "secular" ones.[79] Furthermore, they may have been used at the conclusion of the office during the Christmas season "where 'Benedicamus Domino—Deo gratias' is usually sung."[80] Negatively, they sometimes gravitated to churchyards at the time of Mass, so as to disturb it.[81] Principally they were used at feasts and banquets, sometimes after Mass in the dining hall[82]— which explains why there are so many Christmas carols: they

---

[73] Ibid., p. xxxiii.

[74] John Stevens (ed.), "Medieval Carols," *Musica Britannica: A National Collection of Music, IV* (London: Stainer and Bell Ltd, 1970, 2 ed., rev.), p. xiv.

[75] Routley, *The English Carol*, pp. 107–109.

[76] Greene, *The Early English Carols*, p. xlviii.

[77] Ibid., pp. xxiv, xxvi, cvi. Greene, p. cvi, FN2, mentions Stevens and his absence of evidence. (At another point Greene mentions Routley, p. lxv, FN 4, as dimming rather than illuminating the distinction between the carol and the ballad, "though the whole book has much in it that is lively and stimulating.")

[78] Greene, *The Early English Carols*, p. cxxxix.

[79] Ibid., p. cxlviii.

[80] Ibid., p. cix. ("Let us bless the Lord—Thanks be to God.")

[81] Greene, *The Early English Carols*, p. xxiv.

[82] Ibid., p. lxi.

accompanied the twelve days of Christmas when there were more provisions for feasting than there were at Easter after winter.[83]

In Italy dance and popular song were associated with the *lauda spirituali* of the Franciscans in community activities that included the clergy.[84] These activities happened outside the liturgy, though possibly in cathedrals. Carols may also have been sung at church doors before or after the liturgy. Some have suggested they may not only have been used as processional hymns, but could have been employed as vernacular substitutes for parts of the liturgy itself.[85]

Details are not clear. The scholars disagree. Two things are clear, however. 1) People were denied their voice in worship, though some of their singing may have seeped into it anyway. 2) People sang around worship, about the themes of Christian worship, and in their daily lives. Carols were some of the things they sang, often in a paraliturgical way. The sixteenth-century Reformation, to which we now turn, was a strong impetus in recovering the people's singing, but it was not the first time that Christians sang.

[83] Ibid., p. xxxviii.

[84] John Stevens, "Carol," NGDMM 3, p. 804. See also Greene, *The Early English Carols*, pp. cl–clvii. For *lauda spirituali* see John Stevens and William F. Prizer, "Lauda spirtuale," NGDMM, 10, pp. 538–543.

[85] Ibid., p. 805.

REFORMATION CURRENTS

10

Sound, Silence, and Strictures

At the center of the turbulent sixteenth-century event we call the Reformation stood the question of how humanity is set right with God, or justified before God. Over against the notion that one could gain God's favor by doing something, all the Reformers set their understanding of the biblical message: humanity is justified by grace through faith. That is, human beings can't get right with God by anything they do, by any human merit or meritorious acts at all; God justifies us by grace alone through faith.[1]

On this central matter of justification the Reformers were agreed. But beyond that they disagreed at a number of points, music among them. Those who were forced out or who broke off from the Roman Catholic Church themselves split into an ever-increasing number of divisions. Two major ones were Lutheran and Reformed. These bodies were in large measure controlled by three Reformers, Martin Luther (1483–1546), Ulrich Zwingli (1484–1531), and John Calvin (1509–1564).[2] Luther recovered the congregation's singing, Zwingli denied it, and Calvin restricted it, in ways that are in some sense parallel to Ambrose, Pambo, and Augustine.[3]

---

[1] Bard Thompson's explanation is succinct. The grace of God is a gift shown supremely in the cross of Christ, so irrational that it can only be appropriated by faith. Faith is not belief in certain propositions, but trust in the mercies of God made known in Christ.

[2] For an overview of the positions of these three and Menno Simons of the Radical Reformation, see Timothy George, *Theology of the Reformers* (Nashville: Broadman Press, 1988). For these same four plus several others, see B. A. Gerrish, ed., *Reformers in Profile: Advocates of Reform, 1300–1600* (Philadelphia: Fortress Press, 1967).

[3] These three motifs are not the same as the three Nicholas Temperley calls "three distinct attitudes to the place of music in worship, which can be traced

Luther and Sound

It is relatively easy to demonstrate that Luther had a deep concern for music.

1. He sought advice from and surrounded himself with able musicians. Johann Walter reported that when Luther prepared his *Deutsche Messe* he wanted Conrad Rupff and Walter himself to come to Wittenberg to discuss the nature of the eight Gregorian psalm tones with him. Wanting to make sure the musical setting of the German was right and refusing to hurry the process with mistakes, he prepared the music for the epistles, gospels, and words of institution, asked Walter about his work, and kept Walter in Wittenberg for three weeks discussing how the epistles and gospels might be set in German.[4] The first "hymnal" prepared under Luther's guidance[5] was edited by Walter; and Georg Rhau, the

---

throughout the history of Christianity, and which vary with the theological principles held by different sects and parties." Pambo and Zwingli fit Temperley's first category of those who exclude music; Ambrose, Augustine, Luther, and Calvin all fit his second category of those who harness music for the congregation; the third group denies the "role of music as an actual vehicle of religious expression," but values it "as an ornament of offering to God, as a part of the 'beauty of holiness.'" See Nicholas Temperley, *The Music of the English Parish Church* (Cambridge: Cambridge University Press, 1979), I, p. 4.

David P. McKay and Richard Crawford, *William Billings of Boston: Eighteenth-Century Composer* (Princeton: Princeton University Press, 1975), pp. 3–9, have a different view. They picture an "uneasy truce" between the church and music and define it as a "classic dichotomy between musician and theologian," seen largely in Augustinian-Calvinist terms. Roman Catholic and Lutheran pietist concerns are folded in, but Ambrose and Luther are not included.

[4] Michael Praetorius, *Syntagma Musicum* (Wittebergae, 1615), I, p. 451 f. in Wilibard Gurlitt, ed., *Documenta Musicologica* (Basel: Baerenreiter Kassel, 1959) XXI. For a translation, see Walter E. Buszin, *Luther on Music* (St. Paul: North Central Publishing Company, 1958), p. 17, reprinted from the *Musical Quarterly*, XXXII (January 1964): 80–97, or Carl Schalk, *Luther on Music, Paradigms of Praise* (St. Louis: Concordia Publishing House, 1988), p. 27.

[5] This book, the *Geistliche Gesangbüchlein*, published in 1524, was "a collection of polyphonic motets based on Lutheran chorales." It was intended for the choir, to teach the young something of value (Luther made it clear he was in favor of using the arts in the service of God "who gave and made them") and through the choir's singing to teach the congregation the chorales. See "Liturgy and Hymns" *Luther's Works* (Philadelphia: Fortress Press, 1965) 53, pp. 193 and 315 (hereafter LW). Also in 1524 a hymnal in the stricter sense of the word was published with the title *Etlich Christliche Lyeder Lobgesang und Psalm*. Because it contained eight hymns (four by Luther, three by Paul Speratus, and one by an anonymous writer), it is known as the *Achtliederbuch*. It was republished in Canada in 1984 in a facsimile reprint for

cantor from Leipzig, came to work with Luther at Wittenberg as a music publisher.[6]

2. Luther attempted to enlist the support of the civil authorities on behalf of music and musicians. When John the Steadfast dismantled the *Kantorei* of the Castle Church in Wittenberg, Luther objected and argued that music was more worthy of support than many other endeavors.[7]

3. Luther was a discriminating judge of music who understood polyphony, was delighted with it,[8] and, as indicated earlier, had a high regard for Josquin who was the finest composer of his day.[9]

4. Luther was an able amateur musician. As a boy he was a *Kurrende* singer,[10] loved to sing,[11] and played the lute.[12] He also had ability as a composer. It is probably too much to claim with Paul Nettl that had he not been a reformer Luther would have been a great composer,[13] but the hymn tunes he wrote have proven to be of exceptional quality.

5. Luther regarded music as integral to a child's education[14] and to the education of teachers and ministers.[15] "A schoolmaster," said Luther, "must be able to sing; otherwise I do not look at him."[16]

6. Music often invigorated Luther. The music teacher Lucas Edenberger and some companions once found Luther had fainted in

the Amish Historical Library, Aylmer, Ontario, from the original in the Germanisches National Museum, Nürnberg, with permission.

[6] See Paul Nettl, *Luther and Music*, trans. Frida Best and Ralph Wood (New York: Russell & Russell, 1967), p. 100f., and Schalk, *Luther on Music, Paradigms of Praise*, p. 23.

[7] Martin Luther, Letter to John the Steadfast (1526), *Dr. Martin Luthers Werke, Breifwechsel* (Weimar: Herman Boehlaus Nachfolger, 1933), hereafter WA (Weimar Ausgabe), IV, p. 90, no. 1020. See also Buszin, *Luther on Music*, pp. 8–9.

[8] See, for example, Martin Luther, "Preface to Georg Rhau's Symphoniae iucundae" (1538), LW 53, p. 324.

[9] See, for example, Mathesius, *Dr. Martin Luthers Leben*, p. 227f.

[10] See Nettl, *Luther and Music*, p. 8f.

[11] Praetorius, *Syntagma*, p. 451.

[12] Nettl, *Luther and Music*, p. 12f.

[13] Ibid., p. 62.

[14] Luther, "To the Councilmen" (1524), LW 45, p. 369, and Luther, Letter to Marcus Crodel (1542), WA, *Briefwechsel*, X, p. 134, no. 3783 or LW 50, p. 231. See Schalk, *Luther on Music, Paradigms of Praise*, pp. 28–29.

[15] Martin Luther, "Table Talk," *Dr. Martin Luthers Sämmtliche Werke*, ed. Johann Konrad Irmischer (Erlangen: Verlag von Hender & Zimmer, 1854), LXII, p. 308ff., no. 2848. See Schalk, *Luther on Music, Paradigms of Praise*, pp. 29–30.

[16] Ewald M. Plass, *What Luther Says* (St. Louis: Concordia Publishing House, 1959), p. 980.

his study. They awakened him with their music, and he joined in the singing.[17] In a letter to the musician Ludwig Senfl, Luther remarked how music had often refreshed him.[18]

Luther clearly loved and supported music. Why? Did he simply impart a whim to the church that, against his wishes, bears his name, or is there something more substantive in his position? What was Luther's theology of music?

Luther was not a systematician. He did not write something like John Calvin's *Institutes of the Christian Religion* or Karl Barth's *Church Dogmatics*. He operated out of the moment, with chunks of thought left to hang or fly freely on their way. To ask about Luther's theology of anything requires sorting out the chunks or grabbing them as they go by. Some care has to be exercised lest you make Luther say anything you want him to. Any attempt at systematically summarizing him restricts his brash fullness and freshness; but the task is worth the effort.

Luther said that music is next to theology.[19] We can take that at its face value to mean that music as a discipline of study is next in importance to theology as a discipline of study. Luther also said, however, that "next to the Word of God, music deserves the highest praise."[20] Music is not only next to theology, then; it is next to the word of God. Here we get a more profound and theological sense of what Luther has in mind. Oskar Soehngen expressed it this way.

> That music comes from the *auricularia*, i.e., from the sphere of the miraculous audible things—like the Gospel, that it is a unique gift of God's creation which comes to us in the same way the Word of God does, namely, mediated by the voice, that is a point at which Luther is lost in wonder again and again.[21]

Luther was not simply fond of music. Luther thought music has a theological reason for being: it is a gift of God, which comes from the "sphere of miraculous audible things," just like the word of

---

[17] See Ulrich S. Leupold, "Luther's Musical Education and Activities," *Lutheran Church Quarterly*, XII (1939): 426.

[18] Martin Luther, Letter to Ludwig Senfl (1530), WA, *Briefwechsel*, V, p. 639, no. 1727.

[19] Ibid.

[20] Luther, "Preface to Georg Rhau's Symphoniae iucundae," LW 53, p. 323.

[21] Oskar Soehngen, "Fundamental Considerations for a Theology of Music," *The Musical Heritage of the Church*, ed. Theodore Hoelty-Nickel (St. Louis: Concordia Publishing House, 1963) VI, p. 15–16.

God. Music is unique in that it can carry words. Since words carry
the word of God, music and the word of God are closely related.

As Soehngen pointed out, Luther put the coordination of music
and theology on a new footing. The musica speculativa of the
Pythagorean school was replaced by the "elemental experience of
music as a sounding form."[22] Luther did not approach music first
as a reflection of the numerical laws of the universe; nor did he view
sound ordered in time as first of all a faint resemblance of math or
universal relationships—though those things may also have been
true for him. Rather, he approached music as sound itself, sound
that was regarded as important and indeed critical in its own right.

With that perspective, one can isolate certain elements in Luther's
thought by referring largely to his "Preface to Georg Rhau's Symphoniae iucundae," one of his most complete and "systematic"
statements about music.

First, music is a gift of God's good creation.[23] There are two parts
here. Music is an incredible gift about which Luther was over-
whelmed; he could not find words to describe it. And it is a creation
of God, not of humanity.[24] That distinction does not mean humanity should leave it in its "natural" state. On the contrary,

> when [musical] learning is added to this and artistic music which cor-
> rects, develops, and refines the natural music, then at last it is possible
> to taste with wonder (yet not to comprehend) God's absolute and per-
> fect wisdom in his wondrous work of music.[25]

This gift "of nature and of art" can be "prostituted" by "perverted
minds . . . with their erotic rantings"[26] so that one has to shun those
who do the perverting, but the weight falls on the gift and its goodness.

---

[22] Ibid., p. 9.

[23] See Luther, "Preface to Georg Rhau's Symphoniae iucundae," LW 53, pp. 321
and 324.

[24] See Schalk, *Luther on Music, Paradigms of Praise*, p. 34. In the translation
Buszin, *Luther on Music*, p. 6, gives of this passage one who does not appreciate
music hardly deserves to be called human. Buszin translates, "A person who gives
this some thought and yet does not regard it [music] as a marvelous creation of God,
must be a clodhopper indeed and does not deserve to be called a human being; he
should be permitted to hear nothing but the braying of asses and the grunting of
hogs." The German version (the text is also in Latin) reads as follows. "Wer aber
dazu kein luft noch liebe hat und durch solch lieblich Wunderwerck nicht bewegt
wird, das mus warlich ein grosser Klotz sein, der nicht werd ist, das er solche
liebliche Musica, sondern das wuesste, wilde Eselgeschren des Chorals, oder der
Hunde oder Sewe Gesang und Musica hoere." WA 50, p. 373.

[25] Luther, "Preface to Georg Rhau's Symphoniae iucundae," LW 53, p.324.

[26] Ibid.

Second, music bears the word. "God," says Luther, has the "Gospel preached through the medium of music."[27] This statement has a rich and varied meaning. It almost seems as if Luther sees music in its own right as a parallel to preaching: it is the instrument for the proper work of the Holy Spirit through whom the inclination to virtue was instilled in the prophets,[28] and it casts out Satan. But the weight falls on its association with the word and words that carry the word:

> . . . the fathers and prophets wanted nothing else to be associated with the Word of God as music. Therefore we have so many hymns and Psalms where message and music join to move the listener's soul. . . ."[29]

Or again, "Music and notes . . . do help gain a better understanding of the text."[30] This marriage of message and music is true in the compositions by skillful composers like Josquin,[31] and also when the people participate earnestly in the singing.[32]

Third, Luther joined praise to proclamation. "The gift of language combined with the gift of song," he said, was given to human beings to let us know that we "should praise God with both word and music, namely, by proclaiming the [word of God] through music."[33] To praise is to proclaim, and to proclaim is to praise. They both take sounding form. There is a circle of musical doing here where exegesis and proclamation run into each other on a circuit of sound.

Fourth, a closely related point is sufficiently different to be separated out. The following quotation isolates it.

---

[27] Martin Luther, "Table Talk," *Dr. Martin Luthers Sämmtliche Schriften*, ed. Johann Georg Walch (St. Louis: Concordia Publishing House, 1880ff.), hereafter SL (Saint Louis edition), XXII, 427f., No. 38, and LW, 54, p. 129.

[28] Luther, "Preface to Georg Rhau's Symphoniae iucundae," LW 53, p. 323.

[29] Ibid.

[30] Luther, "Auslegung der letzen Worte Davids, 2 Sam. 23:1–2, SL, III, 1888 (LW 15, pp. 273–274), as translated by Buszin, *Luther on Music*, p. 14.

[31] Luther, "Table Talk," LW, 54, pp. 129–130. Joyce Irwin, *Neither Voice nor Heart Alone: German Lutheran Theology of Music in the Age of the Baroque* (New York: Peter Lang, 1993), p. 147, takes another view of this passage. She thinks Luther is not referring to music's ability to communicate a text here, but is making music analogous to the gospel in opposition to the law. She may well be right, or Luther may have had both ideas going as background for his comment. Either one points to music in relation to preaching—as natural analogue or parallel to preaching, or as exegetical means to break open a text.

[32] Luther, "Auslegung der letzen Worte Davids," SL, III, 1888 (LW 15, p. 274).

[33] Luther, "Preface to Georg Rhau's Symphoniae iucundae," LW 53, p. 323.

For God has cheered our hearts and minds through his dear Son, whom he gave for us to redeem us from sin, death, and the devil. He who believes this earnestly cannot be quiet about it. But he must gladly and willingly sing. . . . [34]

Here is the Christus Victor motif.[35] In Christ God has won the victory. Those who know it are compelled to sing. That is, music is an important way the Christian community celebrates the victory Christ has won. The celebration is especially obvious in the hymns Luther wrote, like the first stanza of *Nun freut euch*, the first two stanzas of *Christ lag*, and the first two stanzas of *Ein feste Burg*.[36] Bold, vigorous rejoicing tells the story of God's victory and our deliverance. The battle is won in Christ, and we sing with jubilation. The tunes Luther wrote, like EIN FESTE BURG, themselves give sounding form to this explosion into song. As Eva Grew said,

Not one of Luther's tunes is sweet, soft, clinging, sentimental . . . nor touched even by the subjective qualities of reflection.[37]

On the contrary, they are bold, confident, joyful. This joyful confidence does not stop prayer or the cry of deep despair, as in Luther's setting of Psalm 130,[38] but it does mean that even such a cry is bold and happens within the context of a community that knows a gracious God who has won the battle on their behalf.

When Carl Schalk sought to sort out Luther's thought about music, he included "Music as Liturgical Song," "Music as the Song of Royal Priests," and "Music as a Sign of Continuity with the Whole Church."[39] This cluster might be subsumed here under a fifth category labeled Luther's ecclesiology of music.

Luther was a conservative reformer. Except for the canon of the Mass, he kept the whole communion liturgy with its chant in Latin and with metrical forms in German. Both the Latin *Formula Missae* of 1523 and the German *Deutsche Messe* of 1526 were sung services; lessons, prayers, the ordinary and the propers of the Mass in their Gregorian and German hymnic versions plus new hymns all

[34] Luther, "Preface to the Babst Hymnal," LW 53, p. 333.

[35] See Gustaf Aulen, *Christus Victor*, trans. A. G. Hebert (New York: The MacMillan Company, 1961).

[36] LBW, #s 299, 134, 228. For all of Luther's texts and tunes, see LW 53.

[37] Eva Mary Grew, "Martin Luther and Music," *Music and Letters*, XIX (1938): 76.

[38] LBW, #295.

[39] Schalk, *Luther on Music, Paradigms of Praise*, pp. 39–49.

were sung by the people and the choir. The offices were also sung. As Schalk points out, this was "the song of the royal priesthood confessing and proclaiming to the world the Good News of God in Christ."[40] And it meant "no parochial exclusiveness, nor provincial self-sufficiency, but a stand in solidarity and continuity with the church catholic."[41] To miss Luther's catholic ecclesiology of music is to misunderstand Luther. He was evangelical, to be sure, but he was also catholic. And sound was central to both positions.

What was the musical result of all this? Luther and the tradition he spawned used Gregorian chant; sacred folk songs; contrafacta, that is, pieces in which a new sacred text replaced an old secular one, keeping the same melody, as in *Vom Himmel hoch*; newly composed pieces such as hymns and motets; instruments along with or in alternation with voices; polyphony for trained groups; and the simpler unison line in its rhythmic form (the isorhythmic form, with a series of essentially equal notes, came later) for the congregation.[42]

In his hymn tune writing Luther followed the Minnesingers and Meistersingers and used *Barform*, a German word that means a poem with more than one stanza, each stanza in the form AAB. It has nothing to do with bars in the sense of pubs. Luther's sources were Gregorian chant, medieval vernacular hymns, and two secular folk melodies that didn't have staying power and themselves were abandoned for new tunes. Luther did not use "popular music."[43] The distinction between sacred and secular was not nearly so strong for him as for us, but he did distinguish what was appropriate to worship.[44] The tune Luther wrote for his metrical version of the Sanctus, for example, is adapted from Gregorian chant and is neither easy nor "popular," though I have heard some Lutheran congregations sing it with love and incredible force.[45] "The very last thing Luther was," says Erik Routley,

> or could have been, was what we now call an adapter of popular styles. He had no use for the 'popular' in the sense of the careless, or the standards of ignorance. His melodies are the kind of melody which would

[40] Ibid., p.44.

[41] Ibid., p. 49.

[42] For detail see Friedrich Blume, rev. Ludwig Finscher, trans. F. Ellsworth Peterson, "The Period of the Reformation," Friedrich Blume et al., *Protestant Church Music* (New York: W. W. Norton & Company, 1974), pp. 3–123.

[43] See Paul Westermeyer, *The Church Musician*, rev. ed., p. 132.

[44] See *Luther's Works, Volume 53: Liturgy and Hymns*, p. 306.

[45] LBW, #528.

appear in a pre-Reformation polyphonic motet, their mixture of basic measure with syncopation being what that style generated. The Minnesinger songs were of the same kind; and it is far removed from the popular music, the carol music.[46]

Luther united old and new, high art and folk art, rural and urban by the chorale itself, which appealed across these lines, and by the ancient principle of alternation. One stanza of a hymn would be sung by the congregation in its simple unaccompanied unison, the next one by a choir or instruments in a more complex polyphonic setting. It is no accident that the Lutheran tradition has stimulated a whole string of hymnwriters, tune writers, and editors who created congregational materials, such as Laurentius Petri (1499–1573), Philipp Nicolai (1556–1608), Johann Crüger (1598–1662), Paul Gerhardt (1607–1676), Nikolai F. S. Gruntvig (1783–1872), Magnus Brostrup Lanstad (1802–1880), and Martin Franzmann (1907–1976). Nor is it an accident that the Lutheran tradition has stimulated a string of composers who created choral and instrumental materials, such as Heinrich Schütz (1585–1672), Dietrich Buxtehude (1637–1707), Johann Pachelbel (1653–1706), the Bach family (throughout the seventeenth and eighteenth centuries), Ludvig Matthias Lindeman (1810–1887), Ernst Pepping (1901–1981), Hugo Distler (1901–1942), and F. Melius Christiansen (1871–1955) with their hymn settings, motets, Passions, cantatas, canticles, etc.

Luther was both radical and conservative. He used all of the past, and he welcomed new texts and music as long as they were well-crafted and durable. Texts that denied the centrality of justification by grace through faith were unacceptable, but a wide variety of fine musical craft from the past and present was warmly welcomed.

Zwingli and Silence

Ulrich Zwingli was at first a humanist, Swiss patriot, and priest. Gradually he became an evangelical reformer. After encountering Erasmus' Greek New Testament in 1516, he began "to preach the word of God that is broken out of Scripture" in his post as chaplain to the pilgrims at the shrine of the Black Virgin at Einsiedeln.[47]

---

[46] Erik Routley, *The Music of Christian Hymns* (G.I.A. Publications, 1981), p. 21. *Cf.* Erik Routley, *Christian Hymns Observed* (Princeton: Prestige Publications, 1982), p. 18.

[47] Bard Thompson, "Ulrich Zwingli," in Gerrish, *Reformers in Profile*, pp. 119–120.

On the first Sunday of January in 1519, when he became priest at the Great Minster in Zurich, he abandoned the lectionary and began preaching from the first chapter of Matthew. By 1525 he had preached *lectio continua*[48] through the New Testament (except for Revelation), and he then began the Old Testament.[49] In 1522 he resigned as "people's priest" of Zurich and was rehired by the city council as preacher to the entire city.[50] In 1523 two disputations were held. They culminated in a decision to abandon images, which was carried out in the summer of 1524.

> In one sweeping action, clergy and craftsmen entered the parish churches; they removed the relics and images, whitewashed the paintings and decorations, carted away the utensils, and nailed the organs shut in token that no music would resound in the churches again.[51]

What was the theology of music behind this? Did Zwingli simply impart to his followers a personal dislike of music?

Zwingli did not dislike music at all. He was probably the best musician of all the reformers. He studied music as a youth and in 1496–1497 was courted by the Dominicans in Bern to enter their monastery because of his beautiful voice. He even agreed to join them until his family intervened and sent him off to Vienna.[52] At Vienna "he was basically grounded in all instruments, such as harp, lute, viol, flute, reedpipe, and cornett, completely educated, a good composer, and so forth."[53] His call as a priest to Zurich was questioned by those who were offended by his "ready talent for music."[54] When he recovered from the plague in 1520, he wrote a poem and composed a polyphonic setting for it; other

---

[48] Since you can't read the whole Bible at every worship service, you have to devise some system to split it up. The church has basically used two systems to discipline its reading so that a single person does not choose his or her own favorite themes week after week. One system is *lectio continua*, that is, reading through a book in course, piece by piece in order week after week. The other is *lectio selecta*, that is, reading selected lections week by week, which match the seasons of the church year.

[49] See Thompson "Ulrich Zwingli," in Gerrish, *Reformers in Profile*, pp. 120–121, and George, *Theology of the Reformers* p. 113.

[50] See George, *Theology of the Reformers* p. 114.

[51] Thompson "Ulrich Zwingli," in Gerrish, *Reformers in Profile*, p. 127.

[52] Charles Garside, *Zwingli and the Arts* (New Haven and London: Yale University Press, 1966), pp. 7–9. Garside's book is the best study of Zwingli's musical position. I have leaned heavily on it.

[53] Garside, *Zwingli*, p. 10. Cf. p. 14.

[54] Ibid., p. 16.

polyphonic pieces followed later in his life.[55] He was not a man who hated or even disliked music. He loved music and cultivated his talent and affection for it. So what drove him to remove it from worship?

Charles Garside in his book *Zwingli and the Arts* has clearly laid out Zwingli's theology of music.[56] It can be summarized in three points.

First, Zwingli asked where in the Scriptures God has commanded singing in worship. Nowhere, he answered.[57] If you want to know what Paul meant about "singing psalms and hymns and spiritual songs with thankfulness in your hearts to God" in Colossians 3:16, Zwingli—like those against whom Niceta of Remesiana argued[58]—says this:

> Here Paul does not teach mumbling and murmuring in the churches, but shows us the true song that is pleasing to God, that we sing the praise and glory of God not with our voices, like the Jewish singers, but with our hearts.[59]

What then about the Old Testament? Zwingli admitted that it reported musical activities, but he said they were not instituted by God. Moses and Hannah prayed "silently in their hearts, exactly as Christ instructed all men to do."[60]

Second, unlike Luther for whom nature was a bearer of grace, Zwingli made a sharp distinction between the two realms. For him "material things could not participate in the holy, or convey grace."[61] Flesh and the physical stood in sharp contrast and opposition to spirit and the spiritual. At Marburg, with John 6:63 close at hand ("the flesh is of no avail"), Zwingli told Luther, "Spirit and flesh contradict each other."[62] This worked itself out for Zwingli in two kinds of worship. One was external forms, "clamor before men"; the other was internal content, "spirit and truth." The first was hypocrisy, the second obedience to the law of Christ.[63] Worship and prayer were synonymous for Zwingli, and the essence of wor-

---

[55] Ibid., pp. 26, 70, and 73.
[56] See FN 52 for the citation.
[57] Garside, *Zwingli*, p. 44.
[58] See chapter 6.
[59] Ibid., p. 45.
[60] Ibid.
[61] Thompson "Ulrich Zwingli," in Gerrish, *Reformers in Profile*, p. 128.
[62] Ibid.
[63] Garside, *Zwingli*, p. 40.

ship was literal obedience to Christ's command in Matthew 6:7 to go into your room, shut the door, and pray to God in secret.[64]

Such a position obviates public worship altogether. You don't need the worship of the Christian community at all if you rigorously follow this logic to its conclusion. But communal worship of the visible church was for Zwingli "a necessity beyond dispute"; "some kind of public worship [was] imperative for the life of the visible church within the city."[65] Zwingli's solution to the dilemma was silence, silence for hearing the word and for contemplation. "The people must be educated in the Word of God," he said, "so that neither vestments nor song have a part in the Mass."[66] Music was unhooked from worship altogether and left to develop in the secular world. In church there was no place for it.

Third, the fundamental issue here is not that music is worldly or theatrical, nor that chant under Gregory the Great is a mark of the fall of the church. Those probably were the arguments of Andreas Karlstadt (c. 1480–1541)[67] whose iconoclasm in Wittenberg evoked Luther's wrath. Zwingli's arguments were far more radical than Karlstadt's and had a theological rather than a historical base.

Luther and Zwingli lived in different worlds in this matter. For Zwingli, music had no relation to the word of God at all. It was related instead to play. Zwingli understood music's tremendous power. In his private life he used it to refresh himself again and again. But he perceived the refreshment to come from music itself, not from any relation to the word of God or to the power of the Holy Spirit, as Luther said.

The musical positions of Luther and Zwingli are closely tied to their eucharistic theologies. There too they were in radically different worlds. Luther's understanding of the real presence of Christ in

---

[64] Ibid., pp. 40–41.

[65] Ibid., pp. 43–45. Zwingli's dilemma here is not unrelated to the one he faced with the Anabaptists over infant baptism and probably never satisfactorily resolved. See Zwingli, "Of Baptism," *The Library of Christian Classics*, XXIV, ed. G. W. Bromiley (Philadelphia: The Westminster Press, 1953), pp. 129–179, and Bromiley's introduction, pp. 126–127; Torsten Bergsten, *Balthasar Hubmaier: Anabaptist Theologian and Martyr* (Valley Forge: Judson Press, 1978), pp. 80–81; and John K. Harms, "Music of the Radical Reformation II," *Church Music* (78/1): 23.

[66] Garside, *Zwingli*, p. 54. Karlstadt set out a similar position in theses for debate, which could be construed as hyperbolic grist. See John K. Harms, "Music of the Radical Reformation II," *Church Music* (78/1): 19–21, where the theses of Karlstadt are given and discussed.

[67] Garside, *Zwingli*, pp. 28–33, 46, and 54–55.

the Lord's Supper, his modest liturgical reforms, and his musical posture resulted, to use Carl Schalk's words, in "solidarity and continuity with the church catholic." Zwingli's denial of the real presence, his removal of the Supper from a weekly to a quarterly celebration with its concomitant iconoclastic liturgical reforms, and his liturgical silence "sundered the unity of word and sacrament that had prevailed since Justin Martyr"[68] and "shattered the unity of art and religion which for centuries had been the greatest single source of higher culture in Western Europe."[69]

Zwingli stimulated no poetic or musical composition in the church, but two observations need to be made. First, in 1525 the Zurich Council out-Zwinglied Zwingli. In his communion service Zwingli included the Gloria in Excelsis in a spoken version which alternated between men and women.[70] The Town Council refused to allow it.[71] Second, over the long haul, Christians will not be silenced. Even in Zurich, where Zwingli obviously had been powerful and persuasive, the church began singing again in 1598.[72]

Calvin and Strictures

John Calvin, unlike Luther and Zwingli, was never a priest and never ordained. He experienced a sudden conversion in 1532–1533, and in 1535 encountered an evangelical community in Basel with psalm-singing in place since 1526.[73] His first edition of the *Institutes of the Christian Religion* was published in 1536 as a 520–page compendium of the Christian faith and an apology of Christian doctrine, organized with the experience of faith at the center and central doctrines carried out as far as possible like spokes on a wheel.[74] A second edition was published in 1539 to train candidates in theology, Calvin translated a third edition into French in 1541, and the definitive edition grew in 1559 to four books: the Father, the Son, the

---

[68] Thompson "Ulrich Zwingli," in Gerrish, *Reformers in Profile*, p. 129.

[69] Garside, *Zwingli*, p. 181.

[70] "Action or Use of the Lord's Supper" in Bard Thompson, *Liturgies of the Western Church* (Cleveland: Meridian Books, 1961), p. 152.

[71] Thompson, *Liturgies*, p. 142.

[72] Garside, *Zwingli*, p. 183.

[73] See Charles Garside, Jr., "The Origins of Calvin's Theology of Music: 1536–1543," *Transactions of the American Philosophical Society* 69:4 (Philadelphia: The American Philosophical Society, August 1979): 9. Again, as for Zwingli, I am indebted to Garside for his work on Calvin's theology of music.

[74] I am indebted to Bard Thompson for this description.

Holy Spirit, and the Church, each divided into numerous chapters and divisions.

In 1536, Calvin was called to Geneva, and on September 1 he began to preach through Paul's letters in lectio continua fashion, like Zwingli. He understood the evangelical community to have two foci, discipline and weekly communion. In 1538, after a crisis with the council over discipline, Calvin was expelled from Geneva.[75] He went to Strasbourg where he was exposed to Martin Bucer's (1491–1551) service and to psalm- and hymn-singing.[76] Bucer, unlike Zwingli, embraced the use of music. He interpreted Paul to mean actual singing, invoked the example of the early church, and pointed out that Christ himself "concluded His Last Supper and final sermon with a song of praise."[77]

After riots in Geneva in 1540, Calvin returned there, and on September 1 of 1541 he began preaching where he had left off in 1538, with no mention of the time-lapse. He supported the textual work of Clement Marot (c. 1496–1544) and Theodore Beza (1519–1605) and the musical work of Louis Bourgeois (c. 1510–1560) in producing the Genevan Psalter. Here is another of history's ironies. Marot's motives "certainly had little to do with the protestant movement,"[78] and metrical psalmody probably began in the French court as "lord and lady vied with each other in finding tunes" for metrical psalms.[79] Marot himself had contributed a French metrical version of Psalm 6 to Miroir d'une âme pécheresse, published between 1531 and 1533, a work of Margaret who was the sister of Francis I, King of France.

The Genevan Psalter went through numerous versions before it reached its final stage in Geneva: Strasbourg in 1539; Antwerp in 1541; then Geneva in 1543, 1545, 1551 (a pivotal edition), 1554, and finally 1562 when all 150 Psalms were present with 125 tunes and 110 different meters (25 melodies for more than one text[80]).

---

[75] See George, Theology of the Reformers, p. 180.

[76] Garside, "Origins," p. 11. Strasbourg was pivotal for contact between the music from Luther's reforming activity and that which would characterize Geneva. See Erik Routley, The Music of Christian Hymns (Chicago: G. I. A. Publications, 1981), pp. 28–34.

[77] Garside, "Origins," pp. 11–12.

[78] Temperley, The Music of the English Parish Church, I, p. 21.

[79] Winfred Douglas, rev. Leonard Ellinwood, Church Music in History and Practice: Studies in the Praise of God (New York: Charles Scribner's Sons, 1961), p. 179.

[80] Erik Routley, The Music of Christian Hymns, (Chicago: GIA Publications, 1981) pp. 33, 36.

What theology of music led to this development? Two initial points must be made. First, Calvin was a careful systematician who, though embroiled in conflict and never granted the book-lined study he desired, nonetheless thought out his position over time. Though he was not a musician, the contours of his thought about music are clear. They are given in the *Institutes* III. xx. 31–32, the preface to the Genevan Psalter of 1542, and the preface to the Genevan Psalter of 1543. The 1543 preface added 917 words to the 1,305 words in the preface of 1542; the two were combined in the 1545 preface to form an unbroken unit of 2,222 words.[81] It is not the case that "Calvin's views on music are unascertainable."[82] Second, Calvin's position of spiritual real presence in and weekly celebrations of the Lord's Supper[83] indicate he was neither a Zwinglian nor a Lutheran. His position on music parallels his eucharistic theology.

The first thing to note is *where* Calvin considered church singing in the *Institutes*. It is in the section on prayer. This is decisive, for it gives Calvin's frame of reference. Both the *Institutes*[84] and the 1542 preface[85] indicate that for Calvin there are two kinds of prayer. One is "with words alone," the other "with singing."[86] Calvin also said,

> Now there are briefly three things which our Lord commanded us to observe in our spiritual assemblies: namely, the preaching of His word, prayers public and solemn, and the administration of the Sacraments.[87]

Since one kind of prayer involves singing, singing then, as Garside says, is for Calvin part of "one of the three fundamental expressions of Christian worship."[88]

Calvin viewed singing in church as no recent invention. It is "very ancient," he said, used "among the apostles."[89] He quoted Paul (I Corinthians 14:15 and Colossians 3:16) to prove his point, Zwingli notwithstanding, but also noted that the practice was not universal. He reported Augustine's observation that men like Hilary attacked

[81] See Charles Garside, Jr., "Calvin's Preface to the Psalter: A Re-Appraisal," *The Musical Quarterly*, XXXVII:4 (October 1951): 569.

[82] Routley, *The Music of Christian Hymns*, p. 30.

[83] See John Calvin, "Institutes of the Christian Religion," ed. John T. McNeill, *The Library of Christian Classics*, XX–XXI (Philadelphia: Westminster Press, 1960), all of IV. xvii and IV. xvii. 43–44.

[84] Calvin, *Institutes*, III. xx. 31.

[85] Garside, "Calvin's Preface," 568.

[86] Ibid.

[87] Ibid.

[88] Ibid.

[89] Calvin, *Institutes*, III. xx. 32. *Cf.* Garside, "Calvin's Preface," 568.

the singing of hymns from the book of Psalms.[90] He also made it clear he did not mean to follow their lead. Rather, he said,

> . . . we do not condemn speaking and singing but rather strongly commend them, provided they are associated with the heart's affection. [91]

What is the point of singing in church? First, music was "peculiarly created to tell and proclaim the praise of God."[92] Second, Calvin saw it as a means "by which the godly may mutually edify one another."[93] These two motifs run together. In the addition to the 1543 preface Calvin began with praise, but quickly moved to edification and the power of music. Music, said Calvin, is "either the first, or one of the principal" things "for recreating" us and giving us "pleasure."[94] He was quite cognizant of music's power.

> . . . there is scarcely anything in the world which is more able to turn or bend this way and that the morals of men, as Plato prudently expressed it. And in fact, we find that it has a secret and almost incredible power to move hearts in one way or another.[95]

In this discussion Calvin even called music a gift of God. That almost sounds like Luther, but, as Oskar Soehngen pointed out, for Calvin it was a gift "in an indirect sense. In the foreground of Calvin's view of music is the idea that it is an invention of human beings and that musical instruments were invented by the descendants of Cain."[96] Calvin also knew, like Luther, that this gift can be perverted, and he spent more energy than Luther warning against the perversion. Music was for him like a funnel that made the word pierce the heart more strongly, so that melodies joined to bad words "distill" the "venom and corruption . . . to the depths of the heart."[97]

If music is so potent and can be misused to our condemnation, what is to be done? How is it to be used rightly?

> It is to have songs not only honest, but also holy, which will be like spurs to incite us to pray to and praise God, and to meditate upon His works in order to love, fear, honor, and glorify Him.[98]

---

[90] Calvin, *Institutes*, III. xx. 32.
[91] Ibid., III. xx. 31.
[92] Ibid.
[93] Ibid., III. xx. 32.
[94] Garside, "Calvin's Preface," 570.
[95] Ibid.
[96] Soehngen, "Fundamental Considerations for a Theology of Music," p. 13.
[97] Garside, "Calvin's Preface," 570–571.
[98] Ibid., 571.

And what songs are holy? The answer is the Psalms of David, "which the Holy Spirit spoke and made through him."[99] When we sing the Psalms, said Calvin, we can be sure that God puts them in our mouths as if God were singing in us "to exalt His glory."[100] John Witvliet notes that "this divine action is construed in Trinitarian terms, where Christ is 'the chief conductor of our hymns' " and the Holy Spirit the prompter.[101]

The next obvious question is how shall the Psalms be sung. How do you go about determining the music? Calvin thought that out. He drew a distinction between the music one makes to entertain people at table in your house and the "Psalms which are sung in the Church in the presence of God."[102] Music in church cannot be "light" or "frivolous," but must have "weight" and "majesty."[103]

This perspective resulted in a series of strictures. Unlike Zwingli, Calvin did not silence music altogether; but, unlike Luther, he did not welcome it so eagerly. The strictures he imposed were metrical psalms, a single monophonic line, one note for each syllable of text, without melismas, without polyphony, without instruments, and without choirs except as a group (of children) led the congregation's unison singing.[104] (Actually it was singing in octaves, of course, since the women and children sang an octave above the men.) The Genevan Psalter, with its tunes such as OLD HUNDREDTH[105] by Louis Bourgeois, was the result.[106] Polyphonic or homophonic settings were made by Clement Jannequin (c. 1474–c. 1560), Claude Goudimel (c. 1514–1572), Philibert Jambe-de-Fer (c. 1515–c. 1566), Claudin Le Jeune (c. 1528–1600), Orlando di Lasso

---

[99] Ibid.

[100] Ibid.

[101] John Witvliet, "The Spirituality of the Psalter: Metrical Psalms in Liturgy and Life in Calvin's Geneva," *Calvin Theological Journal* 32:2 (November 1997): 281–282.

[102] Ibid., 568 (1542 Preface).

[103] Ibid.

[104] See John Witvliet, "The Spirituality of the Psalter," p. 280.

[105] LBW, #245, is one place where OLD HUNDREDTH may be found.

[106] For the tunes in modern notation, with comments, see Waldo Selden Pratt, *The Music of the French Psalter of 1562: A Historical Survey and Analysis, with the Music in Modern Notation* (New York: Columbia University Press, 1939), pp. 79–206. For a summary of recent thought about the sources of the tunes, whether from secular chansons or Gregorian chant, see John Witvliet, "The Spirituality of the Psalter," pp. 14–15.

(1532–1594), and Jan Sweelinck (1562–1621),[107] but they were for use at home or elsewhere outside the liturgy,[108] not when the church gathered for public worship. As usual, the strictures did not always hold. Reformed churches in the Netherlands and Germany brought the organ and polyphony into public worship.[109]

Home use should not be missed here. For both Lutherans and Calvinists the home was important, but for Calvinists there was a musical distinction the Lutherans did not know. In public worship the psalms were sung in unison. At home the same texts could be sung contrapuntally. A fuller musical practice was present than the public face suggests, but behind that stood a fuller worship life in which larger community and home combined to form the whole. People carried their psalters in their pockets. They sang psalms at church and at home, at home in unison if counterpoint exceeded their capabilities. A medieval wholeness was present, unlike our segmented lives where Sunday worship tends to be an isolated activity.

Consequences

Calvin's position may be seen as closest to the early church, but it was not quite the same.[110] Calvin set up restrictions on the texts of worship, psalms only—though the Apostles' Creed and canticles like the Nunc Dimittis were also included in Calvinist psalters—which were more severe than the early church knew. Neither did the early church know the kind of musical restrictions Calvin imposed. It simply adopted the vocal song of the synagogue in its worship while banning instruments outside worship at banquets and the like. More importantly, the song of the early church was what would become chant—not "musica" but "psalms and hymns," which indicated a unique performance practice consciously or unconsciously distinct from the world.[111] Calvin consciously wanted music that was dis-

---

[107] Witvliet, "The Spirituality of the Psalter," p. 292, points to the "explosion of polyphonic settings of Genevan tunes," with 13 volumes of polyphonic music printed between 1554 and 1559, and 28 volumes printed by the end of the century. In all over 2,000 settings of the Genevan texts and tunes were produced."

[108] See Witvliet, "The Spirituality of the Psalter," pp. 293 and 288–294.

[109] See Temperley, *The Music of the English Parish Church*, I, p. 22.

[110] Calvin is obviously closest to Augustine. Luther realized that and said, ". . . but if he were living today, he would hold with us." See Robert M. Stevenson, *Patterns of Protestant Church Music* (Durham: Duke University Press, 1953), p. 9.

[111] McKinnon, "The Meaning," CM: 70–71.

tinct from the world, but he also thought the church had to use
music that was in a "known tongue." [112] He regarded both instruments and chanting as an "unknown tongue" and "an empty
sound." [113] Unlike the early church, which used what it inherited
from the synagogue, Calvin broke with the church's musical past.
The way he got the weight and gravity he sought was through tunes
such as OLD HUNDREDTH. It was music with, if Oskar Soehngen is
right,

> an eye for the inflammability of the Roman temperament and aims in
> this direction. The Psalms of the Geneva Reformation, when seen from
> the standpoint of their musical type, are closely related to the Marseil-
> laise of the French Revolution, the gripping melody of which fascinated
> the people, and it is the same line which leads to the electrifying rhythm
> of Bizet's "Carmen" and Ravel's "Bolero." [114]

Regardless of whether Soehngen is exactly right, Luther and
Calvin spawned different things for the congregation. First, musically Luther embraced the past. Calvin denied it. Second, though
both traditions used unison song for the congregation, Luther's was
"practically based" and Calvin's "theologically based." [115] Finally,
the reformation in Wittenberg produced chorales of bold, vigorous,
objective rejoicing, whereas the reformation in Geneva produced a
song with two prongs—separate from the world, but nonetheless
more subjective than the early church or what the Lutherans knew.
Lutherans looked with some dismay therefore at the seductive
"siren" of Reformed congregations.

The positions of Luther, Zwingli, and Calvin have had consequences and mixes down to our time. 1) Though Reformed people
officially follow Calvin in their confessions and Lutherans follow
Luther and Philipp Melanchthon in theirs, Zwingli has nonetheless
been influential even in some Lutheran communities, especially ones
influenced by Pietism. Such churches have invariably exhibited a
nervousness about music. 2) Where the influence of Calvin is strong,
which again has included some Lutheran communities, the twentieth-century version of his unison singing still often follows the

---

[112] John Calvin, *Commentary on the Book of Psalms* (Grand Rapids: Wm. B.
Eerdmans Publishing, 1949), Psalm XXXIII, vol. I, p. 539.

[113] Ibid. *Cf.* Calvin, *Commentary on the Book of Psalms*, Psalm LXXI, vol. III,
p. 98.

[114] Soehngen, "Fundamental Considerations for a Theology of Music," p. 15.

[115] Erik Routley, *The Music of Christian Hymns*, p. 28. For Routley's take on
Lutheran and Reformed music in more detail, see pp. 21–34.

requirement that harmonizations of hymns are never to be varied from the ones printed in the hymnal. In contrast, Luther's practice easily flowed into changing harmonies or part singing by choir and/or congregation. Lucas Osiander (1534–1604) in 1586 harmonized chorales with the melody in the soprano rather than the tenor so the congregation could hear it better.[116] Practically that was revolutionary and set the model for modern hymnals, but it required no theological adjustments. 3) As to music and art more generally, twentieth-century Reformed art fairs have largely looked to what is outside worship, whereas Lutheran ones have gravitated to what is used in worship.

Psalm singing inevitably spilled over into England, but not without turmoil. To that we will turn after considering some other sixteenth-century European traditions.

---

[116] Lucas Osiander, *Fünffzig geistliche Lieder und Psalmen mit vier Stimmen auff contrapuncstweise (für die Schulen und Kirchen in löblichen Fürstenthumb Würtenberg) also gesetzt, das eine gantze Christliche Gemein durchaus mit singen kann* (Nuremberg, 1586). See Friedrich Blume, trans., Theodore Hoelty-Nickel, "The Age of Confessionalism," Friedrich Blume et al., *Protestant Church Music* (New York: W. W. Norton & Company, 1974), p. 136, and Walter Blankenburg, "Osiander, Lucas," NGDMM 14, 3.

11

A Wider Spectrum

The sixteenth-century spectrum was wider than the positions Luther, Zwingli, Calvin, and their followers took. Not only did the Eastern church continue its practice, but in the West Roman Catholics, Anglicans, and the Radical Reformation all came to their own conclusions as well.

Roman Catholics

Roman Catholic concerns about reforms in worship and music were part of what is sometimes referred to as the Counter-Reformation, systematized at the Council of Trent. Trent was actually not one single meeting, but a series of twenty-five meetings that began a year before Luther's death and spanned almost twenty years, from 1545 to 1563.

Sometimes Trent and Calvin sound alike. In music at worship, said Trent, nothing profane was to be "intermingled." Music was to be constituted so as "not to give empty pleasure to the ear," but rather the words were to be "understood by all, and thus the hearts of the listeners be drawn to the desire of heavenly harmonies, in the contemplation of the joys of the blessed."[1] Calvin may not have expressed these thoughts in exactly the same way and would have argued against Latin and for the language of the people, but the gravity of worship, the opposition to emptiness, and the importance of the heart were his themes, too.

Similarly, Luther wanted the words to be understood, and in other ways he and Trent sometimes sound the same. Clerics, said

---

[1] Hayburn, *Papal Legislation on Sacred Music,* p. 27.

Trent, were to participate in worship themselves, not by proxy (!), and they were to study the arts, including music.[2] Luther too pushed for genuine participation, and he wouldn't look at teachers and clergy who were musical illiterates.

Cleavages, however, hid all common ground or even possibilities for finding it. Luther and Calvin, in their legitimate reaction to Rome's abuses, were prone to intemperate language. Calvin "denounced [the medieval Mass] with raw invective."[3] One of Luther's hymns included a line about the "murderous Pope and Turk."[4] If rhetoric and angry denunciations were the only problems, however, people several generations later might have forgotten the flap and come back together. But under all the nasty fuss was a fundamental disagreement about justification and whether good works could get human beings into God's presence. Both sides of the dispute recognized this basic fissure and have continued to reckon with it to the present day. The rift did not go away, and the early church's ideal of singing with one voice became even more elusive. Disputes between the Eastern and Western portions of the church had led to a schism in 1054 that has not yet healed,[5] in the sixteenth century the West itself divided, and thereafter the Protestant world splintered into an ever-increasing number of pieces. The church's musical life at worship followed these numerous paths. The East continued to use voices alone, while the Western practice became more and more diffuse.

---

[2] Ibid., p. 28.

[3] Thompson, *Liturgies of the Western Church*, p. 185.

[4] See Hayburn, *Papal Legislation on Sacred Music*, pp. 25–26. (Hayburn's quotes from the Bishop of Vienne are helpful, but his editorial aside on this line—literally "des Papst und Türken Mord"—as coming from *Ein feste Burg*, "A Mighty Fortress" (LBW, #228), while accurate in substance, is wrong in detail. The words come from *Erhalt uns, Herr, bei deinem Wort*, "Lord Keep Us Steadfast in Your Word" (LBW, #230), which Luther wrote in response to his Elector's request for Germany's protection. It was later altered to refer generally to enemies of the Word. See W. G. Polack, *The Handbook to the Lutheran Hymnal* (Saint Louis: Concordia Publishing House, 1958), pp. 191–192, and Marilyn Kay Stulken, *Hymnal Companion to the Lutheran Book of Worship* (Philadelphia: Fortress Press, 1981), pp. 308–309. For the original text of *Ein feste Burg*, see Armin Haeussler, *The Story of Our Hymns: The Handbook to the Hymnal of the Evangelical and Reformed Church* (Saint Louis: Eden Publishing House, 1952), pp. 314–315, or, in more modern German, W. G. Polack, *The Handbook to the Lutheran Hymnal*, p. 192.)

[5] See Martin Marty, *A Short History of Christianity*, pp. 152–153, for a summary of this break.

The humanist Erasmus (1469–1536) described the situation Rome faced, curiously close to the way some have described church music in our time.

> We have introduced an artificial and theatrical music into the church, a bawling and agitation of various voices, such as I believe had never been heard in the theatres of the Greeks and Romans. Horns, trumpets, pipes vie and sound along constantly with the voices. Amorous and lascivious melodies are heard such as elsewhere accompany only the dances of courtesans and clowns. The people run into the churches as if they were theatres, for the sake of the sensuous charm of the ear.[6]

In 1562 the Council of Trent sought to clean up the abuses in texts, music, and conduct.

> So that the house of God should truly appear to be rightly called a house of prayer compositions of which there is an intermingling of the lascivious or impure, whether by instrument or voice, and likewise every secular action, idle and even profane conversation, strolling about, bustle, and shouting must be ousted from the churches.[7]

Behind this reprimand stood the "incompetence . . . abysmal ignorance, frivolity, and levity" in worship, which Luther encountered when he visited Rome in 1510.[8] Rome knew the problems and sought to correct them. Fourteen Papal Choir singers were fired.[9]

The deeper musical concern centered on polyphony. In 1563, partly in response to the general bedlam and "scandalous noises" at the Mass, some of the cardinals at Trent called for monophony or even the total absence of music. Emperor Ferdinand I was among those who objected to such suggestions and communicated to the Council a strong defense of polyphony. Radical measures were not taken. An evolutionary approach allowed polyphony to be acceptable as long as worldly forms were excluded and the texts were understood. Though achieving understandable texts meant applying sixteenth-century ideas about Latin accents and "curtailing" melismas, the polyphony of composers such as Tomás Luis de Victoria

---

[6] Quoted in Gustave Reese, *Music in the Renaissance* (New York: W. W. Norton & Company, Inc., 1959, rev. ed.), p. 448. Erasmus, like the early church and Calvin—though apparently more musical than Calvin—had serious qualms about instruments. See McKinnon, "The Fathers and Musical Instruments," p. 286 (including FN 2, which is omitted in the body of the text).

[7] Hayburn, *Papal Legislation on Sacred Music*, p. 28.

[8] Roland Bainton, *Here I Stand: A Life of Martin Luther* (New York: Abingdon Press, 1950), p. 49. Cf. Hayburn, *Papal Legislation on Sacred Music*, pp. 28–29.

[9] Hayburn, *Papal Legislation on Sacred Music*, pp. 29–30.

(c. 1548–1611) and Giovanni Pierluigi da Palestrina (c. 1525–1594) was nonetheless embraced by the Roman Catholic church. The people's song was not yet recovered, but the church's rich choral tradition got even richer.[10]

One should not get the impression, however, that Trent waved a magic wand and made everything everywhere the same. "The immense variety, bordering on anarchy, of liturgies in the latter Middle Ages"[11] was checked, but chant was diffuse and became more so. In the sixteenth century, European chant books were not uniform.[12] Under Pius V a breviary was published in 1568 and a missal in 1570.[13] They did not pay much attention to the chants,[14] which some people were prepared to alter anyway. Chant was "little used" in Italy except for the offices, as themes for polyphonic masses, or as snippets for student's composition assignments.[15] Some thought it needed "correction." Don Fernando de las Infantas (1534–c. 1610), a well-trained Spanish composer and theologian who both served the poor and understood chant, pleaded with Pope Gregory XIII not to make amateurish alterations.[16] Nonetheless, Palestrina and Annibale Zoilo (c. 1537–1592), polyphonic experts but novices about chant, were commissioned by Gregory to make revisions. The project was never finished, but it led to lengthy legal tangles involving the deceit of Palestrina's son.[17]

Diffusion extended well beyond the sixteenth century. In 1582 a new chant book with rhythmic modifications was published by Giovanni Guidetti, a friend of Palestrina. In 1614 and 1615 the Medici Press in Rome published an "improved" new gradual prepared by two other associates of Palestrina, Felice Anerio and Francesco Soriano. Cadences were reshaped, stereotypical melodic lines were intro-

---

[10] See Hayburn, *Papal Legislation on Sacred Music*, pp. 29–30, and Reese, *Music in the Renaissance*, pp. 449–450. For Zarlino's influential rules about how to set texts to polyphony, see Reese, pp. 377–378.

[11] Gordon Rupp, *Patterns of Reformation* (Philadelphia: Fortress Press, 1969), p. 307.

[12] Hayburn, *Papal Legislation on Sacred Music*, p. 33.

[13] For lists of chant books from 1476 to 1987 in the context of a narrative see Robert F. Hayburn, "The Printed Editions of the Chant Books and Their Effect on the Gregorian Tradition," *Cum Angelis Canere*, pp. 98–112.

[14] Ibid., p. 34.

[15] Ibid., p. 36.

[16] Ibid., p. 42.

[17] This situation is detailed with copious quotes from the correspondence in Hayburn, *Papal Legislation on Sacred Music*, pp. 33–57.

duced, melismas were abbreviated, and B flats added in a move toward tonality—the sorts of alterations de las Infantas had feared. In 1602 under Clement VIII and in 1632 under Urban VIII the texts of office hymns were virtually rewritten in a new breviary. In seventeenth-century France "major changes in the liturgy and music" were introduced, and in 1680 a "neo-Gallican" breviary substituted new liturgical formularies for the standard ones. Sophisticated styles of chant performance in eighteenth-century France required highly developed improvisational and contrapuntal skills. None of this was without controversy, and some of it related to broader French nationalistic and antipapal sentiments.[18]

As to composed polyphony itself, some smaller churches wanted to discard the chant in favor of part-written Masses that were not too difficult. Long and difficult polyphonic settings were used, but the typical Western concern for brevity[19] even in larger churches simultaneously led to what Italians called the *Missa brevis*.[20] In Germany parody Masses—that is, settings of the ordinary built on preexistent polyphonic pieces—"continued to be based on compositions of the gayest sort."[21]

The Roman Catholic world encompassed liturgical and musical differences. Word and sacrament with the prayer offices around them were still at the core if you looked deeply enough, but they were certainly obscured. The people's musical office, which always cuts to the core, was still denied.

---

[18] This paragraph summarizes and quotes some of John A. Emerson, "Plainchant," NGDMM, 14, pp. 825–827.

[19] Eastern liturgy can be seen as related to the regal court in which time is unhurried. To enter an Eastern Orthodox church is to enter an antechamber of heaven. One does not rush in the presence of the ruler of the universe, so lavish ceremonial and repetitions lead to services that last several hours. Western liturgy can be seen as related to the legal court where time and juridical action are of the essence. Ceremonial and repetition will therefore be curtailed and services limited to an hour or less—among Roman Catholics and Protestants.

[20] In sixteenth-century Italy, *Missa brevis* meant the whole ordinary of the Mass, each movement short. In seventeenth- and eighteenth-century Lutheran practice it meant settings of the Kyrie and Gloria in Excelsis. See Lewis Lockwood, "Missa brevis," NGDMM, 12, p. 364.

[21] Reese, *Music in the Renaissance*, p. 451. This paragraph relies on Reese, pp. 450–451.

The Reformation in England was associated with a series of historical accidents: England freeing itself of papal control for nationalistic reasons, the divorces of Henry VIII, and his destruction of monasteries for the sake of his own wealth, power, and control. Sometimes Anglicans are viewed as a *via media* between the Roman and Protestant worlds. England had no great theological giant or prophetic voice like Calvin and Luther, though Richard Hooker (c. 1554–1600) was an able Anglican systematician and apologist. For those who want careful confessional logic in worship, these reasons allow them to dismiss the Anglican church without ever getting at its central spirit, namely, that Christianity is to be prayed before it is to be thought.[22] The legacy of the Anglican Reformation is the *Book of Common Prayer,* which, in its language if not always its structure, has influenced Christian worship wherever English has been spoken.

After 1547 when the boy king Edward VI (1537–1553) came to power, Thomas Cranmer (1489–1556), archbishop of Canterbury, became the leader of the Protestant party in England. He was influenced by the continental reformers, mostly by Calvin, though (against canon law[23]) his second marriage was to the niece of the wife of the controversial Lutheran Andreas Osiander (1498–1552).[24] Cranmer probably had a Zwinglian understanding of the Lord's Supper.[25] He also knew more about the liturgy than any of his contemporaries and possessed a remarkable capacity to craft the English language for worship.

[22] Cyril Richardson put it more strongly: for Anglicans "Christianity is not to be thought, but to be prayed."

[23] See Diarmaid McCulloch, *Thomas Cranmer: A Life* (New Haven: Yale University Press, 1996), pp. 72, 577.

[24] Andreas Osiander was the father of Lucas Osiander (1534–1604), mentioned in the last chapter, who in 1586 produced harmonized settings of chorales with the tune in the soprano rather than the tenor and set in motion the kinds of hymn settings that characterize our hymnals.

[25] See Gregory Dix, *The Shape of the Liturgy* (London: Dacre Press, 1960, first published 1945), p. 656. For a fuller description see Bard Thompson, *Liturgies of the Western Church* (Cleveland: Meridian Books, 1961), p. 228, FN. For a still fuller description, see the massive study by McCulloch, *Thomas Cranmer: A Life,* in which the themes of real presence recur throughout and Cranmer is seen to come ultimately to a position of "spiritual presence" (p. 392).

Under Cranmer images and relics were destroyed and old ceremonies abandoned, while at the same time he edited two prayer books that cast the Latin rite into English within simplified yet catholic structures. The first edition of the *Book of Common Prayer* appeared in 1549. Its revision in 1552 included more Reformed ideas and a Zwinglian understanding of the Eucharist. In the revision of 1559, three years after Cranmer's death at the stake under Mary Tudor[26] and one year after Elizabeth I took the throne, the old vestments were restored and the words of delivery at communion from the two earlier books were linked. The former words were Catholic and assumed Christ was present in the Supper. The latter were Zwinglian and assumed Christ was not present in the Supper. This typical Anglican move of linking two things that might not logically go together points to the priority of the life of prayer over the life of thought. In this case it probably reflected for worshipers a sense of real presence, a Calvinist sense of spiritual real presence for some perhaps in which, says Bard Thompson, "the fruit of the sacrament was by no means dissociated from the reception of Holy Communion."[27]

Cranmer's sources for the *Book of Common Prayer*, in addition to his own liturgical knowledge and some elements from Eastern Orthodoxy, included the Sarum Usage (the form of the Western rite in the diocese of Salisbury), the conservative Lutheran Church Order of Brandenburg-Nuremberg, the 1543 Cologne Liturgy from Strasbourg under Martin Bucer, and the Great Bible.[28] The ordinaries and propers of the Mass and the offices, earlier in separate books, were all compressed into one volume.

The *Book of Common Prayer* provided worshipers a largely catholic communion service with additions such as the Comfortable Words and theological ambiguity, as in the preceding paragraphs.

---

[26] If Cranmer was an Erastian, that is, one who advocates the supremacy and authority of the state in ecclesiastical matters, he lived at a particularly vulnerable time. Mary Tudor came to power in 1553, returned England to papal supremacy, and Cranmer was tried for heresy—not without accusations that he recanted, though a recantation in an Erastian context may be hard to decipher. For the drama of Cranmer's final speech and analysis see McCulloch, *Thomas Cranmer: A Life*, pp. 601–605.

[27] See Thompson, *Liturgies*, p. 244.

[28] For more detail see Thompson, *Liturgies*, p. 233–234, and McCulloch, *Thomas Cranmer: A Life*, pp. 414ff. Thompson's whole article, pp. 227–244, provides a careful look at the larger terrain.

For the offices morning prayer was adapted from matins, lauds, and prime, evening prayer from vespers and compline. Though until the nineteenth century morning prayer gradually ousted communion as the central Sunday morning service, the intention was to make short daily prayer services for the people before and after work.[29]

Music

Almost immediately a musical setting appeared, which a congregation could sing. In 1550 John Merbecke (c.1510–c.1585) composed *The Book of Common Praier Noted*. ("Noted" means "with notes.") Merbecke was the organist at St. George's Chapel, Windsor. In 1543 he was arrested for heresy, which in his case meant harboring Calvinist leanings and having largely completed a concordance of the English Bible. Two of his colleagues were put to death, but he was spared. On his release, since his concordance had been confiscated, he began another one. It was published in 1550, the first complete concordance of the English Bible. In its preface to Edward VI, whose accession to power in 1547 removed any threat of punishment to him, Merbecke said he had wasted his early life as a church musician and had given up that vocation. By the end of his life "he opposed the use of even the simplest choral and instrumental music in church."[30]

In *The Book of Common Praier Noted* Merbecke provided music for the ordinary of the communion service and offices, which the people could easily use in parish settings but which may not have been intended for them.[31] It included the characteristic Anglican *Preces* and responses, that is, the versicles and their congregational rejoinders at morning and evening prayer. He followed Cranmer's—and Calvin's—requirements, "for every syllable a note"[32] in monophonic settings. In part Merbecke adapted chant. In part he wrote new music in the same style. He created a functional plainsong, which is what Cranmer, who cared little about polyphony or choral music, desired.[33]

---

[29] See McCulloch, *Thomas Cranmer: A Life*, p. 511.

[30] Judith Blizzard, "Merbecke, John," NGDMM 12, pp. 169.

[31] See Temperley, *The Music of the English Parish Church*, I, p. 15.

[32] Thomas Cranmer, "Letter to Henry VIII" [1544], Strunk, *Source Readings in Music History*, p. 351. See also Temperley, *The Music of the English Parish Church*, I, p. 12.

[33] See McCulloch, *Thomas Cranmer: A Life*, pp. 330–331 (and pp. 264, 629).

The revised prayer book in 1552 and Mary Tudor's coming to power in 1553 sent Merbecke's work into oblivion for a couple centuries. When Elizabeth I (1533–1603) took the throne in 1558 it was not retrieved. Merbecke's settings were only recovered in the nineteenth century and have since been used by many Protestant and Roman Catholic Christians, not only Anglicans.[34] The current *[Episcopal] Hymnal 1982* includes some of them,[35] as did the previous *Hymnal 1940*.[36]

Merbecke seems to have been alone in England in his attempt to provide music for the congregation's parts of the services. Other composers did not follow his example, nor did they forsake their vocations and oppose church music as the "vanity" Merbecke saw in it. They composed for choirs,[37] which started two streams flowing. One is suggested by the printer John Day's publication in 1560, *Certain Notes Set Forth in Foure and Three Parts to Be Sung at the Morning Communion and Evening Prayer*. Choral settings such as these, of the ordinary of the Mass and of the canticles for morning and evening prayer, came to be called "services." Composers also began to write anthems, "which took the place of the motet in the Latin church" and were apparently first sung before and after morning and evening prayer.[38] Christopher Tye (c. 1500–c. 1573) and Thomas Tallis (c. 1505–1585), who managed to live and compose through the ecclesiastical upheavals of the period, stand at the head of both streams, services and anthems. They continued to write polyphony, but in their English choral compositions it was limited by Cranmer's wish for clearly declaimed and understandable syllabic settings.

"Anglican chant," harmonized psalm tones with the intonation omitted and semirhythmic cadence formulas added, was not developed until a century later—though precursors can be found in *fauxbourdon*[39] and Thomas Morley's (1557–1602) *Plain and Easy*

---

[34] I am dependent for much of the material in this and the last paragraph on Judith Blizzard, "Merbecke, John," NGDMM 12, pp. 168–170.

[35] EH, S-67, S-90, S-113, S-157, S-201.

[36] *The Hymnal of the Protestant Episcopal Church in the United States of America 1940* (New York: The Church Pension Fund, 1943), #s701–707.

[37] See Paul Henry Lang, *Music in Western Civilization*, p. 281, and James Robert Davidson, *A Dictionary of Protestant Church Music* (Metuchen: The Scarecrow Press, 1975), p. 46.

[38] Lang, *Music in Western Civilization*, p. 281.

[39] "False bass," a fifteenth-century practice of adding parallel sixths and fourths below a chant melody. See Temperley, *The Music of the English Parish Church*, I, pp. 9–10, and, for an example, II, #2.

Introduction.[40] When the Puritans came to power with Oliver Cromwell (1599–1658) as Lord Protector in 1649, the Anglican services and chant were stopped. When the monarchy was restored in 1660 monophonic chant was recovered and with it harmonized versions that came to be known as "Anglican chant"[41] (which works well when choirs practice it, but easily turns into "Anglican thump" when congregations try it).

Metrical Psalms

Though sixteenth-century English congregations did not sing the service music Merbecke prepared, they did sing. Following the Calvinist model, both Anglicans and the emerging Puritans began to sing metrical psalms. Two years after *Certain Notes*, John Day published the centerpiece of his printing career, *The Whole Booke of Psalmes, collected into Englysh metre by T. Starnhold, I. Hopkins & Others: conferred with the Ebrue, with Apt Notes to synge them withal.* It was the famous Sternhold and Hopkins "Old Version" of the psalms, the English parallel to the French Genevan Psalter, which appeared complete in the same year, 1562. "It ran through an enormous sequence of editions, being reprinted again and again, in some years several times, throughout the next three centuries."[42] At least 65 editions appeared just between 1560 and 1599.[43] The "New Version" of Tate and Brady[44] was not published until 1696, a century and a half later. The "Old Version" became "the foundation stone on which the English tradition of metrical psalmody and hymnody

---

[40] Thomas Morley, *A Plain and Easy Introduction to Practicall Musick* (1597).

[41] Three publications are important here: Edward Lowe, *Short Directions for the Performance of Cathedral Service* 1661, 2d ed., 1664), which gave the tones and endings according to the Roman usage as he had sung at Salisbury before the Rebellion; John Playford, *Introduction to the Skill of Music* (1673), which gave directions for chanting the cathedral service; and James Clifford, *The Divine Service and Anthems Usually Sung in the Cathedrals and Collegiate Choirs of the Church of England* (1663, 2d ed., 1664), which gave monophonic chant and harmonized versions.

[42] Robin Leaver, "English Metrical Psalmody," *The Hymnal 1982 Companion,* I, p. 330.

[43] Horton Davies, *Worship and Theology in England* (Princeton: Princeton University Press, 1970), hereafter *WTE,* I, 386.

[44] *A New Version of the Psalms of David* (1696). Nahum Tate (1652–1715) was the grandson of a Puritan clergyman, preached in Suffolk, published poetry, and was made Poet Laureate by William III. Nicholas Brady (1659–1726) received the B.A. from Christ Church, was a Royal Chaplain, and rector in Stratford-on-Avon.

was built."[45] Metrical psalm singing served as the "principal form of
congregational song, becoming normative for the next three hundred years."[46] In both England and Scotland "congregations sang
with little or no help from choirs, organs, or other instruments,"[47]
just as in Germany. In Germany and wherever Luther's reforms were
influential, the congregation's singing included not only psalms,
however, but chorales that could be free psalm paraphrases or new
hymns, plus metrical settings of the ordinary of the Mass. In England and wherever Calvin's influence was felt, the congregation's
singing was restricted, with minor exceptions,[48] to metrical psalms.

Thomas Sternhold (d. 1549) first began casting the psalms into
meter for the English royalty during the reign of Edward VI.[49] In
1549, the year Sternhold died, thirty-six of his texts were published
with eight by John Hopkins (d. 1570).[50] Routley calls that one
"stream" on the way to the complete Sternhold-Hopkins Psalter of
1562. The other stream was from exiles who fled England to Geneva
under Queen Mary and were influenced by the psalm singing there.[51]
Between 1556 and 1560 they produced several versions of an
"Anglo-Genevan" Psalter. When they returned to England under
Queen Elizabeth they brought their work with them. In short order
The Old Version appeared in 1562 and the complete Scottish Psalter
in 1564.[52]

Unlike the French Genevan Psalter with its 110 meters, the English metricized almost all the psalms into Common Meter (8.6.8.6)

---

[45] Robin Leaver, "English Metrical Psalmody," *The Hymnal 1982 Companion*,
I, p. 330. For a detailed overview of English metrical psalmody before and after
Sternhold and Hopkins, see Leaver's whole article, pp. 321–348.

[46] Robin Leaver, "British Hymnody from the Sixteenth Through the Eighteenth
Centuries," *The Hymnal 1982 Companion*, I, p. 369.

[47] Nicholas Temperley, "The Tunes of Congregational Song in Britain from the
Reformation to 1750," *The Hymnal 1982 Companion*, I, p. 353.

[48] Leaver, "British Hymnody," *The Hymnal 1982 Companion*, I, p. 369ff.

[49] Thomas Sternhold studied at Oxford and was one of the grooms of the robes
of Henry VIII. He contributed 40 psalms to the "Old Version." For more about
Sternhold, see Temperley, *The Music of the English Parish Church*, I, p. 23ff.

[50] John Hopkins received the B.A. from Oxford in 1544 and was a schoolmaster and rector in Suffolk.

[51] For more detail see Temperley, *The Music of the English Parish Church*, I, pp.
26–33.

[52] See Routley, *The Music of Christian Hymns*, pp. 35–39, for more detail. A
table showing the development of both the Old Version and the Scottish Psalter can
be found at pp. 45–47. Authorship and meters are given there, though, for the count
of meters in the Old Version, one has to refer to p. 38.

or Double Common Meter (8.6.8.6 twice),[53] which was regarded as four fourteen-syllable lines. Most of the early English psalm tunes fit this pattern.[54] Rhythmic interest was traded for the flexibility of easily uniting many tunes and texts. From their own oral tradition perhaps,[55] possibly with Genevan and German influences as well, the English created their own idiom in tunes like WINCHESTER OLD[56] or DUNDEE,[57] the latter one of the twelve "common tunes" of the Scottish Psalter of 1615.[58]

When were metrical psalms sung? According to the title of the Sternhold and Hopkins Psalter, "before and after Morning and Evening Prayer, and also before and after Sermons: and moreover in private houses for their godly solace and comfort, laying apart all ungodly songs and ballads, which tend to the nourishing of vice, and corrupting of youth." As in Geneva, note again the relationship to all of life. In 1563 John Day published a four-part harmonized edition. Says Routley, "Four-part singing was as normal a recreation for the educated at home as a game of bridge is today."[59] More significantly, Bible, prayer book, and psalter were published together.[60] Church, home—the whole round of life—were involved.

Anglican Worship

These developments show why Anglican worship is not one easily definable thing. Three forms can be isolated. One type is spoken. It

---

[53] The number of digits indicates the number of lines, the digit itself the number of syllables per line, so that 8.6.8.6, known as Common Meter (C.M.), is four lines of eight syllables, six syllables, eight syllables, and six syllables. Short Meter (S.M.) is 6.6.8.6, and Long Meter (L.M.) is 8.8.8.8.

[54] For examples, see Routley, *The Music of Christian Hymns*, Examples 89–94.

[55] This basis in oral tradition is the view of Temperley, *The Music of the English Parish Church*, I, pp. 33–38. For Temperley's examples of the "Genesis of the metrical psalm tunes, 1520–1570, see Temperley, *The Music of the English Parish Church*, II, #s 7–12.

[56] Routley, *The Music of Christian Hymns*, Example 100.

[57] Ibid., Example 104.

[58] Andro Hart, *The CL Psalms of David* (Edinburgh, 1615).

[59] Routley, *The Music of Christian Hymns*, p. 38.

[60] Two editions illustrate. In 1583 under one cover John Day published the New Testament, the *Whole Book of Psalms*, and a "Table" (concordance). In 1633 under one cover the "Universitie of Cambridge" published the lectionary, the *Whole Book of Psalms*, the *Book of Common Prayer*, the prose translation of the Psalms marked for morning and evening prayer, and the Bible (Old Testament with Psalms in order, Apocrypha, and New Testament).

includes no choir and no singing. The people speak the whole ser-
vice, as in many Episcopal congregations today at 8 A.M. Eucharists
on Sunday morning. A second type is mixed, spoken and sung, by
choir and people. This type fits what Temperley calls harnessing
music "as a vehicle of religious expression" of the people.[61] A third
type, often defined with the label "cathedral," is totally sung by the
choir and priests. The people watch and listen, but are discouraged
from singing. They participate bodily by standing, kneeling, and sit-
ting, the latter possible obviously only as churches were gradually
supplied with pews in the centuries after the Reformation. This type
fits what Nicholas Temperley calls valuing music "as an ornament of
offering to God," which has "encouraged professionalism and has
often led to the virtual silencing of the congregation." Temperley
suggests that the dispute between the second two types has never
been resolved in the Anglican communion and lies behind most of its
conflicts about parish music.[62]

The Radical Reformation

Roman Catholic, Anglican, Lutheran, and non-Separatist Reformed
groups all agreed the church that was presented to them could not
be denied. They regarded the church as a reality sustained by God,
which had to be received as it was, no matter how corrupt. Each
new generation's task in this view is to reform the church and to
build it up on the basis of scripture and perhaps tradition, depending on the way those two entities are regarded. Calvin pushed
toward the edge of this position in that he tried to start over musically. Zwingli fits here even less comfortably and moved to the very
edge, because for him reforms could include iconoclasm. But, even
for Zwingli, the church he inherited was not to be denied, as he indicated by assuming that baptism under the papacy, including baptism
of infants, was "true and valid."[63] Baptism engrafts one into Christ,
said Zwingli, and rebaptism creates an untenable sect.[64]

The radical Reformation which rebaptized, like some English
Puritan Separatists who did the same, took a different view. They

[61] Temperley, *The Music of the English Parish Church*, I, p. 4.

[62] Ibid., I, pp. 4, 42, 243, 342–348.

[63] G. W. Bromiley, ed., Zwingli, "Of Baptism," *The Library of Christian Classics*, XXIV, (Philadelphia: The Westminster Press, 1953), p. 123.

[64] Zwingli, "Of Baptism," *The Library of Christian Classics*, XXIV, ed. G. W.
Bromiley (Philadelphia: The Westminster Press, 1953), p. 152.

felt compelled to repudiate the church they found, to assume the true church had run out. They saw their role as denying what they had received, leaving it, and recovering what they perceived as the church of the New Testament. They were apt to use the Bible severely as the guidebook for their recovery. In such a view nothing can survive unless it matches the understanding of the Bible that a given person or group holds.

This distinction between the church as established and the church as replaced[65] has to be understood in the context of sixteenth-century England and Europe where, like most times and places, positions were often more fluid than their outcomes make them appear in retrospect.[66] Spiritualists like Kaspar Schwenkfeld (1489–1561) and Quakers in England further complicated the picture. Their minimizing of externals and "inner light" led them to be concerned neither with an established church nor a replaced one and to disregard both concerns.[67] The fluidity should not blind us to the fundamental affirmations about the nature of the church that were at stake and stood behind differing practices. The various positions about music in worship that come into view here were not matters of taste or semantics viewed superficially. They reflected critical confessional differences that grew out of what various groups thought about the church, its relation to the world, the Bible, Christ, God, and the faithfulness of God.[68]

The "radical reformation," though it tended to repudiate the church as a given and sought to restore a pristine purity, nevertheless encompassed a wide spectrum in and of itself. Thomas Müntzer (c. 1490–1525),[69] a powerful preacher and reformer who turned

---

[65] Bard Thompson described it with a Latin shorthand. The first perspective is *institutio*, "to institute, to establish, to plant, to set, to fix"; the second *restitutio*, "to replace, to set up again."

[66] For a glimpse at the complexity see John K. Harms, "Music of the Radical Reformation II," *Church Music* (78/1): 27–28.

[67] A hymn by Sebastian Franck ibid., pp. 37–38, is a good illustration. Stanza by stanza each group is rejected: "I will not, cannot, PAPIST be . . . I will not, cannot LUTHERAN be . . . I will not, cannot ZWINGLIAN be . . . No ANABAPTIST will I join. . . . Thus, 'I'm of Christ' says every sect . . . Who would into God's Kingdom go Must flee them so."

[68] For one way to explore some of the issues here, which includes mention of Ernst Troeltsch's church, sect, and spiritualist distinctions, pp. 23–24, see Donald F. Durnbaugh, *The Believers' Church: The History and Character of Radical Protestantism* (New York: The MacMillan Company, 1968).

[69] Müntzer has recently fascinated scholars: Eric W. Gritsch, *A Tragedy of Errors: Thomas Müntzer* (Minneapolis: Fortress Press, 1989), which followed Eric

against Luther and felt more kinship with Andreas Karlstadt, was
tortured and beheaded because of his support for the Peasants' War,
yet his version of the Mass was quite conservative along the lines of
Luther's reforms.[70] Had Müntzer not been killed he might have
made more radical changes. Zwingli's first liturgical reforms, for
example, were also quite conservative.[71]

Conrad Grebel (c. 1498–1526)[72] found a kindred spirit in
Müntzer,[73] but discovered Müntzer encouraged the congregation to
sing German hymns. "That cannot be right," Grebel wrote to
Müntzer.[74] Grebel was a Zwinglian in every regard but two. First,
he rejected infant baptism. He wanted to baptize only professing
Christians. That stance necessitated what opponents called "rebap-
tizing" those who had been baptized (*ana* + baptist = one who bap-
tizes again). He performed the first "rebaptism" in Zurich in January of 1525. Second, whereas Zwingli thought reform came about
by evangelical preaching and discussions by the town council act-
ing as the church council, Grebel wanted immediate action.[75]

As to music in worship, Grebel argued an essentially Zwinglian
position against it.[76] The earliest Anabaptist service we know about
followed Grebel in this matter. It comes from Balthasar Hubmaier
(1482–1528)[77] in 1527 who described a properly celebrated Lord's

W. Gritsch, *Reformer Without a Church: The Life and Thought of Thomas Müntzer*
(1488 [?] – 1525 (Philadelphia: Fortress Press, 1967); Abraham Friesen, *Thomas
Müntzer, a Destroyer of the Godless: The Making of a Sixteenth-Century Religious
Revolutionary* (Berkeley: University of California Press, 1990); Hans-Jürgen Goertz,
Thomas Müntzer: Apocalyptic Mystic and Revolutionary (Edinburgh: T&T Clark,
1993). For studies of Oecolampadius, Karlstadt, and Müntzer, see Gordon Rupp,
Patterns of Reformation.

[70] See John K. Harms, "Music of the Radical Reformation I: Thomas Muentzer
and His Hymns and Liturgy," *Church Music* (77/2): 53–56, for Müntzer's account
of his reforms of the Mass.

[71] See Thompson, *Liturgies*, pp. 141–142.

[72] For a biography see Harold S. Bender, *Conrad Grebel, c.1498–1526, the
Founder of the Swiss Brethren Sometimes Called Anabaptists* (Goshen: The Mennonite Historical Society, 1950).

[73] Harms, "Music of the Radical Reformation II," p. 23.

[74] Ibid.

[75] Ibid., pp. 22–23.

[76] Harms, "Music of the Radical Reformation II," pp. 23–24, gives large quotations from Grebel's letter and discusses them. The musical parts of the letter are
also given in Music, HCSR, pp. 54–55.

[77] For a biography of Hubmaier, see Torsten Bergsten, trans., Irwin J. Barnes, ed.
William R. Estep, *Balthasar Hubmaier: Anabaptist Theologian and Martyr* (Valley
Forge: Judson Press, 1978).

Supper. Not unlike Zwingli's "Action or Use of the Lord's Supper" from 1525,[78] it omitted singing or any other music and added typical Anabaptist characteristics.[79]

The attempt to repudiate the church it found and to reinstate what it understood to be the true church led to excesses that brought disrepute on the Anabaptists. In 1534 and 1535 Anabaptists gained control of Münster in Westphalia. The Melchiorites Jan Beukels and Jan Mathijs set up a communal theocracy under their control, threw out those who would not be rebaptized, practiced Old Testament polygamy, claimed direct revelations, attracted many followers, and awaited an apocalyptic end to the world. The Batenburgers in the Netherlands were even more radical. They thought that anyone who did not agree with them should be killed.[80]

On the other hand, the pacifism of Menno Simons (1496–1561)[81] gives a different perspective on Anabaptism. So does Anabaptist hymnody, which flourished in spite of Grebel's Zwinglian position against it and Hubmaier's service. It flourished "without a trace of violence or hatred"[82] in the face of persecution and martyrdom both Protestants and Catholics served out. According to John Harms, "The doctrine of Christian love is found more than any other single belief in Anabaptist hymns"[83] and has continued to characterize the Anabaptist tradition.[84] Other doctrines and themes are there as

[78] See Thompson, *Liturgies*, pp. 149–156.

[79] It was conceived in the Anabaptist context of a small and closely knit community of followers of Christ who took baptism as the badge of discipleship that might lead to suffering and martyrdom. Meeting in "a suitable time and place," probably someone's house, the order was: confession by the priest on his knees; scripture expounded by the priest, the "servant of the Word"; questions (not frivolous and not by women) asked by the congregation; an exposition of I Corinthians 11 as in Zwingli, with emphasis on service to others and public testimony in which one offers one's own blood; silence; a pledge of love with assent by each person individually; the elements received; and a concluding exhortation. See H. Wayne Pipkin and John H. Yoder, trans., *Balthasar Hubmaier: Theologian of Anabaptism* (Scottdale: Herald Press, 1989), pp. 393–406.

[80] Harms, "Music of the Radical Reformation II," pp. 29–30.

[81] See George, *Theology of the Reformers*, pp. 252–307, for a description of Menno Simons' position.

[82] Harms, "Music of the Radical Reformation II," p. 25.

[83] Ibid.

[84] One form Anabaptist tradition takes is the "right remembering" Dave and Neta Jackson describe. See Dave and Neta Jackson, *On Fire for Christ: Stories of Anabaptist Martyrs Retold from Martyrs Mirror* (Scottdale: Herald Press, 1989), p. 26.

well—baptism, the Lord's Supper, footwashing, the Trinity, sorrow, persecution, martyrdom, loneliness, the use of the ban—all in the context of praise and triumph.[85]

Anabaptist hymnody grew out of martyr ballads. Luther's first hymn was a martyr ballad that celebrated the death of two young men in the Netherlands.[86] Luther never wrote another hymn like it, but between 1537 and 1540 some Anabaptists imprisoned in a castle on the Danube River in Bavaria did.[87] In 1564, fifty-three of their hymns appeared under the title, "Quite a few beautiful Christian hymns as they were composed and sung by Swiss brothers in the prison of the castle of Passau through God's grace." In 1583 the next edition of this book added other hymns, turned the former title into part of a subtitle, and called the result the *Ausbund*[88] (model, paragon, epitome). It is the title of the hymnal, which, with other additions, the group of Mennonites called Amish still use. In one of history's ironies, this group from the radical reformation, which followed the more radical Mennonite elder Jacob Amann (c. 1644–c.1730), became one of the most conservative Christian groups with a hymnal and customs more than four centuries old. The tunes still employed may include some secular ones from the sixteenth century, chorale melodies, at least one melody from the Latin chant repertoire, and a Genevan Psalter influence.[89] They have been transmitted orally, are led by a *Vorsinger* who "sets the pitch and sings the first syllable of each line before the rest of the congregation joins him, singing in unison" without instruments.[90] The

---

[85] Paul M. Yoder, "The Ausbund," *Four Hundred Years with the Ausbund* (Scottdale: Herald Press, 1964), p. 6.

[86] LW 53, pp. 214–216.

[87] See Paul M. Yoder, "The Ausbund," *Four Hundred Years with the Ausbund*, p. 5.

[88] For a bibliographic history of this book, see Nelson P. Springer, "The Editions of the Ausbund," *Four Hundred Years with the Ausbund*, pp. 31–40. The second edition known was published in 1583, increased the number of hymns from 53 to 131, and included "Ausbund" in the title: *Ausbund, Etlicher schöner Christlicher Geseng wie in der Gefengnuss zu Passaw im Schloss von den Schweitzern und auch von andern rechtgläubigen Christen hin und her gedicht worden* (n. p., 1583). For a broader Anabaptist bibliography of hymnody, see Hans J. Hillerbrand, *Anabaptist Bibliography, 1520–1630* (St. Louis: Center for Reformation Research, 1991), pp. 469–480, and Martin E. Ressler, *An Annotated Bibliography of Mennonite Hymnals and Songbooks, 1742–1986* (Gordonville: PA Print Shop, 1987).

[89] Paul M. Yoder, "The Ausbund," *Four Hundred Years with the Ausbund*, pp. 8–9.

[90] Harvey Graber, "The Contemporary Use of the Ausbund in Worship," *Four Hundred Years with the Ausbund*, p. 26.

hymnody can be complex and embellished.[91] It varies in tempo and may be quite slow. The *Loblied* (also called the *Lobsang*, number 131 in the *Ausbund*), has four stanzas of seven lines, which can take from eleven to more than twenty minutes to sing.[92]

Not all Mennonites followed the Amish. Some developed a rich four-part, a cappella hymn-singing tradition for the congregation, sometimes with supremely talented musicians such as Mary Oyer and Kenneth Nafziger in our day to give a pitch and set it off. Others have used the organ, much the same as Protestants generally. Shirley King at Bethel College in North Newton, Kansas, ably represents that tradition.

The Church of the Brethren, an eighteenth-century "anabaptist" group in the Palatinate who were influenced by Pietism and drew their members from Reformed and Lutheran churches, once again found persecution stimulated hymnody. They defied a prohibition against adult baptism, and in 1717 the "Solingen Brethren" were imprisoned. As they were led on a twenty-mile march to the prison in Düsseldorf they sang hymns.[93]

The hymnic heritages of the Mennonites[94] and the Brethren are joined today in the *Hymnal: A Worship Book Prepared by Churches in the Believers Tradition*.[95] That hymnal represents a European lineage. For the English Baptists and their Puritan world, which came to have a strong influence on the American continent, we turn to seventeenth-century England.

[91] Ibid., p. 27. See also the notated version of the *Lobsang*, p. 44.

[92] Ibid., p. 27.

[93] For a study of the hymnody of the Brethren, see Donald R. Hinks, *Brethren Hymn Books and Hymnals, 1720–1884* (Gettysburg: Brethren Heritage Press, 1986), and Hedwig T. Durnbaugh, *The German Hymnody of the Brethren, 1720–1903* (Philadelphia: Brethren Encyclopedia, 1986). For the history of the church itself, see Donald F. Durnbaugh, *European Origins of the Brethren* (Elgin: The Brethren Press, 1958).

[94] For further bibliographic aids in the sixteenth-century Anabaptist heritage, see Anita Breckbill, "The Hymns of the Anabaptist: An English-Language Bibliography," *The Hymn* 39:3 (July 1988): 21–23.

[95] *Hymnal: A Worship Book Prepared by Churches in the Believers Church Tradition* (Elgin: Brethren Press, 1992).

12

Controversies Over Psalm Singing

Psalm Singing

After Calvin and his followers in sixteenth-century Geneva and Strasbourg chose to embrace metrical psalmody as their congregational
song, psalm singing became a staple of much of the English-speaking
church as well. Psalters were produced, singing metrical psalms
became common, and orders of worship included it.

English psalters were produced in profusion throughout the sixteenth and seventeenth centuries.[1] The Sternhold-Hopkins "Old Version" of 1562 is the most obvious example. Less well-known ones
form a long list. In 1612 Henry Ainsworth[2] published *The Book of
Psalms, Englished, both in Prose and Metre*[3] for the Separatist Church
at Amsterdam whom we often call the "Pilgrims." They brought this
book with them to Plymouth in 1620. It's the "well-worn psalmbook
of Ainsworth" on Priscilla's lap in Henry Wadsworth Longfellow's
poem, "The Courtship of Miles Standish." The first book the "Puritans" printed in New England was the "Bay Psalm Book,"[4] in 1640.

---

[1] John Julian and William T. Brooke, "List of Complete and Partial Versions of
the Psalter in English from 1414 to 1889," DH, pp. 926–928, list 106 psalters in the
sixteenth and seventeenth centuries, only one before that. The total from 1414 until
1889 (pp. 926–932) is 326.

[2] Henry Ainsworth (1570–c.1622) was a Hebrew scholar and leader of the
Brownists who left England and led his congregation in Amsterdam.

[3] [Henry Ainsworth], *The Book of Psalms, Englished, both in Prose and Metre*
(Amsterdam: Giles Thorp, 1612).

[4] The actual title is *The Whole Book of Psalmes Faithfully Translated into English
Metre* (1640). See Zoltan Haraszti, ed., *The Bay Psalm Book: A Facsimile Reprint of
the First Edition of 1640* (Chicago: The University of Chicago Press, 1956), Wilberforce Eames, ed., *The Bay Psalm Book: A facsimile reprint of the First Edition with
a list of later editions* (New York: Lenox Hill, n. d.), and Zoltan Haraszti, *The Enigma
of the Bay Psalm Book* (Chicago: The University of Chicago Press, 1956).

In 1641 Francis Rous[5] (1579–1659) revised the "Old Version," then did it again in 1643 and 1646; the last of these revisions was authorized for general use by the Westminster Assembly. In 1644 William Barton[6] (1598–1678) published the first of numerous editions of a metrical psalter. The third edition of Francis Roberts's[7] (1609–1675) *Clavis Bibliorum* included an entire metrical version of the psalms. In 1648 and 1653 John Milton[8] (1609–1674) cast some psalms into English meter. Richard Baxter[9] (1615–1691) worked out a complete metrical psalter that was published after his death in 1692 by Matthew Sylvester under the title *Paraphrase of the Psalms of David, with other Hymns.*

Apart from the psalters, the popularity of psalm-singing is attested to in other ways. The famous letter of John Jewel[10] (1522–1571) is one of these. In 1560 he wrote from London,

> As soon as they had commenced singing in public, in only one little church in London, immediately not only the churches in the neighborhood, but even the towns far distant, began to vie with each other in the same practice. You may sometimes see at St. Paul's Cross, after the service, six thousand persons, old and young, of both sexes, all singing together and praising God.[11]

The Pilgrims from Leyden, before embarking on their journey to the New World, sang psalms.[12] Cromwell's[13] men at Dunbar sang

---

[5] Francis Rous received the B.A. from Oxford and made violent attacks against Arminians and the papacy. He moved from a Presbyterian to an Independent and exuded an intensely mystical and subjective piety.

[6] William Barton, a conforming Puritan, was vicar in Leicester, Mayfield, and Staffordshire.

[7] Francis Roberts received the B.A. and the M.A. from Oxford and joined the Presbyterians at the beginning of the Civil War.

[8] John Milton, author of *Paradise Lost*, was a Puritan who attacked episcopacy, the church establishment, and the orthodox understanding of the Trinity.

[9] Richard Baxter was a self-educated Presbyterian clergyman who attempted to see both sides of issues and perhaps comes the closest among the Puritans to a Lutheran understanding of music.

[10] John Jewel was the Anglican bishop of Salisbury, influenced by Peter Martyr, who wrote the *Apology of the Church of England.*

[11] Bishop Jewel to Peter Martyr (London, March 5, 1560), in Hastings Robinson, ed., *The Zurich Letters* (Cambridge: The University Press, 1842), I, 71. See also Temperley, *The Music of the English Parish Church*, I, p. 43.

[12] See Rowland E. Prothero, *The Psalms in Human Life* (New York: E. P. Dutton and Company, 1941), p. 223f.

[13] Oliver Cromwell (1599–1658), Independent and Lord Protector of England during the Commonwealth, was a brilliant general who chose his soldiers for their religious commitment as well as their military skill.

Psalm 117.[14] Percy Scholes quotes Webster's *The Duchess of Malfi*, IV.2, to indicate how the Puritans overdid psalm-singing: "He makes alum and sells it to Puritans that have sore throats with overstraining."[15] The Puritans have now come into view.

Puritans

By 1570, during the reign of Elizabeth I, a group known as Puritans had arisen in England. They regarded the English *via media* as a patched-up Romanism, a halfway house. They wanted to get on with the Reformation on basically Reformed premises. A university movement that regarded English priests as "dumb dogs," Puritanism at first aimed to reform from within the Church of England. Gradually some Puritans became disillusioned about the possibilities. They are called Separatists. Non-Separatists were in some respects broadly identifiable with Presbyterians, while Separatists were identified with Independents (Congregationalists), Baptists, and other smaller groups. Separatists were less happy with liturgical "set forms" than the non-Separatists, and in 1644 at the Westminster Assembly, when Lord Protector Oliver Cromwell was in power, the "Westminster Directory for the Publique Worship of God" was hammered out as a compromise. Instead of a liturgy, it was a series of rubrics or directions that those who wanted set forms could, by changing the wording here and there, fashion into prayers.[16]

Whatever their perspective Puritans generally sang metrical psalms, and Puritan orders of worship included psalm-singing. John à Lasco (1499–1566) who led the Reformed Church of Strangers (foreign Reformed people of various nationalities) from 1550 to 1553 in London described psalm singing there after the Lord's Prayer and at the end of the service.[17] His example may have influenced the English. *The Forme of Prayers,* which in 1556 issued from the English congregation at Geneva, included a psalm prior to the sermon, one after the creed (during this psalm the elements were brought forward[18]), and one before the final blessing.[19] The

---

[14] Horton Davies, *The Worship of the English Puritans* (Westminster: Dacre Press, 1948), hereafter WEP, p. 180.

[15] Percy Scholes, *The Puritans and Music* (New York: Russell & Russell, 1962), p. 274.

[16] See Thompson, *Liturgies*, pp. 345–371.

[17] Temperley, *The Music of the English Parish Church*, I, p. 18, gives à Lasco's directions.

[18] See Bard Thompson, ed., *Liturgies of the Western Church* (Cleveland: The World Publishing Company, 1961), p. 307.

[19] Ibid., pp. 295–305.

Middleburgh Liturgy of 1586[20] added more psalm-singing: prior to
the service, as the people gathered (for an hour or so), the Bible was
read in course with psalm-singing between the readings;[21] in the service itself a psalm preceded the sermon, preceded the final blessing,
and probably served as an offertory when the Lord's Supper was
celebrated.[22] In the Westminster Directory of 1644 a psalm followed the reading of the word prior to the confessional prayer
before the sermon, and a psalm preceded the final blessing.[23]
Richard Baxter's Savoy Liturgy of 1661[24] indicated more latitude
and dependence on the *Book of Common Prayer*. There a psalm
could be sung or the Te Deum said between the Old Testament and
New Testament lessons, a psalm or the Benedictus or Magnificat
could follow the New Testament lesson, and at the close of the
communion service "the Hymn in metre, or some other fit Psalm of
praise" preceded the final blessing.[25]

Objections

Though psalm singing enjoyed broad support, that support was not
universal. As early as 1539 "the Puritans . . . apparently fanned
opposition to singing with 'conjoint voices' and contributed to the
eventual burning of Coverdale's *Goostly Psalmes and Spiritualle
Songs*."[26] In 1586 Puritans proposed

> That all Cathedral Churches may be put down where the service of God
> is grievously abused by piping with organs, singing, ringing, and trowl-
> ing of Psalms from one side of the choir to the other.[27]

Separatist groups tended to be most suspicious of singing metrical
psalms. The Barrowists (flourishing from 1587 to 1593[28]) at first did
not use psalms or hymns at all.

---

[20] Ibid., pp. 322–340.

[21] Ibid., p. 315.

[22] Ibid., p. 334.

[23] Ibid., pp. 354–371.

[24] Ibid., pp. 385–404.

[25] Ibid., p. 404.

[26] Davies, WEP, p. 168. Miles Coverdale's *Goostly Psalmes* is one of the earliest
metrical psalters, dependent on German Lutheran models rather than Genevan ones.
Coverdale (1487–1569) was a rector who was educated at Cambridge, came into
contact with the continental reformers, espoused their cause, and in 1535 translated
the Bible.

[27] Davies, WEP, p. 168.

[28] Horton Davies, *WTE*, I, 327f.

Francis Johnson, a Barrowist pastor in Kamden and Naarden, however, introduced psalm-singing in his congregation. Franc-Iohnson (being advised by one that talked with him thereabouts in the *Clinke* at London) did presse the use of our singing Psalmes (neglected before of his people for Apocrypha;) whereupon his Congregation publikely in their meetings used them. . . .[29]

Henry Barrowe[30] himself did not oppose singing of psalms as such, but was against metrical psalms and hymns. In a dispute with Gifford he wrote that he was not

against that most comfortable and heavenly harmony of singing psalms, but against the rhyming and paraphrasing the Psalms as in your Church; nor yet . . . so much against that, as against the apocrypha erroneous ballads in rhyme sung commonly in your Church instead of the Psalms and holy songs of the canonical Scriptures.[31]

Robert Browne[32] and his followers (Brownists) rejected singing metrical psalms because singing of a group ("with conjoint voices") required a "set form" and because singing a metrical psalm was an alteration of the words and possibly the thoughts of scripture.[33] Psalms also reminded Browne of antiphonal psalm-singing, which he considered vanity and "gaming" in worship.[34] Extemporaneous singing of a single person was apparently acceptable.[35]

[29] Quoted in Davies, *WTE*, I, 331.

[30] Henry Barrowe (c. 1550–1593) was converted at a preaching service in London, gave up law, and was one of the founders of congregationalism.

[31] Benjamin Hanbury, *Historical Memorials Relating to the Independents or Congregationalists* (London: Fisher, Son, & Co., 1839), I, 61.

[32] Robert Browne (c. 1550–c. 1633), like Henry Barrowe, was from Cambridge and founded an Independent congregation. He went to Holland, but returned to England, rejoined the Anglican church, and was episcopally ordained. His *Treatise of Reformation without Tarrying for Any* is a staple of Congregationalism.

[33] See Davies, WEP, 168f. and J. Spencer Curwen, *Studies in Worship Music* (London: J. Curwen & Sons, 1880), p. 80.

[34] "Their tossing to & fro of psalmes & senteses, is like tenisse plaie vvereunto God is called a Iudge vvho can do best & be most gallant in his vvorship: as bie organs, solfaing, pricksong, chauting, bussing & mumling verie roundlie, on diuers handes. Thus thei haue a shevve of religion but indeed thei turne it to gaming & plaie mock holidaie vvith the worship of God." Robert Browne (?), *A True and Short Declaration* (1583?) in Albert Peel and Leland H. Carlson, ed., *The Writings of Robert Harrison and Robert Browne* (London: George Allen and Unwin Ltd, 1953), p. 415.

[35] See Curwen, p. 80. Paul Richardson has supplied me with a copy of Katherine Sutton, *Christian Womans [sic] Experiences of the glorious working of Gods [sic] free grace* (Rotterdam: Henry Goddaeus, 1663), which indicates the importance

A similar position was taken by the early Baptists. John Smyth,[36] pastor of the Gainsborough Separatists who fled to Amsterdam in 1608, wrote the following in that year.

We hould that the worship of the new testament properly so called is spirituall proceeding originally from the hart: & that reading out of a book (though a lawful ecclesiastical action) is no part of spiritual worship. . . .

We hould that seeing singing a psalme is a parte of spirituall worship therefore it is unlawful to have the book before the eye in time of singing a psalme.[37]

In his *Certain demaundes* Smyth asked the following rhetorical questions:

Whither the Apostles did not pray, prophesy, & sing Psalmes as the holy ghost gave them vtterance?

Whither as in prayer & prophesy one alone speaketh, & the rest pray & prophesy by consent. I cor. 11.4 so in a Psalm one onely must co[n]set. I cor. 14. 16.

Whither in a Psalme a man must be tyed to meter & Rithme, & tune, & whither voluntary be not as necessary in tune & words as in matter?

Whither meter, Rithme, & tune, be not quenching the Spirit?[38]

In 1609 Henry Ainsworth responded, asking why Smyth allowed singing in worship but did not practice it.[39] The query indicates that

---

of immediate experience and therefore of extemporaneity. Sutton recounts the hymns she extemporized, and concludes her book with these words; "I assure you COURTEOUS READER these are not studed [sic] things, but are given in immediately."

[36] John Smyth (c. 1544–1612) came from Cambridge and was a priest in the Church of England before he left the Anglicans and joined the Gainsborough Separatists.

[37] John Smyth, *The Difference of the Churches of the Separation* (1608), in W. T. Whitley, ed., *The Works of John Smyth* (Cambridge: University Press, 1915), I, 273.

[38] John Smyth, *Certayne demaundes from the auncyent brethren of the Separation, whereto wee desire direct & sound answer, with proof from the Scripture,* in Whitley, *The Works of John Smyth,* II, pp. 324–325.

[39] Henry Ainsworth, *A Defense of the Holy Scriptures, Worship, and Ministerie, used in the Christian Churches separated from Antichrist: Against the challenges, cavils and contradiction of M. Smyth: in his book intituled The Differences of the Churches of the Separation* (Amsterdam: Giles Thorp, 1609), p. 22. See Curwen, *Studies in Worship Music,* p. 80f., and Robert H. Young, "The History of Baptist

even the extemporaneous singing by an individual, which was permitted, did not happen.

The objections to psalm singing in the latter half of the seventeenth century were sufficiently strong to produce a series of treatises for and against the practice, including the following:[40]

- *The Preface* to the *Bay Psalm Book* (1640)
- Francis Cornwell,[41] *Some Reasons Against Stinted Forms of Praising God in Psalms* (1646)
- John Cotton,[42] *Singing of Psalmes a Gospel Ordinance* (1647)
- Edward Drapes,[43] *Gospel-Glory Proclaimed Before the Sonnes of Men in the Visible and Invisible Worship of God* (1649)
- Thomas Ford,[44] *5 Sermons on Singing of Psalms the Duty of Christians under the New Testament* (1653)
- Cuthbert Sydenham (also Sidenham),[45] *A Christian, Sober, and Plain Exercitation of these Times; Infant Baptism and Singing of Psalms* (1653)
- William Kaye,[46] *Baptism Without Bason or Plain Scripture— Proof Against Infant Baptism* (1653)
- Thomas Grantham,[47] *Christianismus Primitivus* (1678)
- Hercules Collins,[48] *An Orthodox Catechism* (1680)

Hymnody in England from 1612 to 1800" (Los Angeles: University of Southern California, Doctor of Musical Arts diss., 1959), pp. 10–13.

[40] For detailed descriptions of the Baptist components of this controversy, see Young, "The History of Baptist . . . ," and Carry Edward Spann, "The Seventeenth Century English Baptist Controversy Concerning Singing," Master of Church Music dissertation (Fort Worth; Southern Baptist Theological Seminary, 1965). Spann, pp. 220–222, also gives a chronology.

[41] Francis Cornwell was a Particular Baptist.

[42] John Cotton (1564–1652) was a graduate of Cambridge and lecturer and dean at Emmanuel College who gradually took a non-Separating Puritan stance. He was forced to flee from London in 1632 and became teacher at First Church in Boston.

[43] Drapes followed Smyth. See Young, "The History of Baptist . . . ," p. 20.

[44] Thomas Ford was a minister in Exeter, England.

[45] Cuthbert Sydenham (1622–1654) was a Presbyterian pastor and lecturer.

[46] William Kaye was a Particular Baptist minister at Stokesley. See Young, "The History of Baptist . . . ," p. 22.

[47] Thomas Grantham was a leading General Baptist minister, baptized in 1653, who became president of the General Association of General Baptists. See Young, "The History of Baptist . . . ," p. 15, and Spann, "The Seventeenth Century English Baptist Controversy Concerning Singing," pp. 40–57, 77.

[48] Hercules Collins, a Particular Baptist minister, countered Grantham by arguing for congregational singing. See Spann, "The Seventeenth Century English Baptist Controversy Concerning Singing," pp. 42–57.

- Isaac Marlow, *A Brief Discourse Concerning, or rather Against Singing* (1690)
- Isaac Marlow, *An Appendix* (1691)
- Benjamin Keach, *The Breach Repair'd in God's Worship: or, Singing of Psalms, Hymns, and Spiritual Songs proved to be an Holy Ordinance of Jesus Christ. With an Answer to all Objections. As Also an Examination of Mr. Isaac Marlow's two papers, one called, A Discourse against singing, &c. the other an Appendix* (1691).[49]

The Issues

John Cotton (1564–1652), a nonseparating Congregationalist who fled England in 1632 and became a leading teacher at First Church in Boston, in *Singing of Psalmes a Gospel Ordinance*[50] summarized the central issues of this seventeenth century dispute. He divided them into four categories: the duty, the matter, the singers, and the manner of singing.

As to the duty,[51] Cotton was convinced that singing of psalms with the actual voice is a duty for Christians. He proposed three "proofs": first, Ephesians 5:19, Colossians 3:16, and I Corinthians 14:15–16 all meant for him the actual use of the voice, not just singing with the heart; second, the New Testament provides numerous examples: Christ and the disciples after the Lord's Supper (Matthew 26:30), and Paul and Silas singing in prison (Acts 16:25); third, the Old Testament prophecies—Isaiah 52:8, Psalm 100:1, and Psalm 95:1ff.—foretell the New Testament duty. Cotton's most telling point is, perhaps, that if our hearts sing with joy and our glory (our tongue) is silent, we dishonor our "chief singer Christ" because Christ himself rejoiced with his glory (his tongue) at his last supper.

As to the matter,[52] Cotton sounds like a true Calvinist. In private, he says, Christians may use psalms or other scriptural songs or even newly composed ones. Instruments may even be employed. In pub-

---

[49] This was not the end of the controversy. Marlow especially continued it, others also got involved, and between 1696 and 1698 it started all over. See Spann, "The Seventeenth Century English Baptist Controversy Concerning Singing," pp. 8off.

[50] John Cotton, *Singing of Psalmes a Gospel Ordinance* (London, 1650). Both Haraszti and Davies refer to a 1647 edition, but the one I worked from at the Newberry Library in Chicago is from 1650.

[51] Cotton, *Singing of Psalmes a Gospel Ordinance*, p. 2ff.

[52] Ibid., p. 14ff.

lic gatherings of the church, however, though a special occasion may
call forth a psalm composed by a member of the congregation, normally it is the Psalms of David that are to be employed. Why?
Because both Ephesians 5:19 and Colossians 3:16 tell us to sing
Psalms, Hymns, and Spiritual Songs, which, says Cotton, are the
titles of David's Psalms (an interesting notion!).

The question of whether it is acceptable to use set, or precom-
posed, forms then arises. Cotton says there is a difference between
set forms of prayer and set forms of psalms. The former are of
human devising, while the latter are appointed by God.

Finally, Cotton tells us that Colossians 3:16 instructs us to use
psalms for instruction, admonition, and for praise and thanksgiving to God. Then, he says, since no ordinance appoints someone to
"psalmistry" as they do for preaching, prayer, and rule (that is,
elders), the whole body of believers has to sing the psalms.

The third problem concerns who is supposed to sing. It encompasses three subheads: whether one person ought to sing followed
by a corporate "Amen," whether women may join men, and
whether "carnall Men or pagans" may join Christians.

First, says Cotton, all ought to sing.[53] This gets convoluted in
usual Puritan fashion, with copious biblical citations, but essentially
Cotton says singing is not prophecy in which only one person
speaks, it is not confusion when all sing together though it has no
scriptural example, scriptural warrant for it is there, and singing
together does not make everyone a teacher since only the one who
appoints the psalm is the teacher.

Second,[54] women are not permitted to teach or ask questions in
church, but they may confess their sins and may sing.

Third,[55] Cotton argues that the church is called to sing for mutual
edification, that praising God with psalms is comely for the upright
whether or not they are members of the church, and that the chief
ground for psalm singing is that it is a duty laid on all people.
Singing instructs the wicked, he says, and it is the job of the whole
creation to glorify God.

The last big issue, the manner of singing,[56] refers in the first
instance to whether it is lawful to devise meter and tunes. Well, says

[53] Ibid., p. 37ff.
[54] Ibid., p. 46ff.
[55] Ibid., p. 44ff.
[56] Ibid., p. 54ff.

Cotton, if it's lawful to translate the Bible, it must be lawful to translate the psalms. And since God has hidden from us the music that
originally accompanied those psalms, in typical Calvinist language
Cotton says it must be that God allows us

> to sing them in any such grave, and solemne, and plain Tunes, as doe
> fitly suite the gravitie of the matter, the solemnitie of God's worship, and
> the capacitie of a plaine People.[57]

Further, says Cotton, meters and tunes help the memory and stir
up the affections.

The other issue here is lining out, an expedient adopted "for the
present" by the Westminster Assembly of 1644 to make singing of
psalms possible if people could not read or did not have books. A
precentor or other leader spoke or sang each line, answered by the
people who repeated the very same line. This practice creates a call
and response pattern that not only lengthens, but substantively
alters the form of the hymn. It's the form Idelssohn called "didactic."[58] Where people have books, said Cotton, it is needless. Otherwise it is necessary and done by one of the elders.

Benjamin Keach

Like John Smyth, Baptists in seventeenth-century England were generally opposed to psalm singing in worship.[59] In 1689 the General
Baptist Assembly concluded that psalm singing was "so strangely
foreign to the evangelical worship that it was not conceived anyways
safe to admit such carnal formalities."[60] Benjamin Keach
(1640–1704), a Particular Baptist[61] minister, at first opposed singing
with "conjoint voices" in the usual Baptist fashion, but changed his

---

[57] Ibid., p. 56.

[58] See chapter 2.

[59] William J. Reynolds, *Companion to Baptist Hymnal* (Nashville: Broadman
Press, 1976), p. 349.

[60] W. T. Whitley, ed., Minutes of the General Assembly of the General Baptist
Churches, I, 27, quoted in Davies, WTE, III, 127.

[61] Particular Baptists were less opposed to singing than General Baptists. See
Spann, "The Seventeenth Century English Baptist Controversy Concerning
Singing," p. 16. [Particular Baptists believed in "particular" election and predesti-
nation. The General Baptists were Arminian and believed God's offer of grace was
universal, that human beings could respond in faith. The first Baptist churches in
America—Roger Williams in Providence, Rhode Island (1630), and John Clarke in
Newport, Rhode, Island (1641)—were Particular Baptists.]

mind. Between 1671 and 1675 he introduced singing into his church
at Horselydown at the Lord's Supper.[62] Between 1677 and 1679 he
introduced the practice "in mixt Assemblies on Days of Thanksgiving," at Baptisms, and on other occasions.[63] Sometime before 1691
his congregation decided with only five or six negative votes to sing
on Lord's Days after the sermon and "when Prayer ended."[64] This
decision split the congregation: twenty-two people left and founded
the Maze Pond Church (which later, in the eighteenth century,
admitted singing).[65]

At about the same time a lay member of a church in Mile End
Green named Isaac Marlow who opposed singing in worship put his
thoughts in writing in a tract called *A Brief Discourse Concerning
Singing in the Public Worship of God in the Gospel Church*.[66] Keach
responded with *The Breach Repair'd*. Before Keach's pamphlet was
off the press, Marlow published an Appendix, to which Keach
responded with an Appendix of his own.[67] A hot pamphlet war followed.[68]

Keach wrote half a century after Cotton. He quoted him, Sydenham, Francis Roberts, Barton, and others. Keach's writing can be
viewed as a freewheeling, rambling summary of Cotton and those
who followed him, with additions and specific answers to Marlow.
However, he expanded Cotton's Calvinist stance: he saw no reason
to restrict congregational song to psalms and wanted to include
hymns as well.[69]

For Keach the "breach" was the "lost and neglected ordinance of
singing Psalms, Hymns, and Spiritual Songs."[70] Restoration of

---

[62] See Benjamin Keach, *The Breach Repair'd in God's Worship* (London, 1691),
p. vii, and *An Answer to Mr. Marlowe's Appendix* (bound with *The Breach Repair'd*
with separate pagination), p. 8. *Cf.* W. R. Stevenson, "Baptist Hymnody, English,"
in John Julian, DH, I, 111.

[63] Keach, *The Breach Repair'd in God's Worship*, p. 8.

[64] Ibid.

[65] See Spann, "The Seventeenth Century English Baptist Controversy Concerning
Singing," p. 72, and J. Spencer Curwen, *Studies in Worship Music* (London: J. Curwen & Sons, 1880), p. 96ff.

[66] See Keach, *The Breach Repair'd*, p. vii; *An Answer*, p. 8.

[67] See Young, "The History of Baptist . . . ," pp. 37–40.

[68] See Spann, "The Seventeenth Century English Baptist Controversy Concerning
Singing," pp. 8off.

[69] Keach, though not a very good hymnwriter, is nonetheless justly credited with
introducing hymnody into the worship of the Dissenters. With Baxter he is important in the hymnological development that led to Isaac Watts.

[70] Keach, *The Breach Repair'd*, p. vi.

singing, said Keach, would make the congregation "compleat in the whole will of God."[71] It was very strong language, but it is even stronger if you consider the choice of the words "ordinance" and "breach." To call singing an "ordinance" puts it on a par with baptism and the Lord's Supper, which Baptists call "ordinances." And Keach used the word "breach" in one of his hymns to describe the break between God and humanity caused by sin.

> A Breach most sore there was between
> > Poor Sinners, Lord, and thee;
> Before the Fall nought then was seen
> > But perfect amity.[72]

This "breach" was clearly a very serious matter for Keach. He pointed out that just because a group such as Roman Catholics or Quakers holds some errors is no reason to suppose that they hold no truth at all.[73] Singing needed to be restored, he argued, no matter how hard that restoration may be and no matter who else did or did not do it. Keach launched therefore into a lengthy section that essentially says it's nonsense to talk of singing with the heart and without the voice, and then he was off to all the other issues Cotton and the others had covered.

Quakers (*Society of Friends*)

The Quakers to whom Keach referred stood at the opposite end of the spectrum from him. They took the Puritan potential for mysticism and the logic against set forms the farthest of any group. They outdistanced even Marlow or Zwingli in removing music.

George Fox (1624–1692)[74] was an unlearned shoemaker who wandered about England in quest of faith.[75] He found no help from existing groups and concluded that a person's life should be guided by the light within. Several years after the Westminster Assembly, perhaps around 1647, he began a ministry that recruited especially

---

[71] Ibid., p. v.

[72] Benjamin Keach, *Spiritual Melody, Containing near Three Hundred Sacred Hymns* (London: John Hancock, 1691), hymn 17, p. 35.

[73] Keach, *The Breach Repair'd*, p. 1. *Cf.* p. 123.

[74] See H. Larry Ingle, *First Among Friends: George Fox and the Creation of Quakerism* (New York: Oxford University Press, 1994).

[75] Fox's autobiography is available as *The Journal of George Fox* (Cambridge: University Press, 1952).

from "dissatisfied Baptists and Independents."[76] Those who joined
the Quakers, like Anabaptists, were persecuted. Their pacifism alone
was sufficient to make them seem dangerous. They grew and organized nevertheless, and Fox managed to travel through England,
Wales, Scotland, Ireland, Europe, the West Indies, and the American
colonies. From the community in Scotland Robert Barclay
(1648–1690)[77] emerged as a Quaker apologist. His *Apology for the
True Christian Divinity* from 1676 is a standard explanation of
Quaker thought.[78]

Cyril Richardson summarized the Quaker position in this manner.[79] You don't need ordained ministers. You need "professors,"
that is, people who earnestly profess the faith with simplicity. Fox's
mystic visions had the consequence of rescuing him from affectation,
one of the greatest temptations. To lead a simple and earnest life
meant for seventeenth-century Quakers that they did not call someone else "you," a plural form that made one seem as important as
a whole colony. They did not take their hat off to someone else
because that unduly elevated the other person. Males and females
were equal. Quakers dressed simply, did not sign a letter "Your
humble servant" because they were only God's humble servants, did
not swear an oath in court because one's allegiance should be to God
alone, refused all luxuries, and would not participate in warfare,
which they regarded as contrary to the gospel. Lest this seem like a
series of negatives, Quakers have regarded their lifestyle as affirmative love of God, the neighbor, and Christ's kingdom of peace.[80]
Their way of making decisions points to this affirmative commitment. The community operated by a sense of the meeting.[81] There
were no Roberts's Rules of Order. Neither side was to attempt to

[76] "Quakers," *The Westminster Dictionary of Church History*, ed. Jerald C.
Brauer (Philadelphia: The Westminster Press, 1971), p. 684.

[77] For a biography, see Elton Trueblood, *Robert Barclay* (New York: Harper &
Row, 1968).

[78] Robert Barclay, *An Apology for the True Christian Divinity Being an Explanation and Vindication of the Principles and Doctrines of the People Called Quakers* (Philadelphia: Friends' Book Store, 1908), dedication to Charles II, signed 1675.

[79] Notes from two lectures on the Quakers by Cyril Richardson at Union Seminary, New York, New York, March 17 and 22, 1966.

[80] John S. Rowntree, *The Society of Friends: Its Faith and Practice* (London:
Headley Brothers, 1901).

[81] See Howard Haines Brinton, *Friends for Three Hundred Years; the History
and Beliefs of the Society of Friends Since George Fox Started the Quaker Movement* (New York: Harper, 1952), pp. 99–117.

convince the other side. Instead everyone was to share disagreements until a mystic unity arose, striving for such a unity even if it took a long time.

At worship this position worked itself out as holy silence, interpreted as "Holy Obedience."[82] The silence was regarded as fullness, not as emptiness. The point was to enter the depth of one's self and come upon God, the inner light. Since the internal was seen as so important, the external was correspondingly devalued. If you go to a Quaker service, you will find it held in a plain room, with no symbols or vestments or icons—as little as possible of what is external. This plainness means no prepared sermon or prayers, and no singing or music of any kind.[83] Robert Barclay said bluntly, "But as for the formal customary way of singing, it hath no foundation in scripture nor any ground in true Christianity."[84] As if that were not clear enough, Barclay reiterated the point and expanded it. "But as to their artificial music, either by organs, or other instruments, or voice, we have neither example nor precedent for it in the New Testament."[85] People enter a Quaker service quietly, sit, and at the appointed time the service is understood to begin. After an hour or so, a leader raps, the service ends, and announcements are made that usually concern needs for the world. A meal may follow in a nearby room.

Though there may be no speaking at all in a Quaker service, there is a discipline. It is called "centering down."[86] To "center down" is to come away from the superficial and hurried world to engage in a vital relaxation and wait on God. This practice may sound individualistic, but it is not understood that way. You "let thyself go" in the presence of God and of the community. You risk letting go to the community and blending with it. When this blending occurs

[82] Elton Trueblood, *The People Called Quakers* (New York: Harper & Row, 1966), p. 86.

[83] Some Quakers have modified their position to include "programmed" and "unprogrammed" services. The former are closer to Protestants with hymn singing before or after them, sometimes as part of them. The "unprogrammed" type expresses the classic Quaker position.

[84] Robert Barclay, *An Apology for the True Christian Divinity*, p. 386.

[85] Ibid., p. 387.

[86] A concise description is given in Marshall Hodgson, *So We Enter* (Chicago: 57th Street Meeting of Friends, 1966), [pp. 7–8]. Allan Glatthorn, "The Stages of Worship," *The Friends Journal* (December 1, 1961, reprinted by the Friends General Conference, Philadelphia), traces silent meditation through a series of "stages."

Quakers speak of a "gathered meeting." When it does not occur, they call the meeting "dry." A gathered meeting for the Quaker is mystical and could be regarded as what some Christians call sacramental: ". . . the ground and foundation of the gathered meeting is . . . the Real Presence of God."[87]

As the worshiper you do not seek out a subject for meditation. You let it emerge. If outward noises and disturbances occur, you accept them. Resistance is destructive. Mostly, you do not come prepared to speak—or not to speak.[88] A cardinal temptation is to rush into speech—or to avoid speaking when the current of worship is powerful.[89] You speak only if constrained to do so out of the communal mystical experience. Anyone who attends some Quaker meetings will sense how those who have lived the Quaker discipline speak little and with wisdom, while those who are newer to it speak more often and much more superficially but are nonetheless to be treated with respect and kindness.[90]

Reflections

The seventeenth-century English squabble about psalm singing, partly because of the detail Puritans exercised in their debates, may in some ways seem more quaint and antiquarian than earlier collisions we have encountered. But, like all the chapters in the history of the church's song, it too can teach us some things. Now that we have read a number of these chapters, a longer pause to reflect may be in order.

First, though singing at worship may seem self-evident to us, for some traditions it has been won through considerable struggle. Maybe vigilance is always necessary to retain it.

Second, we again encounter here the question of whether women should sing at worship. Even the permission for them to sing is less than satisfactory because it is linked to making public confession of

---

[87] Thomas R. Kelly, *The Gathered Meeting*, (Philadelphia: The Tract Association of Friends, n. d.), [p. 8]. For more detail see Howard Haines Brinton, *Friends for Three Hundred Years*, pp. 59–98.

[88] Trueblood, *The People Called Quakers*, p. 86.

[89] Kelly, *The Gathered Meeting*, [p. 4].

[90] For further description and thoughts, see M. A. Creasey, "Quaker Worship," *The New Westminster Directory of Liturgy and Worship* (Philadelphia: The Westminster Press, 1986), pp. 454–456.

their sins as one of the two things women may do when the church gathers. How tempted the church has been to back away from its New Testament roots that in Christ there is neither male nor female. How tempted the church has been to back away from the early church's ideal of singing with one voice. Vigilance is necessary not only for the song itself, but for the birthrights of all the singers.

Third, once more we encounter the idea that texts such as Colossians 3:16 can be understood to mean silent singing in the heart and not with the voice. We are not likely to argue the case for silent singing the way Zwingli or the opponents of Niceta of Remesiana or of Cotton and Keach did it. We are more likely not to argue it at all, but to do it in practice. We practice congregational silent singing every time we set up the leaders of worship as a self-contained unit so that the people and their singing become irrelevant. It can happen with organs and choirs, amplified vocalists and bands, synthesizers and other electronic equipment, in any style or in any place—wherever the sonic environment is made to appear complete without the congregation.

Our danger may actually be closer to the Middle Ages than it is to the seventeenth century. I have never heard anyone among us, other than Quakers, argue for a silent congregation. But I have often witnessed worshiping communities which, if the sounds of organs or choirs or bands or amplified equipment were removed, would be nearly or totally silent. There are "high art" churches where the congregation is asked not to sing and "contemporary Christian music" churches where things are so complex that the congregation can't possibly sing. Although some justification may be found for such places, they certainly cannot be normative for most Christian churches. When they become normative our congregational silence parallels the Middle Ages and is but another form of priestly substitution for an assembly of spectators. With the exception of Zwingli, the reformers in the sixteenth century all argued against such a state of affairs. With the exception of Pambo, so did the church of the first centuries. So did the Second Vatican Council in our century.

Fourth, Cotton makes an interesting observation, that elders are appointed to preach, pray, and rule. But no similar appointment to "psalmistry" is made, he says, and therefore responsibility for it falls to the congregation.

These thoughts of Cotton lead to questions about polity—how a worshiping group is organized, whether it has bishops or elders or other sorts of overseers, who is responsible to whom, how lines of authority flow, whether spiritual leaders are called ministers, rectors, pastors, elders, or priests. Those concerns have exercised the church at length. What we have been less concerned about is the point Cotton makes, which the early church embodied, that singing belongs essentially to the congregation. It suggests the uniqueness of the musician's "office" or "role" or "vocation." The musician's job is to get out of the way so the people can in fact sing. The musician turns out to be invisible in a way the preacher and presider are not.

In other words, the presider and preacher—the ones whom Christians call by the name of minister, rector, pastor, elder, clergy, preacher, or priest—can be identified and defined with a clarity in a way the musician cannot. As became obvious already in the Old Testament, the musician is close to the people and has an "office" that is, whether by biblical design or sociological analysis, difficult if not impossible to regard as distinct from them.[91]

[91] The difficulty of defining the role of the church musician can be seen in widely disparate places well before the twentieth century and our discussions about "ordaining" musicians.

Edward Foley, *Ritual Music: Studies in Liturgical Musicology* (Beltsville: The Pastoral Press, 1995), pp. 65–66, indicates how hard it is to identify a "cantor" in the early church apart from the congregation's singing at worship.

Cotton seems to suggest the "office" of "psalmistry" is literally identified with the congregation, but when he says the elder lines out the psalms where needed he admits a person has to lead, and he assumes the person is the "clergy."

At the beginning of the eighteenth century, when Watts took Keach's position and began to argue for hymns as well as psalms, he hinted at an office of "psalmistry" in a person. He said that the early church's "gifts of the spirit" included preaching, prayer, and song. Ministers are to study and acquire gifts of preaching and praying. Why then, he asked, should they—and, could one add, other Christians too?—not cultivate the capacity to compose spiritual songs as well? [See Louis F. Benson, *The English Hymn* (Richmond: John Knox Press, 1962), p. 110.] The logical extension of this question is to suggest not only that there should be authors and composers to write texts and music, but also musicians to lead them in worship.

J. S. Bach understood his office as church musician to relate to proclamation of the word. He did not tie it to ordination, but to I Chronicles and a Davidic relationship. See Robin A. Leaver, ed., *J. S. Bach and Scripture: Glosses from the Calov Bible Commentary* (St. Louis: Concordia Publishing House, 1985), pp. 93–94.

For a Roman Catholic view in our period, which presumes a wide historical range, includes proclamation and other motifs, but ties the church musician finally to a "priestly duty," see Johannes Overath, "The Office of the Church Musician: A Genuine Apostolate," (ed.), *Crux et Cithara*, pp. 64–69.

Fifth, the question of set forms is isolated quite clearly in this seventeenth-century dispute about whether to sing. If you argue that corporate worship cannot have set forms, but must be "immediate" rather than "mediated" through someone else's words or forms, you will obviously not sing anything except possibly what is improvised on the spot. As we have seen that will seldom if ever happen because it is impossible unless it is a solo, and even then very unlikely. If you are consistent you will also not read lessons or speak the Lord's Prayer together, because you will regard all of that as set forms that "quench the spirit." Such a position is understandable in response to habit that has become deathly, though its liability is the arrogance of those who inhabit a specific historical moment. Apart from such considerations, however, the quite practical problem is that for a community to gather more than once and not repeat itself in words or gestures defies comprehension. I suspect the opponents of Keach and Cotton created for themselves an impossible contradiction, which ultimately had the effect of destroying all corporate worship. Maybe it is why they have had little or no ongoing existence and why the singing position has been the more usual practice—even with the contradictory opposition to set forms that has been so influential on the American scene. Whether that is true or not, this conflict clearly isolates the issue. We do well to note both the presuppositions and the implications.

Sixth, Christians will invariably sing, though it has been possible to "restrict when and where their singing is allowed."[92] What Christians do naturally is not simply a reflex, however.[93] It is a very serious matter. Keach's choice of "breach" was not too strong. The

[92] Foley, *From Age to Age*, p. 102.

[93] My friend Francis Williamson challenges my choice of words here, saying they hide my Lutheran bias. He suggests that those who take what he calls the eucharistic sacrificial position would not say this because in that perspective the community only sings the song through the ordained priest. He then cites Susan E. Schreiner, *The Theater of His Glory: Nature and the Natural Order in the Thought of John Calvin* (Durham: The Labyrinth Press, 1991) to press another response, this time the Calvinist one. As related to church music he formulates the question like this: "When the gathered congregation sings do they sing 'naturally' or in the restored relation with 'nature'? [If the latter, is it] as perceived through the Law or in the reestablished right relation with nature through Christ? If one answers [through Christ], then . . . this goes beyond Luther. It is no longer imputed righteousness but experienced sanctification." I will leave my phrase as it is, but note that Williamson raises issues here that church musicians need to sort out with their communities of faith.

church that is healthy will sing. To be human is to sing; to worship is to sing.[94] Or, as Karl Barth in our time put it,

> The praise of God which constitutes the [Christian] community and its assemblies seeks to bind and commit and therefore to be expressed, to well up and be sung in concert. The Christian community sings. It is not a choral society. Its singing is not a concert. But from inner, material necessity it sings. . . . What we can and must say quite confidently is that the community which does not sing is not the community.[95]

Keach said it less precisely than that, but he was on to the same thing. He could not tolerate the breach of congregations forced into silence. If we are faithful, neither will we.

But what then about the Quakers? Why even consider those who in their worship have no music at all? Quaker leadership in prison reform, women's rights, and against slavery, positive though it may be, is not the topic of this book.[96] Dealing with disputes that touch music does concern us, however, and at that point paradoxically the church could learn much from the Quakers. Their "sense of the meeting" suggests that in Christ we can find an alternative to pious manipulative treacle that can masquerade as prayer or worldly power plays of force, which the church often adopts as weapons to "settle" differences. Quakers also set several things out in bold relief, which are directly related to music and worship.

1. Worship classes I have taken to visit Catholic Masses and Quaker services have noted a curious similarity between the two. They can be equally formal, and they can both be "gathered" or "dry." It is worth observing that the presence or absence of externals does not seem to protect against formalism nor guarantee depth of meaning.

2. Quakers raise questions about the nature of worship and the Christian faith. Is the inner light Christ? Without words about Christ can he be encountered? If you dispense with all outward forms have you denied the body and the incarnation? Some Quakers would tell you they and their worship have indeed pushed to the limits of or even outside the Christian fold.

---

[94] See Paul Westermeyer, "To Be Human Is to Sing," *The Luther Northwestern Story* (Winter 1990), pp. 4–8.

[95] Karl Barth, *Church Dogmatics*, IV, part three, second half, trans. G. W. Bromiley (Edinburgh: T. & T. Clark), pp. 866–867.

[96] See Lucille Salitan, Eve Lewis Perera, ed., *Virtuous Lives: Four Quaker Sisters Remember Family Life, Abolitionism, and Women's Suffrage* (New York: Continuum, 1994).

3. The most helpful insight Quakers have for churches that use music is that they remind us of silence, which almost everyone else tends to forget or is nervous about. Virtually every Christian service of worship has within it places where silences need to be kept.[97] Keeping silence is not only a rubrical matter, though neglected rubrics often do call for silence. More importantly, the nature of worship itself demands silence—which, of course, is why the rubrics got there in the first place. At certain points a pregnant silence is the only appropriate preparation or response.[98] In Bonhoeffer's words, "Silence is the simple stillness of the individual under the Word of God."[99] Our propensity to rush into sound garbles our worship, hurries it, and confirms our nervous frenzy[100] apart from the word. It also destroys our song, which needs the backdrop of silence to have any character at all.

---

[97] Discussions of worship almost invariably affirm this notion. See, for example, "Constitution on the Sacred Liturgy," *The Documents of Vatican II* (New York: Guild Press, 1966), p. 148.

[98] For reflections about silence, see Joseph Dougherty, "Silence in the Liturgy," *Worship* 69:2 (March, 1995): 142–154.

[99] Bonhoeffer, *Life Together*, p. 79.

[100] Silence, understandably, is almost impossible to find in our technological age, though there is no reason to succumb to the numbing mask of honest looks at our innermost selves. Buildings, even libraries, hum with motors. So do our neighborhoods, highways, and air spaces. And beyond them, where we go for "recreation," as Robert Hughes learned, "The rarest thing in the Great American Outdoors is a moment of silence. Every time we turned on a camera in some national park or other, a chain saw began howling a mile away, or children in beanies appeared over a nearby rock asking what we were up to." *Time Special Issue: American Visions* (Spring, 1997): [4].

AFTER THE REFORMATION

English Hymns

Benjamin Keach opened the door to English hymnody, as in poetry for the congregation to sing that was not restricted to psalmody.[1] (Hymns are texts. They imply the presence of music, but a hymn strictly speaking—and as I am using the term here—refers to words.) The hymns he wrote, however, were not of a quality that congregations would want to sing for very long if at all, and there was no body of hymnody elsewhere to which the English-speaking church could turn. Isaac Watts stepped into this breach. He argued persuasively for hymn singing and, though "he could descend to bathos,"[2] as a whole his hymns have proven to be worth the church's time and effort to learn and use. He did for the English-speaking world what Luther had done for the German-speaking world two centuries earlier and what Ambrose had done for the Latin world twelve centuries before that.

Isaac Watts

Isaac Watts (1674–1748) stands in the Puritan line of Independent (Congregational) ministers. He served the wealthy Mark Lane Church in London[3] where he was called in 1702. "His sermons were

---

[1] For Keach's importance in the development that led to Watts, see Harry Escot, *Isaac Watts: Hymnographer* (London: Independent Press, Ltd., 1962), chapter 3, particularly pp. 81–87; and Erik Routley, *Hymns and Human Life* (Grand Rapids: Wm. B. Eerdmans Publishing, 1959), p. 148.

[2] Erik Routley, *A Panorama of Christian Hymnody* (Collegeville: The Liturgical Press, 1979), p. 17.

[3] Selma L. Bishop, *Isaac Watts, Hymns and Spiritual Songs, 1707–1748: A Study in Early Eighteenth Century Language Changes* (London: The Faith Press, 1962), p. xv, gives a succinct description of the society Watts moved in and served.

written with care; and the hymns adjusted to the meanings of the sermons."[4] The congregation grew. In 1702 it had sixty members. In 1708 it constructed a church on Bury Street to accommodate more than 400.[5] In 1712 ill health forced Watts to relinquish his duties, though officially he remained the pastor of the church that never allowed him to resign.[6] Sir Thomas Abney, once the Lord Mayor of London, and his second wife opened their house to him. There he spent the remainder of his life as guest, unofficial tutor, and chaplain to the family.[7]

Bright and learned, a prolific author of almost sixty books who had studied several languages and whose *Logic* was used at Harvard, Watts is best known as the father of English hymnody. He was not happy with the quality of the metrical psalms that were in use, nor happy that the people's song was restricted to psalmody. "The accepted story" is that, when he was about sixteen, he complained to his father about what was being sung in church. His father responded, "Then write something better," which is what he did.[8] "Behold the Glories of the Lamb"[9] resulted and after that hymns still sung by English-speaking Christians, such as "When I Survey the Wondrous Cross,"[10] "Jesus Shall Reign,"[11] "O God, Our Help in Ages Past,"[12] and "Joy to the World."[13]

Though Watts began writing hymns in the last decade of the seventeenth century, they were not published until the eighteenth century, in four collections: 1) *Horae Lyricae* in 1705, with hymns and other poems, intended as poetry "to entertain educated, polite society;"[14] 2) *Hymns and Spiritual Songs* in 1707, for the "common, uneducated Christian's understanding,"[15] in three books—scripture paraphrases, spiritual songs "compos'd on divine subjects" and not

---

[4] Bishop, *Isaac Watts . . A Study*, p. xvi.

[5] E. Routley, *Isaac Watts* (London: Independent Press, 1961), p. 7.

[6] Bishop, *Isaac Watts . . . A Study*, p. xvi.

[7] For a description of Thomas Abney and his world, see Arthur Paul Davis, *Isaac Watts: His Life and Works* (New York: The Dryden Press, 1943), pp. 32–38. Routley, *Isaac Watts*, a succinct sketch, relies on David for his "factual matter" (p. 15).

[8] Routley, *A Panorama*, p. 16.

[9] Ibid., p. 17.

[10] LBW, #482.

[11] LBW, #530.

[12] LBW, #320.

[13] LBW, #39.

[14] Bishop, *Isaac Watts . . . A Study*, p. xx.

[15] Ibid.

tied to particular biblical passages, and hymns for the Lord's Supper; 3) *Divine and Moral Songs . . . for the Use of Children* in 1715; and 4) *The Psalms of David Imitated in the Language of the New Testament* in 1719 with 138 psalms, the remaining twelve deemed by Watts to be unsuitable for the use of Christians.[16] Watts wrote about 700 hymns altogether.[17] The ones from 1707 and 1719 are best known.

Hymns and Spiritual Songs in its first edition of 1707 included "A Short Essay Toward the Improvement of Psalmody."[18] There, in typically detailed Puritan fashion, Watts signaled his intentions. After listing the texts in the New Testament where singing is mentioned[19] and explaining the meaning of the terms "psalm," "hymn," and "song,"[20] Watts asked how the Psalms were to be translated. Like the Bible generally, the Psalms are God's word to us, he thought, but congregational song is our word to God. Translations for singing the Psalms should therefore speak in *contemporary* ways—which took strange twists: Judah and Israel could be translated England and Scotland, and the land of Canaan could be Great Britain.[21] More significantly, if David were alive today, said Watts, he would write in the language of the New Testament that sings *of Christ*. So should we.[22]

Translating the Psalms was not enough. Watts wanted newly composed hymns as well and supported them by five arguments. First, since content, not form, is important, let us have hymns "suited to the present case and experience of Christians."[23] Second, the "ends and designs" of singing at worship are to express to God "what sense and apprehensions we have of his essential glories." That goal can "never be sufficiently attained by confining ourselves

---

[16] I have detailed these omissions and discussed implications in *Let Justice Sing: Hymnody and Justice* (Collegeville: The Liturgical Press, 1998), pp. 34–38.

[17] Bishop, *Isaac Watts . . . A Study*, p. xxiv, says he authored 697 hymns. Routley, *A Panorama*, p. 16, says "700-odd pieces."

[18] The full title is "A Short Essay Toward the Improvement of Psalmody: or, An Enquiry how the Psalms of David ought to be Translated into Christian Songs, and how lawful and necessary it is to compose other Hymns according to the clearer Revelations of the Gospel, for the Use of the Christian Church." It can be found in *The Works of the Rev. Watts, D. D. in Seven Volumes* (London: Edward Baines, 1800), pp. 1–20.

[19] Watts, "An Essay," *The Works of the Rev. Isaac Watts*, pp. 1–2.

[20] Ibid., pp. 2–4.

[21] Ibid., p. 6.

[22] Ibid., p. 9.

[23] Ibid., p. 10.

to David's psalms" or paraphrases of words from the Bible.[24] Third, Ephesians 5:19–20 and Colossians 3:16–17, contrary to Zwingli, command us to sing and give thanks in Christ's name. Praying, preaching, baptism, and the Lord's Supper are expressed in language suited to the gospel. Why not our song as well?[25] Fourth, the book of Psalms does not cover the "almost . . . infinite number of occasions for praise and thanksgiving" in the life of the Christian.[26] Finally, worship includes preaching, prayer, and song. Ministers are to acquire the gifts of preaching and praying. Why then, asked Watts, should not Christians cultivate the capacity to compose spiritual songs as well?[27]

Many Christians today would probably regard Watts's logic as self-evident. But we live on this side of him. That he had to make his case so strongly—he clearly was the aggressor against public opinion[28]—indicates the inertia metrical psalm singing had generated. Watts met resistance at first. Benjamin Franklin printed his *Psalms* in Philadelphia in 1729, but it did not sell. Franklin did not reprint it until 1741. By then reprints were being made in Boston and New York. At the time of Watts's death in 1748 "only sixteen editions" of *Hymns and Spiritual Songs* "were known in London, with a handful in America,"[29] but by 1800 there were more than 228 editions and from 1800 to 1900 at least 516.[30] Watts was increasingly used in both England and New England. By the nineteenth century he was everywhere.[31] "Among the Congregationalists" he "attained complete dominance by 1836."[32] Outside his denomination he was also in control.

- About one-third of *Psalms and Hymns*, 1834, the hymnal of the German Reformed Church—a body in the United States with German, not English roots—was by Watts, and much of

---

[24] Ibid., pp. 10–11.

[25] Ibid., p. 12.

[26] Ibid.

[27] Ibid., p. 14.

[28] Bishop, *Isaac Watts . . . A Study*, p. xxi.

[29] Selma L. Bishop, *Isaac Watts's Hymns and Spiritual Songs (1707): A Publishing History and a Bibliography* (Ann Arbor: The Pierian Press, 1974), p. xv.

[30] Ibid., p. xvii.

[31] Louis F. Benson, *The English Hymn: Its Development and Use in Worship* (Richmond: John Knox Press, 1962, reprinted from 1915), pp. 108–218, explains Watts' position and then traces its influence in detail.

[32] Davis, *Isaac Watts*, p. 208.

the rest of the book by authors in a style similar to Watts.[33]

- In 1865, 60,000 copies of *Psalms and Hymns* by Watts were sold.[34]
- When 750 hymn books were checked in 1891, two-fifths of the hymns were by Watts.[35]
- In 1898 five of the 32 most popular hymns in English were by Watts.[36]

Watts assumed the psalm tunes that were in use. By casting his hymns mostly into Common Meter, Short Meter, and Long Meter, the tunes that were known could easily carry his texts. He also made lining out, a practice he said "cannot presently be reformed," less confusing by matching one complete thought with one line of poetry.[37]

The Wesleys

Watts's hymnody was grafted into the evangelical activity of the eighteenth century, which brings the Wesleys into view. John (1703–1791) and Charles (1707–1788)—part of the large Wesley family whose lives, poetry, and music had a notable impact on church and world before and after them[38]—were Anglican priests who spanned the eighteenth century and symbolize much of it. Sacramental renewal with the *Book of Common Prayer* as back-

---

[33] *Psalms and Hymns for the Use of the German Reformed Church in the United States of America* (Chambersburg: Publication Office of the German Reformed Church, 1834). Of the 520 hymns 100 are by Watts, and of the 299 entries for the 150 Psalms 169 are by Watts.

[34] Davis, *Isaac Watts*, pp. 212–213.

[35] Ibid., and Bishop, *Isaac Watts . . . A Study*, p. xxiii.

[36] Davis, *Isaac Watts*, p. 213.

[37] Isaac Watts, "The Preface," *Hymns and Spiritual Songs*, 1709, reprinted in Bishop, *Isaac Watts, Hymns and Spiritual Songs*, p. liii.

[38] Including father Samuel (1662–1735); mother Susanna Annesley (1669–1742); oldest brother Samuel (1691–1739)—first of seventeen children; Charles and Sarah Gwynne's son Charles (1757–1834), a child prodigy, organist, harpsichordist, and composer; Charles and Sarah Gwynne's son Samuel (1766–1837), organist, extemporizer, violinist, composer, conductor, and ardent apologist for J. S. Bach; and Samuel and Sarah Suter's (illegitimate) son Samuel Sebastian (1810–1876), organist with a reach of an octave and a half, conductor, composer. Erik Routley, *The Musical Wesleys* (London: Herbert Jenkins, 1968), covers John, Charles, Charles II, Samuel, and Samuel Sebastian, not always positively.

ground was a central component of the Wesleyan movement.[39] Eighteenth century Anglicans neglected the Eucharist.[40] Early Methodists, on the other hand, "flocked to the celebration of Holy Communion in such numbers that the clergy were really embarrassed with the multitude of communicants with which they had to deal."[41] (In the nineteenth century Methodists succumbed to the Anglican example and neglected the Lord's Supper, whereupon the tables were reversed: Anglicans engaged in the recovery and objected to the Methodist's neglect.)

Frequent communion for early Methodists is not too surprising, given the example of their leaders. As an undergraduate at Oxford University, Charles organized the "Holy Club" with several fellow students. Its members, led by John, "followed a strenuous and consistent routine."[42] They rose early, studied the Greek New Testament, fasted on Wednesdays and Fridays, received communion weekly, observed the church's fasts and feasts, and visited prisoners and the sick. Because of their "methods"—their "methodical . . . observance of the rites and statutes of the church"[43]—other students poked fun at them and labeled them "Methodists." They were "neither sour Puritans nor pious sentimentalists," however. They were simply "out of tune with contemporary cynicism and indifference."[44] Study, sacramental recovery, and serving the needy characterized their upbeat activity.

Throughout their lives these same themes persisted. John, the organizer of the movement, communed "more often than not, twice a week."[45] He preached on "constant communion"[46] and had a lively

[39] J. Ernest Rattenbury, *The Eucharistic Hymns of John and Charles Wesley* (London: The Epworth Press, 1948), p. 3.

[40] Ibid., p. 4.

[41] Ibid.

[42] Frederick C. Gill, *Charles Wesley, the First Methodist* (New York: Abingdon Press, 1964), p. 41.

[43] Oliver A. Beckerlegge, "The Development of the Collection," *The Works of John Wesley*, vol. 7, ed. Franz Hildebrandt, Oliver A. Beckerlegge, and James Dale (Oxford: Clarendon Press, 1983), p. 22.

[44] Ibid.

[45] See James White, Intro., *The Sunday Service of the Methodists in North America* (The United Methodist Publishing House, 1984), p. 17, and J. Ernest Rattenbury, *The Eucharistic Hymns of John and Charles Wesley*, p. 8. For the full picture Rattenbury gives, see J. Ernest Rattenbury, *The Evangelical Doctrines of Charles Wesley's Hymns* (London: The Epworth Press, 1941).

[46] Rattenbury, *The Eucharistic Hymns of John and Charles Wesley*, pp. 171–172.

understanding of Christ's real presence in a Calvinist sense with a
converting twist added in.[47] The background of worship for the
Wesleyan movement was the 1662 edition of the *Book of Common
Prayer*. In 1784, when John revised it for use in North America as
The Sunday Service of the Methodists,[48] he shortened it in part so
that the Lord's Supper could be received every Sunday.[49] The normal
Sunday practice for eighteenth century Anglicans was morning
prayer, the litany, and antecommunion (the word service of the
Eucharist without communion), with the full Eucharist three times a
year.[50] As to the Prayer Book, John said, "I BELIEVE there is no
LITURGY in the World, either in ancient or modern language,
which breathes more of a solid, scriptural, rational Piety, than the
COMMON PRAYER of the CHURCH of ENGLAND."[51]

Charles,[52] the primary hymnwriter of the movement, drew mostly
from the Bible for his texts, but "the debt of the Book of Common
Prayer" cannot be missed either.[53] His hymns encompassed the
church year,[54] and he penned numerous Eucharistic hymns that were
published in 1745 as *Hymns on the Lord's Supper*.[55] This hymnal
was "the most widely circulated and continuously used of all the

[47] See Rattenbury, *The Eucharistic Hymns of John and Charles Wesley*, pp.9–11,
13, 16, 41, 50–51, 57, 64, 78, and Thompson, *Liturgies*, pp. 412–413.

[48] Published in England in 1786.

[49] Letter of John Wesley to Coke, Asbury, and "our Brethren in NORTH
AMERICA," September 10, 1784, printed with *The Sunday Service* in Thompson,
Liturgies, p. 416. It can also be found in White, *The Sunday Service of the
Methodists in North America*, p. [39].

[50] White, *The Sunday Service of the Methodists in North America*, pp. 15 and
17.

[51] Letter of John Wesley to Coke, Asbury, and "our Brethren in NORTH
AMERICA," September 10, 1784, printed with *The Sunday Service* in Bard Thompson, *Liturgies*, p. 416. It can also be found in White, *The Sunday Service*, p. [A1].

[52] More of "a strict high churchman" than his brother John. See Temperley, *The
Music of the English Parish Church*, I, p. 208.

[53] Oliver A. Beckerlegge, ed., *The Works of John Wesley*, vol. 7, p. 5.

[54] See Timothy Dudley-Smith, "Charles Wesley—A Hymnwriter for Today," *The
Hymn* 39:4 (October 1988): 7, and Alfred Burton Haas, "The Papers of the Hymn
Society of America, XXII: Charles Wesley" (Springfield: The Hymn Society of Amer-
ica, 1957), pp. 10–17.

[55] *Hymns on the Lord's Supper . . . With a Preface concerning the Christian
Sacrament and Sacrifice, extracted from Doctor Brevint* (Bristol: Farley, 1745)
republished in J. Ernest Rattenbury, *The Eucharistic Hymns of John and Charles
Wesley*, with a book-length discussion of their significance.

[Methodist] hymn-books, except the General Collections."[56] John Newton probably took the line "Was blind, but now I see" for "Amazing Grace" from one of these hymns where seeing meant perceiving the mystery of the grace of Christ conveyed with the bread and wine.[57]

When one thinks of the Wesleys, the sacramental background, the *Book of Common Prayer*, and origins in "the high-church religious societies of Queen Anne's time"[58] are not what come to mind. The Wesleys are better known for their opposition to formalism; John for abbreviating the prayer book to get more time for preaching, extemporaneous prayer, and hymnody; the drift of the Methodists away from the Anglican church;[59] and for their "conversions." For Charles the date was Pentecost, May 21, 1738, via Martin Luther's commentary on Galatians. For John it was three days later (the "Aldersgate experience") via Martin Luther's Preface to Romans after hearing an anthem that afternoon, "Out of the Deep" (Psalm 130), at St. Paul's Cathedral.[60] Underlying these experiences was the "heart religion" of the Moravians (see the next chapter), who were on board ship with them on their way to Georgia in 1735. After their conversions the brothers were known for itinerant preaching outside to large throngs of people.

Though the Wesleys knew of "no conflict between the evangelical reality and the sacramental reality of Christian experience,"[61] the forces of their period out-Wesleyed them. The Puritan strain that called for experience unmediated by set forms and the frontier of the American continent with neither a communally disciplined life of

---

[56] Rattenbury, *The Eucharistic Hymns of John and Charles Wesley*, p. 11.

[57] Here is the second stanza of Hymn 59 (Rattenbury, *The Eucharistic Hymns of John and Charles Wesley*), p. 213.

> How He did these creatures raise,
>   And make this bread and wine
> Organs to convey His grace
>   To this poor soul of mine,
> I cannot the way descry,
>   Need not know the mystery;
> Only this I know—that I
>   Was blind, but now I see.

[58] Temperley, *The Music of the English Parish Church*, I, p. 204.

[59] Ibid., p. 205.

[60] See Routley, *The Musical Wesleys*, pp. 26–27.

[61] Thompson, *Liturgies*, p. 414. Cf. Rattenbury, *The Eucharistic Hymns of John and Charles Wesley*, pp. 18–19.

faith nor enough clergy to go around yielded a mindset that wanted
to tell time by a massive once-for-all conversion, not repeated conversions and repentance across a lifetime. Word and sacrament
under the guidance and reminders of the church year were correspondingly devalued. Jesse Lee's comments about John's revision of
the prayer book are symbolic. Preachers, he said, thought they could
pray better extemporaneously, and "after a few years the prayer
book was laid aside, and has never been used since in public worship."[62] Lee exaggerated—for baptisms, eucharists, weddings, funer-
als, and ordinations, Methodists continued to rely on Wesley's *Sunday Service*[63]—but he captured the spirit of the late eighteenth
century and what was to follow. The Wesleys had assumed the structures of the church's life and sought to allow them their intrinsic
evangelical fervor.[64] Those who followed in many cases thought they
could have the latter without the former.

When the public liturgical bones of communal worship are dismissed, the church's song is left in a free fall. As we have seen, it can
disappear altogether in such a context, at least for a time, if you
oppose it the way Zwingli or some Anabaptists and Puritans did.
The Wesleys did not favor that choice at all. They championed
hymns. Charles wrote ten times as many as Watts,[65] a goodly number still in use: "O, for a Thousand Tongues to Sing,"[66] "Come,
Thou Long Expected Jesus,"[67] Hark! the Herald Angels Sing,"[68]
"Christ the Lord Is Risen Today,"[69] and "Love Divine, All Loves
Excelling."[70] In hymnody Wesleyans followed their leaders. Hearty
hymn singing characterized Methodist societies and reflected John's
directions about singing together lustily, modestly, in time with the
leaders, not too slow, and spiritually.[71]

---

[62] Quoted in Thompson, *Liturgies*, p. 410, and White, *The Sunday Service*, p.
13.

[63] See White, *The Sunday Service*, p. 13.

[64] Cf. Temperley, *The Music of the English Parish Church*, I, p. 208.

[65] The number given varies from 5,000 to 9,000. Frank Baker said 8,989. See
Routley, *The Musical Wesleys*, p. 30.

[66] UMH, #57.

[67] UMH, #196.

[68] UMH, #240.

[69] UMH, #302.

[70] UMH, #384.

[71] [John Wesley], *Directions for Singing*, in *Select Hymns*, 1761, reprinted in *The
Works of John Wesley*, Vol. 7, p. 765, and in the UMH, p. vii.

John was not enamored of anthems and omitted them,[72] but already in Georgia he prepared *A Collection of Psalms and Hymns* for congregations, printed at Charleston in 1737.[73] Watts was represented in ample supply,[74] but the chief of John's hymnals came in 1780 with *A Collection of Hymns for the Use of the People Called Methodists*[75] which he fashioned as "a book of Christian experience,"[76] mostly including Charles' hymns filtered through his own editorial sieve. His other collections continued to have lives of their own. The eucharistic hymns remained in circulation, and the Charleston *Collection*,[77] in its revised version of 1741, was published in "over thirty editions, well into the nineteenth century."[78] John commended its use in public worship, and it was reissued in a "slightly abridged form entitled *A Collection of Psalms and Hymns for the Lord's Day*" when it was published with *The Sunday Service* in 1784.[79]

John had strong ideas about hymns. He was adamant about not allowing anyone to change texts in his collections. He used and edited mostly the hymns of his brother, but of others such as George Herbert (1593–1633) as well, plus translations from the Spanish, French, and German. The published result, he thought, comprised "no doggerel, no botches, nothing . . . to patch up the rhyme, no feeble expletives . . . nothing turgid or bombast . . . nor low and creeping . . . no *cant* expressions, no words without meaning, [but] the purity, the strength, and the elegance of the English language."[80]

---

[72] White, *The Sunday Service,* p. 10.

[73] *A Collection of Psalms and Hymns* (Charlestown: Lewis Timothy, 1737, reprinted Nashville: The United Methodist Publishing House, 1988). For some detailed reflections about this hymnal, see Carlton R. Young, "John Wesley's 1737 Charlestown Collection of Psalms and Hymns," *The Hymn* 41:4 (October 1990): 19–27.

[74] Frank Baker and George Walton Williams, ed., *John Wesley's First Hymnbook* (Charleston: The Dalcho Historical Society, 1964), pp. xxvii–xxviii, gives the sources, about half from Watts.

[75] This *Collection* with introductory material can be found in *The Works of John Wesley*, vol. 7, ed. Franz Hildebrandt, Oliver A. Beckerlegge, and James Dale (Oxford: Clarendon Press, 1983).

[76] Oliver A. Beckerlegge, "John Wesley as Hymn-book Editor," *The Works of John Wesley*, vol. 7, p. 58.

[77] [John Wesley], *A Collection of Psalms and Hymns* (London: Strahan, 1741).

[78] Oliver A. Beckerlegge, ed., *The Works of John Wesley*, vol. 7, p. 23.

[79] Ibid., pp. 28–29.

[80] John Wesley, "The Preface," *A Collection of Hymns for the Use of the People*

Others should not attempt to "mend" the texts, he said, "for they really cannot"; he did not want to be held "accountable" for "the nonsense" or "the doggerel" of anyone else.[81]

He also had ideas about the music of hymns. The normal practice in the eighteenth century was "words only" editions of hymnals without tunes. Local churches used tunes they knew, and their musicians compiled manuscript collections themselves or found ones that were available. John was not content to let this practice of laissez faire prevail. In 1786 for the fifth edition of the 1780 *Collection of Hymns* he "indicated at the head of each hymn the tune to which he intended it to be sung."[82] He chose the tunes normally used, but he guided the norm so tunes would be common from one group to another. The tunes came "from a wide variety of sources"—psalm tunes, German chorales, earlier eighteenth-century collections, and local musicians such as John F. Lampe (1703–1751).[83] Lampe was a bassoonist and composer, a friend of Charles Wesley, who in 1746 published a set of tunes for a number of Charles' texts.[84]

John's foray into matters musical for hymns began before 1786. In 1742 he had published a set of tunes known as the "Foundery Collection."[85] The title refers to the Foundery, a cannon factory in London that had been wrecked by an explosion. John bought it in 1739 and rebuilt it as a "preaching-house, schoolroom and living quarters (later adding a dispensary and an almshouse)."[86] The "Foundery Collection," unlike the texts he edited, was a botch. As Bryan Spinney asks, what does the title "tunes set to music mean?"

Called Methodists (London: J. Paramore, 1780), in *The Works of John Wesley*, vol. 7, p. 74.

[81] Ibid., p. 75.

[82] Oliver A. Beckerlegge, Franz Hildebrandt, Appendix J, "Wesley's Tunes for the *Collection*, 1786," *The Works of John Wesley*, vol. 7, p. 770. In their printing of the *Collection*, Beckerlegge and Hildebrandt give the tune names from the 1786 edition with the hymns, then in Appendix J, after a brief introduction, alphabetically list all of the tunes with comments about their origins and the texts Wesley married to them (pp. 772–787).

[83] Oliver A. Beckerlegge, Franz Hildebrandt, Appendix J, "Wesley's Tunes for the *Collection*, 1786," *The Works of John Wesley*, vol. 7, p. 770.

[84] John F. Lampe, *Hymns on the Great Festivals* (1746). For a sketch of Lampe's life, see Roger Fiske, "Lampe, John Frederick," NGDMM, 10, pp. 419–421.

[85] [John Wesley], *A Collection of Tunes Set to Music, As they are commonly Sung at the Foundery* (London: A. Person, 1742, reprinted with an Introduction and Notes on the Tunes by Bryan F. Spinney, 1981, n. p.).

[86] Ibid.

Tunes were "wrongly barred," had rhythmic errors, and the pitch of some of them was "quite incredible"—above the range of normal human beings.[87] Printed pitch can be considered irrelevant, because in practice tunes could have been pitched anywhere. But there is no reason for tessituras to lie at the top of the treble clef with ledger lines when they could just as easily have been centered on the staff.[88] Though the printing was a botch, fortunately John's judgment about the tunes themselves was much better. The tunes in the "Foundery Collection" included ones he continued to choose for future collections and give the flavor of his intent and of early Methodist hymn singing. Some of them remain in use today,[89] indicating pretty sturdy choices. They include

- Hanover[90] called Bromswick Tune[91] and later Tallis's[92]
- Easter Hymn[93] called Salisbury Tune[94] or Salisbury[95]
- Something similar to Orlando Gibbons's Song 34[96] called Angel's Hymn Tune[97] or Angel Hymn (also Angel Song and Angel's Song)[98]
- A version of Tallis' Canon[99] called Cannon Tune[100] or Canon[101]
- Vater Unser[102] called Playford's Tune[103] and 112th Psalm[104]

---

[87] Ibid.

[88] JERICHO TUNE, p. 5, is an example.

[89] Carlton R. Young, *Music of the Heart: John and Charles Wesley on Church Music and Musicians* (Carol Stream: Hope Publishing, 1995), p. 55, lists the tunes in the current Methodist hymnal, which Wesley himself chose: Amsterdam, Carrey's (Surrey), Easter Hymn, Hanover, Old 113th, Savannah, Tallis' Canon, Uffingham, Vater Unser, Wer nur Den Lieben Gott.

[90] UMH, #181.

[91] "Foundery Collection," p. 6.

[92] Oliver A. Beckerlegge, Franz Hildebrandt, Appendix J, "Wesley's Tunes for the *Collection, 1786*," *The Works of John Wesley*, vol. 7, p. 785.

[93] UMH, #302.

[94] "Foundery Collection," p. 11.

[95] Oliver A. Beckerlegge, Franz Hildebrandt, Appendix J, "Wesley's Tunes for the *Collection, 1786*," *The Works of John Wesley*, vol. 7, p. 783.

[96] LBW, #505.

[97] "Foundery Collection," p. 21.

[98] Oliver A. Beckerlegge, Franz Hildebrandt, Appendix J, "Wesley's Tunes for the *Collection, 1786*," *The Works of John Wesley*, vol. 7, p. 772.

[99] UMH, #682.

[100] "Foundery Collection," p. 22.

[101] Oliver A. Beckerlegge, Franz Hildebrandt, Appendix J, "Wesley's Tunes for the *Collection, 1786*," *The Works of John Wesley*, vol. 7, p. 775.

[102] UMH, #414.

[103] "Foundery Collection," pp. 33–34.

- WINCHESTER NEW[105] called SWIFT GERMAN TUNE[106] and later FRANKFORT[107]
- OLD 113TH[108] called THE 113TH PSALM TUNE,[109] a "great favourite" of John Wesley,[110] perhaps the tune he sang on his deathbed just before he died.[111]

In 1761 Wesley published another tune book entitled *Sacred Melody*, this one with a hymnal called *Select Hymns: With Tunes Annext*.[112] He explained that he wanted Methodists to sing the tunes in common use among them, available in one portable and inexpensive volume. He said he had been trying for twenty years to get such a book as this, but had not found musicians who would do what he wanted. What was that? Not "*mending* our tunes, but setting them down neither better nor worse than they were." This book, he said, contained "all the tunes in *common use* among us," printed "exactly as I desire our congregations may sing them."[113] There were 102, 104 in 1786.

What lay behind John's concern about not "mending" the published texts or tunes? Like Luther, Wesley knew a body of Christians couldn't have many continually changing versions of hymns and hymn tunes without creating confusion which endangered their song. Carlton Young speaks of "Wesley's lifelong efforts to standardize the rhetoric and music of congregational song—the unity of emotion and the cognate, the heart and the head."[114] Two related concerns were at work here. 1) Wesley knew, again like Luther, that

[104] Oliver A. Beckerlegge, Franz Hildebrandt, Appendix J, "Wesley's Tunes for the *Collection*, 1786," *The Works of John Wesley*, vol. 7, p. 782.

[105] PH, #10.

[106] "Foundery Collection," p. 34.

[107] Oliver A. Beckerlegge, Franz Hildebrandt, Appendix J, "Wesley's Tunes for the *Collection*, 1786," *The Works of John Wesley*, vol. 7, p. 777.

[108] UMH, #60.

[109] "Foundery Collection," pp. 35–36.

[110] Spinney, "Foundery Collection," p. 40.

[111] Oliver A. Beckerlegge, Franz Hildebrandt, Appendix J, "Wesley's Tunes for the *Collection*, 1786," *The Works of John Wesley*, vol. 7, p. 783.

[112] *Select Hymns: With Tunes Annext; Designed chiefly for the Use of the People called Methodists* (London: n. p., 1761). The *Tunes Annext* had a separate title page: *Sacred Melody: or a choice Collection of Psalm and Hymn Tunes*.

[113] John Wesley, "The Preface" to *Select Hymns: With Tunes Annext*, reprinted in *The Works of John Wesley*, vol. 7, p. 738.

[114] Young, *Music of the Heart*, p. 74.

the quality of the texts and music had to be high or the song would be ephemeral and would evaporate very quickly.[115] Erik Routley's summary of Wesley is apt: "Give us the best music we can have, but make it *friendly* to the people."[116] 2) And he knew congregations had to learn to sing. That knowledge explains his preparation of two manuals of instruction for reading music[117] as well as his admonitions: learn the tunes, sing them exactly as printed, and join the singing even if "it is a cross to you."[118] It will turn out to be a blessing, he added! Carlton Young's summary of Wesley follows:

> . . . Wesley is the paradigmatic enabler of that brand of vital congregational song that combines the singable, the heartfelt, and the appropriate—a repertory that since his time has often been the enigma and sometimes the nemesis of clergy and musician alike.[119]

Wesley was not always consistent. His position as a whole[120] suggests a pivotal move toward Romanticism and music's role in arousing emotions. Singing too many hymns back to back for him enervated or enfeebled rather than strengthened a community. He was worried about "vain repetitions" and did not like either repeated choruses or polyphony. He thought modern harmony and counterpoint drained music of its more primal monophonic power, though

---

[115] Luther and Wesley are not alone in realizing that perpetual change and poor quality destroy a congregation's singing. Richard Schuler, a Roman Catholic concerned about the congregation's participation, makes the same points. See Richard J. Schuler, "The Congregation: Its Possibilities and Limitations in Singing," *Cum Angelis Canere*, p. 326.

[116] Erik Routley, *The Church and Music: An Enquiry into the History, the Nature, and the Scope of Christian Judgment on Music* (London: Gerald Duckworth & Co. Ltd., 1950), p. 161.

[117] *The Gamut, or Scale of Music*, 1761, reprinted in *The Works of John Wesley*, vol. 7, pp. 739–751, and *The Grounds of Vocal Music*, 1765, reprinted in *The Works of John Wesley*, vol. 7, pp. 752–764. In their introductory notes Franz Hildebrandt and Oliver Beckerlegge indicate that, at least for the first of these, Wesley probably "collaborated" with Thomas Butts, his secretary at the Foundery who became a music publisher and on whose *Harmonia Sacra* Wesley relied for *Sacred Melody*, 1761.

[118] [John Wesley], *Directions for Singing*, in *Select Hymns*, 1761, reprinted in *The Works of John Wesley*, vol. 7, p. 765, and in the UMH, p. vii.

[119] Young, *Music of the Heart* , p. 113.

[120] See Young, *Music of the Heart*, especially pp. 84–105. Young prints, then comments on, Wesley's "Thoughts on the Power of Music," 1779, which can also be found in *The Works of John Wesley*, vol. 7, pp. 766–777.

he was attracted to Handelian opera and eighteenth-century tunes with figured bass.[121] (For figured bass, see the next chapter.) The inconsistency here resulted in publications of tunes both mono-phonic and harmonized. The "Foundery Collection" and *Sacred Melody* from *Select Hymns: With Tunes Annext* were melody-only editions, but the latter was reissued in 1780 as *Sacred Harmony* in two or three parts with harpsichord and organ.[122] John was similar-ly ambivalent about organs. In them he sometimes found "an uncommon blessing," yet he resisted them—a resistance his follow-ers seem to have ignored.[123]

In one sense Wesley was a Puritan, uninterested in music with-out words. Yet he had "no use for music of the intellect." In spite of his opposition to repeated words or those "obscured by counter-point," he nevertheless liked Handel's *Messiah*.[124] Erik Routley clar-ifies the contradictions.

> there is in him a creative conflict . . . between the residue of Puritanism and a proleptic Romanticism. . . . No seventeenth-century Puritan would have dreamed of saying that it was music's purpose, in or out of church, to arouse emotions; if it did, they did not approve it. But to John, music's primary purpose was just this.[125]

Other Writers, Collections, and Tunes

Writers

Isaac Watts and Charles Wesley were the chief English-speaking hymnwriters of the eighteenth century, but they were not the only ones. Philip Doddridge (1702–1751)—friend of Isaac Watts, sup-porter of the Wesleys and Whitefield though not always with Watts's blessing,[126] and Congregational pastor of a poor church at

---

[121] See Young, *Music of the Heart*, pp. 89–91, especially points 2 and 9.

[122] *Sacred Harmony: or a choice Collection of Psalms and Hymns set to Music in two or three parts for the Voice, Harpsichord and Organ* (London: Bennett, 1780).

[123] Young, *Music of the Heart*, pp. 98–99. For further quotes and reflections see Routley, *The Musical Wesleys*, pp. 10–13, and Temperley, *The Music of the Eng-lish Parish Church*, I, pp. 214–215.

[124] Routley, *The Musical Wesleys*, pp. 22–23.

[125] Ibid., p. 23. Francis Williamson objects to Routley's calling Wesley a prolep-tic Romantic for whom music was to arouse emotions. He thinks the primary aim of the Wesleys was "to teach scriptural holiness, to confront people with the moral claims of the gospel."

[126] See Davis, *Isaac Watts*, pp. 46–49.

Castle Hill, Northampton—wrote over 400 hymns, mostly to follow his sermons. His "Hark, the Glad Sound!"[127] and "O God of
Jacob"[128] are still sung today. Anne Steele (1716–1778), a Baptist,
wrote over 200 poems, some of them metrical psalms but most
of them hymns. Many became quite popular both in England and
in this country. In an American Lutheran hymnal from 1828,
Hymns, Selected and Original,[129] she was represented with more
hymns than anyone else except Isaac Watts. Watts had 149; she
had 49. Her "Father of Mercies, in Your Word" is still in use
today.[130] Augustus Toplady (1740–1778), a feisty Anglican
Calvinist who launched some of the more intemperate attacks on
Wesley, wrote "Rock of Ages, Cleft for Me."[131]

Olney Hymns

The most important eighteenth-century hymn collection, apart from
the ones by Watts and the Wesleys, was *Olney Hymns*, 1779, of
John Newton (1725–1807) and William Cowper (1731–1800).
John Newton, a rough, bawdy sea captain and slave trader, was converted under the influence of George Whitefield and John Wesley. He
renounced his former ways and became the Anglican curate at the
parish in Olney. Later he was the center of the evangelical movement
within the church of England as a rector in London. William Cowper, a sensitive poet and would-be lawyer given to suicidal fits of
depression, came to Olney when Newton was there. John Newton's
"Amazing Grace"[132] comes from *Olney Hymns*,[133] as do his "Glorious Things of Thee Are Spoken"[134] and "How Sweet the Name of
Jesus Sounds."[135] Cowper wrote some remarkable texts, like "God

---

[127] LBW, #35.

[128] LBW, #477.

[129] *Hymns Selected and Original, for Public and Private Worship. Published by
the General Synod for the Evangelical Lutheran Church* (Gettysburg: General Synod
of the Evangelical Lutheran Church, 1828).

[130] LBW, #240.

[131] UMH, #361.

[132] UMH, #378.

[133] *Olney Hymns, in Three Books. Book I. On Select Texts of Scriptures. Book
II. On Occasional Subjects. Book III. On the Progress and Changes of the Spiritual Life* (London: W. Oliver, 1779).

[134] UMH, #731.

[135] LBW, #345.

Moves in a Mysterious Way"[136] and "Sometimes a Light Surprises."[137] The first of these celebrates God's grace though the clouds of paradox. The latter, because of its not easily altered male pronouns, has fallen out of use, though it remains a cheerful account of the surprising presence and faithfulness of God coming to consciousness in singing a hymn.[138]

Whitefield and the Countess of Huntingdon

George Whitefield (1717–1770), just mentioned in connection with Newton, was a member of the Holy Club at Oxford, well acquainted with the Wesleys. Though not so given to organizational skills as John Wesley, he was the better-known preacher. He got the idea of open air preaching from the Welsh and gave it to John.[139] He made seven preaching trips to the United States and also preached through Wales, Scotland, Ireland, and England.

Whitefield, like the Wesleys, was an Anglican priest. Unlike them, he was a more strict Calvinist. They were "Arminians,"[140] objected to predestination, and broke with Whitefield over this matter. With that Selina Hastings, the Countess of Huntingdon (1707–1791), threw her sympathies to Whitefield, appointed him as one of her chaplains, and supported other chaplains throughout England.[141] Edward Perronet (1762–1792) was among them. He wrote "All Hail the Power of Jesus' Name"—as well as a scurrilous attack on his own Church of England,[142] which incensed John Wesley who managed to suppress it.

Before her death the Countess of Huntingdon organized her more than sixty "Calvinist Methodist" chapels into an association called the "Countess of Huntingdon's Connexion." From 1757 hymnals were compiled for this group. The final authorized version came in

---

[136] LBW, #483, EH, #677.

[137] RL, #159, EH, #667.

[138] For concise summaries of the *Olney Hymns* and their authors, see H. Leigh Bennett, "Olney Hymns," DH, I, pp. 867–868; H. Leigh Bennett, "Cowper, William," DH, I, pp. 265–266; and H. Leigh Bennett and John Julian, "Newton, John," DH, I, pp. 803–804.

[139] Alan Luff, *Welsh Hymns and Their Tunes* (Carol Stream: Hope Publishing, 1990), p. 65.

[140] A movement in the Dutch Reformed Church, named for Jacobus Arminius (1560–1609), which objected to strict Calvinism and particularly to predestination.

[141] See Temperley, *The Music of the English Parish Church*, I, p. 205.

[142] Edward Perronet, *The Mitre* (London, 1757).

1780,[143] the same year as John Wesley's *Hymns for the Use of the People Called Methodists*. The hymnals of the Countess of Huntingdon included a wide spread of eighteenth-century evangelical hymnwriting—from the Moravians, Watts, Wesley, Newton, and Cowper, among others.

Welsh Hymns and Tunes

Whitefield's contacts with the Welsh point to yet another piece of the eighteenth-century story. An evangelical revival in Wales paralleled the one in England. In 1735, three years before the Wesleys' conversion experiences, a teacher from Trevecca named Howel Harris (1714–1773) attended church on Palm Sunday and heard his vicar encourage the people to come to communion on Easter no matter how unworthy they felt. Harris was moved, received communion, began devotional reading, and organized a small group whose central activities were preaching, exhorting, mutual support, and regular attendance at the parish church for the Lord's Supper. From this beginning Harris became the lay leader of the Welsh evangelical revival. In 1752 he established an almshouse and school at Trevecca. A chapel was added in 1758. About ten years later the Countess of Huntingdon began a seminary there, with rooms added for her.

In the same year that Harris responded to his vicar, Daniel Rowland (c. 1711–1790) was ordained to the priesthood and began to draw large throngs by powerful preaching in his parish church at Llangeitho and beyond. At the same time that people were coming to live at Trevecca, they were making pilgrimages to Llangeitho, especially for the "last Sunday of the month" communion services. Rowland preached on Saturday, and 1,200 to 1,500 people received communion on Sunday.[144]

The interaction between the Welsh and English evangelical activity extended beyond George Whitefield and Lady Huntingdon. There were contacts with the Wesleys as well. Charles Wesley's wife Sarah (Sally) Gwynne was the daughter of Marmaduke Gwynne of

---

[143] *A Select Collection of Hymns to be universally sung in all the Countess of Huntingdon's Chapels, Collected by her Ladyship* (London, 1780). The various editions leading up to this one are detailed in William T. Brooke, "Huntingdon's Hymn-Books, Countess of," DH, I, pp. 543–544.

[144] For this history, where it is given in greater detail, I am dependent on Alan Luff, *Welsh Hymns*, pp. 62–72.

Garth near Llangamarch who supported Harris.[145] Watts was translated into Welsh by Dafydd Jones, Caio (c. 1710–1777).[146]

The most characteristic Welsh hymnody had its own flavor. William Williams, Pantycelyn (1717–1781)[147] is the Welsh parallel to Charles Wesley, Ann Griffiths (1776–1805) a close second.[148] The world beyond Wales, because of translation barriers, knows but one Welsh hymn, Williams's "Guide Me, O Thou Great Jehovah."[149] Welsh tunes, however, are sung throughout the world, like: ABERYSTWYTH,[150] AR HYD Y NOS,[151] BRYN CALFARIA,[152] CWM RHONDDA,[153] EBENEZER,[154] HYFRYDOL,[155] LLANFAIR,[156] LLANGLOFFAN,[157] RHOSYMEDRE,[158] RHUDDLAN,[159] ST. DENIO,[160] and THE ASH GROVE.[161] These tunes were written in the eighteenth and nineteenth centuries in an eighteenth-century musical style. They grew out of the evangelical revival. They relate to the strong Welsh tradition of singing, sometimes in parts, but they are not "archaic" or usually minor as is often suggested.[162]

At Century's End

The Welsh and English revivals, like all similar movements, were not all positive. They generated their own deep fissures and hostil-

---

[145] Ibid., p. 63. The marriage of Charles and Sarah was one of the few happy ones in the Wesley clan. John's was like the unhappy norm.

[146] Luff, *Welsh Hymns*, p. 104.

[147] That is, William who had an ancestor named William, which gave him the surname Williams, who lived at a farm called "Pantycelyn." See Luff, *Welsh Hymns*, p. 19.

[148] Luff, *Welsh Hymns*, pp. 93–124, lists and discusses these and other Welsh hymnwriters.

[149] UMH, #127.

[150] UMH, #479.

[151] UMH, #688.

[152] LBW, #156.

[153] UMH, #127.

[154] UMH, #108.

[155] UMH, #196.

[156] UMH, #312.

[157] UMH, #425.

[158] UMH, #447.

[159] LBW, #418.

[160] UMH, #103.

[161] UMH, #664.

[162] See Luff, *Welsh Hymns*, pp. 236, 86, 134, and, for a summation of Welsh tunes with their composers and comments, pp. 130–236.

ities[163] and drove wholesome folksong, dance, and celebration underground.[164] Emotional excesses were created, which leaders often resisted.[165] John Wesley regularly condemned such things as "bringing the real work into contempt,"[166] and they have sometimes given Christianity a bad name.

The Middle Ages had liturgical structures that implied but left out the people's singing. The evangelical movement generated song but left out the structures to support it. Both postures sowed the seeds of their own destruction. Liturgical structures without their inherent congregational involvement become intolerably legalistic and dry, but "a 'free' order of worship which has solidified into a custom"[167] becomes equally or more inflexible, arid, and nonparticipatory.

But not everything was negative. A wholesome moral life underlay what sometimes became unwholesome moralistic strictures. And song was let loose. By the end of the eighteenth century the poor quality and strait jacket of metrical psalms, which Watts had lamented a hundred years earlier, had been broken. Watts's small stream of English hymns had by the end of the century reached flood stage. It began to overrun its churchly settings. Watts was sung at the indoor and outdoor meetings of Wesley, Whitefield, and other preachers such as Jonathan Edwards in this country, but also "through the streets, and in Ferry-boats" before and after the meetings—which seemed ostentatious to some though not objectionable to others.[168] The flood also overran psalm tunes and Welsh tunes. William Billings (1746–1800) and other Americans began to use Watts in their music.[169] African Americans would call Watts's texts "Dr. Watts's Hymns" and set them to their rhythms.[170]

[163] See Luff, *Welsh Hymns*, pp. 64–69.

[164] Ibid., pp. 26, 83.

[165] Ibid., pp. 71, 73, 99, 140.

[166] E. P. Thompson, *The Making of the English Working Class* (New York: Vintage Books, 1963), p. 381. Charles Wesley too "had little patience with hysterical converts." Frederick C. Gill, *Charles Wesley, the First Methodist* (New York: Abingdon Press, 1964), p. 84.

[167] Luff, Welsh Hymns, p. 78. Luff says such orders are "permanent." He is right. I would add that the permanence is inflexible. It ultimately ossifies and cracks.

[168] Louis F. Benson, *The English Hymn* (Richmond: John Knox Press, 1962, reprinted from the edition of 1915), p. 164.

[169] Ibid., pp. 169–170.

[170] Wyatt Tee Walker, "*Somebody's Calling My Name,*" *Black Sacred Music and Social Change* (Valley Forge: Judson Press, 1992, first printing, 1979), pp. 73–96.

At the beginning of the nineteenth century, the English-speaking world had a repertoire of hymns and tunes that had not existed one hundred years earlier and that was gaining momentum. But before we get to the nineteenth-century developments, we need to back up a bit and cross the English Channel into Germany, then work forward again into other places.

14 | Music

The last chapter was restricted to English hymnody. Moravians played a role in its development and could have been considered there. They also fit here because, like currents chronicled in this chapter, they moved to music beyond hymn tunes.

The Moravians, or *Unitas Fratrum*, in this country known as the Moravian Church in America, trace their lineage to the Bohemian Brethren who developed as followers of Jan Hus (c. 1369–1415), the Czech reformer burned at the stake by the Council of Constance in 1415. The Bohemian Brethren produced numerous hymnals in the sixteenth century, beginning before the Lutheran ones. They became part of a complex interplay with the Genevan Psalter and Lutheran hymnody.[1] Jan Roh, also known as Johannes Horn (1490–1547), and Michael Weisse (1480–1534) are among the editors and writers from this period. The text "Once He Came in Blessing"[2] and the tunes AVE HIERARCHIA[3] (also called GOTTES SOHN IST KOMMEN[4]), BEATUS VIR,[5] GAUDEMUS PARITER,[6] SONNE DER

---

[1] For detailed overviews of the Moravian heritage, see Walter Blankenburg, trans. Hans Heinsheimer, "The Music of the Bohemian Brethren," in Friedrich Blume, *Protestant Church Music: A History* (New York: W. W. Norton & Company, 1974), pp. 593–607; J. T. Mueller, "Bohemian Brethren's Hymnody," DH, I, pp. 153–160; and J. T. Mueller, "Moravian Hymnody," DH, I, pp. 765–769.

[2] *Moravian Book of Worship* (Bethlehem: Moravian Church in America, 1995), hereafter MBW, #270.

[3] MBW, #270.

[4] LBW, #312.

[5] LBW, #419.

[6] MBW, #525.

GERECHTIGKEIT,[7] and FREUEN WIR UNS ALL IN EIN[8] come from this heritage.

Michael Weisse, who paid Luther repeated visits in the 1520s, created hymns in much the same fashion as Luther did and from the same medieval materials, without adapting them to congregations as skillfully as Luther. He didn't have to be so concerned about that because the Bohemian Brethren were a closely knit community, which met daily for worship and engaged therefore in a more intense musical formation and practice than Luther or other reformers could assume. *Ein New Gesengbuchlen,* which Weisse edited in 1531, was organized not only according to the church year, but also had hymns for various times of the day.[9] The community sang in the vernacular without instruments or counterpoint, up to thirty hymns daily.[10]

The Bohemians were persecuted, often had to meet in secret, and were sometimes homeless. In 1722 Nicholas Ludwig, Count von Zinzendorf (1700–1760), offered them asylum on his estates, which came to be called "Herrnhut" (*Hut des Herrn,* "under the protection of God"). Zinzendorf not only sheltered them, he also led them as "The Renewed Church of the Brethren." His leadership included hymnody and music.[11] Zinzendorf edited hymnals for the Moravians and in one of them called himself "Minister and Cantor, known to the congregation."[12] He began as a boy to write hymns and completed more than 2,000 during his lifetime. Only a couple are known beyond the Moravian world, "Jesus, Your Blood and Righteousness," a translation by John Wesley,[13] and "Jesus, Still Lead On," a translation by Jane Borthwick (1813–1897).[14]

That more of Zinzendorf's hymns are not better known is understandable. Their "deep and personal devotion to and fellowship

---

[7] MBW, #375.

[8] MBW, #519, and LBW, #37 (in different rhythmic versions).

[9] Walter Blankenburg, "The Music of the Bohemian Brethren," *Protestant Church Music,* pp. 594–595.

[10] Ibid., pp. 599–600.

[11] For a sketch with its ecumenical context, see A. J. Lewis, *Zinzendorf the Ecumenical Pioneer: A Study in the Moravian Contribution to Christian Mission and Unity* (Philadelphia: The Westminster Press, 1962), pp. 161–169.

[12] Blankenburg, "The Music of the Bohemian Brethren," *Protestant Church Music,* p. 601.

[13] LBW, #302.

[14] LBW, #341.

with the crucified Saviour" too easily turned into "perverted fervor" without "self-restraint."[15] But what he intended is clear. He thought song "was the best method to bring God's truth to the heart and to preserve it there."[16] And what he did is clear. In 1727 he introduced "hours of song" to the Moravians. These were occasions when he strung together pieces of hymns in a "sermon in song." The whole assembly—"cantor, organist, teacher, and audience"—responded in kind: took "whole or half verses from 20 or 30 songs that illustrate[d] the subject [of the sermon] in a clear and orderly fashion" and sang them from memory.[17] Zinzendorf said his ten-year-old son played "the hours of song in the house," shifting "imperceptibly from one melody to another so that nobody knows whether the entire hour of song had not been expressly so composed."[18] Complete hymns were not neglected. They were sung at the Sunday services.[19] Zinzendorf apparently also invented hymns on the spot to go with his sermons, lining them out for the congregation.[20]

As one might anticipate, this musical activity altered the earlier practice. After Zinzendorf the Moravians did not limit themselves to unaccompanied congregational singing. Organs, polyphony, and solos even by women were introduced, and from 1731 wind instruments were used. Trombone choirs developed. So did cantata-like pieces.[21] Christian Gregor (1723–1801) brought order to these developments. He was a Moravian bishop, organist, composer, hymnwriter, and editor who, from 1742, acted as music director at Herrnhut.[22] He took the disorganized musical and textual materials he inherited from Zinzendorf, wove them together, created anew as necessary, and in 1778 edited a hymnal[23] of 1,750 hymns, which

[15] James Mearns, "Zinzendorf, Nicolaus Ludwig, Count von," DH, II, p. 1302. For an instance of fervor out of hand, see John R. Weinlick, *Count Zinzendorf* (New York: Abingdon Press, 1956), pp. 198–206.

[16] Blankenburg, "The Music of the Bohemian Brethren," *Protestant Church Music*, p. 600.

[17] Ibid., p. 600.

[18] Ibid., p. 601.

[19] Ibid.

[20] Harry Eskew and Hugh T. McElrath, *Sing with Understanding*, 2d rev. ed. (Nashville: Church Street Press, 1995), p. 107.

[21] Blankenburg, "The Music of the Bohemian Brethren," *Protestant Church Music*, p. 604.

[22] Ibid.

[23] *Gesangbuch, zum Gebrauch der evangelischen Brüdergemein* (Barby, 1778).

served the Moravians for the next century. He also published four-voice settings and stimulated Moravian composers to write anthems and cantata-like pieces for various days of the church year.[24]

The Moravians who were on board ship to Georgia with the Wesleys in 1735 abandoned their colony there in 1740 because they refused to take up arms in a war with Spain about territorial rights. A year later they settled in Bethlehem, Pennsylvania, then in other places as well, notably Salem, North Carolina. A vigorous musical life accompanied them.[25] Congregations sang, trombone choirs and orchestras developed, vocal choirs were organized, music from Europe was imported, Moravian composers in this country set to work, and David Tannenberg (1728–1804) built organs.[26]

The point to be noted, which will become more obvious as we proceed, is this: A rich musical development grew out of the congregation's song. It grew beyond that song—as in the Bethlehem Bach Choir, founded by J. Fred Wolle late in the nineteenth century—but it is inconceivable without the context that spawned it.

Pietism

Zinzendorf was educated as a Pietist. His godfather was Philip Jacob Spener (1635–1705), the progenitor of German Lutheran Pietism. Pietism is often identified with Lutheranism, but it relates to a much broader range. One can trace individual connections: Spener studied in Strasbourg, which was associated with the Reformed tradition; spent a year in Geneva, which was the center of the Reformed tradition; and was influenced by reading English Puritans and Dutch Calvinists. He influenced Zinzendorf who led the Moravians. They influenced the Wesleys who with Whitefield

---

[24] John R. Weinlick, "Gregor, Christian Friedrich," NGDMM, 7, 690.

[25] For an account see James Henry, *Sketches of Moravian Life and Character* (Philadelphia: J. B. Lippincott, 1859), pp. 264–275. For a broader overview, see Fred Graham, "Moravian Church Music in America: A Model for Living," *GIA Quarterly* 8:3 (Spring 1997): 16–17, 41–42.

[26] See Karl Kroeger, "Moravians, American," NGDMM, 12, pp. 562–563; Donald M. McCorkle, "The Moravian Contributions to American Music," *Music Library Association Notes*, Second Series, XIII:4 (September 1956): 597–606; and William H. Armstrong, *Organs for America: The Life and Work of David Tannenberg* (Philadelphia: University of Pennsylvania Press, 1967). The Moravian Music Foundation in Winston Salem, North Carolina, has published pieces of Johann Gottfried Geisler. They are not as profound as the work of J. S. Bach and gravitate to major keys, but they indicate a vigorous musical life.

influenced the American "Great Awakening." Wesley also had continuing contacts with John Martin Boltzius (1703–1765), the pastor of the Lutheran Salzburgers in Ebenezer, Georgia, just up the river from Savannah where Wesley was the rector of the Episcopal church in 1736 and 1737.

Individual connections such as these were but small pieces of a much broader seventeenth- and eighteenth-century context. After the demise of the Commonwealth under Oliver Cromwell and the restoration of the monarchy in England in 1660, Puritans lost political control and turned inward. Methodists and other evangelicals reacted against rationalism and Deism: René Descartes' (1596–1650) "I think, therefore I am," to John Locke's (1632–1650) *The Reasonableness of Christianity*, 1695, to John Toland's (1670–1722) *Christianity not Mysterious*, 1696, to David Hume's (1711–1776) being skeptical of his own skepticism. In France and the Low Countries Cornelius Jansen (1585–1638) responded negatively to what he perceived as the wooden casuistry of the Jesuits, though the Jesuits strongly supported Sacred Heart devotion, which became a public rite in the seventeenth century. Jansenism was connected to Gallicanism and to loosening papal authority over the French church. Blaise Pascal's (1623–1662) "conversions" and his dictum, "The heart has its reasons which reason does not know," had their origins in the piety of Jansenism. Jean Jacques Rousseau (1712–1778) was convinced the heart was more important than the head. Voltaire (1694–1778) sneered at the church's institutions and their hypocrisy, superstition, and deceit. In Germany after the Thirty Years War (1618–1648) there were more than three hundred "states." No attacks on the church from without like those of Voltaire were launched, but internally the vitality of the Reformation had solidified into a controversial but often lifeless scholastic orthodoxy. Reformed and Lutheran protagonists appeared to hate one another more than they hated Rome, while attendance at church was often mechanical. Sleeping during sermons, which might be about the follicles of one's hair, was normal. Structures were cracking, and structures in the colonies of the new world were forming.

Creaky, divided, or yet-to-emerge institutions were unable to provide a vital common life. Christianity was denuded of its mystery and attacked as superstition. In such a context many Christians turned inward to individual piety. This individual piety is one reason the Wesleys' "conversions" and their "heart religion" are paradigmatic of the period. Sixty years before their contact with the Moravians and 63 years before their conversions, Spener had laid a groundwork in *Pia Desideria*.[27] The "principal thing," he said, was that

> our whole Christian religion consists of the inner man or the new man, whose soul is faith and whose expressions are the fruits of life, and all sermons should be aimed at this.[28]

He was concerned "that we lay the right foundation in the heart."[29] In addition to preaching, he urged the reading of the Bible both aloud in the family and in private, book by book.[30] He thought groups of pastors and lay people should gather to discuss the Bible and edify one another.[31] These groups came to assume more importance, were called *collegia pietatis*, and yielded the term "Pietism." The laity, said Spener, should establish and diligently exercise "the spiritual priesthood,"[32] not simply know, but practice the faith.[33] He wanted to curb controversy, "beware of invectives and personal insinuations," practice "heartfelt love toward all unbelievers and heretics," and assume that disputation is not the only way to truth or union with other Christians.[34]

As happened with Wesley a century later, Spener's followers out-Spenered him too. The collegia pietatis became divisive and sometimes wanted to separate from the church. Spener tried to check these tendencies, not always successfully. Pietists, more strongly than their leader, opposed the opera, the theater, dancing, playing cards, and drinking,[35] trying to make these activities essentials rather than the nonessentials of more classic Lutheranism. Pietism spread but was resisted,[36] especially at the universities of Wittenberg and Leipzig. Hostilities arose between Orthodox and Pietists, which have continued to this day. Pietists, like all groups, present a mixed picture. Some reflected their theory in irenic and gracious lives, while others responded to the invective they opposed with equal if not more cruelty, viciousness, and brutality than their enemies.

---

[27] Philip Jacob Spener, trans., ed., and intro. by Theodore Tappert, *Pia Desideria* (Philadelphia: Fortress Press, 1964).

[28] Ibid., p.116.

[29] Ibid.

[30] Ibid., pp. 88–89.

[31] Ibid., p. 89.

[32] Ibid., p. 92.

[33] Ibid., p. 97.

[34] Ibid., pp. 97–102.

[35] Ibid., p. 22.

[36] Theodore Tappert, "Introduction," *Pia Desideria*, pp. 19–23.

Halle, where the composer George Frederic Handel (1685–1759) was born and the American Lutheran patriarch Henry Melchior Muhlenberg (1711–1787) taught before he came to this country, became a center of Pietism. When Pastor August Hermann Francke (1663–1727) and his followers faced opposition in Leipzig, they moved to Halle and in 1694 founded a new university there. Francke also led an orphanage and other educational and missionary enterprises. Zinzendorf was one of Francke's students and probably got the idea for his "hours of song" from Francke's practice in Halle[37] where there were plenty of hymns. Johann Anastasius Freylinghausen (1670–1739) stood at their center.

Freylinghausen was Francke's son-in-law. He assisted Francke and, at his death, followed him as pastor of St. Ulrich's and director of the orphanage. More importantly for our story, he edited a massive hymnal called the *Geistreiches Gesang-Buch*,[38] the first part in 1704 with 683 hymns and 173 melodies, the second part in 1714 with 815 hymns and 154 melodies. The collection included old and new hymns and tunes, his own among them. John Wesley translated his *Wer ist wohl wie du* as "O Jesu, Source of Calm Repose" and included it in the Charleston Collection. Tunes from Freylinghausen's *Gesangbuch* which are still in use include MACHT HOCH DIE TÜR,[39] GOTT SEI DANK,[40] and DIR, DIR, JEHOVA,[41] the last a relative of WINCHESTER NEW.

Zinzendorf's hymns moved beyond Freylinghausen's example to an ingrown lack of restraint. Freylinghausen in like manner had pressed Lutheran hymnody to the limits of or even beyond its balance. In one sense this was not a radical move. The rugged chorales of Luther had progressed through Philipp Nicolai's (1556–1608) "king" and "queen" of the chorales ("Wachet auf"[42] and "Wie schön leuchtet"[43]) to the warmth of Paul Gerhardt's (1607–1676) texts and Johann Crüger's (1598–1662) tunes. Crüger edited the major German hymnal of the seventeenth century. Its very title,

---

[37] Blankenburg, "The Music of the Bohemian Brethren," *Protestant Church Music*, p. 600.

[38] *Geistreiches Gesang-Buch den Kern und neuer Lieder* (Halle: Wèaysenhauses, 1704 and 1714).

[39] LBW, #32.

[40] LBW,#379.

[41] LBW, #382.

[42] LBW, #31, "Wake, Awake," text and tune.

[43] LBW, #76, "O Morning Star," text and tune.

Praxis Pietatis Melica, which might be translated something like "Practice of Musical Piety," presaged Pietism.

In another sense, however, the hymnic and musical currents that seemed to go with the flow were part of seventeenth- and eighteenth-century mindsets, which undermined the church and its worship. Mark Bangert has listed some contributors.

- Heinrich Mueller (1631–1675), a precursor of Pietism, in his *Geistliche Seelenmusik* of 1659 viewed music as "part of the soul's devotional exercise."
- Rousseau and German advocates of the Enlightenment "stressed the absolute independence of music (art for art's sake) and its potential to better humanity."
- Pope Benedict XIV (1675–1758) in his encyclical *Annus qui* saw music as "useful for 'arousing the sentiments of the faithful so that they may be more joyfully excited to piety and devotion.' "
- Friedrich Schleiermacher (1768–1834), a child of the Enlightenment and Pietism, wanted music that was simple and popular, which in turn meant "learned" music was scorned.[44]

One could add that Pietists tended to discount all music in services except simple and often sentimental hymns.[45] In Routley's view, Wesley was a "proleptic Romantic" for whom music was to arouse emotions,[46] and Schleiermacher—who was educated at Moravian schools and Halle and became the most influential Protestant theologian of his day—systematized the whole mindset when he defined piety as "essentially a state of feeling."[47] If everything is

[44] Mark Bangert, "Theology of Music, Pietism and Rationalism," *Key Words in Church Music,* ed. Carl Schalk (St. Louis: Concordia Publishing House, 1978), p. 342.

[45] Basil Smallman, *The Background of Passion Music: J. S. Bach and his Predecessors* (New York: Dover Publications, 1970), p. 16.

[46] Francis Williamson does not think Wesley fits this description. See chapter 13, FN 125.

[47] Friedrich Schleiermacher, *The Christian Faith,* ed. H. R. Mackintosh and J. S. Stewart (New York: Harper & Row, Publishers, 1963, English trans. of the 2d German ed., 1830), vol. I, p. 11. It should be noted that this is the linchpin of Schleiermacher's systematic theology, not an accommodation he made when he addressed the "cultured despisers" in *On Religion: Speeches to Its Cultured Despisers,* trans. John Oman (New York: Harper & Brothers, 1958, trans. from the 3d German ed., 1821; 1st ed., 1799).

reduced to feelings, and music is to arouse them, the implication is clear: Why are the church and its worship needed at all? Why are words or even faith needed? Why not let music do its thing outside the church at wordless symphony concerts, or at rock concerts where words become unimportant vocables to carry many decibels of liminal sound? Questions such as these, which people in the nineteenth and twentieth centuries either asked or assumed, had their roots in the seventeenth and eighteenth centuries. Here we have music not being pushed out of the church, but a whole frame of reference that quietly carried it out. If Zwingli along with some Anabaptists and Puritans consciously excluded music from the church, this mindset unconsciously removed it.

The point is not that the leaders in the church intended to undermine the church's worship and its music, though some Pietists have been viewed that way. Pope Benedict XIV was obviously not a Protestant Pietist. His context was the Roman Catholic church and its liturgy. He was quoting the Council of Trent and could be interpreted as countering seventeenth- and eighteenth-century tendencies.[48] Mueller, Spener, Wesley, and Schleiermacher likewise all presumed the church and theological categories that transcended their period and ran counter to it. Nor was the heart absent from music in the church before these leaders. It was obviously there from the Psalms to Calvin. The point is that in the seventeenth and eighteenth centuries the heart was moved to such a central place that music's historic anchors to the church and its worship—carrying praise, prayer, the story, and proclaiming the word—were obscured or removed.

Pietists set up a complex conflict, another of the prophetic and priestly dichotomies. Their emphasis on how the heart was oriented and what people ought to do often sounded as if works could set humanity right with God—precisely what Luther had opposed so vigorously. Pietists have affinities therefore with what Mary Catherine Hilkert calls the catholic sacramental imagination rather than the more Lutheran dialectical one,[49] but Pietism has nevertheless opposed catholic liturgical forms much more than classic Lutheranism, which retained them. Pietism's danger was to erect a means to reach God with the heart rather than in catholic sacra-

---

[48] Benedict XIV, *Annus qui*, in Hayburn, *Papal Legislation*, pp. 92–107, especially p. 97.

[49] See Mary Catherine Hilkert, *Naming Grace: Preaching and the Sacramental Imagination* (New York: Continuum, 1997), p. 20.

mental means—which Luther saw as gift and not a reaching to God at all. Where Pietists kept strong preaching traditions, they were able to stay in touch with the church's historic faith. Where they lost both preaching and sacraments, they easily slid into a cultural moment. When Pietists expected everybody to feel the same way, they undermined the church's worship with its freedom and welcome for people of various pieties at different stages or developments in their lives. Musically they have been prone to trade the bold rejoicing of Luther's chorales for something more intent on creating a response rather than voicing it.

If Pietism sounded as if the orientation of the heart could get you into God's presence, Orthodoxy had it own version of works righteousness in which the orientation of the head could do it—that if you thought the right thing and had the right doctrine you would be saved. The cleavages between Orthodox and Pietists confounded the church's song and witness in the world. One can see this perhaps most obviously among Lutherans, but the whole church since the eighteenth century has tended to drive a wedge between head and heart, between body and pulse. Luther maintained the balance, but it was upset soon after his death when Lutheran Orthodoxy created a shell that seemed heartless. Gerhardt and Crüger point to an undertow of hymnic health that countered the external and mechanical appearance of that shell. They too maintained the balance, as their durability indicates: Gerhardt's "O Sacred Head, Now Wounded"[50] and nine other texts in the *Lutheran Book of Worship (LBW)*,[51] Crüger's NUN DANKET ALLE GOTT[52] and ten other tunes in the *LBW*. But after them Pietism moved to a heart that seemed to have no head or body. Since then the church has often been paralyzed into thinking head and heart or body and pulse oppose one another and have to be divided, without realizing the obvious—that one without the other is death and yet another reason for music and musicians to migrate outside the church.

Music Spilling Beyond the Congregation

Music not only migrated out of the church for negative reasons. It also spilled out in an exuberant overflow. Unlike Watts, Charles

[50] LBW, #116, 117.
[51] One of them a translation by John Wesley: "Jesus, Thy Boundless Love to Me," LBW, #336.
[52] LBW, #533, 534.

Wesley wrote many hymns in many meters, influenced, as we have seen, in part by contact with the German "Herrnhut Moravians and with the lyric chorale school of Freylinghausen."[53] Hymnals were growing. Crüger's *Praxis Pietatis Melica,* first published in the 1640s, went through more than 40 editions into the next century, picking up other editors, texts, and tunes as it went. In 1690 it included 1,220 hymns. In 1702 Spener wrote its preface, and the book became the first Pietist hymnal, two years before Freylinghausen's *Gesang-Buch,* which itself expanded in successive editions until 1778. In 1736 *Praxis* had 1,316 hymns. This penchant for huge hymnals turned toward anthology. In 1735 the first hymnal Zinzendorf published for the Moravians[54] already had 999 hymns. In 1753 and 1754 his "London Songbook"[55] required two volumes to get all 3,265 hymns in it.

The evangelical hymnic activity spun itself out musically beyond leaders' control. In Germany the Wittenberg University faculty said the tunes of Freylinghausen's hymnal were "not in the slightest compatible with the elevated mysteries which ought to be contained therein."[56] In England John Wesley, though he adapted tunes from secular sources—Temperley regards the "typical" Methodist tune to be one like HELMSLEY[57]—was not in favor of florid hymn tunes.[58] Yet

> the music which came naturally to the composers who furnished the tunes for the early evangelical hymnbooks was the music of the opera house and the concert room, the music of solo and chorus, melody and bass, aria and continuo.[59]

Though Charles Wesley "always deplored Lampe's involvement with theater music,"[60] the new tunes that Lampe composed for his

[53] Ibid., p. 35.

[54] *Das Gesang-Buch der Gemeine in Herrnhut.*

[55] *Etwas vom Liede Mosis des Knechts Gottes und dem Liede des Lammes, das ist: Alt- und neuer Brüder-Gesang von den Tagen Henochs bisher, für alle Kinder und Seelen Gottes gesammelt* (London, vol. I, 1753; vol. II, 1754).

[56] Walter Blankenburg, "Freylinghausen, Johann Anastasius," NGDMM, 6, p. 840.

[57] Temperley, *The Music of the English Parish Church,* I, p. 212. HELMSLEY can be found in the UMH, #718. Martin Madin's arrangement of it is given in Temperley, *The Music of the English Parish Church,* II, #46.

[58] Routley, *The Musical Wesleys,* p. 25. See Temperley, *The Music of the English Parish Church,* I, pp. 207–208.

[59] Routley, *The Musical Wesleys,* p. 34.

[60] Roger Fiske, "Lampe, John Frederick," NGDMM, 10, p. 421.

texts were solo music with grace notes and trills,[61] which came
directly out of the theater. Here we have incipient oratorios developing.[62] Since congregations could not sing such complex music,
choral and instrumental groups were formed to do it.[63] Martin
Madan (c. 1726–1790) was at the center of some of this activity.

233

Music
Spilling
Beyond the
Congrega-
tion

Madan cut short a legal career after hearing John Wesley preach,
was ordained in the Church of England, and became the chaplain
at Lock Hospital,[64] a home for women who were venereal patients.
Though he was a popular preacher and a skillful composer, an out-
cry forced him from view when he suggested that polygamy would
solve the problems Lock Hospital represented.[65] Before that curious
episode he had introduced concerts and oratorios into the chapel
there, with support from the Countess of Huntingdon and John
Wesley, but disapproval from his first cousin William Cowper.[66] He
also edited a hymnal[67] and a tunebook.[68] The "tunebook" was less
than congregational. It had "duets and trios with figured bass, . . .
symphonies, [and] florid melodies."[69] The composers included
Samuel Arnold (1740–1802) who wrote operas and the violinist
Felix Giardini (1716–1796) whose oratorio *Ruth* was performed
twice at the Lock Hospital Chapel. Madan himself contributed
tunes, some "so extended as to amount almost to anthems."[70]

Music spilled beyond the congregation and its worship, but
would have been inconceivable without the congregational spring
that fed it.

[61] Routley, *The Musical Wesleys*, p. 36. Gilbert Chase, *America's Music: From
the Pilgrims to the Present*, rev. 2d. ed. (New York: McGraw-Hill, 1966), p. 49,
gives the example of Lampe's tune for "Ah, Lovely Appearance of Death."

[62] Routley, *The Musical Wesleys*, p. 38.

[63] Ibid., p. 41. For the ambivalent attitude of Evangelicals to anthems, see Temperley, *The Music of the English Parish Church*, I, p. 213.

[64] Hospitals and proprietary chapels were centers of gravity for Evangelicals. See
Temperley, *The Music of the English Parish Church*, I, pp. 206–207.

[65] The work he wrote was called *Thelyphthora* (London, 1780). The title was
"fancifully formed from the Greek for 'female' and 'destruction', probably meaning 'the destruction of woman'" (Routley, *The Musical Wesleys*, p. 73).

[66] Nicholas Temperley, "Madan, Martin," NGDMM, 11, p. 453.

[67] [Martin Madan], *A Collection of Psalms and Hymns Extracted from Various
Authors* (London, 1760).

[68] [Martin Madan], *Collection of Psalm and Hymn Tunes sung at the Chapel of
the Lock Hospital* (1769).

[69] Nicholas Temperley, "Madan, Martin," NGDMM, 11, p. 452.

[70] Ibid., p. 453.

Concerts and oratorios would have been just as inconceivable without the musical developments that made them possible. Musically the period we are dealing with has been labeled the Baroque.[71] It stretches from about 1600 with Giulio Caccini's collection called *Le Nuove Musiche* (1602) to the death of J. S. Bach in 1750.

Le Nuove Musiche was a set of solo songs with figured bass. In his foreword[72] to it Caccini expressed the ideas of a Camerata he met with in the 1570s and 1580s. In this circle Renaissance polyphony with its "number of voices singing together"[73] was regarded with suspicion because it obscured the words and their expression. In response Caccini developed monody, a term that can mean monophony but in this context means a solo line with a characteristic accompaniment. The solo voice expressed the words with whatever motives and ornamentation were appropriate, and a "figured bass" or basso continuo accompanied it. Figured bass meant a bass line played by bass and keyboard instruments, with "figures" (numbers and other conventional signs) under it. The keyboardist "realized" the figures that signified chords and nonharmonic notes. The melodic lines at the "top" and "bottom" of a piece served as borders. In between an organ or harpsichord filled in the implied harmonies. A sixteenth-century version of a jazz chart resulted. The keyboard continuo player was expected to improvise within the given harmonic structures. Caccini described this already in 1600 in the dedication to his opera *Euridice*.[74]

This *stile recitativo* gave composers a dramatic tool, which developed in two directions—operas and oratorios. Claudio Monteverdi's (1567–1643) *L'Orfeo* is an example of the former, Giacomo Carissimi's (1605–1674) *Jephte* the latter. Several additional points will give the musical scope at work here. 1) Figured bass remained the

---

[71] To study this period see Manfred F. Bukofzer, *Music in the Baroque Era from Monteverdi to Bach* (New York: W. W. Norton & Company, 1947); Donald Jay Grout, Claude V. Palisca, *A History of Western Music*, 5th ed. (New York: W. W. Norton & Company, 1996), chapters 9–11; Paul Henry Lang, *Music in Western Civilization* (New York: W. W. Norton & Company, 1941), chapters 10 and 11; Claude V. Palisca, "Baroque," NGDMM, 2: 172–178; and Claude V. Palisca, *Baroque Music*, 3d ed. (Englewood Cliffs: Prentice-Hall, 1991) .

[72] Giulio Caccini, "Foreword," *Le Nuove Musiche* [1602] in SRMH, pp. 377–392.

[73] Ibid., p. 379.

[74] Giulio Caccini, "Dedication," *Euridice* [1600] in SRMH, p. 371.

characteristic underlay of the entire Baroque period. Crüger's *Praxis*
Pietatis Melica, or its progenitor *Newes vollkömliches Gesang-*
buch,[75] was the first chorale book to use it. Freylinghausen did the
same. So did Lampe and Madan. 2) Along with the figured bass,
tonality developed from the modal system into the major and minor
keys we now take for granted. Tonality increased the possibilities for
both drama and length of musical pieces. After a key was established, another (related) key could be introduced to set up a longing for the home key. The return to the initial key fulfilled the expec-
tation. Baroque da capo arias were constructed in this manner, and
later Classic and Romantic symphonies "developed" the possibilities
of key contrast in more complex ways. 3) Caccini and his circle did
not curtail polyphony. It continued but was influenced, so that by
the time of Bach the vertical harmonies of figured bass and the horizontal lines of polyphony had achieved a tensile strength and
balance.

Large Works

The historical forces we have been observing led to large-scale oratorios, passions, masses, and requiems, which, though stimulated by
the church and inconceivable without it, came to be viewed as freestanding pieces with their own purely musical interest. "Church
music" today often refers to just such pieces. Some people might
regard the subtitle of this book as misleading because it has taken so
long to get to them, because they will be mentioned briefly, and
because I obviously define church music much more broadly as fundamentally the people's song at worship from which these larger
freestanding works have grown. Shorter medieval and Renaissance
masses, motets, and anthems (later pieces too, such as cantatas) can
be taken out of their worshiping context and also viewed indepen-
dently, but the theological and musical forces of the Baroque pow-
erfully increased the possibility and resulted in immense musical
gifts from the church to the world. They stand on their own with
symphonies and operas as marvelous large human creations.

Some view this development with despair, as the church pulling
away from its former creativity and abandoning music and the arts
more generally to the world around it. There is some truth to such

[75] Johann Crüger, *Newes vollkömliches Gesangbuch, Augspurgischer Confes-*
sion (1640).

a view, though renewed nerve rather than despair may be a more appropriate response.[76] Others view these pieces with disdain as "learned music," which is not worth anything—the eighteenth-century idea the twentieth century has often vehemently perpetuated. This view is more unhealthy. A healthy church will celebrate the amazing gifts it has given to the world and, with discrimination, love them and the world to whom they were given.

Oratorios

An oratorio generally can be defined as a musical setting of a religious text, often a dramatic one from the Bible, which requires soloists, chorus, and instrumentalists, and which is intended to be performed in a church or concert hall, without action or scenery. It can be traced to liturgical dramas that were acted out in the liturgy in the tenth to twelfth centuries, in connection with tropes, when the story was portrayed at an appropriate point as in the Mass at the introit on Christmas or Easter.[77] Larger medieval dramas[78] can also be seen as leading to oratorios,

> but the real beginnings of the genre are to be found in the late Renaissance and early Baroque periods, where an ever-increasing interest in settings of dramatic and narrative texts gave rise first to opera and then to oratorio.[79]

In response to the reforms of the Council of Trent, Philip Neri (1515–1595)—a priest who sold all his books and gave himself to instruction, prayer, and the care of pilgrims and convalescents—attracted men and boys to conferences at the church of San Girolamo in Rome where he lived in community with other priests. At first a few men gathered with him informally to pray, discuss spiritual things, and sing spiritual lauds[80]—Italian devotional and vernacular hymns, derived from Francis of Assisi (1182–1226) and the Franciscans, such as Francis's "Canticle of the Sun."[81] As the number in the group increased, an "oratory" (house of prayer) was built

---

[76] The response of Quentin Faulkner, *Wiser Than Despair*, p. 213, is to be patient and "wiser than despair."

[77] See Reese, MMA, pp. 193–197.

[78] See John Stevens and Jack Sage, "Medieval drama," NGDMM, 12, pp. 21–58.

[79] Howard E. Smither, "Oratorio," NGDMM, 13, p. 656.

[80] Ibid., pp. 656–657.

[81] LBW, #527, now "All Creatures of Our God and King."

above the nave where those who gathered could hold their "spiritual exercises." These "oratoriani" (that which belongs to prayer) included Bible readings, sermons, and spiritual lauds, which involved fine musicians such as Palestrina and were done more and more by professionals as time progressed. From these lauds, or perhaps from the whole context, the oratorio was born.[82] In 1575 Pope Gregory XIII approved the Congregazione dell'Oratorio, which spread throughout Europe.

Oratorios include a wide spectrum. They have sometimes been liturgical, sometimes paraliturgical, sometimes freestanding. They can be viewed not only as gift of the church to the world, but as a tradition of proclamation in the world. In seventeenth-century Italy, for example, they characteristically had two parts with a sermon placed between them. Formally oratorios sometimes have had ties to cantatas or Passions. They are often dramatic, as in Carissimi's *Jephte,* which tells the story in Judges 11 where Jephte's vow forced him to kill his beloved daughter and only child. Felix Mendelssohn's *Elijah,* Arthur Honegger's (1892–1955) *King David,* and William Walton's (1902–1983) *Belshazzar's Feast* also recount dramatic Old Testament incidents. The best-known of all oratorios, however, George Frederik Handel's (1685–1759) *Messiah,* is not dramatic in the sense of *Jephtha,* which Handel also set, nor like his *Israel in Egypt.* It fits none of the usual categories, not even his own.[83] If one includes Johannes Brahms' (1833–1897) *German Requiem* in the category of the oratorio, it too is less than characteristic. Neither dramatic nor a Requiem Mass for the dead, it is a series of biblical texts in the face of death. It has provided comfort at "concerts" and on recordings in living rooms and listening rooms for people who have lost loved ones. Heinrich Schütz's (1585–1672) *Easter Oratorio* and *Christmas Oratorio,* Franz Joseph Haydn's (1732–1809) *Seven Last Words* and *Creation,* and Igor Stravinsky's (1882–1971) *Threni: Lamentations of Jeremiah* (a twelve-tone piece) further suggest how wide the scope is here both in content and musical style.[84]

[82] Howard E. Smither, "Oratorio," NGDMM, 13, p. 657.

[83] Bukofzer, MBE, p. 337.

[84] For the range, history, and many titles, see Howard E. Smither, "Oratorio," NGDMM, 13, pp. 656–679.

Masses and Requiems

When polyphony developed, settings of the propers of the Mass were at first more common than those of the ordinary, as in the Notre Dame School of Pérotin and Léonin. By the time settings of propers had declined, a huge set called *Choralis Constantinus* was nonetheless composed by Heinrich Isaac (c.1450–1517)—who also wrote the ubiquitous tune INNSBRUCK[85] (also known as INNSBRUCK, ICH MUSS DICH LASSEN or O WELT, ICH MUSS DICH LASSEN).

The primary period for settings of the ordinary of the Mass, in the sense of Kyrie, Gloria, Credo, Sanctus, and Agnus Dei,[86] came between 1400 and 1600, from Dufay to Palestrina. In this period composers employed musical devices that unified the movements into cycles in the context of actual worship services. In a motto mass each movement began with the same or similar musical motives. In the more usual cantus firmus mass, a preexistent melody—which could be from a secular source—served as the basis for the various movements.

In the Classical period, Franz Joseph Haydn (1732–1809) and Wolfgang Amadeus Mozart (1756–1791) wrote fine settings, which nonetheless pushed the limits of liturgical use not only by length, but because symphonic and operatic qualities tended to assume center stage. J. S. Bach's (1685–1750) *B Minor Mass* and Ludwig van Beethoven's (1770–1827) *Missa Solemnis* simply broke out of all liturgical limits into huge—and remarkable—freestanding pieces. Some settings of the Requiem, the mass for the dead, are in the same huge and remarkable category, notably those by Mozart, Hector Berlioz (1803–1869), and Giuseppe Verdi (1813–1901). The greatest twentieth-century setting of the Mass is probably the one by Igor Stravinsky. Its proportions are liturgical.[87]

Passions

The Passion and death of Christ stand at the center of the Christian faith. 1) The central Christian symbol has been a cross. 2) The earliest announcement to the world of what Christianity was about,

---

[85] UMH, #631; LBW, #s 222, 276, 282.

[86] This common designation "is a strictly musical rather than a liturgical" one: Richard L. Crocker, "Mass," NGDMM, 11, p. 774.

[87] For the range, history, and many titles of mass composition, see Ruth Steiner, Maurus Pfaff, Richard L. Crocker, Frederick R. McManus, Theodor Göllner, Lewis Lockwood, and Denis Arnold, "Mass," NGDMM, 11, pp. 769–797. For Requiems, see James W. Pruett, "Requiem Mass," NGDMM, 15, pp. 751–755.

called *kerygma* or "proclamation," included Christ's death as a central ingredient. (See, for example, I Corinthians 15:3 and Acts 2:23.) 3) The earliest yearly celebration of the church was Pascha, from which our Easter derives. It related to the Jewish Passover and meant passover from death to life or the Passion of Christ as victory. 4) By far the largest part of the New Testament Gospels point to and recount Christ's Passion and death.

The Passion narrative is therefore central to the Christian message. That it became important to the church's music is no surprise. Pascha was refracted into a period of feasting and celebration after it, fasting and instruction before it. The week prior to Pascha came to be called Holy Week. By the fifth century the St. Matthew Passion was used on the Sunday of the Passion (Palm Sunday, a week before Easter), and the St. John Passion on Good Friday. Those pairings have remained fairly constant. Other Passions on other days of Holy Week have been less consistent, and versions that mixed pieces of the four accounts together have also been made.

Like other liturgical texts, Passions were not simply spoken, but were sung. Originally a single person sang the whole narrative on reciting tones, varying pitch, volume, and tempo to match the words of the evangelist, of Jesus, and of the crowd or individuals in the story. Various letters were used to prompt the singer: like *c* for *celeriter* (rapid)—the evangelist's narration; *t* or *l* for *tenere* (to hold) or *trahere* (to drag) or *tarde* or *lento* (slow)—the words of Jesus; *s* for *sursum* (high)—the crowd and the individuals. From the thirteenth century on more than one person began to sing the story. Then *c* came to mean *cronista*, the chronicler; *t* turned into a cross for Christ; and *s* meant *synagoga*, the congregation or crowd.[88] In the fifteenth century polyphonic settings were composed.

Once polyphonic settings began the range broadened. Parts of the story were set polyphonically, the whole thing was done that way, chordal settings were made, oratorio-like works included interpolations into the narrative, and chorales were used as melodic material or as interpolations.[89] J. S. Bach's St. John and St. Matthew Passions are two of the most remarkable settings. They were part of the liturgical life in Leipzig, though their proportions extend beyond

[88] See Basil Smallman, *The Background of Passion Music: J. S. Bach and His Predecessors* (New York: Dover Publications, 1970), and Kurt von Fischer, "Passion," NGDMM, 14, p. 277–278.

[89] For the range, history, and many Passion settings, see Kurt von Fischer and Werner Braun, "Passion," NGDMM, 14, pp. 276–186.

what most churches today could conceive as part of their worship in Holy Week. Heinrich Schütz (1585–1672), as an octogenarian, wrote a St. Matthew Passion that is equally amazing, though quite different from Bach's. Bach used soloists and orchestra, and interpolated arias and chorales that freeze the action for meditation. Schütz's setting is a cappella and, with the exception of the opening announcement and closing chorus, uses only the text from Matthew with newly composed monophony for individuals and polyphony for groups. Kryzsztof Penderecki's (b. 1933) St. Luke Passion is related to Bach's settings, but employs huge forces and a mix of twentieth-century compositional techniques.

J. S. Bach

More than anyone else, J. S. Bach symbolizes music that grows out of, yet moves beyond worship. Resources about Bach and his large musical family that stretched before and after him seem limitless and are easily accessible. They need not be recounted here,[90] nor is this the place for lengthy commentary. Instead, here are a few ideas to stimulate your research, agreement, and disagreement. They assume that Bach is the musical result of Luther.

---

[90] For a glimpse, see Denis Arnold, *Bach* (New York: Oxford University Press, 1984); Howard H. Cox (ed.), *The Calov Bible of J. S. Bach* (Ann Arbor: UMI Research Press, 1985); Hans T. David and Arthur Mendel, *The Bach Reader: A Life of Johann Sebastian Bach in Letters and Documents*, rev., with Supp. (New York: W. W. Norton & Company, 1966); Douglas R. Hofstadter, *Gödel, Escher, Bach: an Eternal Golden Braid* (New York: Basic Books, Publishers, 1979); Joyce Irwin, *Neither Voice nor Heart Alone: German Lutheran Theology of Music in the Age of the Baroque* (New York: Peter Lang, 1993); Robin Leaver (ed.), *J. S. Bach and Scripture: Glosses from the Calov Bible Commentary* (St. Louis: Concordia Publishing House, 1985); Michael Marissen, *The Social and Religious Designs of J. S. Bach's Brandenburg Concertos* (Princeton: Princeton University Press, 1995); Jaroslav Pelikan, *Bach Among the Theologians* (Philadelphia: Fortress Press, 1986); Albert Schweitzer, *J. S. Bach*, trans. Ernest Newman (Boston: Bruce Humphries Publishers, 1962, first published 1905), two volumes; Basil Smallman, *The Background of Passion Music: J. S. Bach and his Predecessors* (New York: Dover Publications, 1970); Philipp Spitta, *Johann Sebastian Bach: His Work and Influence on the Music of Germany, 1685–1750*, trans. Clara Bell and J. A. Fuller-Maitland (New York: Dover Publications, 1951), three volumes bound as two; Günther Stiller, *Johann Sebastian Bach and Liturgical Life in Leipzig*, trans. Herbert J. A. Bouman, Daniel F. Poellot, Hilton C. Oswald, ed. Robin A. Leaver (St. Louis: Concordia Publishing House, 1984, first published 1970); Christoph Wolff, Walter Emery, Richard Jones, Eugene Helm, Ernest Warburton, Elwood S. Derr, "Bach," NGDMM, 1, pp. 774–877.

1. For much of his life J. S. Bach served as cantor at St. Thomas Church in Leipzig. He lived at a point in history where tonality was being established and where polyphony and homophony were engaged in a dynamic interplay. The builders Arp Schnitger (1648–1719) and Gottfried Silbermann (1683–1753) brought the organ to new musical heights during his lifetime. Bach did nothing new, but as a craftsperson used the occasions, resources, and possibilities at hand in a way that transcended craft.

2. Bach has been called the fifth evangelist. His cantatas only make sense as proclamation of the word in the word portion of Leipzig's four-hour Sunday morning Eucharists where cantatas were expected,[91] his music is loaded with Christian symbolism (ingeniously hidden), and he exegetes texts in all sorts of ways that include word painting. Yet his music—even his vocal music—is instrumental in character and could be considered in its totality (not only in the obvious pieces like the *Brandenburg Concertos* or the *Well-Tempered Clavier*) as absolute, not programmatic. Proclaiming the gospel and liberating music to be its most intrinsic essence as music were not contradictory for Bach, but two parts of a common reality—in the service of God and free. There are many implications, one of which may be that the church needs to value the finest and purest music, no matter its source.

3. Bach lived with the tensions of his age about dramatic music in worship and used to the fullest the resources that were available to him, responsive to word and sacrament in the discipline of the church's historic worship.

4. Order epitomizes Bach, yet freedom does too.

5. Bach inherited Luther's chorales not in their original rhythmic forms, but in their smoothed-out isometric versions, then gave them new vitality with stellar harmonizations.

6. Bach's music is complex, yet it grows out of and affirms the congregation's song.

7. Bach lived with but refused to be captive to the conflicts between Orthodoxy and Pietism. He wrote with form for the pious heart and with heart for the orthodox form.

Think on these things—*soli Deo gloria.*

---

[91] For a description of a Sunday in Leipzig see "The 18th Century, Leipzig Church Orders at the Time of Bach (c. 1725)," *A Handbook of Church Music,* ed. Carl Halter and Carl Schalk (St. Louis: Concordia Publishing House, 1978), pp. 72–74.

Before and After the French and American Revolutions

15

American Developments

At the end of the eighteenth century the French and American Rev-
olutions created a sense of starting from scratch. In Europe the old
order was overturned or being rejected. In the colonies that would
become the United States of America a new church and state relationship was being forged, and American Indian culture would be
wiped out by Europeans and their descendants.[1] But, as always, the
past was not absent from the present. The evangelical engine of the
eighteenth century rolled into the nineteenth. Heart religion, the part
of the Puritan strain that did not want religion mediated by set
forms, and the American frontier with no structured church life all
pointed toward a future that would presumably avoid the marks of
the church's history, liturgy, and music.[2] The train was headed for
nineteenth century revivalism. Before we get there, however, we need
to back up to trace some outlines of church music on the American
continent.

---

[1] For the intensity of the Indian campaign see Brian Wren, *What Language Shall
I Borrow? God-Talk in Worship: A Male Response to Feminist Theology* (New
York: Crossroad, 1989), pp. 78–79.

[2] This chapter and the next two rely partly on and use sections from my articles,
"Religious Music and Hymnody," *Encyclopedia of the American Religious Expe-
rience*, ed. Charles H. Lippy and Peter W. Williams (New York: Charles Scribner's
Sons, 1988), III, pp. 1285–1305; "Hymnody in the United States from the Civil War
to World War I (1860–1916)," *The Hymnal 1982 Companion*, ed. Raymond F.
Glover (New York: Church Hymnal Corporation, 1990), I, pp. 447–473; and
"Twentieth Century American Hymnody and Church Music," *New Dimensions in
American Religious History: Essays in Honor of Martin E. Marty*, ed. Jay P. Dolan
and James P. Wind (Grand Rapids: William B. Eerdmans Publishing, 1993), pp.
175–207, part of which is replicated in *With Tongues of Fire: Profiles in 20th-Cen-
tury Hymn Writing* (St. Louis: Concordia Publishing House, 1995), pp. 15–25.
These may be consulted for additional detail.

Catholic Marks

When Christopher Columbus and his fellow explorers came to America, they brought with them their Spanish Roman Catholic liturgy and its music. A choir of sorts sang Mass in San Domingo in 1494. A Dominican cathedral with a singer and organist was approved in 1512. In 1524 the Franciscan Father Pedro de Gante organized a school at Texcoco to train native musicians. Many similar schools sprang up in the next two centuries. During the sixteenth century at the cathedral in Mexico City Europeans and Indians sang chant as well as polyphony by Palestrina, Orlando di Lasso (1532–1594), Tomás Luis de Victoria (1548–1611), and other Renaissance composers. In 1539 a printing press was established at Mexico City, and in 1556 the *Ordinarium* (ordinary of the Mass) was printed there, the first printed American book with music.

Within what would become the continental United States, Father Cristóbal de Quiñones installed an organ and taught the San Felipe Indians the music of the liturgy at the San Felipe Mission in New Mexico between 1598 and 1604. The Indians also developed vernacular folk hymns called *alabados*, along with medleys of Gregorian chant, Spanish, and Indian melodies. These, as well as some four-part masses, became part of the culture as Roman Catholicism left its mark in southwestern portions of the United States.[3]

In the French Canadian colonies music was likewise associated with the liturgy, with devotional singing, and with the conversion of the Indians who were attracted to European music. "Possibly the earliest composition in Canada was a piece of plainsong attributed to the priest Charles-Amador Martin (1648–1711)."[4]

The Reformed Heritage

The Reformed heritage had a more significant impact on America. The Huguenots who came to South Carolina and Florida between 1562 and 1565 brought French metrical psalms and tunes with

---

[3] For more detail see Leonard Ellinwood, *The History of American Church Music* (New York: Morehouse-Gorham Company, 1953), pp. 3–17, on whom I am dependent here. See also Gilbert Chase, *America's Music: From the Pilgrims to the Present*, rev. 2d ed. (New York: McGraw-Hill, 1966), p. 59. For hymnody among the Indians see J. Vincent Higginson, "Hymnody in the American Indian Missions," *The Papers of the Hymn Society*, XVIII (Wittenberg: The Hymn Society of America, 1954).

[4] Carl Morey, Roxanne Connick Carlisle, "Canada," NGDMM, 3, p. 667.

them. Indians learned snatches of these and continued to sing them
after Spain had laid waste to the Huguenots. The Indians were
attracted to the psalm singing of Sir Francis Drake and his compatriots who brought English psalms to the coast of California in
1579. Early in the seventeenth century the Jamestown settlers carried English psalms and tunes with them.[5] Huguenots also carried
their psalters to New France.[6] Dutch Reformed merchants came to
what is now New York in 1613 and, though they did not provide
well for their worship at first,[7] sang from Peter Datheen's translation of the Genevan Psalter in a slow, unaccompanied, and unison
style.[8]

The "Pilgrims" and "Puritans" had the most significant impact.
The "Pilgrims" who landed at Plymouth, Massachusetts, in 1620
were psalm-singing English Separatists. Before coming to Plymouth, they had taken refuge in Holland where in 1612 Henry
Ainsworth, a minister and biblical scholar, had prepared for them a
more literal metrical psalter[9] than Sternhold and Hopkins. The
non-Separatist "Puritans," who decided reform of the church in
England from within would not work and formed the Massachusetts Bay Colony in New England after 1629, also thought that
Sternhold and Hopkins was not literal enough. In 1636, the same
year Harvard College was founded, they appointed thirty ministers
to prepare a new translation. The result was the "Bay Psalm Book,"
published in 1640.[10] Ainsworth had fifteen meters and thirty-nine
tunes like OLD 124TH, OLD 100TH, and WINDSOR. The "Bay Psalm

[5] Ellinwood, *The History of American Church Music*, pp. 10–12.

[6] See John Beckwith, ed., *The Canadian Musical Heritage, 5, Hymn Tunes*
(Ottawa: Canadian Musical Heritage Society, 1986), p. vi.

[7] Jerald C. Brauer, *Protestantism in America: A Narrative History*, rev. ed.
(Philadelphia: The Westminster Press, 1965), pp. 27–28.

[8] See Bert F. Polman, "Dutch Reformed Church, music of the," NGDAM, I, p.
663. For more detail about the Reformed Church in America and the Christian
Reformed Church, bodies which stem from the Dutch Reformed, see W. A. Weber,
"The Hymnody of the Dutch Reformed Church in America, 1628–1953," *The
Hymn* XXVI: 2 (April 1975): 57–60; Rudolf Zuiderfeld, "Some Musical Traditions
in Dutch Reformed Churches in America," *The Hymn* 36:3 (July 1985): 23–25;
James L. H. Brumm, "Coming to America: RCA Hymnals in the 18th and 19th Cen-
turies," *The Hymn* 41:1 (January 1990): 27–33; and Bert F. Polman, "Church Music
and Liturgy in the Christian Reformed Church of North America" (University of
Minnesota diss., 1981).

[9] See chapter 12.

[10] *The Whole Book of Psalmes*, or "Bay Psalm Book." See chapter 12.

Book" had only six meters, favoring Common Meter. In 1698, when tunes were included, there were only thirteen, OLD 100TH and WINDSOR among them.

Within a generation or two the vitality and variety of the Pilgrims' practice waned, and they abandoned Ainsworth for their compatriots' "Bay Psalm Book." They began to line out around 1682, following the Bay Colony's practice, which was already common by 1647.[11] Lining out slowed the pace of singing, broke the shape of a psalm into a line-by-line, call-and-response pattern, and encouraged improvised turns and flourishes. To keep afloat in this drifting sea people had to sing loudly. Finally nobody sang the same thing any more in a cacophony so slow that two breaths were required on one note.[12] Thomas Walter (1696–1725), a minister in Roxbury, Massachusetts, said tunes were "miserably tortured, and twisted, and quavered . . . into an horrid Medly of confused and disorderly Noises."[13] He pronounced it "something so hideous . . . as is beyond expression bad."[14]

Singing Schools

At about the same time that Watts was stimulating a concern for hymn texts in England, in New England Walter and a couple other ministers, Thomas Symmes (1677–1725)[15] and John Tufts (1689–1750),[16] were less concerned about texts and more concerned about what would become a continuing American refrain—the

[11] Irving Lowens, *Music and Musicians in Early America* (New York: W. W. Norton & Company, 1964), p. 18.

[12] Thomas Walter, *The Grounds and Rules of Music Explained: Or, An Introduction to the Art of Singing by Note. Fitted to the Meanest Capacities* (Boston: Benjamin Mecom, [1760], 1st ed., 1721), p. 5. Temperley, *The Music of the English Parish Church*, I, pp. 91ff. has explained how it developed that a congregation could take an hour to sing thirty stanzas of a psalm, two to three seconds per note.

[13] Walter, *The Grounds and Rules of Music Explained*, p. 3.

[14] Ibid., p. 5.

[15] Thomas Symmes, *The Reasonableness of Regular Singing: or Singing by Note* (1720).

[16] [John] Tufts, *An Introduction to the Singing of Psalm-Tunes In a Plain and Easy Method. With a Collection of Tunes in Three Parts*, 5th ed. (Boston: Samuel Gerrish, 1726), reprinted with an Introduction by Irving Lowens (Philadelphia: Albert Saifer, 1954). See also Irving Lowens, *Music and Musicians in Early America* (New York: W. W. Norton & Company, 1964), pp. 40–41.

musical state of affairs.[17] They argued for a return to "regular singing" or singing "by note," that is, "according to the rules of music," not "by rote."[18] Though lining out "by rote" was in this case the innovation, within a generation or so it had become traditional. People were not of a mind to change. The standoff that resulted ultimately was solved more by sociology than debate. Urban churches were the first to adopt lining out and the first to dispense with it. The Brattle Street Church in Boston had abandoned it already in 1699 at the same time that more rural churches were first beginning it.[19] It rose in popularity until the middle of the eighteenth century, died out in New England by 1800, then moved south and west with the frontier—migrating to some German groups in Pennsylvania and to places like Blackey, Kentucky, where Old Regular Baptists still practice it today.[20] It had a parallel in England that Nicholas Temperley has described.[21]

Though advocates of "regular singing" did not sway everyone with their arguments, almost immediately they stimulated singing schools,[22] which became established institutions after the middle of the eighteenth century and important cultural forces in New England, Pennsylvania, and other areas well into the nineteenth century. At first ministers or lay persons found patrons, hired a teacher, and reserved a meeting room in a church, private house, or tavern. The teacher instructed the students in the rudiments of music so they could sing the psalms. Students paid a fee and were expected to bring a candle and instruction book with a board to hold them. Courses usually lasted for a period of twenty-four sessions or less. By the middle of the nineteenth century itinerant "singing school masters" went from community to community, organizing students into schools for about fifty cents a lesson for some thirteen lessons.

---

[17] The English had similar concerns. See Temperley, *The Music of the English Parish Church*, I, pp. 100ff.

[18] For more detail and a longer trajectory see McKay and Crawford, *William Billings of Boston*, pp. 9–29.

[19] See Gilbert Chase, *America's Music: From the Pilgrims to the Present*, rev. 2d ed. (New York: McGraw-Hill, 1966), p. 39.

[20] Among Presbyterians lining out was dying out by mid-nineteenth century. See Ernest Trice Thompson, *Presbyterians in the South, Volume One: 1607–1861* (Richmond: John Knox Press, 1963), p. 219.

[21] Temperley, *The Music of the English Parish Church*, I, pp. 91–99.

[22] See H. Wiley Hitchcock, *Music in the United States: A Historical Introduction* (Englewood Cliffs: Prentice-Hall, 1969), p. 8.

Toward the end of the nineteenth century recreation and courting, never absent from these gatherings,[23] became more important than the original instructional intent.[24]

Many things could be said about singing schools. Here are some of them. 1) Singing schools exerted a considerable influence on America's musical and cultural life beyond their potential for matchmaking. They generated hundreds of instruction books, which, by the end of the eighteenth century, were printed in their characteristic oblong shape. These "tunebooks" introduced the rudiments of music with an anthology of metrical psalms. Hymns, fuging tunes, and anthems were included as the repertoire expanded beyond psalmody. Newly composed hymn tunes were also stimulated, like Oliver Holden's (1765–1844) CORONATION for "All Hail the Power of Jesus' Name."[25]

2) Singing schools pushed into Canada. James Lyon (1735–1794) took his tune book *Urania*[26] to Nova Scotia with him when he went there in 1764 as a minister and singing school instructor. John Beckwith points to the social and religious importance of singing schools in maritime Canada and the Loyalist settlements of the Upper and Lower Colonies.[27]

3) Singing schools produced church choirs and choral societies, especially in urban centers. The choral societies moved beyond affiliations with a given church and gravitated to European art music and concerts. The Handel and Haydn Society of Boston, founded in 1815 and the first oratorio society in America, is a prime example. It grew out of a fine choir at Boston's Park Street Church and set as its goals presenting concerts and publishing tunebooks.[28] The important tunebook it published, which Lowell Mason (1792–1872) compiled, points to the same progression: the usual psalm and hymn tunes were there plus "beautiful extracts" from Haydn, Mozart, and Beethoven.[29]

---

[23] Ibid.

[24] See Richard Byron Rosewall, "Singing Schools of Pennsylvania" (University of Minnesota Ph.D. diss., 1969), pp. 136–140.

[25] CORONATION first appeared in Holden's tunebook *Union Harmony* (1793).

[26] James Lyon, *Urania* (Philadelphia, 1761).

[27] Beckwith, ed., *The Canadian Musical Heritage, 5, Hymn Tunes*, p. vi.

[28] George N. Heller and Carol A. Pemberton, "The Boston Handel and Haydn Society Collection of Church Music (1822): Its Context, Content, and Significance," *The Hymn*, 47:4 (October 1996): 27.

[29] [Lowell Mason, comp.], *The Handel and Haydn Society Collection of Church Music Being a Selection of the Most Approved Psalm and Hymn Tunes Together with Many Beautiful Extracts from the Works of Haydn, Mozart, Beethoven, and Other Eminent Modern Composers. Never Before Published in This Country: The*

4) Singing schools used pitch pipes and bass viols.[30] These naturally crept into worship services and ran headlong into the Reformed
stricture against instruments. "Catgut churches" and strict
Reformed proponents were set against one another. By the nineteenth century many churches used and even bought their own pitch
pipe and bass viol.[31] The way was paved for the introduction of
organs.

Hymns

When Whitefield came preaching to the American colonies in 1739,
he brought with him Wesleyan hymns. When he protested the Wesleys' Arminian stance, he abandoned Wesley for Watts. The theological dispute was lost in hymn singing, however, as both Wesley
and Watts were adopted by worshipers.

American hymn singing had its homegrown aspects. At First
Church, Northampton, Massachusetts, the minister Solomon Stoddard (1643–1729) favored "regular singing." Stoddard's grandson
Jonathan Edwards (1703–1758) joined him as assistant and became
the pastor at his death. Edwards championed a spiritual awakening
and hearty congregational singing. From about 1734 his preaching
stimulated the "Great Awakening" in New England.[32] Upon his
return to Northampton after a trip in 1742, he found that his congregation had out-done his zeal by substituting Watts for metrical
psalmody. He favored the presence of Watts but not the absence of
the psalms. A compromise was reached so that both Watts and metrical psalms were used.[33]

*Whole Harmonized for Three and Four Voices, with a Figured Base for the Organ
or Piano Forte Calculated for Public Worship or Private Devotion* (Boston: Richardson and Lord, 1822). Unabridged republication of the first edition (New York: Da
Capo Press, 1973). For a discussion of this book see Heller and Pemberton, "The
Boston Handel and Haydn Society Collection of Church Music," pp. 26–39.

[30] In England a bassoon or cello was the "most essential instrument" in the
church bands, which were common from 1780 to 1830. See Temperley, *The Music
of the English Parish Church*, I, p. 197 (and pp. 196–201 for a fuller description).

[31] See Henry Wilder Foote, *Three Centuries of American Hymnody* (Cambridge:
Harvard University Press, 1940), p. 112–113, and Ellinwood, *The History of American Church Music*, pp. 23–24.

[32] See William Warren Sweet, *The Story of Religion in America* (New York:
Harper & Brothers, Publishers, 1950), pp. 127–154, for one of the classic
descriptions.

[33] Henry Wilder Foote, *Three Centuries of American Hymnody*, pp. 147–149.

Not everybody approved of Whitefield, Edwards, Watts, or the Awakening. As in England, so in America: heated conflicts were set in motion. Charles Chauncy (1705–1787), the pastor for sixty years at First Church in Boston who was the great-grandson of the second president of Harvard and a force to be reckoned with, opposed the excesses of the "Great Awakening," like singing Watts as a kind of recreation "through the streets and in ferry boats."[34] Jonathan Edwards was not so disturbed by this, though he disliked disorderly and careless singing as much as Chauncy.[35]

As for use in worship, little by little New England's Congregational churches adopted Watts. In what was to become an American pattern, they compared Watts, Tate and Brady's "New Version" of 1696, and the "Bay Psalm Book"; then they made trials, voted, referred the matter to committees, and worked out compromises. After the Revolution Watts was pretty much in place, but, because he had made the psalmist speak like an English patriot, he had to be modified for American use. This necessity gave rise to numerous publications, which were called by their editors' names. Joel Barlow's (1755–1812) was "Barlow's Watts,"[36] Timothy Dwight's (1752–1817) was "Dwight's Watts,"[37] and Samuel Worcester's (1770–1859) was "Worcester's Watts and Select" (or "Watts and Select," most used up to the Civil War).[38]

The Presbyterians engaged in the fiercest strife about hymns. First organized from scattered Puritan congregations in New England, Scotch-Irish immigration augmented the denomination and changed the ethnic balance by the early eighteenth century. Disputes over organization and doctrinal standards were exacerbated by the Great Awakening. In 1741 the more experiential "New Side" party and the more orthodox "Old Side" advocates split into separate groups. The "Old Side," mostly Scotch-Irish, clung to *The Psalms of David*

---

[34] Benson, *The English Hymn*, p. 164.

[35] Ibid.

[36] Joel Barlow, *Psalms Carefully Suited to the Christian Worship in the United States of America, Being Dr. Watts's Imitation of the Psalms of David as Improved by Mr. Barlow* (1786).

[37] Timothy Dwight, *The Psalms of David, & . . . By I. Watts, D. D. A New Edition in which the Psalms omitted by Dr. Watts are versified, local passages are altered, and a number of Psalms versified anew in proper metres By Timothy Dwight, D. D, & . . .To the Psalms is added a Selection of Hymns* (1800).

[38] Samuel Worcester, *The Psalms, Hymns, & Spiritual Songs of the Rev. Isaac Watts, D. D. To Which Are Added Select Hymns from Other Authors; and Directions for Musical Expression* (Boston: Samuel T. Armstrong, 1819).

in English Meter,[39] originally prepared by Francis Rous (1579–1659) in 1643, or they used William Barton's (1603–1678) psalter of 1644.[40] The "New Side" gravitated toward Tate and Brady or Watts. After the Revolution and in the nineteenth century, Presbyterians generally adopted Watts and other hymns, but nasty conflicts and divisions arose in the process. The most intense partisan was the Kentucky pastor Adam Rankin who vigorously opposed hymns and led some congregations into the "Rankinite Schism" by forming the Associate Reformed Presbyterian Church.[41]

In 1688 Benjamin Keach's son Elias became the pastor of a Baptist church in Philadelphia and, before returning to London, was a force in introducing singing among Baptists here.[42] Just over a decade prior to the Revolution Baptists began to publish hymnals with the hymns of Watts, Philip Doddridge, Anne Steele, and other writers. They tended to favor the Great Awakening, adapted to the American frontier, and grew with a wide influence.[43]

Methodist societies began to gather by 1766 and formed a national organization in 1784. As Anglicans and with Wesley's opposition to the colonial cause, they suffered in the Revolution but rebounded with their organizational skills.[44] They had available to them the 1740 Philadelphia reprint of John and Charles Wesley's *Hymns and Sacred Poems* from 1739 and other English hymn publications of the Wesleys.[45] In 1781 Melchior Steinberg collected three of these into a single volume, probably for St. George's Church in Philadelphia, then the largest Methodist church in the United States. As noted earlier, the prayer and hymnbook Wesley prepared for use

[39] Francis Rous, *The Psalmes of David in English Meter* (1643; 1st ed., 1641; rev., 1646).

[40] William Barton, *The Book of Psalms in Metre* (1644; 2d ed., 1645; 3rd ed., 1646; 4th ed., 1654).

[41] See Ernest Trice Thompson, *Presbyterians in the South*, I, pp. 218–219, and E. H. Gillett, *History of the Presbyterian Church in the United States of America* (Philadelphia: Presbyterian Publication Committee, 1864), I, pp. 291–292, 410–414.

[42] See Beverly Bush Patterson, *The Sound of the Dove: Singing in Appalachian Primitive Baptist Churches* (Urbana: University of Illinois Press, 1995), pp. 26–27.

[43] See Brauer, *Protestantism in America*, pp. 99–100. For an overview of some Baptist contributions to American hymnody see Harry Eskew, David W. Music, and Paul A. Richardson, *Singing Baptists: Studies in Baptist Hymnody in America* (Nashville: Church Street Press, 1994).

[44] See Brauer, *Protestantism in America*, p. 100.

[45] See Foote, *Three Centuries of American Hymnody*, p. 146.

in the United States in 1784 were not always followed, even though a Methodist Conference in 1784 said that the way to "reform our singing" was to "keep close to Mr. Wesley's tunes and hymns."[46]

Unitarians have their roots in the seventeenth century or even earlier in sixteenth-century Socinianism,[47] but the eighteenth century saw organizational beginnings: King's Chapel in Boston became Unitarian in 1785, Hosea Ballou (1771–1825) was part of a Universalist Convention in Massachusetts in 1791, Joseph Priestley founded a Unitarian Church in Pennsylvania in 1794, and William Ellery Channing (1780–1842) organized the American Unitarian Association in 1825. Unitarians and Universalists came together in 1961 to form the Unitarian Universalist Association.

Unitarians contributed some hymns to the common pool. Samuel Longfellow (1819–1892), the brother of Henry Wadsworth Longfellow, wrote "Holy Spirit, Truth Divine"[48] and "Now, on Land and Sea Descending."[49] James Russell Lowell (1819–1891), not a member of any church but virtually a Unitarian, in 1845 wrote the antiwar poem "The Present Crisis" from which "Once to Every Man and Nation"[50] was extracted.

Unitarians, given their view of Jesus as example but not saviour or conqueror of sin and death, have emphasized ethical and artistic concerns in their worship and have employed music in those contexts. Robert Shaw (b. 1916), for example, one of the premier conductors of the twentieth century, expressed the musical telos of the Unitarian position. He was installed as Minister of Music at the First Unitarian (Universalist-Unitarian) Church, Cleveland, Ohio, in 1960. In his inaugural sermon, "Music and Worship in the Liberal Church," worship and its music were related to art, beauty, and form.[51] Shaw and Robert Killam, the minister, assumed "that noth-

---

[46] Louis F. Benson, *The English Hymn*, p. 285.

[47] Some Unitarians would say earlier than that. See Jack Mendelssohn, *Meet the Unitarians* (Boston: Unitarian Universalist Association, n. d.), pp. 13–16.

[48] UMH, #465.

[49] UMH, #685.

[50] *The Hymnal of the Protestant Episcopal Church in the United States of America 1940* (New York: The Church Pension Fund, 1943), #519. This hymn has fallen out of use because of the generic use of "man" in the first line and because it can be understood to imply progressive revelation, but earlier in this century it was sung fervently as a call to do battle against evil.

[51] Parts of this address are given in Joseph A. Mussulman, *Dear People . . . Robert Shaw: A Bibliography* (Bloomington: Indiana University Press, 1979), pp. 182–184.

ing which man had created that was of quality should be foreign to a service of worship."[52] So they did "Hindu chants, Buddhist or Jewish religious music[,] . . . went through the complete Bach Resurrection cantatas[, . . . had] Beethoven string quartets [and] a series of sermons on the ethical and moral situation in Shakespearean drama, or a series on great American poets."[53]

Composers

During the latter half of the eighteenth century American composers became evident. They were stimulated by psalmody, the trend toward hymnody, singing schools, choirs, and the birth of the nation. William Billings (1746–1800) was one of the most colorful of these.[54] Though his trade was tanning, he was consumed by music. Not very tall, with one leg shorter than the other, one eye, an "unkempt mien," and no formal schooling after the age of fourteen, Billings made up in voice, personal force, and study what he lacked in appearance and education. He tirelessly taught, composed, conducted, published, and promoted music. The *New England Psalm-Singer*,[55] *The Singing Master's Assistant*,[56] and *Continental Harmony*[57] were three of his six collections. In *Poganuc People*, Harriet Beecher Stowe characterized fuging tunes, specifically Billing's MAJESTY,[58] as "a grand, wild freedom, an energy of motion." They suggested to her the strife of the period versus the

---

[52] Ibid., p. 184.

[53] Ibid.

[54] For more detail see McKay and Crawford, *William Billings of Boston*, and David P. McKay, "Billings, William," NGDMM, 2, pp. 703–705.

[55] William Billings, *The New England Psalm-Singer: or, American Chorister. Containing a Number of Psalm-Tunes, Anthems and Canons. In Four and Five Parts. (Never Before Published)* (Boston: Edes and Gill, 1770).

[56] William Billings, *The Singing Master's Assistant, or Key to Practical Music. Being an Abridgement from the New-England Psalm-Singer; Together with Several Other Tunes, Never Before Published* (Boston: Draper and Folsom, 1778).

[57] Hans Nathan, ed., *The Continental Harmony of William Billings* (Cambridge: The Belknap Press of Harvard University Press, 1961), reprint of William Billings, *The Continental Harmony, Containing A Number of Anthems, Fuges, and Chorusses, in Several Parts. Never Before Published* (Boston: Isaiah Thomas and Ebenezer T. Andrews, 1794).

[58] One place this tune may be found is A. Davisson, *Kentucky Harmony or A Choice Collection of Psalm Tunes, Hymns, and Anthems* (1816), p. 65; facsimile edition with introduction by Irving Lowens (Minneapolis: Augsburg Publishing House, 1976), p. 85.

"measured motion of the mighty sea in calm weather," which is how she defined "Church chant."[59]

Fuging tunes were characteristic of Billings and other composers during the last half of the eighteenth century.[60] They were psalm and hymn tunes a bit too elaborate for congregations, written in three or four parts—or, in Irving Lowens' definition, a psalm-tune with a fuge tacked onto it.[61] They began with homophony and broke into energetic polyphonic imitation.[62] Anthems for solo and chorus also came from this period, with texts supplied by Watts, other poets, and the Bible.

Supply Belcher (1752–1836) and Jeremiah Ingalls (1764–1838) were tavern keepers and composers in Billings's rustic mold. So was Daniel Read (1757–1836) who ran a general store in New Haven, Connecticut. He rivals Billings in importance. Other composers were not so enamored with what they perceived as crude music with jig-like frivolity, "A Virgin Unspotted" by Billings, for example. As in the "rote" versus "note" controversy, they wanted to improve musical standards. Andrew Law (1749–1821), a Calvinist minister and the grandson of a Connecticut governor, preferred European models, though in 1803 he worked out a shape-note method without a staff to teach music.[63] The Baptist Oliver Holden—general store owner, real estate dealer, and Massachusetts representative—composed tunes such as CORONATION, wrote many anthems, and compiled over a dozen collections.[64] Samuel Adams Holyoke (1762–1820) was prolific but died penniless.[65] Oliver Shaw (1779–1848), another of the world's many blind organists, was one of Lowell Mason's teachers who cared little for fuging tunes and helped organize the Handel and Haydn Society.[66]

[59] Harriet Beecher Stowe, *Poganuc People: Their Loves and Lives* (New York: AMS Press, 1967), p. 49.

[60] For a description of the English parallel see Temperley, *The Music of the English Parish Church*, I, pp. 173–176; for examples, II, #s 41–43.

[61] Quoted in McKay and Crawford, *William Billings of Boston*, p. 92.

[62] See Irving Lowens, *Music and Musicians in Early America*, pp. 240–241, and Richard Crawford, "Fuging-tune [fuguing-tune, fugue-tune]," NGDAM II, pp. 175–176.

[63] For more detail see Richard Crawford, "Law, Andrew," NGDMM, 10, p. 556.

[64] See David Music, "Oliver Holden," in Harry Eskew, David W. Music, and Paul A. Richardson, *Singing Baptists*, pp. 17–25, and Richard Crawford, "Holden, Oliver," NGDMM, 8, pp. 643–644.

[65] See Richard Crawford, "Holyoke, Samuel (Adams)," NGDMM, 8, p. 668.

[66] See James William Thompson, "Shaw, Oliver," NGDMM, 17, p. 235.

Though Puritans followed the characteristic Reformed practice and permitted no instrumental music in church, at home it was acceptable. The popular notion that Puritans were dour and bereft of all music except unaccompanied monophonic metrical psalmody cannot be substantiated, as Percy Scholes has demonstrated[67] (and Billings' fuging tunes too!). By 1708 the wealthy Bostonian Thomas Brattle had imported an organ for his house. When he died in 1713 he left it to his Brattle Street Church, which rejected it. He anticipated such a possibility in his will and provided that the Episcopal King's Chapel would then receive it. Their acceptance made it the first permanent organ installation in a New England church.[68]

It was not the first organ used in a North American church. That distinction belongs to Quebec where an organ was used by 1661.[69] Within what would become the United States the Wissahickon Pietists and Swedish Lutherans probably first used an organ. Lacking pastors, the Swedish Lutherans in America received permission to ordain Justus Falckner, a native of Saxony who had studied for the ministry in Halle. The ordination took place in 1703 at the Swedish Lutheran Gloria Dei Church in Philadelphia. According to Julius F. Sachse, a late nineteenth- and early twentieth-century writer on the history of German sects in Pennsylvania, "Jonas the organist" and the Wissahickon Mystics (or Pietists) supplied the music. Sachse is not always reliable, his account is not without its problems, and where the organ came from is not clear, but the presence of an organ is at least probable—and the first reference to organ music in the colonies.[70]

In the middle of the eighteenth century David Tannenberg was building organs for his own Moravians and for German Reformed and Lutheran churches as well.[71] By 1800 there were about twenty

---

[67] Percy A. Scholes, *The Puritans and Music in England and New England* (New York: Russell & Russell, 1962), pp. 336–344, and the whole book!

[68] See Orpha Ochse, *The History of the Organ in the United States* (Bloomington: Indiana University Press, 1975), p. 20. This book is an extensive historical study up to 1970.

[69] Morey and Carlisle, "Canada," NGDMM, 3, p. 667.

[70] See Edward Christopher Wolf, "Lutheran Music in America During the Eighteenth and Early Nineteenth Centuries" (University of Illinois Ph.D. diss, 1960), pp. 17–21.

[71] The organs Tannenberg built are listed in Armstrong, *Organs for America: The Life and Work of David Tannenberg*, pp. 89–113, and Ochse, *The History of the Organ in the United States*, pp. 58–60.

organs in New England,[72] mostly in Episcopal churches. Puritan scruples against instruments in church continued well into the nineteenth century. As organs were adopted, the reed or pump organ became most common in the nineteenth century. Some of them could still be found in rural churches as late as the 1940s.[73]

Other Groups

Episcopalians

As has been obvious in the foregoing descriptions, other groups than Reformed ones and Moravians were gradually turning the American landscape into its richly textured variety. Actually, already by 1646, "18 languages could be heard along the Hudson River."[74]

Anglicans, known as Episcopalians in the United States, struggled to keep a regular schedule of worship in the face of widely scattered parishes and a shortage of clergy. But, with Congregationalists and Presbyterians, at the end of the eighteenth century they were "the largest and best equipped churches in the new nation."[75] Before that they inaugurated singing schools in Virginia by 1710 where masters and slaves played instruments. Philip Pelham became organist in 1755 at Bruton Parish Church in Williamsburg, Virginia, and by the last quarter of the century singing and playing of four-part hymns and anthems overflowed the church into homes. In Charleston, South Carolina, organs, organists, bells, printers, and composers were imported from Europe. Charles Theodore Pachelbel (1690–1750), son of Johann Pachelbel (1653–1706), was organist at St. Philip's from 1737 to 1750.

[72] Foote, *Three Centuries of American Hymnody*, p. 85.

[73] In England from the 1790s to the 1860s mechanical barrel organs, which operated by turning a handle, were popular. Thereafter the harmonium, in which the direction of air was the reverse of the American reed organ, became more common. See Temperley, *The Music of the English Parish Church*, I, pp. 234–239, 310–313. For a transcription of a barrel organ setting, see Temperley, *The Music of the English Parish Church*, II, #s 56, 57. *Cf.* C. Henry Phillips, *The Singing Church: An Outline History of the Music Sung by Choir and People* (London: Faber and Faber Ltd, 1945), p. 120.

[74] Brauer, *Protestantism in America*, p. 28.

[75] Ibid., p. 98.

In 1638 Swedish Lutherans settled along the Delaware. They maintained the sung liturgy of the Church of Sweden, with matins and High Mass on Sunday and sometimes matins and vespers daily. Within two centuries, however, they had disappeared as one by one their churches joined the Episcopalians.

Other Lutherans who came later in the eighteenth century stayed with their confessional roots. By 1780 there were more than 225 Lutheran churches in Pennsylvania and nearby states with people largely from the palatinate. Their German Reformed sisters and brothers from the same region, with whom they sometimes shared buildings, had more than 200 churches by that time.[76] They brought hymnals from Germany and reprinted them in this country.

Henry Melchior Muhlenberg (1711–1787), himself a musician and the organizer of the early Lutherans, is often called the "patriarch of the Lutheran Church in America." He was ordained in Leipzig in 1739. J. S. Bach played the organ for the service.

Mennonites and Amish

Less mainstream groups were also present. From 1683 Mennonites, followers of Menno Simons (1496–1561), began to migrate to Pennsylvania. In the eighteenth and nineteenth centuries the Amish came to the United States. They were a more radical Anabaptist group with even more social cohesion, named for their leader Jakob Amann (c.1644–c.1730).[77]

Pietist Separatists

The Wissahickon Pietists who participated in Falckner's ordination settled on the Wissahickon Creek near Philadelphia in 1694. They were a group of celibate millennialists with esoteric theosophical and mystical tendencies, led by Johann Kelpius (1673–1708) who had graduated with a degree in theology from the University of Altdorf.[78] He compiled a "hymnal" called "The Lamenting Voice of the Hidden Love at the Time When She Lay in Misery and Forsaken." It

---

[76] See Edwin Scott Gaustad, *Historical Atlas of Religion in America* (New York: Harper & Row, 1976), pp. 18, 28.

[77] See chapter 11.

[78] See Robert Stevenson, "Kelpius, Johann," NGDMM, 9, pp. 856–857.

contained ten Baroque melodies with figured bass. The community played instruments, sang, and were well known for their music. They died out within a generation.

Their spiritual successors were the Ephrata Community led by Conrad Beissel (1690–1768). Like Kelpius, Beissel was a Pietist from Germany. In 1732 he gathered a group at Ephrata, Pennsylvania. They wore habits and observed the seventh-day Sabbath, celibacy, separation of the sexes, and sharing of property. They, especially Beissel himself, wrote hymns and hymn tunes plus lengthier compositions with primitive parallel intervals and little dissonance. These pieces were transcribed onto illuminated manuscripts. The community formed itself into a choir with women at its core. Beissel conducted rehearsals for four hours each night. The singing was known for its contemplative and ethereal qualities.[79]

The African American Heritage

The "American dilemma"[80] of enslaved African Americans created not only a societal cancer for American civilization, but a separate musical strand that may ironically be one of the lasting contributions of the United States to human civilization. Because of laws that restricted slaves' freedom of assembly, by 1790, when the slave trade had reached its height, local churches in the South were made up of blacks and whites, with blacks restricted to a separate section for worship. At St. George's Methodist Church, Philadelphia, in 1792, when blacks were asked to sit separately from their accustomed places with whites, they walked out.[81] Richard Allen then formed a group in 1794 which became the African Methodist Episcopal Church. Twenty years earlier a separate Baptist church had organized.[82] An invisible black church had taken shape long before there were organized separate black

[79] See Russell P. Getz, "Ephrata Cloister," NGDMM, 6, p. 211; Russell P. Getz, "Beissel, J(ohann) Conrad," NGDMM, 2, pp. 418–419; and Betty Jean Martin, "The Ephrata Cloister and Its Music, 1732–1785: The Cultural, Religious, and Bibliographical Background" (University of Maryland Ph. D. diss., 1974).

[80] The phrase is from Gunner Myrdal, *An American Dilemma* (New York: McGraw-Hill, 1964).

[81] The famous account of this incident is quoted in William D. Watley, *Singing the Lord's Song in a Strange Land: The African American Churches and Ecumenism* (Geneva: WCC Publications, 1993), p. 5.

[82] Albert J. Raboteau, *Slave Religion: The 'Invisible Institution' in the Antebellum South* (New York: Oxford University Press, 1978), p. 139.

churches, however.[83] Clandestine "praise houses" developed in the woods or in plantation chapels where "ring shouts" with clapping and dancing resounded, sometimes out of the master's hearing.[84]

In their sermons African American preachers pushed speech to an elevated chant-like state that called forth responses by the congregation.[85] It is not an "exclusively black tradition,"[86] but it developed in a style derived from West African roots.[87] Spirituals developed in which moans, shouts, groans, slides, and spoken interjections combined with energetic bodily movement, hand clapping, foot stamping, and dancing. African songs were there with white Protestant psalms, hymns, and revival songs filtered through the African tradition.

African American music in the seventeenth and eighteenth centuries has been described by Wyatt Tee Walker as the moans, chants, and cries for deliverance that he calls slave utterances.[88] The oral tradition resulted in "spirituals," which developed between the middle of the eighteenth and end of the nineteenth centuries.[89] They combined African and American elements. Their verses and refrains that alternated between soloist and people came from an African call-and-response form that easily adapted lining out. The form invited extensive improvisation in which slides and turns abounded. Pitches were shaded to the flat side of the Western norm, and syncopation shifted accents. Black spirituals could be exceedingly sorrowful, like "Nobody Knows the Trouble I've Seen" or "Sometimes

[83] See Wyatt Tee Walker, *"Somebody's Calling My Name," Black Sacred Music and Social Change* (Valley Forge: Judson Press, 1992, 1st printing, 1979), pp. 19, 31ff. See also Raboteau, *Slave Religion*, pp. 68–75, 137, 212–219.

[84] See Portia K. Maultsby, "Afro-American Religious Music: A Study in Diversity," *The Papers of the Hymn Society of America*, XXXV (Springfield: The Hymn Society of America, [c. 1979]), pp. 8–11. Interesting schemes, some perhaps symbolic as well as acoustic, were devised to keep from being heard. See Raboteau, *Slave Religion*, p. 215–217.

[85] Maultsby, "Afro-American Religious Music," pp. 6–8. See also Albert J. Raboteau, *A Fire in the Bones: Reflections on African-American Religious History* (Boston: Beacon Press, 1995), pp. 141–151 (chapter 7, "The Chanted Sermon"), and Jon Michael Spencer, *Protest and Praise: Sacred Music of Black Religion* (Minneapolis: Fortress Press, 1990), pp. 225–243 (chapter 10, "Sermon and Surplus: Musicality in Black Preaching, *The Chanted Sermon*").

[86] Raboteau, *A Fire in the Bones*, 142.

[87] For a description of the music of West Africa see Gilbert Chase, *America's Music: From the Pilgrims to the Present*, rev. 2d. ed. (New York: McGraw-Hill, 1966), pp. 71–76.

[88] Wyatt Tee Walker, *"Somebody's Calling My Name,"* p. 38.

[89] For a description see Raboteau, *Slave Religion*, pp. 243–266.

I Feel Like a Motherless Child." They could also be jubilant, like "In That Great Gettin' Up Mornin'" or "Didn't My Lord Deliver Daniel."[90]

At Century's End

By 1800 the American Revolution had been won with the contradiction of oppressive slavery and the music its suffering fostered. The United States was increasing in diversity, in church music as well as other areas of life. In another of history's ironies, the New England reformers who had advocated singing by note "as a guarantee of musical uniformity" generated a "skill that had become just the opposite: an agent of musical diversity."[91] By 1760 there were "seventy-odd tunes available . . . approximately four hundred tunes printed before 1770," and by 1800 "well more than a thousand different compositions had been printed in American tunebooks."[92] Watts, Wesley, and Billings were in place. And a Second Great Awakening was brewing.

[90] Erskine Peters, ed., *Lyrics of the Afro-American Spiritual* (Westport: Greenwood Press, 1993) is a comprehensive collection of the texts.

[91] McKay and Crawford, *William Billings of Boston*, p. 24.

[92] Ibid., p. 23.

16

Revivalism, Liturgical Renewal, and Spirituals

Revivalism

Dwight

The Second Great Awakening began in two centers.[1] One started at Yale under the school's president, Timothy Dwight, the grandson of Jonathan Edwards whose edition of Watts was the most popular hymnal for Congregationalists and Presbyterians during the first quarter of the nineteenth century. Dwight fostered hymn singing and with Lyman Beecher (1775–1863) opposed Deism while stressing morality and good government.

Cane Ridge

On the western frontier a more emotional and less intellectual revivalism developed. In July of 1800 Presbyterians gathered at Gasper Ridge in Kentucky for an outdoor "sacramental meeting," which culminated in the Lord's Supper.[2] In 1801 at Cane Ridge, Kentucky, more than 12,000 people came to what was now called a "camp meeting," jointly sponsored by Methodists and Presbyterians. It lasted several days and involved the converted in sighs, moans, jumping, jerking, and trances.[3] This sort of revivalism spread throughout the Midwest. It did not lend itself to psalm or hymn singing of the type a group of worshipers who gathered regularly might do with texts they knew in hymnals. It stimulated instead an immediate emotive response and used music as part of the stimulus.

---

[1] See Sweet, *The Story of Religion in America,* pp. 223–242.
[2] Brauer, *Protestantism in America,* pp. 108–109.
[3] Ibid., pp. 109–111.

264

Revivalism,
Liturgical
Renewal,
and
Spirituals

This took the form of choruses fashioned from Watts or others that throngs of persons could learn quickly and remember easily. As Henry Wilder Foote noted, many anonymous publications appeared that were barely above the level of doggerel.[4]

Nettleton

Revivalism and evangelistic services became part of the nineteenth-century landscape. Sensing a need for a hymnal that would serve this type of worship, Asahel Nettleton (1783–1844), a Calvinist evangelist, in 1824 assembled *Village Hymns for Social Worship*[5] and a tunebook called *Zion's Harp* to go with it.[6] He rejected "the cheaper type of revival hymn"[7] and avoided the excesses of revivalism. He was hard-pressed to find "in the style of genuine poetry, a greater number of hymns adapted to the various exigencies of a revival,"[8] and he left out the "ephemeral" ones that were "entirely destitute of poetic merit."[9] Those "should be confined to seasons of revival," he said.

Finney

Charles Grandison Finney (1792–1875), whose emotionalism Nettleton opposed, moved toward the more ephemeral.[10] He introduced the "anxious bench" in the front of churches. There sinners were called, addressed, and prayed for by name. His campaigns needed a more immediate hymnody than Nettleton's *Village Hymns*, and in 1831[11] the Congregational minister Joshua Leavitt (1794–1873)

---

[4] Foote, *Three Centuries of American Hymnody*, p. 187.

[5] Asahel Nettleton, *Village Hymns for Social Worship, Selected and Original, Designed as a Supplement to the Psalms and Hymns of Doctor Watts* (Hartford: Brown and Parsons, 1848, 1st ed., 1824), p. iii.

[6] Asahel Nettleton, *Zion's Harp* (New Haven: N. & S. S. Jocelyn, 1824).

[7] Henry Wilder Foote, *Three Centuries of American Hymnody*, p. 189.

[8] Asahel Nettleton, *Village Hymns*, p. v.

[9] Ibid., p. vi.

[10] For a biography of Finney, see Charles E. Hambrick-Stowe, *Charles G. Finney and the Spirit of American Evangelicalism* (Grand Rapids: Wm. B. Eerdmans Publishing, 1996).

[11] Eskew, "Lowell Mason," NGDAM III, p. 188 gives 1830 as the date. Carol A. Pemberton, *Lowell Mason: His Life and Work* (Ann Arbor: U. M. I. Research Press, 1985), p. 56, gives April of 1831.

supplied *The Christian Lyre*[12] to meet the need.[13] This book was
designed to be "of a different character from [the hymns and music]
normally heard in church,"[14] the ones Leavitt thought *Village
Hymns* and *Zion's Harp* provided for. On the whole, as Henry
Wilder Foote said, it was "on a distinctly lower literary and musical level" than *Village Hymns*,[15] but it included a curious mix of
things: a wandering chorus ("A chorus which may be sung after any
suitable tune") with the text "Come to Jesus,"[16] the Marseilles with
the text "The Host of Heaven,"[17] "O Sacred Head, Now Wounded,"[18]
and Lowell Mason's tune MISSIONARY HYMN for "From Green-
land's Icy Mountains."[19] Leavitt printed texts and tunes together,[20]
the tunes in two staves with melody and bass. Two thousand copies
were sold in the first few months,[21] and twenty-six editions were
published by 1842.[22]

Waves of emotional response greeted Finney's campaigns, even
carrying along portions of the German Reformed and Lutheran
groups who were tempted to trade both their confessional and Germanic heritages for an almost wholesale embrace of Watts, Nettleton, and Leavitt. Though that temptation was checked by renewed
confessional responses, the lure was great.

Hastings and Mason

The Christian Lyre set in motion another typical American reaction
against it for a better quality of music. Thomas Hastings

---

[12] Joshua Leavitt, *The Christian Lyre*, vol. I, 5th ed., rev. (New York: Jonathan Leavitt, 1831, 1st ed., 1830?).

[13] For the issues involved here that led to Nettleton's and Leavitt's collections, see Sandra S. Sizer, *Gospel Hymns and Social Religion: The Rhetoric of Nineteenth-Century Revivalism* (Philadelphia: Temple University Press, 1978), pp. 67–68 (52ff).

[14] Leavitt, *The Christian Lyre*, Preface.

[15] Foote, *Three Centuries of American Hymnody*, p. 203.

[16] Leavitt, *The Christian Lyre*, p. 73.

[17] Ibid., p. 70.

[18] Ibid., p. 196.

[19] Ibid., p. 24.

[20] In "Religious Music and Hymnody," *Encyclopedia of the American Religious Experience*, ed. Charles H. Lippy and Peter W. Williams (New York: Charles Scribner's Sons, 1988), III, p. 1301, I said John Zundel's and Charles Beecher's *Plymouth Collection* of 1855 was the first to do this. That is wrong.

[21] Carol A. Pemberton, *Lowell Mason*, p. 56.

[22] Paul C. Echols, "Leavitt, Joshua," NGDAM, III, p. 23.

266

Revivalism,
Liturgical
Renewal,
and
Spirituals

(1784–1872) and Lowell Mason (1792–1872) led the charge this time. Hastings had little formal musical training, but educated himself and became a music teacher, editor, composer, and writer.[23] In addition to his 1,000 hymn tunes and fifty music books, he wrote a *Dissertation on Musical Taste*.[24] There he argued that "music is a language of sentimental feeling, and the excellence of any music is directly proportional to the effect it produces in the listener."[25] He assumed a European musical model as opposed to "a multiplicity of ephemeral productions, that fall infinitely beneath criticism" from "our country,"[26] though he confined the ideal sacred style to one that was "correct" but not too complex. He also assumed progress in the arts both historically and by individuals who could cultivate their taste and ability, in spite of his recognition that attempts by "theorists and compilers" to regulate "the public taste . . . have never been attended with entire success."[27]

Lowell Mason, who read the *Dissertation*,[28] worked as hard as Hastings—and was even more influential—in his efforts to improve church music on a European model.[29] He directed his church choir by the time he was 16, though his first full-time work was not music. He published voluminously and taught successfully enough to get music introduced into the public schools of Boston, the first such instance in the United States. That introduction was no accident.

> Mason's career hinged on one central belief and on his tireless efforts to carry out that belief: namely, that church music could not improve until everyone learned to read music, and consequently that teaching music to children in the public schools was . . . essential.[30]

---

[23] See Richard Crawford, "Hastings, Thomas," NGDMM, 8, pp. 298–299, and James E. Dooley, "Introduction," in *Thomas Hastings, Dissertation on Musical Taste or General Principles of Taste Applied to the Art of Music* (New York: Da Capo Press, 1974, republication of the 1st ed., 1922), pp. v–xii.

[24] See the previous footnote for the citation.

[25] James E. Dooley, "Introduction," in *Thomas Hastings, Dissertation on Musical Taste*, p. xiv. I am quoting Dooley's apt summation here. If you want to check the convoluted way Hastings says this, see p. 5.

[26] *Thomas Hastings, Dissertation on Musical Taste*, pp. 203–204.

[27] Ibid., pp. 187–188.

[28] George N. Heller and Carol A. Pemberton, "The Boston Handel and Haydn Society Collection of Church Music (1822): Its Context, Content, and Significance," *The Hymn*, 47:4 (October 1996): 29.

[29] See Harry Eskew, "Lowell Mason," NGDMM, 11, pp. 748–750 and Pemberton, *Lowell Mason* for studies of Mason.

[30] Heller and Pemberton, "The Boston Handel and Haydn Society Collection of Church Music (1822)," p. 29.

Mason wrote tunes like BETHANY[31] and OLIVET.[32] Hastings wrote
TOPLADY.[33] For all their correctness, Richard Crawford accurately
calls their style "pallid."[34] With it they wanted to counter Leavitt's
"trivial melodies,"[35] even though Mason's MISSIONARY HYMN was
in Leavitt's book. They produced *Spiritual Songs for Social Wor-*
ship.[36] Like Leavitt, they intended the book for revivals and special
occasions,[37] and put texts and tunes together.

Bradbury

In another of history's ironies, William Bradbury (1816–1868), a
student of Mason, set in motion a sort of quality that hardly squared
with the improvement of church music on a European model that
his teacher Lowell Mason had sought. He took the predictable harmonies and melodies of Mason and Hastings plus the characteristics
of camp meeting songs—catchy tunes with refrains—and introduced
them as Sunday school hymns, published in collections with titles
such as *Golden Chain, Golden Shower,* and *Golden Censer*.[38] When
he died William H. Doane (1832–1915) and Robert Lowry
(1826–1899) continued to write, compile, and edit collections of this
sort which Biglow and Main published. Bradbury wrote the tunes
CHINA[39] for "Jesus Loves Me" and SWEET HOUR[40] for "Sweet Hour

[31] UMH, #528.

[32] UMH, #452.

[33] UMH, #361.

[34] Crawford, "Hastings, Thomas," NGDMM, 8, p. 299.

[35] Pemberton, *Lowell Mason,* p. 56.

[36] *Spiritual Songs for Social Worship, adapted to the use of families and private*
circles in seasons of revival meetings, to the monthly concert, and other occasions of
special interest (Utica: W. Williams, 1833, 1st ed., 1832?).

[37] For fuller details and context, see Sizer, *Gospel Hymns and Social Religion,*
pp. 68–69.

[38] *The Golden Chain of Sabbath School Melodies* (New York: Ivison, Phinney,
1861), *Golden Shower of S. S. Melodies: A New Collection of Hymns and Tunes for*
the Sabbath School (New York: Ivison, Phinney Co., 1862), *Golden Censer: A Musi-*
cal Offering to the Sabbath Schools (New York: William B. Bradbury, 1864), published together in *The New Golden Trio, or, Bradbury's Golden Songs of Sabbath*
School Melodies, comprising the New Golden Chain, New Golden Shower, and
Golden Censer (New York: Biglow and Main, c. 1866). The titles are interesting in
their allusions to incense.

[39] BH, #344.

[40] BH, #445.

268

Revivalism,
Liturgical
Renewal,
and
Spirituals

of Prayer." Doane wrote PASS ME NOT[41] for "Pass Me Not, O Gentle Savior," and Lowry the words and music of "Shall We Gather at the River."[42]

When adults began to carry hymns of this sort from the Sunday school to urban revivals and church services, they became known as gospel songs or gospel hymns. Large gatherings of spirited singing fostered them: Eben Tourjée (1834–1890), founder of the New England Conservatory of Music, in 1851 began holding "praise services" or "sings"; Philip Phillips (1834–1895), a singer of sacred songs who sang before President Lincoln in 1865, organized singing schools and led "services of song" at Sunday school gatherings; and large conventions of the YMCA included singing.[43]

Moody and Sankey

Dwight Moody (1837–1899), shoe salesman turned evangelist, began his revivalist activities in Chicago and eventually took his campaigns to England. Ira Sankey (1840–1908) joined him in 1870 as his song leader. Sankey's baritone voice, harmonium, and compositions—such as the music for Elizabeth C. Clephane's text, "The Ninety and Nine"[44]—popularized gospel hymns, which even came to be called "Sankeys" in England.

In 1875 Sankey and Philip P. Bliss (1838–1876) published the first edition of *Gospel Hymns*. Over the next twenty years Sankey was joined by James McGranahan (1840–1907) and George C. Stebbins (1846–1945) who continued to add hymns until 1895 when *Gospel Hymns Nos. 1 to 6 Complete*[45] was published with 739 entries. Much of this activity centered around Chicago and what became the Moody Bible Institute.

---

[41] BH, #308.

[42] BH, #518.

[43] See William J. Reynolds and Milburn Price, *A Survey of Christian Hymnody* (Carol Stream: Hope Publishing, 1987), pp. 99–100. For larger contexts and summaries see William Jensen Reynolds, *Hymns of Our Faith* (Nashville: Broadman Press, 1964), pp. xxv–xxviii, and Harry Eskew, James C. Downey, and Horace Clarence Boyer, "Gospel Music," NGDAM, II, pp. 248–261.

[44] Ira Sankey, James McGranahan, George C. Stebbins, Philip P. Bliss, *Gospel Hymns Nos. 1 to 6 Complete* (New York: Da Capo Press, 1972, unabridged reproduction of the "Excelsior Edition," 1895), Introduction by H. Wiley Hitchcock, #570.

[45] See the previous footnote for the citation.

Fanny Crosby (1820–1915), one of the most important gospel hymnwriters, was not associated with Chicago. Blind almost from birth, she studied and taught at the New York City School for the Blind. At the age of forty-four she began writing gospel hymns.[46] By the time she died she had created more than 8,500 of them, including "Blessed Assurance," "Jesus, Keep Me Near the Cross," and "Rescue the Perishing." Her texts were set by gospel tune writers and published by Biglow and Main, located in New York and Chicago, which became the largest nineteenth-century publisher of gospel hymnody.[47]

The Twentieth Century

Revivalists and their musicians continued into the twentieth century.[48] Homer Rodeheaver (1880–1955) sang and played his trombone with Billy Sunday (1862–1935). Charles Alexander (1867–1920),[49] song leader for R. A. Torrey (1856–1928) and J. Wilbur Chapman (1859–1918), developed massed choirs who sat behind the preacher and became regular features of revivals. Cliff Barrows and George Beverly Shea (b. 1909) have been part of Billy Graham's (b. 1918) crusades.

The music of gospel hymnody employed triplets and dotted rhythms, predictable melodies and harmonies, major keys, mild chromaticism, and no dissonance or musical argument to create tension. Its choruses could be thunderous or quietly hushed. After Moody's death in 1899, during the Billy Sunday (1862–1935) era, it became lighter, semi-sacred, and commercial.[50] Examples are "His Eye Is on the Sparrow" (1905) and "Ivory Palaces" (1915) from Charles Alexander's collections, Ina Ogden's (1872–1964) "Brighten

---

[46] The first was "We Are Going, We Are Going" for Bradbury and published in his *Golden Censer* of 1864.

[47] Hope Publishing Company is the successor to Biglow and Main, whom Hope bought out.

[48] For an overview see Talmage W. Dean, *A Survey of Twentieth Century Protestant Church Music in America* (Nashville: Broadman Press, 1988), pp. 63–85.

[49] For interesting sidelights see Mel R. Wilhoit, "Alexander the Great: Or, Just Plain Charlie," *The Hymn* 46:2 (April 1995): 20–28.

[50] See Eskew, Downey, and Boyer, "Gospel Music," NGDAM, II, p. 251. [I am tempted to say "optimistic and cheery," but I have omitted those adjectives at the urging of my friend Francis Williamson who thinks they are inaccurate.]

270

Revivalism,
Liturgical
Renewal,
and
Spirituals

the Corner Where You Are" (1912),[51] George Bennard's (1873–1958) "The Old Rugged Cross" (1913), and C. Austin Miles's (1868–1946) "In the Garden," which Homer Rodeheaver popularized.

Liturgical Renewal

Solesmes

The camp meeting moved away from its character as a sacramental congregation to a social aggregation and, like the general momentum of the period, suggested the historic marks of the church's worship and music would be forgotten. Liturgical movements in the same period were not disposed to forget.

We already encountered one of these movements in Solesmes, a priory in France from 1010 until 1791, which the Benedictine monk Prosper Louis Pascal Guéranger (1805–1875) revived in 1833. Pope Gregory XVI appointed him abbot in 1837.[52] The monks who joined him worked from an ideal of Gregorian chant in its primal unaccompanied form and attached to Latin. In one sense they represent a reaction against classical masses whose musical architecture and logic was seen to obscure texts and crowd out worship. Solesmes's massive research was even more directed, however, at retrieving the chant that underlay its alterations after the Reformation.

Pius X

Pius X (1835–1914, pope from 1903), who had an intense interest in church music and "wrote more [about it] than all the popes together,"[53] embraced the work of Solesmes and issued his *motu proprio* soon after becoming pope. It was very close to a *votum* he had prepared in 1893 as patriarch of Venice. He said "sacred music

---

[51] See J. H. Gardner, "Hymn Story, Hymn Myth: The Case of Ina Ogden," *The Hymn* 37 (July 1986): 30–34.

[52] See Hayburn, *Papal Legislation on Sacred Music,* p. 169, for more details. Hayburn, pp. 169–193 surveys the work of Solesmes as do Eugène Cardine and Richard Sherr, "Solesmes," NGDMM, 17, pp. 452–454, and Hiley, *Western Plainchant,* pp. 624–627.

[53] Hayburn, *Papal Legislation on Sacred Music,* p. 195. For the reforms of Pius X see Hayburn, pp. 195–250.

should possess in the best possible grade the qualities which are
proper to the liturgy," namely, holiness, goodness, beauty, excellence
of form, and universality. Gregorian chant was understood to
embody these qualities most perfectly and was therefore regarded as
the "highest model of church music."[54] Palestrina's Renaissance
polyphony also fit the standards. The church has "always recognized and encouraged progress in the arts," said Pius X, and modern
music has "produced compositions good and serious and dignified
enough to be worthy of liturgical use;" but "nothing profane" is to
be allowed.[55] The theatrical style is least fitted, especially the one "so
much in vogue during the last century" in Italy.[56] Pianos and "all the
instruments which are too noisy or nimble, such as drums, kettle-
drums, bells, cymbals, triangles, and the like" were forbidden. Bands
were "strictly forbidden" except in some circumstances where "a
certain number of specially chosen wind instruments" were allowed.
The music they played had to be "reverent, appropriate, and in
every way like that of the organ."[57]

As Pius X's motu proprio indicates, the labors of Solesmes were
officially embraced by the Roman Catholic Church[58] and can be
seen in summary fashion in the *Liber Usualis*.[59] The motu proprio
and similar legislation has not been without some effect.[60] Pius X
himself had restored High Mass singing of the chant at Salzano,
Tambalo, Mantua, and Venice.[61] There were qualified successes in
France.[62] Congregations in Baltimore and Indiana made efforts.[63]
Richard Schuler says "parochial schools, seminaries, novitiates and
abbeys were the scene of greatest chant activity" and "singing by

[54] Hayburn, *Papal Legislation on Sacred Music*, p. 224.

[55] Ibid., p. 225.

[56] Ibid., p. 226.

[57] Ibid., p. 229.

[58] Ibid., pp. 251–293.

[59] *The Liber Usualis with Introduction and Rubrics in English,* ed., the Benedictines of Solesmes (Tournai: Desclee Company, 1958), pp. vii–x.

[60] Hayburn, *Papal Legislation on Sacred Music*, pp. 295–386.

[61] Gerald Ellard (ed.), *On the Sacred Liturgy, Encyclical Letter, Mediator Dei
(Nov. 20, 1947) of Pope Pius XII* (New York: The American Press, 1954), p. 5.

[62] J. Robert Carroll, "Cold Facts on the Congregational Singing of Gregorian
Chant," *The Gregorian Review,* III: 3 (May–June 1956): 18.

[63] Paul David Hume, *Catholic Church Music* (New York: Dodd, Mead & Company, 1956), p. 86f.

272

Revivalism,
Liturgical
Renewal,
and
Spirituals

even large congregations developed."[64] But, partly because Solesmes was rigidly interpreted and chant made too precious,[65] these ultimately were isolated examples. "Despite multiple invitations and prompting, congregations singing the High Mass chants did not quickly materialize."[66] Pius X's motu proprio has often served as an ideal well beyond Roman Catholicism as well, but neither it nor other legislation on church music has successfully controlled most Roman Catholics or other church bodies.[67] The church has a mind of its own about these matters.[68] Behind what might seem to some like legalistic fictions, however, there has been a struggle with central concerns. Pius X represents part of that struggle. At some points he and John Calvin seem to have made similar moves. "Nothing profane" sounds like Calvin's weight and majesty. At other points they responded quite differently. Calvin rejected chant. Pius X embraced it.

Mercersburg

There were other nineteenth-century movements of liturgical renewal. One of the most creative took its name from the little town of Mercersburg, Pennsylvania, where at the German Reformed Seminary there Philip Schaff (1819–1893) and John Williamson Nevin (1803–1886) worked at an evangelical catholic yet confessional Reformed theological position.[69] Nevin was among the first to challenge revivalism.[70] Liturgically and ecumenically their work was

---

[64] [Richard J. Schuler], "A Chronicle of the Reform," *Cum Angelis Canere,* p. 354.

[65] Ibid., pp. 354–355.

[66] Ellard (ed.), *On the Sacred Liturgy,* p. 26.

[67] See Hayburn, *Papal Legislation on Sacred Music,* pp. 403–404.

[68] Cf. Nicholas Temperley, *The Music of the English Parish Church,* I, p. 1.

[69] For an overview of this movement see James Hastings Nichols, *Romanticism in American Theology: Nevin and Schaff at Mercersburg* (Chicago: The University of Chicago Press, 1961), for the worship more specifically Jack Martin Maxwell, *Worship and Reformed Theology: The Liturgical Lessons of Mercersburg* (Pittsburgh: The Pickwick Press, 1976). Brief studies of Schaff and Nevin can be found in George Shriver, *Philip Schaff: Christian Scholar and Ecumenical Prophet* (Macon: Mercer University Press, 1987) and Richard E. Wentz, *John Williamson Nevin: American Theologian* (New York: Oxford University Press, 1997).

[70] See John W. Nevin, *The Anxious Bench* (Chambersburg: Publication Office of the German Reformed Church, 1844), republished with an introduction in *Catholic and Reformed: Selected Theological Writings of John Williamson Nevin,* ed. Charles Yrigoyen, Jr., and George H. Bricker (Pittsburgh: The Pickwick Press, 1978), pp. 1–126.

remarkable. Though there were many musical implications, few found expression.[71]

Lutheran

More musical roots formed an intrinsic part of Lutheran liturgical renewal in Germany and this country, the beginnings of which can be dated with the three hundredth anniversary of the Reformation in 1817. By the end of the nineteenth century the roots had sprouted and flowered. Congregational singing was revived, enormous hymnic research was done, and the rhythmic Reformation chorale was recovered—sometimes in theory and sometimes in practice. In either case it served as a confessional Lutheran signature. Liturgically the Common Service of 1888 in this country recovered the Lutheran heritage and became the basis for twentieth-century liturgical editing.[72]

Oxford-Cambridge

The Oxford Movement carried the most influence among Protestants.[73] Like Solesmes, the year 1833 dates its beginning. In July of that year John Keble (1792–1866), probably best-known among us for his poem-turned-hymn "New Every Morning Is the Love,"[74]

[71] See Paul Westermeyer, "What Shall We Sing in a Foreign Land? Theology and Cultic Song in the German Reformed and Lutheran Churches of Pennsylvania, 1830–1900" (University of Chicago, Ph.D. diss., 1978).

[72] For a concise overview, see Carl Schalk, "German Church Song," HC, I, pp. 304–307. For further literature, see Carl Schalk, *The Roots of Hymnody in the Lutheran Church—Missouri Synod* (St. Louis: Concordia Publishing House, 1965); Paul Westermeyer, "What Shall We Sing in a Foreign Land?"; Paul Westermeyer, "Church Music at the End of the Nineteenth Century," *Lutheran Quarterly* VIII:1 (Spring 1994): 29–51. For the background of church life and liturgy from one portion of the Lutheran confessional renewal, see Thomas H. Schattauer, "Announcement, Confession, and Lord's Supper in the Pastoral-Liturgical Work of Wilhelm Löhe: A Study of Worship and Church Life in the Lutheran Parish at Neuendettelsau, Bavaria" (Notre Dame University Ph. D. diss., 1990).

[73] Much of the following relies on my article, "The Hymnal Noted: Theological and Musical Intersections," *Church Music* 73:2: 1–9.

[74] This is from the first poem, "Morning," of John Keble, *The Christian Year: Thoughts in Verse for the Sundays and Holidays Throughout the Year* (London: Frederick and Warne and Co., [1827]), pp. 2–4, a book that "became a bestseller [and] helped to pay for the renovation of Keble's parish church." Glover, *The Hymnal 1982 Companion*, III, p. 22.

274

Revivalism,
Liturgical
Renewal,
and
Spirituals

preached his sermon on National Apostasy. In September of the same year John Henry Newman (1801–1890) published the first *Tract for the Times,* which defended apostolic succession. These tracts began as short leaflets by various writers and gave the name "Tractarian" to the Oxford Movement. The last tract, number 90 in 1841, was also by Newman who explained the Anglican 39 Articles in a way that resembled the Council of Trent. The controversy it caused brought the tracts to a close. Four years later Newman officially joined the Roman Catholic Church—a tempting move for many in this period.

The Oxford Movement began like the Wesleyan one, at Oxford University, but Cambridge University was soon involved as well. In 1839 two undergraduates at Cambridge, John Mason Neale (1818–1866) and Benjamin Webb (1819–1895), founded the Cambridge-Camden Society. It was renamed the Ecclesiological Society in 1845 when its formerly undergraduate members were becoming leaders in the church.[75] This society began with architecture as its chief concern, but quickly bumped into church music because organs and choirs take up space. Already in Volume III of the society's journal, aptly named *The Ecclesiologist,* organs were discussed in a not altogether positive way. Church music, it was argued, is "almost exclusively vocal." Organs are unnecessary and may be negative: they cost money, which could be spent on art and architecture; they require organists who also cost money; and they turn churches into practice studios and concert rooms. It was agreed that the "occasional and judicious use" of the organ can "increase the grandeur and propriety of public worship," but if organs were permitted they should be placed at the west end of the nave or at the end of either aisle on the ground, in other words, away from the altar.[76] When Neale's opinions that the choir should be in the chancel became normative, however, the organ moved there too.[77]

Articles appeared in *The Ecclesiologist* by Thomas Helmore (1811–1890). Helmore, the son of a Congregational minister, became an Anglican priest and precentor and thought out the nature of church music. He concluded it had two branches. One was the strictly congregational. The other pertained to the clergy and choir.

---

[75] See A. G. Lough, *The Influence of John Mason Neale* (London: S.P.C.K., 1962), pp. 6–11.

[76] "Organs," *The Ecclesiologist* III (September 1843): 1–4.

[77] Temperley, *The Music of the English Parish Church,* I, p. 254 (also pp. 256–257).

The complexity of music varies, he said, from the simple monotone for prayers to slightly varied formulas for Scripture readings, to psalm tones, to Gregorian hymns tunes, to more figured music. Unison Gregorian chant was considered the ideal, not Anglican chant, and operatic music was totally unfit.[78] Because of its relation to the modal framework of chant, the ideal choral music was that of the sixteenth-century composers Palestrina and Vittoria, with a nod to "Sebastian Bach."[79] That is, there is a style of church music versus oratorio, opera, theatre, concert room, and military parade music just as the Christian architecture of the Middle Ages stands versus that of classical Greek and Rome, modern Italy, classicized church architecture under Christopher Wren, and so-called "Gothic" architecture at the beginning of the nineteenth century.[80] Church music was not just theory for Helmore. He practiced it quite successfully in unaccompanied services, which he led, notably but not only at St. Mark's College, Chelsea.[81]

Before Helmore worked on music, John Mason Neale worked on hymnody and came to similar musical conclusions. Neale represents the path the Oxford-Cambridge movement took toward an embrace of hymnody. He grew up in a strict Evangelical home where he memorized many of Watts's *Divine and Moral Songs for Children*. As a youth he was terrified by a strict Calvinism coupled with the threat the Evangelical teaching on conversion seemed to him to con-

[78] See Thomas Helmore, "Ecclesiastical Music," *The Ecclesiologist* X, New Series VII (February 1850): 342–349; Thomas Helmore "Ecclesiastical Music, The Cantus Collectarum," *The Ecclesiologist* X, New Series VII (April 1850): 378–386; and Thomas Helmore, *The Ecclesiologist* XI, New Series VIII (August 1850): 104–110.

[79] See Thomas Helmore, "Ecclesiastical Music," *The Ecclesiologist* X, New Series VII (February 1850): 347; Thomas Helmore, "On Hymnody," *The Ecclesiologist* XII, New Series IX (June 1851): 172–178, and Thomas Helmore, "On the Music of the Hymnal Noted," *The Ecclesiologist* XII, New Series IX (August 1851): 250–253.

[80] Helmore, "On Hymnody," p. 173. Temperley, *The Music of the English Parish Church*, I, p. 251, explains the Tractarian perspective as eclectic, with these elements: theology from the first centuries interpreted through the seventeenth century, an architectural ideal of the fourteenth century, liturgy from the sixteenth, musical models of chant believed to be from the early church, and vestments and ceremonial from the later Middle Ages.

[81] See Bernarr Rainbow, *The Choral Revival in the Anglican Church* (1839–1872) (London: Barrie & Jenkins, 1970), pp. 58–73, and Temperley, *The Music of the English Parish Church*, I, pp. 257–258.

276

Revivalism,
Liturgical
Renewal,
and
Spirituals

tain.[82] He therefore disliked hymns[83] and vowed to "free our poor children from the yoke of Watts."[84] *Hymns for Children, 1842,* was the result.[85]

The negative approach of freeing children from the "yoke of Watts" forced Neale to think about hymnody and to study its history. His thoughts found expression in 1843 in an article that moved from a negative to a positive position.[86] Because hymns were so associated with nonconformists, they were at first viewed with suspicion. Benjamin Webb, a moderate about ceremonial who never wore eucharistic vestments,[87] nonetheless had serious qualms about hymns and wrote to Neale that he expected to

> loathe your Methodistical snuffling hymnizing article. It is the oddest thing to me that you have never slipped off that Evangelical slough: and is due, I take it, to your own facility of versifying.[88]

The key to embracing hymns was the discovery that they were not simply associated with Evangelicals, but with the daily office before the Reformation. Neale responded to Webb that he was guilty of "high-and-dryism" and that attributing a concern for hymns to facility in versifying was like pooh-poohing pictures in churches because one does not paint.[89] Neale was prepared to adapt

---

[82] See Mary Sackville Lawson, *Letters of John Mason Neale* (London: Longmans, Green, and Co., 1910), p. 45; Eleanor A. Towle, *John Mason Neale, D.D.: A Memoir* (London: Longmans, Green, and Co., 1906), pp. 245–246; and [John Mason Neale], "English Hymnody: Its History and Prospects," *The Christian Remembrancer* XVIII (October 1849): 335f. (Towle's book is not the same as a bound volume of articles with the same title by Sister Miriam. See Lough, *The Influence of John Mason Neale,* p. 1, FN 3.)

[83] Lawson, *Letters,* p. 22.

[84] Ibid., p. 46.

[85] This was followed by *Hymns for the Young, 1844, Hymns for Children, Second Series, 1846,* and the three then bound together. Neale later said that, though they "teach no false doctrine, and . . . are written in easy measures, . . . many of them are intolerably prosaic." See [Mary Sackville Lawson, ed.], *Collected Hymns[,] Sequences[,] and Carols of John Mason Neale* (London: Hodder and Stoughton, 1914), p. viii, and Neale, "English Hymnody," p. 337.

[86] [John Mason Neale], "Hymns for Public Worship," *The Christian Remembrancer* V (January 1843): 39–52.

[87] For an overview of the ritualistic controversy, see Temperley, *The Music of the English Parish Church,* I, pp. 252–253; for more detail and relation to music, pp. 268–276. Temperley's comment, p. 275, that the two extremes had so much in common but could not see it might summarize many conflicts.

[88] Lawson, *Letters,* p. 124.

[89] Ibid., pp. 124ff.

the hymns of Evangelicals, though he regarded the Breviary as the starting point for a core of hymnody. He realized it had its own "trashy hymns" and bad translations, which he wanted to avoid,[90] but hymns fit into the context of worship like this:

> There will then be *chanting* of the psalms, canticles, and responses, by the people; the *anthem* sung by the choir,—and the metrical *hymns*, such as we have suggested, completing the whole.[91]

The choir was not to take away from the singing of the congregation, but to lead it.[92]

With a committee that included Webb, Helmore and Neale teamed up to produce the *Hymnal Noted*.[93] Neale began to prepare translations, and Helmore adapted chant to English in a collection of 105 primarily morning and evening hymns for the church year. There were three versions: with words alone; with Gregorian notation on a four line staff, not the usual five lines of modern Western musical notation; and with accompanying harmonies, though Helmore regarded unaccompanied unison chant as the norm.[94]

We have here an English version of something like Solesmes. In both cases the central issue was about rhythm. Gregorian chant, with its gentle speech rhythm and characteristic modality and notation, was perceived to reflect a sacred sphere as opposed to a secular sphere where regular pulsations have heavy beats with attendant tonality and modern notation.[95] Perspectives like this have been profoundly influential as an ideal in wide portions of the church right up into our period, even where their "priestly" origins and theological presuppositions have not been known or held. No matter how

---

[90] Ibid., p. 125.

[91] Neale, "Hymns for Public Worship," p. 52.

[92] See Temperley, *The Music of the English Parish Church*, I, p. 255. Cf. William J. Gatens, *Victorian Cathedral Music in Theory and Practice* (Cambridge: Cambridge University Press, 1986), p. 7, 31.

[93] *Hymnal Noted*, Part I, 1851, bound with Part II, 1854 (London: Novello, Ewer and Co., 1871).

[94] Helmore cited authority for harmonization from the time of Guido on. See Thomas Helmore, "Lecture on Gregorian Music at Brighton," *The Ecclesiologist* XIV, New Series XI (February 1853): 54. Helmore has, of course, been criticized for harmonizing chant. See Percy A. Scholes, *The Mirror of Music* (Freeport: Books for Libraries Press, 1970), II, p. 554. For an example of a harmonized plainsong hymn from the *Hymnal Noted*, see Temperley, *The Music of the English Parish Church*, II, #63.

[95] I have explained this in more detail in "The Hymnal Noted: Theological and Musical Intersections," pp. 6–7.

278

Revivalism,
Liturgical
Renewal,
and
Spirituals

influential or ideal, however, the *Hymnal Noted* was never a best-seller,[96] though hymns such as "All Glory, Laud, and Honor,"[97] "O Come, O Come, Emmanuel,"[98] "Of the Father's Love Begotten,"[99] and "Now That the Daylight Fills the Sky,"[100]—later sometimes altered—appeared there. The Oxford movement's influence at the level of practice came with *Hymns Ancient and Modern*, not only a bestseller but the model of the modern hymnal.

Hymns Ancient and Modern

In 1858 a number of Anglican parish priests discovered they were each planning to compile hymnals and decided to work together on a single book.[101] A "distinctly Tractarian"[102] editorial committee was formed, chaired by Henry W. Baker (1821–1877). Keble and Neale served as advisors. Baker "defined three priorities."[103] First, hymns from the Sarum Breviary were to be translated anew or taken from the *Hymnal Noted*. Second, the editorial committee would check with all the correspondents for approval of the hymns selected. Third, some hymns "suitable for mission rooms, at lectures in cottages, etc." would be included, which gave the committee more latitude in its choices.[104]

William Henry Monk (1823–1889), choirmaster and organist at King's College, London, became the musical editor. By Advent of 1860 the words edition was to be ready, and by March of the next year the music edition appeared.[105] There were 273 hymns with 110 translations from the Latin, organized according to the church year.

---

[96] For details of its adoption, see Temperley, *The Music of the English Parish Church*, I, p. 264.

[97] EH 82, #154, #155.

[98] EH 82, #56.

[99] EH 82, #82.

[100] EH 82, #3, #4.

[101] For a concise history of *Hymns Ancient and Modern*, see Robin A. Leaver, "British Hymnody in the Nineteenth Century," HC I, pp. 436–441. For a bit more detail, see W. K. Lowther Clarke, "Hymns Ancient and Modern," *Historical Companion to Hymns Ancient and Modern*, ed. Maurice Frost (London: William Clowes & Sons, 1962), pp. 119–124.

[102] Leaver, "British Hymnody in the Nineteenth Century," HC I, p. 437.

[103] Ibid.

[104] Ibid.

[105] *Hymns Ancient and Modern for Use in the Service of the Church* (London: Novello, 1860–1861).

In 1868 a supplement was added. By then 4.5 million copies of the hymnal had been sold. In this country the book was reprinted "at least fourteen times in New York and Philadelphia between 1866 and 1888."[106]

Hymns Ancient and Modern had focus and breadth. A churchly concern had clearly set it in motion, but that concern was construed broadly, not in narrow Tractarian terms. The excellent translations of Neale were there, altered with his permission.[107] Catherine Winkworth (1827–1878) had made a number of her remarkable translations of German chorales by this time. The committee wisely used some of them.[108] And a wide array of new texts were there, such as Baker's "The King of Love My Shepherd Is."[109] *Hymns Ancient and Modern* paved the way for the rich ecumenical mix of hymns that has been typical of most hymnals since then. The book also left an indelible mark in its pairings of texts and tunes, which became unbreakable throughout the English-speaking world: "All Glory, Laud, and Honor" with VALET WILL ICH DIR GEBEN,[110] "Holy, Holy, Holy" with NICAEA,[111] "O God, Our Help in Ages Past" with ST. ANNE,[112] and "The Church's One Foundation" with AURELIA,[113] for example. In Temperley's view, the musical result, which *Hymns Ancient and Modern* symbolizes, was that the Victorian hymn tune brought all parties together and gave the congregation a new folk song.[114]

---

[106] Leaver, "British Hymnody in the Nineteenth Century," p. 438.

[107] Clarke, "Hymns Ancient and Modern," p. 120.

[108] The ones the committee had access to were from *Lyra Germanica: Hymns for the Sundays and Chief Festivals of the Christian Year. Translated from the German* (London, 1855), and *Lyra Germanica: Second Series. The Christian Life* (London, 1858). Later, in her *Chorale Book for England: A Complete Hymnbook for Public and Private Worship, in Accordance with the Services and Festivals of the Church of England* (London, 1863), she modified her translations so that they could be sung with their melodies. For the life and work of Catherine Winkworth, see Robin A. Leaver, *Catherine Winkworth: The Influence of Her Translations on English Hymnody* (St. Louis: Concordia Publishing House, 1978).

[109] EH 82, #645.

[110] EH 82, #154.

[111] EH 82, #362.

[112] EH 82, #680.

[113] EH 82, #525.

[114] Temperley, *The Music of the English Parish Church*, I, p. 314. See also pp. 296–310.

Revivalism and liturgical renewal represent two major streams on the nineteenth-century landscape, but there were other ones.

African American Congregational Song

The "spirituals" that African Americans sang in praise houses and beyond expressed the faith and hope that Christians of all races have sung about. They also had multiple meanings with signals about where to meet or the next underground railroad,[115] dressed in a form the white culture, if it heard them, interpreted as harmless.[116] They spilled out of their native worship environment in the 1870s when the Fisk Jubilee Singers of Fisk University in Nashville, Tennessee, sang them in choral arrangements and toured the United States and Europe with them.[117] They were introduced to a wide audience, which spanned the globe, and created a rich repertoire that black and white church, high school, college, community, and professional choirs began regularly to incorporate into worship services and concerts. Harry Burleigh's (1866–1949) arrangement of "Deep River" in 1916 served as a model, which Robert Nathaniel Dett (1882–1943), William Dawson (b. 1899), and others followed.

African Americans not only sang spirituals. In the early nineteenth century they also adapted the hymns of Isaac Watts into "Dr. Watts hymns," called "meter music," because the texts were in a metrical form.[118] These hymns were integrated into the oral tradition as they were lined out and "Africanized" so that the rhythmic and melodic characteristics of spirituals became evident in them. Meter music reached its peak around 1875 without ever displacing spirituals.[119]

---

[115] See Melva Costen, *African American Christian Worship* (Nashville: Abingdon Press, 1993), pp. 41, 45; Walker, *"Somebody's Calling My Name,"* p. 46, Watley, *Singing the Lord's Song in a Strange Land: The African American Churches and Ecumenism,* p. 30, and Raboteau, *Slave Religion,* pp. 246–266 (cf. pp. 296–297).

[116] Howard Thurman, *Deep River and the Negro Spiritual Speaks of Life and Death* (Richmond: Friends United Press, 1975), pp. 44–52, perceptively discusses how the weak have survived by fooling the strong. In his "General Introduction" Thurman also recounts the persistence into the twentieth century of African Americans hiding their song from whites when his college student body refused "to sing our songs to delight and amuse white people."

[117] See Eileen Southern, *The Music of Black Americans: A History,* 2d ed. (New York: W. W. Norton & Company, 1983), pp. 225–228.

[118] See Wyatt Tee Walker, *"Somebody's Calling My Name,"* pp. 73–96.

[119] Ibid., pp. 76–77.

African Americans not only sang in an oral tradition. Richard Allen (1760–1831), who founded the African Methodist Episcopal Church in 1794, compiled *A Collection of Spiritual Hymns and Songs* in 1801[120] and began the stream of African American hymnal production.[121] Like Leavitt after him, his hymnal included typical camp meeting "wandering choruses" from the period.[122]

African American congregational song was at first unaccompanied by instruments. Organs were introduced into African Methodist Episcopal and African Methodist Episcopal Zion churches in the 1820s and thereafter, with opposition, into independent African American churches.[123] Native hand clapping, foot stomping, and spoken interjections provided a percussive frame to which tambourines, drums, and other percussive instruments were easily added. Wind instruments, piano, and eventually the Hammond organ were also added, providing the instrumental resources that black gospel music employed in the twentieth century.

Black gospel appeared at the end of the nineteenth century at the same time as ragtime, blues, and jazz. White tunes in the Lowell Mason tradition were "Africanized" by syncopation. The genre reached a composed state and entered mainstream African American churches after 1900, when the Methodist minister Charles A. Tindley (1851 or 1859–1933) began composing hymns such as "I'll Overcome Someday" (1901), "We'll Understand It Better By and By" (1905), and "Stand By Me" (1905). Thomas A. Dorsey (b. 1899),[124] Baptist jazz pianist and accompanist for Mahalia Jackson and Bessie Smith, developed Tindley's beginning by using blues and ragtime melodic and harmonic patterns.[125]

---

[120] Richard Allen, comp., *A Collection of Spiritual Hymns and Song, Selected from Various Authors* (Philadelphia: John Ormrod, 1810).

[121] For this history see Jon Michael Spencer, *Black Hymnody: A Hymnological History of the African-American Church* (Knoxville: The University of Tennessee Press, 1992).

[122] Southern, *The Music of Black Americans,* pp. 85–86.

[123] For lists of and essays about African American groupings, see Wardell J. Payne, ed., *Directory of African American Religious Bodies: A Compendium by the Howard University School of Divinity* (Washington: Howard University Press, 1991).

[124] Not the same person as the jazz trombonist and band leader Tommy Dorsey (1905–1956).

[125] See Michael W. Harris, *The Rise of Gospel Blues: The Music of Thomas Andrew Dorsey in the Urban Church* (New York: Oxford University Press, 1992).

282

Revivalism,
Liturgical
Renewal,
and
Spirituals

Black gospel is an intense form of congregational hymnody. It may be perceived as bearing a relationship to what began in independent Holiness churches as an oral, communal creation. The highly emotional services of newly formed Pentecostal churches, typified especially by the prolonged Azusa Street Revival in Los Angeles that ran from 1906 to 1909,[126] however, should not be confused with black gospel. The African American community has often been as divided as the white one about its worship and music for similar reasons of theology, denominational configurations, and social class. Some blacks opposed Pentecostal practices, some argued for spirituals as opposed to gospel, and some sought to distance themselves from such styles altogether. One of my African American students suggested to me that there were successive layers of changing styles and opposing postures in his congregation alone. In any event, black gospel became widespread in many African American Protestant churches by World War II and in Catholic parishes in the 1970s after the Second Vatican Council. Dorsey's "Precious Lord, Take My Hand" spread to white churches as well and indicates the flexibility of the gospel style. It can be sung by individuals, duos, trios, quartets, choirs, and whole congregations. The vocal quality has been rough, even raspy, utilizing high registers and vibrato to be heard over instruments and loud congregations, often performed in a slow or moderate tempo to allow ample time for improvisation.

White Spirituals

Black spirituals and their jazz relatives grew out of intense suffering. As one of America's unique gifts to human civilization, they are widely known. They are not the only "spirituals" America has produced, however. Hidden away in rural areas, white spirituals have tenaciously contributed their haunting contours to American church music. George Pullen Jackson did the pace-setting research that introduced this part of America's rich heritage to many Americans and to the rest of the world.[127]

---

[126] For an analysis of the significance of this event, see Joe Creech, "Visions of Glory: The Place of the Azusa Street Revival in Pentecostal History," *Church History* 65:3 (September 1996): 405–424.

[127] George Pullen Jackson, *White Spirituals in the Southern Uplands: The Story of the Fasola Folk, Their Songs, Singings, and "Buckwheat Notes"* (New York: Dover Publications, 1965, republication of 1st ed., 1933).

Singing school teachers employed a system in which pitches were described by four syllables: fa (or faw), sol, la (or law), and mi. Since the diatonic scale has more than four pitches, these syllables were repeated like this: fa, sol, la, fa, sol, la, mi, fa. In 1801 William Smith and William Little published a book called *The Easy Instructor* in which they applied shapes to the syllables. Fa was given a triangle, sol a circle, la a square, and mi a diamond. *The Easy Instructor* was first published in Philadelphia, then in New York, and went through numerous editions in Albany from 1805 to 1831. It became popular throughout the country. Its shape-note notation took hold as a successful sight-singing system, especially in rural areas and among those who emigrated to the South and West.[128] This system is often called "fasola" solmization. Solmization means naming pitches by syllables rather than letters.

Nineteenth-century urban centers were influenced by Mason. They and he were embarrassed by rural self-educated singing school instructors who were cobblers and carpenters, and by their "buckwheat" or "dunce" (shape) notes.[129] Mason set out to make a "scientific improvement" of American music by European do-re-mi-fa-sol-la-ti-do solmization.

The indigenous American musical material that used shape-notes came largely from the British Isles and was filtered through the New England singing school instructors. It was an oral tradition in which composers and compilers used old tunes, altered old tunes, or newly composed ones in the same idiom. It began to take printed form in the early nineteenth century. Contemporary copyright issues and concern for who composed what were unimportant. The living tradition took precedence over individual contributors to it. The pentatonic tune New Britain, associated with John Newton's text "Amazing Grace," is a good example. Its origin is unknown, and it appears in many fasola books with no composer indicated.

Like New Britain, the tunes in this tradition often employed "gapped" features and appeared in the tenor voice. The most natural setting was three parts, though four were also used. Traditional Western rules of "correct" harmony were not observed: parallel fifths, octaves, and unisons, for instance, were permitted; disso-

---

[128] See Irving Lowens, "Introduction," *Wyeth's Repository of Sacred Music Part Second* (New York: Da Capo Press, 1964), pp. xv–xvi.

[129] The rural and urban division was not new to America or this period. See Temperley, *The Music of the English Parish Church*, I, pp. 100, 141 (and the whole book).

284

Revivalism,
Liturgical
Renewal,
and
Spirituals

nances did not have to be prepared or resolved; and voices were allowed to cross. The result was a haunting, rustic, and rugged music without the thick harmonic palette of the late nineteenth-century Romantic European tradition. It has attracted twentieth-century composers and congregations without a fasola heritage, as another way around the Romantic impasse.

A number of songbooks in the oblong tradition printed white spirituals and fuguing tunes in the nineteenth century. Examples are John Wyeth's (1770–1858) *Repository of Sacred Music, Part Second*,[130] Ananias Davisson's (1780–1857) *Kentucky Harmony*,[131] William Walker's (1809–1875) *Southern Harmony*,[132] and Benjamin F. White's (1850–1879) and E. J. King's (1821–1844) *Sacred Harp*.[133] *Sacred Harp*, in print yet today, is still used at Sacred Harp

[130] See Irving Lowens, "Introduction," *Wyeth's Repository of Sacred Music Part Second*, pp. v–xvi, for details about this book, shape notes, and an unabridged republication of John Wyeth, *Wyeth's Repository of Sacred Music. Part Second—* (2d ed.) *Original and Selected from the Most Eminent and Approved Authors in That Science for the Use of Christian Churches, Singing-Schools and Private Societies. Together with a Plain and Concise Introduction to the Grounds of Music, and Rules for Learners* (Harrisburgh: John Wyeth, 1820, 1st ed., 1813). For additional material, see Irving Lowens, "Introduction," *Wyeth's Repository of Sacred Music* (New York: Da Capo Press, 1974), pp. vii–xvii, and the accompanying unabridged republication of John Wyeth, *Wyeth's Repository of Sacred Music Selected from the Most Eminent and Approved Authors in That Science for the Use of Christian Churches, of Every Denomination, Singing Schools & Private Societies Together with a Plain and Concise Introduction to the Grounds of Music and Rules for Learners*, 5th ed. (Harrisburgh: John Wyeth, 1820).

[131] A. Davisson, *Kentucky Harmony or A Choice Collection of Psalm Tunes, Hymns, and Anthems. In Three Parts* (1816), Facsimile Edition with Introduction by Irving Lowens (Minneapolis: Augsburg Publishing House, 1976).

[132] Glenn C. Wilcox, ed., *The Southern Harmony* (Berea: The University of Kentucky Press, 1987), reprint of William Walker, *The Southern Harmony & Musical Companion; Containing a Choice Collection of Tunes, Hymns, Psalms, Odes, and Anthems; Selected from the Most Eminent Authors in the United States: Together with Nearly One Hundred New Tunes, Which Have Never Before Been Published; Suited to Most of the Metres Contained in Watts's Hymns and Psalms, Mercer's Cluster, Dossey's Choice, Dover Selection, Methodist Hymn Book, and Baptist Harmony; and Well Adapted to Christian Churches of Every Denomination, Singing Schools, and Private Societies: Also, An Easy Introduction to the Grounds of Music, the Rudiments of Music, and Plain Rules for Beginners* (Philadelphia: E. W. Miller, [1854], 1st ed., 1835).

[133] George Pullen Jackson, "The Story of the Sacred Harp," in *The Sacred Harp* (Nashville: Broadman Press, 1968), an unabridged republication of an 1860 imprint of the third edition of 1859 of B. F. White & E. J. King, *New And Much Improved and Enlarged Edition. The Sacred Harp, A Collection of Psalm and Hymn Tunes,*

of the country. Chicago is a particularly vital center.

The shape-note tradition found its home primarily among English-speaking white Baptists and Methodists, but it influenced other
groups as well, including German ones. *The Easy Instructor* was
translated into German by Joseph Doll in a book called *Der leichte*
Unterricht. It combined Smith and Little's shapes with German texts
and elements of the German chorale tradition and achieved some
popularity among less revivalistic German Reformed and Lutheran
groups.

Pennsylvania Spirituals

There is another set of white spirituals that used neither books nor
shape-notes.[134] Don Yoder calls them the "Pennsylvania Spirituals"
of the "Bush-Meeting Dutch," whom he defines as the United
Brethren, the Evangelicals, and the Church of God to distinguish
them from both the "Church"-type Lutheran and German
Reformed and the "Plain"-type Amish, Mennonites, and
Dunkards.[135] "Dutch" here does not mean from the Netherlands,
but the Pennsylvania German dialect called "Dutch," a variant on
"Deutsch," which is the German word for "German." The "Pennsylvania Dutch" bear affinities with more revivalistic groups that
date from the Second Great Awakening[136] and hold "that church-
going and the sacraments do not of themselves bring salvation,"[137]
but they need to be distinguished from those who practice mass
evangelism and once-for-all conversions. They were German Wesleyan pietists who connected "revivalism" with small groups, informal occasions, and ongoing sanctification as well as conversion.[138]
Their gospel songs in the Pennsylvania Dutch dialect without the use
of books related to this perspective.[139]

Odes, Anthems, Selected from the Most Eminent Authors: Together with Nearly
One Hundred Pieces Never Before Published; Suited to Most Meters, and Well
Adapted to Churches of Every Denomination, Singing Schools, and Private Societies
(Philadelphia: S. C. Collins, 1860, 1st ed., 1844).

[134] Don Yoder, *Pennsylvania Spirituals* (Lancaster: Pennsylvania Folklife Society,
1961), p. 185.

[135] Ibid., p. vii.

[136] Ibid.

[137] Ibid., p. 391.

[138] As Francis Williamson forcefully reminds me.

[139] See Yoder, *Pennsylvania Spirituals*, for copious examples and a broad discussion of them.

Yet another group of white spirituals were produced by the Shakers. Shakers were English Quakers led by Mother Ann Lee (1736–1784) who brought eight followers with her to Watervliet, New York, in 1774. Some increase in membership came during the Revolution, but it was the Second Great Awakening that stimulated groups in Massachusetts, Connecticut, Kentucky, Ohio, and Indiana, as well as New York. The Shakers flourished throughout much of the nineteenth century, but declined toward the century's end. By the mid-twentieth century they had virtually disappeared. They lived in spotless celibate communities characterized by common property, faith healing, and separation from the world. Mother Ann Lee was viewed as a feminine incarnation of the second coming of Christ.

The Shakers or "Shaking Quakers" were so named because they employed group dancing in their worship. It could reach frenzied heights with complex configurations and movements. The songs came out of an European-American folk tradition, which, at least until the mid- to late-nineteenth century, eschewed instruments and harmony. Shape-notes were sometimes used with music that bore some relation to that of the broader culture, but most characteristically Shakers isolated themselves musically as well as communally. They devised their own arcane notational systems, sometimes sang in vocables known as "unknown tongues," and considered many of their compositions "inspired." "Simple Gifts" is perhaps the best-known Shaker spiritual of the more than 8,000 they produced.[140]

Mormons

Shakers pushed the Christian envelope by positing a second incarnation in Mother Ann Lee. The Mormons, officially the Church of Jesus Christ of Latter-Day Saints, did another sort of pushing at the edges of the Christian confession. They have split into sub-groups, but they all regard Joseph Smith (1805–1844) as their founder and the one who discovered and translated the Book of Mormon, which they place on equal ground with the Bible. Like Anabaptists, they assume the church ran out[141] and that through them and Joseph Smith's discovery it has been reconstituted.

[140] See Daniel W. Patterson, *The Shaker Spiritual* (Princeton: Princeton University Press, 1979).
[141] See chapter 11, FN 65.

Latter-Day Saints became an aggressive missionary body in the twentieth century. Musically they have employed much of the Protestant musical heritage.[142] Their Mormon Tabernacle Choir programs from Salt Lake City have reached many people by radio with choral and organ music. The Mormons' westward trek to Utah stimulated William Clayton's (1814–1879) hymn "Come, Come Ye Saints," sung to the tune ALL IS WELL.[143] Other denominations have sometimes used it in altered forms.

Salvation Army

The Salvation Army was founded by William Booth (1829–1912). Successively an Anglican, Methodist, and minister of the Methodist New Connection, in 1861 he became a traveling evangelist. Concerned about the poor and outcast, he organized a mission in the East End of London in 1865 from which the Salvation Army grew, modeled on the discipline of the British Army. It spread to the United States in 1880, to Australia and France in 1881, and now can be found in 100 countries. It champions the cause of the dispossessed and is often the first on the scene to help in natural disasters or accidents.

Booth encouraged singing of the people and "had no time for professional choirs."[144] Tunes, he thought, "must have plenty of rhythm and life, and people must learn to sing the songs by heart."[145] Good singing needed "plenty of repetition," a good chorus, and variety in volume and tempo. The musical upshot was brass bands and popular tunes. Charles Fry and his three sons stimulated this development when they came from Salisbury to London to join William Booth and began using musical instruments. Soldiers were

---

[142] For a history see Michael Hicks, *Mormonism and Music: A History* (Urbana: University of Illinois Press, 1989).

[143] *Hymns of the Church of Jesus Christ of Latter Day Saints* (Salt Lake City: The Church of Jesus Christ of Latter-Day Saints, 1985), #30.

[144] From "Sing Glory! Hallelujah!: The Music and Mission of the Salvation Army," p. 1, a paper with no ascription of authorship, prepared by the Salvation Army and given with examples and a band at the International Hymn Conference at York, England, August 10–17, 1997, where the Hymn Society of Great Britain and Ireland, the Hymn Society in the United States and Canada, the International Arbeitsgemeinschaft für Hymnologie, and the Cymdeithas Emynau Cymru came together to consider "Quality in Hymnody—Is This an Aesthetic or Theological Imperative?"

[145] Ibid.

288

Revivalism,
Liturgical
Renewal,
and
Spirituals

encouraged to play instruments, stringed ones as well as winds. String quartets were first used indoors and brass bands at the open air meetings. In 1883 more than 5,000 instruments were sold from Salvation Army stores, and later the Army opened its own instrument factory.[146]

The statement, "Why should the devil have all the good tunes?"—understood to mean the church should employ secular and lively tunes in its worship—has been attributed without authentication to many people, among them Martin Luther, John Calvin, John and Charles Wesley, opponents of the four just mentioned, and William Booth. Among these the theory and practice of General William Booth probably embody what we take it to mean, although Booth may not have said it either.[147]

[146] Ibid.

[147] See Carlton R. Young, *Music of the Heart*, p. 104, who cites Nicholas Temperley and Frank Baker as "narrowing the source of this oft-quoted phrase to E. W. Broome's book published in 1881, on the Anglican clergyman Rowland Hill, 1744–1833, a critic of John Wesley. Broome says of Hill, 'He did not see any reason why the devil should have all the good tunes.'"

17

Recurrent American Themes and Richer Textures

Recurrent Themes

By the beginning of the twentieth century recurrent themes of American church music were in place. Here are some of them.

Reading and Singing

The eighteenth-century conflict about singing by rote or singing by note was solidified and furthered by Mason. Mason deserves gratitude for his efforts to help Americans to be musically literate. There is no doubt that many individuals and the culture as a whole have benefited from his work. However, he also left the abiding impression that the reading of music preceded the singing of music. The obvious corollary has been drawn by those who were not good readers or singers: they could not and should not sing in church with their congregations.

Elitism and Taste

The inherent elitism in such a stance was deepened by Hastings's *Dissertation on Musical Taste,* which, with the "scientific" European model of both Hastings and Mason, made people assume they had to work up to the proper level to be able to sing. Failing that, they should remain silent, and if their taste was not right something was wrong with them, which it was best not to express. Congregational singing was itself cast into the realm of taste.[1]

---

[1] *Cf.* H. Wiley Hitchcock, "Introduction," [Lowell Mason, comp.], *The Handel and Haydn Society Collection of Church Music* (New York: Da Capo Press, 1973), n. p.

290

Recurrent
American
Themes and
Richer
Textures

This message is not the same as what Ralph Vaughan Williams said in the preface to *The English Hymnal* in 1906, which Erik Routley later referred to as taste.[2] Vaughan Williams had not used that word and had even admitted that tastes could differ.[3] Hastings was trying to pull people up to a "correct" (and pallid) version of a European model. Vaughan Williams worked with both folk song and "art music" and realized that "musically correct" was meaningless, that "the only 'correct' music is that which is beautiful and noble," which could also be simple like St. Anne or Old Hundredth. He saw the issue as moral rather than musical, that the "miasma of the languishing and sentimental hymn tunes which so often disfigure our services . . . would not be tolerated in any place of secular entertainment,"[4] and "that a tune has no more right to be dull than to be demoralizing."[5] Vaughan Williams gave a charter for singing at worship, not for silence. Hastings meant to do that, but inadvertently imparted as much reason for silence as for singing.

Music and Feeling

Hastings, unlike those from earlier periods of the church's history, assumed what has become more and more axiomatic since the seventeenth and eighteenth centuries, that music is fundamentally related to feelings, the problems of which I have addressed elsewhere.[6]

Immediacy and Sustenance

White gospel hymnody meant to appeal immediately. Its liability was lack of stamina. Wiley Hitchcock called it "at its best . . . a kind of religious art almost irresistible in its visceral appeal; at its worst, an embarrassingly trivial sacred counterpart of the sentimental 'songs of hearth and home' of the same era."[7] William Benbow (1865–1939), a Lutheran church musician, isolated the problem

---

[2] Erik Routley, *Church Music and the Christian Faith* (Carol Stream: Agape, 1978), p. 96.

[3] *The English Hymnal with Tunes* (London: Oxford University Press, 1933, 1st ed., 1906), p. x.

[4] Ibid., p. ix.

[5] Ibid., p. x.

[6] See chapter 14 and Paul Westermeyer, *Let Justice Sing: Hymnody and Justice*, chapter 4.

[7] Hitchcock, "Introduction," *Gospel Hymns Nos. 1 to 6 Complete*, first page.

more forcefully when he said "that music having an easy and delightful swing and well-sugared is the kind that people will love most readily and afterward loathe most heartily."[8]

Since gospel hymnody meant to appeal immediately, it is easy to understand. Confessional and liturgical movements were concerned about sustained discipline, which is always more difficult. If the seventeenth, eighteenth, and nineteenth centuries moved toward forgetting or denying the marks of the church's history, liturgy, and music, groups of confessional and liturgical renewal remembered and affirmed those marks. These groups are often portrayed as Romantics who wanted to take the church back to some pristine nostalgia of their authors' own makings. There is some truth in that interpretation, especially as they lost their original vision and were identified in the late nineteenth century with what is called Victorian. But, considered more broadly and at their inceptions, they pointed to the church's more radical stamina that has always refused to be controlled by momentary fads and fancies. They were stands against the cultural tide, refused to identify Christ with fragmentary popularity, and perceived a depth of meaning in the Christian gospel, which transcends the moment.

Sustenance over time is one of the central issues that has troubled American church music. It has troubled American civilization generally because westward expansion after a revolution presumably meant the past was forsaken for an ever upward and onward push that could forget about continuity, human habit, or durability. Not until recently have realizations about limits on expansion and resources chastened such a presumption. Donald P. Hustad (b. 1918), a musician who directed music at the Moody Bible Institute from 1950 to 1963 and who served as organist for Billy Graham's crusades, isolated the problem for church music. He saw the "chief pitfalls" of traditional evangelism "not actually related to the 'revival' or 'crusade'," but to canonizing "evangelism's pattern and style, the preaching and music . . . as the norm for regular church worship."[9] "The effectiveness of historic preaching events," he said, "was due partly to the fact that they were extraordinary events and

---

[8] William Benbow, "The Function of Music in the Service of the Church," *The Lutheran Church Review*, XVII (July, 1989): 482.

[9] Donald P. Hustad, *Jubilate! Church Music in the Evangelical Tradition* (Carol Stream: Hope Publishing, 1981), p. 143.

292

Recurrent
American
Themes and
Richer
Textures

that normal church life needs a pattern of worship that is less specialized and more complete."[10]

American churches have often canonized the specialized worship to which Hustad referred. James White describes it as "common today in American Protestantism," traceable to the camp meeting. A "tripartite . . . service of the word," it begins with "a service of song and praise which places great emphasis on music" and employs gospel hymns followed by prayer and a scripture reading. Then comes the sermon, "highly evangelistic, calling souls to conversion." It reaches a climax in "the final act, a call to those who have been converted to acknowledge this change in their lives by coming forward, being baptized, or making some other indication of their new being."[11]

Hustad points to one of the problems that has dogged American church music, namely, trying to make the occasional normative. William Warren Sweet's description of what happened in the eighteenth century explains the problem. "During the years from 1740 to 1742," he says, "there was a wonderful ingathering of members into the New England churches. Out of a population of 300,000, from 25,000 to 50,000 were added," and the "general moral effect . . . was clearly manifest."[12] But "the revival interest passed away almost as quickly as it had arisen." Sweet said that from 1744 to 1748 Jonathan Edwards himself pronounced the church at Northampton as "utterly dead."[13] Sweet then continued, "The fifty years following the Great Awakening may be characterized as one of spiritual deadness, a period of religious and moral indifference throughout New England," full of bitter doctrinal controversy.[14] In the nineteenth century John G. Morris (1803–1873), the first editor of the *Lutheran Observer*, noted a similar rhythm. After a successful revivalist left a community, "divisions ensued," interest waned, and the crowds dissipated.[15]

Not all of life is a season of revival. If the presence of God and the worship and music around that presence are tied exclusively, pri-

---

[10] Donald P. Hustad, *Jubilate II: Church Music in Worship and Renewal* (Carol Stream: Hope Publishing, 1993), p. 243. This is the update of *Jubilate!* and the best book about music in the evangelical tradition.

[11] James F. White, *Introduction to Christian Worship*, rev. ed. (Nashville: Abingdon Press, 1990, 1st ed., 1980), pp. 154–155.

[12] Sweet, *The Story of Religion in America*, p. 133.

[13] Ibid., p. 134.

[14] Ibid., p. 137.

[15] John G. Morris, *Fifty Years in the Lutheran Ministry* (Baltimore: James Young, 1878), p. 356.

marily, or even ideally to such seasons, the dark places of life are made darker because God's faithfulness is denied. The possibility of sustained and disciplined growth in the communal Christian life around word and sacrament along with the music that attends that life are threatened, destroyed, or not even allowed to take root. And the conflicts the American church has known are inevitable.

Racism

The racism of the culture has exacerbated the conflicts and driven them to deeper, tangled, and angry confusion. Whites have sometimes viewed black music as backward, tribal, and primitive in a negative sense. At the same time they have been drawn to its power, which their oppression and persecution have only increased. The conflict and guilt that whites know have bound them in their own slavery, and the syntax of black music has increased the potential for bondage. African Americans have filtered the music of white culture, including gospel hymnody, through their own ethnic heritage. They have not only used their own heritage, but they have adapted and recreated the white one within the context of their own in a way that affirmed their being—with what liberation theologians might call the freedom and "epistemological privilege of the poor" and oppressed.[16] The result has looked to whites like their gospel hymnody with no "basic dichotomy . . . between folk music and art music,"[17] but that superficial look has missed the freedom, ethnic roots, and durability of a "functional, social, and communal music."[18]

It is possible for oppressors to sing the music of the oppressed and be liberated. However, when whites have tried in their guilt to imitate black music as if it were normative for all people all the time, they have often denied their own ethnic roots in an inverse self-hatred and racism of its own. It has left them more guilty and more paralyzed, either for using black music or for not using it. The occasional African Americans who, in legitimate anger at white oppression, have mistakenly sought to impose their music as normative for everyone have lost their epistemological privilege and set in motion a new round of bondage for themselves and others.[19]

[16] See Hilkert, *Naming Grace*, p. 172.

[17] Ibid., p. 13.

[18] Eileen Southern, "Afro-American Music," NGDAM, I, p. 14.

[19] For the more usual prophetic yet amazingly hospitable stance of black churches, see Watley, *Singing the Lord's Song in a Strange Land: The African American Churches and Ecumenism.*

294

Recurrent
American
Themes and
Richer
Textures

The way we treat one another has profound and long-lived consequences for church music as well as the rest of life.

Richer Texture

These recurrent themes in the twentieth century have been imbedded in an increasingly rich texture, which could be broadly compelling or a cacophonous welter. Singing provides a way into the layers of this texture.

Quartets, Choirs, and Congregational Song

Singing schools generated choirs, and here and there a southern Episcopal choir of boys and men followed the English tradition. But in the nineteenth century quartets or "quartet choirs" developed and often replaced choirs.[20] Volunteers were augmented by a quartet of paid professionals who "led" their sections. When amateurs could not be motivated, hired quartets took over altogether, often with singers who had more interests in opera and entertaining than in worship. In the 1890s leading urban Presbyterian churches were designed for quartets. Above the central pulpit a narrow choir loft for four singers was provided in front of the organist. When the singers sat down a velvet curtain hid them from the congregation's view. In spite of objections to quartets from mid-nineteenth century onward, they remained popular in Protestant churches until after World War I.

The contradiction of professional quartets entertaining a congregation was most apparent in liturgical churches like the Episcopal, but the alternative of men and boys in vestments was virtually nonexistent in the early nineteenth century. In 1828 William Augustus Muhlenberg (1796–1877), an Episcopal priest who was the great-grandson of the Lutheran patriarch Henry Melchior Muhlenberg (1711–1787), organized a boy choir on Long Island, one of the few exceptions to the more common practice. The Oxford-Cambridge movement, however, was the major stimulus for vested choirs of boys and men who sang services in the Episcopal church.[21] Parishes with boy choirs increased after the Oxford-Cambridge

---

[20] For the English version of this movement, see Temperley, *The Music of the English Parish Church*, I, p. 231.

[21] Not the only stimulus, but a major one. See Temperley, *The Music of the English Parish Church*, I, pp. 249–250.

impulse, sometimes with parochial schools.[22] They did not decline until after World War II when extracurricular public school activity crowded out rehearsal time.

The liturgical movement was not limited to the Episcopal church. Virtually all American churches, especially mainstream Protestant ones, adopted robed choirs in the twentieth century, often in many colors and with the curious presence of stoles, the traditional symbol of the clergy. Even so-called nonliturgical churches had choirs that sang responses in place of the people in a way that contradicted the liturgical movement they were imitating and again silenced the people.

What quartets represented and reactions to it were not limited to Protestants. In spite of all his careful qualifications, Benedict XIV, in his edict *Annus qui* of 1749, had admitted orchestral music to worship.[23] Entertaining theatrical and operatic music flourished in the Roman Catholic church of Europe in the nineteenth century. When poor German, Italian, or Irish congregations in America could afford it, they hired soloists and quartets to sing what they had heard in Europe. The boy choir at the Jesuit Church of St. Francis Xavier in New York City was one of the few exceptions. Another was the chant and polyphony nurtured at St. John's Abbey in Collegeville, Minnesota, a Benedictine house founded in the middle of the nineteenth century.

Franz Xaver Witt (1834–1888), a German church musician and composer, countered the general practice by organizing the Caecilian Society at Bamberg, Germany, in 1868.[24] In the United States, John Baptist Singenberger (1848–1924), a Swiss conductor who emigrated to Cincinnati, "formally instituted the American Caecilian Society" in 1873 and began to publish the magazine *Caecilia* in 1874.[25] *Caecilia*, printed in German, influenced German Catholic parishes in Cincinnati, Chicago, Milwaukee, and Midwestern states.

The Caecilian Society attempted to reintroduce and reform Gregorian chant, to revive polyphony in place of operatic music, and

---

[22] For the English version of this, see Bernarr Rainbow, *The Choral Revival in the Anglican Church (1839–1872)* (London: Barrie & Jenkins, 1970).

[23] See Hayburn, *Papal Legislation*, pp. 92–108, especially pp. 103–105.

[24] Or 1869. Karl Gustav Fellerer, *The History of Catholic Church Music* (Baltimore: Helicon Press, 1961), p. 187, says 1868. August Scharnagl, "Witt, Franz Xaver Witt," NGDMM, 20, p. 466, says 1869.

[25] Fellerer, *The History of Catholic Church Music*, p. 190. For a description of the broader outlines of the Caecilian movement, see pp. 187–191, and Karl Gustave Fellerer, "Cecilian Movement," NGDMM, 4, pp. 47–48.

296

Recurrent
American
Themes and
Richer
Textures

to encourage congregational song. Its aims paralleled and were supported by Solesmes and Pius X's motu proprio,[26] though its results were not always salutary. "A flood of poor Caecilian church music was printed . . . often prepared from a few cadences and stereotyped phrases" so that "mere externalism" and "shallowness" resulted."[27] This tendency to degenerate to something pious and precious was typical of the period.[28]

The strongest stimulus for church choirs in this country came in the twentieth century with two choral conductors, John Finley Williamson (1887–1964) and F. Melius Christiansen (1871–1955). Though they both studied for a time in Leipzig, they represent quite different approaches to choral singing. Williamson formed a choir at Westminster Presbyterian Church in Dayton, Ohio, which led to his founding of Westminster Choir College in 1926 for the training of church musicians.[29] He set up a system of choirs for all age groups, with a big, dark choral sound. Christiansen organized the St. Olaf Choir in 1912 and was more interested in a blend of straight tones (some would say minimized vibrato) with a common color and flexible movement.[30] Both men had an enormous influence on church and college choirs throughout the country, not only through their touring choirs, but through the choral series Williamson edited[31] and the Lutheran chorales and Norwegian folk songs Christiansen arranged.[32] Williamson and Westminster Choir College radiated

[26] Richard Schuler sees Solesmes and the Caecilian movement as "separate but similar paths," one French and the other German, which led to the *motu proprio* of Pius X in 1903. See [Richard J. Schuler], "A Chronicle of the Reform," *Cum Angelis Canere*, pp. 349–350.

[27] Fellerer, *The History of Catholic Church Music*, pp. 188–189. *Cf.* [Schuler], "A Chronicle of the Reform," *Cum Angelis Canere*, pp. 352–353.

[28] For additional examples, see "Hymnody in the United States from the Civil War to World War I (1860–1916)," *The Hymnal 1982 Companion*, ed. Raymond F. Glover (New York: Church Hymnal Corporation, 1990), I, pp. 465f.

[29] See Charles Harvey Schisler, "A History of Westminster Choir College" (Indiana University Ph. D. diss., 1976).

[30] For a history of the St. Olaf Choir see Anton Eugene Armstrong, "Celebrating 75 Years of Musical Excellence: The Evolution of the St. Olaf Choir" (Michigan State University Ph. D. diss., 1987).

[31] Westminster Series of Choral Music.

[32] "His St. Olaf Choir Series, published by the Augsburg Publishing House in Minneapolis between 1919 and 1944, included 216 works in 12 volumes, many of which have become the mainstay of small-town choral literature." (One could add "and large-town.") Carol J. Oja, "Christiansen, F(rederick) Melius," NGDAM I, p. 439.

from a Protestant Presbyterian perspective, Christiansen from a
Lutheran one, though their influence transcended these roots.

The twentieth century has witnessed a remarkable flowering of
choral music in the United States beyond Williamson and Christiansen. Howard Swan organized it into six groupings or types:
Williamson; Father William J. Finn (1881–1961); Christiansen; Fred
Waring (1900–1984); a "scientific," mechanistic approach by teachers
like Joseph J. Klein, Douglas Stanley, and John C. Wilcox; and
Robert Shaw (b. 1916).[33] Many church choirs have learned from
one or more of these types and have been superb. Churches have
benefited immensely. Their singing improved, and their worship was
enriched by choral sounds from a wide spectrum.

This choral development would have been inconceivable without
the church and its worship, which spawned it, but again it spilled
out beyond its original locus. The downside has been that, though
these choirs in their origins often were conceived to enliven and
renew congregational song, their very success sometimes ironically
silenced it by turning congregations into listeners only.[34] When this
choral treasury was turned into partisanship instead of celebration,
things got worse.[35] Then the song was further silenced.

A number of layers of the increasingly rich American texture have
just been implied. We need to sort them out.

Immigrations

F. Melius Christiansen came to the United States from Norway as part
of the immigration of Norwegians and the Norwegian Lutheran
Church. The development of church music Gerhard Cartford has
detailed for Norwegian Lutherans from the old to the new country[36]

---

[33] See Harold A. Decker and Julius Herford, ed., *Choral Conducting Symposium*, 2d ed., (Englewood Cliffs: Prentice-Hall, Inc., 1988, 1st ed., 1973), pp. 11–43.

[34] See John Ferguson, "Hymnody and St. Olaf: I, The Hymn in the St. Olaf
Christmas Festival," *The Hymn* 38:4 (October 1997): 30–33; John Ferguson,
"Hymnody and St. Olaf: II, The Hymn and the St. Olaf Tradition," *The Hymn* 39:1
(January 1988): 31–32, especially p. 31; and Gerhard M. Cartford, "Music in the
Norwegian Lutheran Church: A Study of Its Development in Norway and Its Trans-
fer to America, 1825–1917," (University of Minnesota Ph.D. diss., 1961), p. 296.

[35] For an English parallel, see Temperley, *The Music of the English Parish
Church*, I, pp. 151ff.

[36] Cartford, "Music in the Norwegian Lutheran Church." See also J. C. K. Preus,
The History of the Choral Union of the Evangelical Lutheran Church, 1847–1960
(Minneapolis: Augsburg Publishing House, 1960).

298

Recurrent
American
Themes and
Richer
Textures

can be multiplied for Scandinavian Lutherans generally and other nationalities and confessional groups even more broadly.[37] Singenberger came from Switzerland as part of the German-speaking Roman Catholic Church's immigration. German and Slovakian Lutherans came. Irish, Italian, and German Roman Catholics came. Greek and Russian Eastern-rite Christians came. ". . . The period from around 1840 to World War I was one of tremendous influx of Irish, Germans, Scandinavians, and southern Europeans."[38] Between 1860 and 1900 alone more than 14,000,000 people fled "terrible living conditions . . . persecution [and] military service" for freedom in the United States.[39]

Not all these people or populations were Christian. Jews from Spain and Portugal came with their Sephardic musical traditions. Later in the nineteenth century larger waves of Jewish immigrants from Germany, Austria, Poland, and Russia brought their Ashkenazic traditions. The Jewish community itself was no monolith. In addition to Orthodox and conservative groups, the Jewish Reform movement in the United States adopted organs, choirs, and even hymns in a Protestant style. Professional organists and singers, often Christian ones, found themselves playing and singing in Jewish temples on Friday night and in their Christian churches on Sunday morning. More recently Muslims joined the ranks of immigrants.[40] Buddhists and Hindus have come. New groups have sprung up with amalgams of various religions. By the end of the twentieth century somewhere in the United States one could probably find almost every ethnic and religious music in the world. The exhilarating complexity of this situation has challenged the church in its music as well as in other ways.

[37] For the struggles of different ethnic groups within one confession, see Carl Schalk, *God's Song in a New Land: Lutheran Hymnals in America* (St. Louis: Concordia Publishing House, 1995), and the companion volume, Carl Schalk, *Source Documents in American Lutheran Hymnody* (St. Louis: Concordia Publishing House, 1996).

[38] Gaustad, *Historical Atlas*, p. 45.

[39] Brauer, *Protestantism in America*, p. 190.

[40] For an introduction to the Muslims from a sensitive Christian perspective, see Roland E. Miller, *Muslim Friends, Their Faith and Feeling, an Introduction to Islam* (St. Louis: Concordia Publishing House, 1995).

Westminster Choir College and St. Olaf College signal the development of schools. Among others, several that have been significant for church music might be mentioned. One is the Department of Church Music, which Peter Christian Lutkin (1858–1931) established at Northwestern University in Evanston, Illinois, in 1896. It reached beyond the school's Methodist roots and the Midwest. A second is a cluster that Justine Bayard Cutting Ward (1876–1975) founded, in response to her Solesmes-like concern for Gregorian Chant: the Pius X School of Liturgical Music in New York City in 1918,[41] the Dom Mocquereau Foundation in New York in 1928, and the Schola Cantorum at the Catholic University of America in Washington, D. C., in 1929.[42] Yet another is the School of Sacred Music at Union Theological Seminary, which Clarence Dickinson (1873–1969) founded in 1928 with his wife Helen Adell Snyder Dickinson (1875–1975).[43] Utilizing the rich resources of New York City, it served churches and their musicians from around the world with a remarkable ecumenical breadth and capacity. In 1973 it was transplanted to Yale University in New Haven, Connecticut. Another group are the church music schools that Southern Baptists developed at their seminaries in Louisville, Kentucky; Fort Worth, Texas; and New Orleans, Louisiana.

Societies

The twentieth century has seen the formation of various societies related more or less directly to church music. Many of these have been denominational in scope. Others have been more broadly ecumenical. The latter have included the American Guild of Organists, founded in 1896; the Hymn Society of America (later "in the United States and Canada") in 1922, with a concern for congregational song; the Chorister's Guild in 1949; and the American Choral Directors Association in 1959. Schools and societies have overlapped or

---

[41] [Richard J. Schuler], "A Chronicle of the Reform," *Cum Angelis Canere*, p. 353, says 1916.

[42] See Catherine Dower, "Patrons of the Arts, The Wards: Justine and George, Symbolic Illusions," *Cum Angelis Canere*, p. 151.

[43] For a history until 1953, see Ellouise W. Skinner, *Sacred Music at Union Theological Seminary, 1836–1953: An Informal History* (New York: Union Theological Seminary, 1953).

300

Recurrent
American
Themes and
Richer
Textures

related to one another. Lutkin and Dickinson, for example, were founding members of the American Guild of Organists.

Organs and Organists

The formation of the American Guild of Organists signals the unexpected presence of organs. After struggling to be accepted in American churches who had Calvinist predispositions against them, in the twentieth century organs became an expected part of all but a few American churches. A seventeenth- or eighteenth-century citizen who returned a couple centuries later would probably have been shocked not only at the presence of organs, but by their variety. Organs and organ builders in all sorts of styles, with numerous electronic imitations, have covered the land. Some of them, like some choirs, have not been very good. But a surprisingly large number have been remarkable. Orpha Ochse grouped them historically in the twentieth century into the orchestral organ, the American Classic organ, and the neo-Baroque organ.[44] Somewhere in the United States, mostly in churches, by the end of the twentieth century one could find almost any kind of organ imaginable. Though acoustical settings often have made both congregational singing and organ music a struggle, the organs are there nevertheless.

The twentieth century has also been blessed with talented church organists and organ teachers around the world. W. Lynnwood Farnum (1885–1930), Marcel Dupré (1886–1971), E. Power Biggs (1906–1977), Jean Langlais (1907–1991), Helmut Walcha (1907–1991), Virgil Fox (1912–1980), David Craighead (b. 1924), Catherine Crozier (b. 1914), Fred Swann (b. 1931), and Marilyn Keiser (b. 1941) suggest the range of players. They and their students have played music from all periods. If it were possible to freeze time and space and move randomly from church to church on Sunday mornings—sometimes even in one church—in the latter half of the twentieth century, one would hear an incredible range of music: pre-Bach; Bach; Classic; the French Romantic school of César Franck (1822–1890); the twentieth-century breadth of Paul Hindemith (1895–1963), Paul Manz (b. 1919), Calvin Hampton (1938–1984), John Ferguson (b. 1941), David Cherwien (b. 1957), and gospel styles. The last four composers mentioned are among the American organists who have revitalized improvisation in their ser-

---

[44] Ochse, *The History of the Organ in the United States*, pp. 321–426.

vice playing, which, while ongoing in Europe, has not been so common until recently in the United States.

Organs, organists, and organ music have mostly been cause for celebration in churches, but such celebration usually occurs in a given community or among those grateful for the presence of so many different sorts of instruments. Organ-building fads and partisans choosing to support one organ design by attacking other ones have attracted more attention. Congregations pulled unknowingly into such conflicts have usually experienced the all too familiar result: their song has been neglected. The instrument which got into churches in the first place to support and enliven congregational song sometimes took on its own life as a weapon.

Ives and a Twentieth-Century Dilemma

Churches and their choirs, schools, societies, and organists all require composers. The twentieth century has produced many besides Christiansen. Of those born and trained in the United States in the late nineteenth and early twentieth centuries, Charles Ives (1874–1954) is the most colorful. He forcefully poses one of the period's dilemmas.

Using quotations from Protestant hymn tunes, Ives celebrated the sacred events, people, places, and festivals of his country along with its faith in progress and the ultimacy of a broad consensus.[45] That would presumably have evoked wide and popular support from many mainstream churches who themselves supported the mindset Ives represented. But Ives wove his native musical raw materials together with the threads of twentieth-century compositional techniques. As David Ewen said, he worked with polyrhythms before Stravinsky, dischords before Bartók, polytonality before Stravinsky and Milhaud, atonality before Schönberg, quarter tones before Hába, tone clusters before Henry Cowell, and chance music before Boulez.[46] These techniques, not unexpectedly, honestly reflected the twentieth century. They were dissonant and angular, not soothing or easy to understand. Ives realized the dilemma. Until 1902 he was a

---

[45] For a biography of Ives, see Henry and Sidney Cowell, *Charles Ives and His Music* (New York: Oxford University Press, 1955). For a more recent overview and bibliography, see John Kirkpatrick (with Paul C. Echols), "Ives, Charles (Edward)," NGDAM II, pp. 503–520.

[46] David Ewen, *The World of Twentieth Century Music* (Englewood Cliffs: Prentice-Hall, 1968), p. 394.

302

Recurrent
American
Themes and
Richer
Textures

church organist in New England and New York City. He quit because his stacks of thirds above a soprano line and consecutive dissonances denied the "rights" of the congregation.[47] Compelled by conscience to write what he heard and knowing it could be misunderstood or disturbing, Ives supported himself as an insurance agent rather than a full-time composer so that he would not have to go "ta-ta for money!"[48]

As I have indicated elsewhere,[49] the fundamental problem here is much broader than church music. It has to do with the twentieth century's rupture between the arts and the public at large, and the individual freedom of the artist versus the corporate selfhood of a people. Whether this situation bespeaks esoteric compositions,[50] a public lost in a nostalgic dead end, or some of both, only time will tell. For churches, however, the dilemma was particularly acute because, while all kinds of music can be used in worship by choirs or organists or other instrumentalists as long as it is broken to word and sacrament, at the central locus of the people's song a folk idiom is required or the people can't sing. As Bela Bartók (1881–1945) discovered in his research, an atonal folk song is "not possible . . . because folk tunes are always tonal,"[51] by which Bartok also meant modal.

Technology

The broad problem of congregational participation in song was exacerbated after Ives as technology increased and microphones became more and more ubiquitous. Libby Larsen, a composer and perceptive analyst, has described the electronic realities of our technological revolution as a sound revolution. She considers the twentieth century to be the end of the Romantic period and suggests that instruments, ensembles, performance venues, notational systems, and composed music are changing as always happens when one

[47] Cowell, *Charles Ives and His Music*, p. 44.

[48] Ibid., p. 37.

[49] "Twentieth Century American Hymnody and Church Music," *New Dimensions in American Religious History: Essays in Honor of Martin E. Marty*, ed. Jay P. Dolan and James P. Wind (Grand Rapids: William B. Eerdmans Publishing, 1993), pp. 180–181.

[50] For a trenchant statement of this view, see Henry Pleasants, *The Agony of Modern Music* (New York: Simon and Schuster, 1955).

[51] Elliot Schwartz and Barney Childs, ed., *Contemporary Composers on Contemporary Music* (New York: Holt, Rinehart and Winston, 1967), p. 77.

common practice gives way to another. Whether she is right and how this will play out over the next centuries remains to be seen, but she and others have isolated a critical ingredient of our culture. It is at heart an epistemological crisis. This text is not the place to explore the issues that may be raised, except to make the following brief comments, which relate most directly to church music and the church musician. At the end of the twentieth century the "sound revolution" has to do with manipulating sound, carrying it in headsets, listening to others manufacture it, or allowing groups with microphones and mixers to give the impression that a large group is singing. The result is in part like the problems posed by Ives and other composers with techniques similar to his, namely, to silence communal singing generally and congregational singing specifically. At a deeper level the problem is that the musical learning process of a people is circumvented by a preexistent package. Congregational song and church musicians face the dilemma of creatively using all the sounds that lay before them without silencing the people and without denying them their part in the learning curve.

Other Composers

Though Ives is unique, he is but one of many twentieth-century composers who have enriched the church's music. The best we can do here is to hint at the spread that recent composers from around the world have provided the church: the influence of composition teachers such as Nadia Boulanger (1887–1979); the hymn tunes of Carl Schalk (b. 1929); the huge variety of anthems that include Randall Thompson's (1899–1984) "Alleluia" and "The Last Words of David"; Igor Stravinsky's (1882–1971) *Symphony of Psalms*, among other pieces; the French Catholic mysticism of Olivier Messiaen (b. 1908); the works of Healey Willan (1880–1968), Harry Burleigh (1866–1949), Robert Nathaniel Dett (1882–1943), Leo Sowerby (1895–1968), William Levi Dawson (b. 1899), Benjamin Britten (1913–1976), Ralph Vaughan Williams (1872–1958), Hugo Distler (1908–1942), Alice Parker (b. 1925), Emma Lou Diemer (b. 1927), Carolyn Jennings (b. 1936), Krzysztof Penderecki (b. 1933), John Rutter (b. 1945), and so on in a seemingly endless list.

Music from past periods has accompanied this twentieth-century feast, with research about performance practice, performing editions, and sounds in multiple styles. The same church choir at a single Sunday morning service might do a spiritual arranged by Dawson, a motet by Palestrina, and a chorale harmonized by J. S. Bach.

304

Recurrent
American
Themes and
Richer
Textures

I write this on the first Monday in May of 1997. Yesterday I attended two typical Sunday morning services near my home. It was the Sixth Sunday of Easter and the commemoration of Monica, the mother of Augustine. At the small Lutheran church where I am a member the adult choir did two pieces with African roots, one in Swahili and one in English. The children's choir drew on Mozart. The congregation sang a Celtic "Alleluia." They also sang a psalm, the service setting, and five hymns, which taken together represented five different periods covering the sixth to the twentieth centuries and came from Germany, Italy, England, the Netherlands, and the United States. In addition to the service music he led, partly improvised, at the organ and piano with help from an eighth grader playing Conga drums, our cantor also played a twentieth-century French organ piece. At another church, more than four times larger than mine and with a full-time rather than a part-time musician, the spread was almost equally as wide. An amazingly large musical palette has become available to congregations of all sizes. At the services I attended yesterday the breadth fit the flow of word and sacrament very well. I have been to other services where it has yielded chaotic confusion or simply called attention to itself.

Explosions

The breadth has been increased by the "hymn explosion." To see its scope we need to begin early in the century.

Gospel hymnody at the end of the nineteenth century was challenged by Walter Rauschenbusch (1861–1918) and the Social Gospel, an optimistic movement that sought to renew society by bringing in the kingdom of God. Rauschenbusch had translated gospel hymns into German,[52] but after the turn of the century he attacked Christian hymnody generally and gospel hymnody specifically for avoiding service to humanity and postponing correction of social ills to a future life.[53] Henry Sloane Coffin's (1877–1954) *Hymns for the Kingdom of God*[54] and Mabel Mussay's (b. 1873)

[52] Walter Rauschenbusch and Ira D. Sankey, *Evangeliums-Lieder, Gospel Hymns mit deutschen Kernliedern* (New York: The Biglow & Main Co., 1890).

[53] See John Michael Spencer, "Hymns of the Social Awakening: Walter Rauschenbusch and Social Gospel Hymnody," *The Hymn* 40 (April 1989), 18.

[54] Henry Sloane Coffin and Ambrose White Vernon, ed., *Hymns for the Kingdom of God* (New York: A. S. Barnes, 1931, 1st ed., 1909 or 1910).

Social Hymns of Brotherhood and Aspiration[55] embodied Rauschenbusch's concerns, but their challenge to the society was no match for gospel hymnody's enticements. Hymns with societal themes were not absent from this period,[56] but they did not have the proportions or attractions of gospel hymnody.

Throughout the twentieth century hymnals increased in ecumenical breadth, such as the Episcopal *Hymnal 1940*. The breadth was criticized, however, for being "a frozen repertory reshaped according to denominational needs."[57] That frozenness changed in the 1960s in response to a perennial cry of the period that "nobody's getting down to writing the hymns for our time."[58] With Erik Routley as the catalyst, meetings of clergy, poets, musicians, teachers, and scholars were held between 1961 and 1969 at the Scottish Churches House in Dunblane, Scotland. The result was *Dunblane Praises*[59] and *New Songs for the Church*.[60]

There was no comparable meeting in this country, but publications such as *Songs for Today*,[61] *Hymns for Now*,[62] and the *Hymnal for Young Christians*[63] gave voice to the same need. The ferment on both sides of the Atlantic created a whole body of new hymns from writers such as Albert Bayly (1901–1984), Fred Pratt Green (b. 1903), Martin Franzmann (1907–1976), Jaroslav Vajda (b. 1919), Jane Parker Huber (b. 1926), Joy Patterson (b. 1932), Brian Wren (b. 1936), Gracia Grindal (b. 1943), Thomas Troeger (b. 1945), Sylvia Dunstan (1955–1993), and many more.[64]

---

[55] Mabel Hay Barrows Mussay, ed., *Social Hymns of Brotherhood and Aspiration* (Boston: Universalist Publishing House, 1914).

[56] See Westermeyer, "Hymnody in the United States from the Civil War to World War I (1860–1916)," pp. 449–451.

[57] Russell Schultz-Widmar, "Hymnody in the United States Since 1950," HC, I, p. 600.

[58] Ian M. Fraser, "Beginnings at Dunblane," *Duty and Delight: Routley Remembered*, ed. Robin A. Leaver and James H. Litton (Carol Stream: Hope Publishing, 1985), p. 171.

[59] *Dunblane Praises* (Dunblane: Scottish Churches' House, 1965).

[60] *New Songs for the Church*, vols. I and II (Norfolk: Galliard, Ltd., 1969).

[61] *Songs for Today*, ed. Ewald Bash and John Ylvisaker (Minneapolis: American Lutheran Church, 1964).

[62] *Hymns for Now: A Portfolio for Good, Bad, or Rotten Times* (Chicago: Walther League, 1961).

[63] *Hymnal for Young Christians* (Chicago: Friends of the English Liturgy Church Publications, 1967).

[64] Some of these and others are given in Paul Westermeyer, *With Tongues of Fire*.

306

Recurrent
American
Themes and
Richer
Textures

Several interlocking issues about language were part of this explosion. One was putting the texts in the vernacular to avoid "thee," "thy," and similar words or phrases no longer in use. Less often up-down language, which refers to a three-story universe with heaven on top, was regarded with suspicion because we no longer held such a worldview. A second concern was inclusive language. Racist words and thought patterns were excluded, like washing us "whiter than snow." Generic male words for humanity were avoided or imagery that was patriarchal such as "king." As the discussion worked its way into male language for God, there was less clarity and agreement.[65] Other questions also increased the complexity. Could language about the deaf and dumb or walking be used? Does such usage discriminate against the disabled? What about militaristic imagery? Does it program singers to violence or idolatrous tribal persuasions? A third issue was how to apply the first two to old hymns. Could the church's repertoire of hymns be mended without damage? Should it be? And, finally, in spite of the positive intent, was the effect to wipe out metaphor and poetry altogether and to usher in a legalistic use of language? Madeleine Marshall pointed to the danger of a new asceticism in which "linguistic absolutists" reason with an "objective" scientific clarity that says if this is that, then that is this.[66]

The hymnwriting also had to reckon with what Brian Wren in one of his hymns called "The Horrors of Our Century":[67] two world wars, Auschwitz and Hiroshima, Vietnam and South Africa, Hitler and Stalin. Social justice and the kinds of issues Rauschenbusch had raised could not be avoided any longer. Within the larger context of doxology they found expression late in the century. They were chastened by the century's horrors and the realism of theologians such as Karl Barth (1886–1968) and Reinhold Niebuhr (1892–1971), which

[65] For overviews of issues related to language, see Gail Ramshaw, *God Beyond Gender: Feminist Christian God-Language* (Minneapolis: Fortress Press, 1995) and Gabriel Fackre, "Ways of Inclusivity—the Language Debate," *Prism*, 9:1 (Spring 1994): 52–65. For Erik Routley's pilgrimage about this matter, see Glenn Phillip Eernisse, "The Views of Erik on Inclusive Language," *The Hymn* 47:1 (January 1996): 34–40.

[66] Madeleine Forell Marshall, " 'The Holy Ghost Is Amorous in His Metaphors': The Divine Love Hymn Reclaimed," *Cross Accent* 5A: 9 (January 1997): 22.

[67] *Faith Looking Forward: The Hymns and Songs of Brian Wren* (Carol Stream: Hope Publishing, 1983), # 46.

some hymnwriters themselves articulated beyond their hymns.[68] The
social consciousness that accompanied the hymn explosion was not
the optimistic Social Gospel that Rauschenbusch had in mind, but
a social consciousness nonetheless.

The hymn explosion not only created new hymn texts and translations. It also stimulated new metrical psalms and rejuvenated
psalm singing of the biblical texts themselves. Composers were
impelled to write new hymn tunes, harmonizations, psalm tones,
refrains, and service music. Calvin Hampton and Carl Schalk have
already been mentioned. They fit here. So do Richard Dirksen (b.
1921), Hal Hopson (b. 1933), Carol Doran (b. 1936), Richard
Proulx (b. 1937), Peter Cutts (b. 1937), Marty Haugen (b. 1950),
and David Hurd (b. 1950), a few of the many other tunesmiths who
suggest once again the spread of what has been created.

In addition to all this the ostinatos, litanies, acclamations, and
canons that Jacques Berthier (1923–1994) composed for the French
monastic community at Taizé swept across the church.[69] A little later
came the hymns and music created by John Bell (b. 1920) and the
Iona Community in Scotland[70] plus African, Latino, and Asian
materials.[71]

By century's end the musical resources were greater than anyone
could fully comprehend. Beginning with the *Lutheran Book Worship* of 1978 a cluster of denominational hymnals, perhaps just now
coming to a close,[72] responded to the hymn explosion, each hymnal

[68] See, for example, the chapters on Fred Kaan, Thomas Troeger, and Brian Wren
in Westermeyer, *With Tongues of Fire*, pp. 93–107, 123–136, and 155–166

[69] In a series of publications like Jacques Berthier, *Music from Taizé* (Chicago: G.
I. A. Publications, Inc., 1978). See also J. L. Gonzalez Balado, *The Story of Taizé*
(London: A. R. Mowbray & Co. Ltd., 1994, first English edition, 1980).

[70] John Bell and Graham Maule, *Heaven Shall Not Wait* (Chicago: GIA, 1987,
rev. 1989); *Enemy of Apathy* (Chicago: GIA, 1988, rev. 1990); *Love from Below*
(Chicago: GIA, 1989).

[71] For an overview with underpinnings see C. Michael Hawn, "Vox Populi:
Developing Global Song in the Northern World," *The Hymn* 46:4 (October 1995):
28–37. For a more detailed theological and ethnomusicological study see Mark
Bangert, "Dynamics and New World Musics: A Methodology for Evaluation," *Wor-
ship and Culture in Dialogue*, ed. S. Anita Stauffer (Geneva: The Lutheran World
Federation, 1994), pp. 183–203.

[72] Carlton Young, "The New Century Hymnal, 1995," *The Hymn* 48:2 (April
1997): 37, suggests that *The New Century Hymnal* (Cleveland: The Pilgrim Press,
1995) of the United Church of Christ in its "ideological and doctrinaire" consisten-
cy appears to be the work "of a sect, rather than a church" and may be the first

308

Recurrent
American
Themes and
Richer
Textures

with more resources to draw from. Supplements and pieces prepared for congregations on single handouts have added more and more. Some churches employed Broadway tunes with vigor;[73] others with equal vigor employed chorus and orchestra for settings of the ordinary of the Mass by Haydn and Mozart as part of their regular weekly Latin worship.[74] Multicultural materials have abounded. Those who have been able to harness the resources for their specific place found the result compelling. Others perceived the welter of possibilities to be cacophonous. The common themes have not been obliterated, but some found the texture so dense that they could not penetrate it.

"post-denominational hymnal." This book may be idiosyncratic, or it may signal the end of the current cluster of hymnals after the *Lutheran Book of Worship*. An article by John P. Nordin, "Breaking the Hymnal Logjam: a Second Edition of the *LBW*," *Lutheran Partners* 13:3 (May/June 1997): 24–30, suggests the beginning of a new round.

[73] As at St. Joan of Arc Church in Minneapolis, Minnesota.

[74] As at the Church of St. Agnes, St. Paul, Minnesota.

N o w

18

Postscript

Two Histories

The history of the church and its music in the twentieth century could be written as two histories, both equally accurate. One would be titled ecumenical cooperation, the other sectarian conflict.

Ecumenical Cooperation

Ecumenical cooperation has its roots in the nineteenth century. Missionary meetings from 1854 on led in 1908 to the Federal Council of Churches in the United States and the World Missionary Conference at Edinburgh in 1910, which led to the World Council of Churches in 1948 and the National Council of Churches in the United States two years later. Liturgical renewal of the nineteenth century spawned massive scholarship right up to the present[1] as well as cooperation and consensus among groups with a wide variety of confessional postures.[2] *Hymns Ancient and Modern* provided an ecumenical hymnic vision that led to the common hymnic and musical quarry from which twentieth-century editors of hymnals have drawn their materials.

Though its roots are in the nineteenth century, at the center of ecumenical cooperation in the twentieth century stands the Second Vatican Council, which Pope John XXIII (1881–1963, pope from 1958) called as part of his aggiornamento and which met between

---

[1] See Bard Thompson, *A Bibliography of Christian Worship* (Metuchen: The American Theological Library Association and the Scarecrow Press, 1989), 786 almost solely bibliographical pages.

[2] A comparison of denominational hymnals and worship books shows a similarity of structures and texts.

1962 and 1965. From the Reformation to Vatican II Protestants and Roman Catholics could attack one another from behind fortresses with caricatures. After Vatican II that was not so easy. Suddenly the Mass was in the vernacular, a "rigid uniformity" was not to be enforced, and "gifts of various races and peoples" were to be respected and fostered.[3] The Roman Catholic Church was still the Roman Catholic Church, but it seemed not to be the monolith many had perceived it to be, it appeared to have voiced some Reformation themes, and, in any case, it opened its doors and welcomed dialogue. Warfare was hard to sustain.

In the same spirit as Vatican II, the twentieth century has seen numerous mergers of related denominations, all sorts of cooperative endeavors between denominations and between local congregations from different traditions, societies that transcend normal divisions where learning has crossed historic boundaries, common schools where clergy from different denominations have studied, and common theological teachers and writers who have influenced people from widely divergent backgrounds.

Sectarian Conflict

But everything has not been sweetness and light. Sectarian conflict has accompanied the ecumenical cooperation, not necessarily the way one might anticipate. As would be expected, there have been voices of opposition to the thaw between Protestants and Roman Catholics, to mergers, or to cooperative ventures. The most bitter feuding has not been between denominations, however, but within them, especially after Vatican II. The disputes have concerned ethical and hermeneutical questions such as the role of the church in social justice versus personal morality or differences about racism, abortion, homosexuality, the role of women, and biblical interpretation. Sometimes these issues have been a screen for attempts to exercise control. Often the conflicts have been about worship and music. Within the same denomination (choose almost any one of them) different groups have wanted to use worship and music for high art, folk art, popular currents, concerts, education, social justice, personal morality, or evangelism.

Disputes became more accentuated in the turbulence of the 1960s with the Vietnam War and the assassinations of John F. Kennedy

---

[3] "Constitution on the Sacred Liturgy," *The Documents of Vatican II* (New York: Guild Press, 1966), p. 151.

and Martin Luther King, Jr. A dream died, as Don McLean expressed it in his popular song, "American Pie." U. S. President Dwight D. Eisenhower's quip, "It doesn't matter what you believe as long as you're sincere about it," and the artificial bubble of church attendance that went with it after World War II did not hold. Coali-
tions and financing came apart, symbolized most forcefully for church music when the School of Church Music at Union Seminary closed its doors in the early 1970s.

After Vatican II English Masses replaced Latin ones for Roman Catholics. There was a scramble to set the new, hastily devised English texts to music. The speed with which guitar masses were ground out often produced less than durable fare for congregations. "Polka Masses,"[4] "hootenanny Masses,"[5] and eventually "heavy metal Masses"[6] sprang up. Since then Roman Catholics have struggled again with the nature and quality of their liturgical music.[7]

The influx of guitars was not restricted to Roman Catholics. Protest songs, a few guitar chords, throwaway choruses and melodic lines swept briefly across many churches, not without conflict. As for Roman Catholics, choirs were out of favor in many places, and organs were turned off or used less.

---

[4] See Robert A. Skeris, "To Sing With the Angels," *Cum Angelis Canere*, pp. 2–3.

[5] [Richard J. Schuler], "A Chronicle of the Reform," *Cum Angelis Canere*, p. 379.

[6] Heavy metal Masses were later. I first heard about them in the early 90s when I was on a panel with a Roman Catholic priest.

[7] *The Milwaukee Symposia for Church Composers: A Ten-Year Report* (Washington: The National Association of Pastoral Musicians and Chicago: Liturgy Training Publications, 1992), gives the nature of this struggle, as do a review and a response to the review: James E. Frazier, "The Milwaukee Symposia for Church Composers," *Worship* 70:3 (May 1996): 274–279, and Jan Michael Joncas, "Forum: Continuing the Conversation: The Milwaukee Symposia for Church Composers," *Worship* 70:4 (July 1996): 328–335. *The Snowbird Statement on Catholic Liturgical Music* (Salt Lake City: The Madeleine Institute, 1995) is another piece of the dialogue. So are large portions of Robert A. Skeris (ed.), *Crux et Cithara*; and Robert A. Skeris (ed.), *Cum Angelis Canere*, especially [Richard J. Schuler], "A Chronicle of the Reform," pp. 349–416, particularly pp. 369ff., where internal squabbles become especially apparent. For a description and discussion of nine twentieth century documents about the nature of music in Roman Catholic worship see Jan Michael Joncas, *From Sacred Song to Ritual Music: Twentieth-Century Understandings of Roman Catholic Worship Music* (Collegeville: The Liturgical Press, 1997).

Geoffrey Beaumont (1904–1970), an Anglican priest, had already experimented with a "popular" liturgical music. Having written songs for the "Footlights" as an undergraduate at Cambridge University, in 1956—while chaplain at Trinity College, Cambridge—he published his "Twentieth-Century Folk Mass." A musical setting of the Eucharist of the Church of England in a "popular" style, it and other sacred music with a "pop," "folk," or "rock" character spread through England and was picked up in the United States.[8] First considered too "secular," congregations sorted out what was for entertainment and what was for worship, not without disagreements. Questions of what might be termed "fittingness" (see below for a few thoughts about this) were raised, which have not yet been resolved.[9] Then came the hymn explosion described in the last chapter, not without its disagreements as well.

From Conflict to Competition

As organs and choirs returned and guitars became harder to find by the mid 1970s, the character of the debate changed, and disagreements turned into competitions. Praise choruses or "teeny hymns,"[10] often with bands and many decibels produced by electronic equipment, emphasized the Holy Spirit and praise. Charismatics and Holiness groups that developed from Wesleyan sanctification motifs used these with integrity not only as their "tradition," but because they did not have to concern themselves with tradition. For them the Holy Spirit alights where and when it will. Some Anabaptists have integrated charismatic motifs into their worship.[11] Groups with his-

---

[8] For more detail see Temperley, *The Music of the English Parish Church*, I, pp. 334–335, 341–342. For Beaumont's setting of the Lord's Prayer, see Temperley, *The Music of the English Parish Church*, II, # 91.

[9] For a detailed discussion of "fittingness" as related to our period from the standpoint of a Reformed Christian philosopher, see Nicholas Wolterstorff, *Art in Action: Toward a Christian Aesthetic* (Grand Rapids: William B. Eerdmans Publishing Company, 1980), pp. 96–121. For the question applied to music in worship by some Roman Catholics, see Robert A. Skeris, "To Sing With the Angels," *Cum Angelis Canere*, p. 3 and 1–6, as well as the following essays in the same volume: Giles D. Dimock, "The Beauty of Holiness? Liturgical Music Today," pp. 23–27; Mary Oberle Hubley, "Some Reflections on 'Contemporary' Hymns," pp. 29–63; Robert A. Skeris, "Wanted: Reverence in Worship," pp. 65–79; and Richard J. Schuler, "The Sacred and the Secular in Music," pp. 303–312.

[10] See George Shorney, *The Hymnal Explosion in North America* (Carol Stream: Hope Publishing, 1988), p. 7.

[11] As at the Reba Place community in Evanston, Illinois.

toric liturgical traditions, some Roman Catholics[12] and Episcopalians, for example,[13] have done the same in their services, but
these more catholic traditions generally have bumped into their histories when they sought to use praise choruses with a wholesale
embrace. Lutherans bumped into Luther, Presbyterians into Calvin,
Methodists into Wesley. Baptists too had the inertia of a large
singing institution, which made it hard for them to "replace" their
church and its traditions as their origins might suggest they could.
They too were distanced from what might be called contemporary
"spiritualists."

New-start megachurches began. Though not charismatic, they
sometimes used praise choruses as they sought to appeal to the culture in seeker services. They regarded the historic marks of the
church as putting people off. Willow Creek Community Church in
South Barrington, Illinois, usually serves as the model for these.
Market research and analysis done before the church was established in 1975 controlled the church's decisions for its seeker services.[14] "Professional men between the ages of twenty-five and fifty
are the target audience. Women tend to be more open, forgiving and
easier to please in church matters," so it was assumed that if men
came so would the women.[15] As the seeker

> sits down in the auditorium he will find himself listening to taped music
> that is designed to allow him to feel comfortable since silence is unset-
> tling for most people. Examining the auditorium he finds nothing that is
> offensive or even questionable. There are no crosses or other religious
> symbols that may distract him. The entire experience is designed to put
> him at ease and allow him to be receptive to the message.[16]

"The music performed is upbeat and contemporary,"[17] which
means in the style of recent popular culture, not that of Charles Ives,
Igor Stravinsky, Krzysztof Penderecki, or Olivier Messiaen. "Musical selections may be performed by members of the vocal team,

---

[12] See Giles R. Dimock, "The Beauty of Holiness? Liturgical Music Today," *Cum
Angelis Canere*, p. 25.

[13] Like Saint Andrew's-by-the-Sea Episcopal Church in Destin, Florida, or St.
Michael-le-Belfrey Anglican Church in York, England.

[14] Willow Creek Community Church Leaders, "Seekers' Service/Believers' Worship," *The Complete Library of Christian Worship, Volume 3, The Renewal of Sunday Worship*, ed. Robert E. Webber (Nashville: Star Song Publishing Group, 1993),
p. 124.

[15] Ibid., p. 125.

[16] Ibid., p. 126.

[17] Ibid., p. 126.

orchestra, or band,"[18] and there is little communal song. "The seeker is asked to participate in one chorus during the service. . . ."[19] Willow Creek consciously sought to start "its own tradition *sui generis* that is not derived directly from any denominational or sectarian source."[20] Existing churches who wanted to imitate Willow Creek have bumped into their own traditions, but those whose worship already fit the American canon of "evangelism's pattern and style . . . as the norm for regular church worship"[21] could feel a kinship. Though Willow Creek eschews the sawdust trail of the camp meeting as its concern for immaculate grounds symbolizes,[22] it nonetheless fits the same tradition where worship is regarded fundamentally as an agent to convert people.[23]

The language charismatics and megachurches have used has not been concerned with inclusivity. More liberal groups have opposed them at this point, but, ironically, have sometimes joined them in rejecting classic hymnody and organs or anything connected with the "old order" and the historic marks of the church. They did it for different reasons, however. For charismatics and the megachurches historic marks of the church are out of touch with the Spirit or current culture and get in the way of evangelism. For liberals they are tied to racism, sexism, homophobia, and forms of oppression. The outcome was the same. Something new had to be done, though charismatics, Willow Creek, and liberals disagreed about what that should be.

Because charismatics and megachurches—and sometimes Eastern Orthodox churches as well—seemed to be attracting more people than "mainline churches" who perceived their numbers to be dwindling, a scramble from denominational and local church leaders developed to respond to what was often described as a "paradigm shift." In many churches in the 1990s "alternative" services on the Willow Creek model were constructed alongside "traditional" ones,

---

[18] Ibid.

[19] Ibid.

[20] Steve Burdan, "The Seekers' Service/Believers' Worship Churches," *The Complete Library of Christian Worship, Volume 3, The Renewal of Sunday Worship*, p. 94.

[21] See chapter 17.

[22] Willow Creek Community Church Leaders, "Seekers' Service/Believers' Worship," p. 124.

[23] See Lester Ruth, "Lex Agendi, Lex Orandi: Toward an Understanding of Seeker Services as a New Kind of Liturgy," *Worship* 71:5 (September 1996): 387, FN1, 402–405.

imitating the cafeteria style of "folk" and "traditional" Masses that
Roman Catholics had devised after Vatican II. Then a menu of services that included "blended" possibilities was introduced.

Sometimes this blending has led to healthy discussions about the culture and how to address it, part of a much larger debate about a bifurcated culture.[24] Sometimes it has promoted if not ecumenical cooperation, at least gratefulness for various perspectives and practices. More often, however, the divisive history of the twentieth century was played out again, this time into competitions. Some leaders

[24] A substantial literature is developing. It includes the following: Allan Bloom, *The Closing of the American Mind* (New York: Simon & Schuster, 1987); Marva J. Dawn, *Reaching Out without Dumbing Down: A Theology of Worship for the Turn-of the-Century Culture* (Grand Rapids: William B. Eerdmans Publishing, 1995); Os Guiness, *Dining with the Devil: The Megachurch Movement Flirts with Modernity* (Grand Rapids: Baker Book House, 1993); James Davison Hunter, *Culture Wars: The Struggle to Define America* (New York: BasicBooks, 1991); Gordon Lathrop, ed., *Open Questions in Worship* (Minneapolis: Augsburg Fortress, 1994), eight pamphlets , three authors in each; Barry Liesch, *The New Worship: Straight Talk on Music and the Church* (Grand Rapids: Baker Book House, 1996); Kenneth A. Myers, *All God's Children and Blue Suede Shoes: Christians and Popular Culture* (Wheaton: Crossway Books, 1989); Ted Peters, ed., "Worship Wars," *Dialogue* 33:3 (Summer 1994); Don E. Saliers, "Contemporary/Traditional: The Dilemma of the Church Today," *The Covenant Companion*, LXXXV, 1 (January 1996): 18–20; Thomas Schattauer, "A Clamor for the Contemporary: The Present Challenge for Baptismal Identity and Liturgical Tradition in American Culture," *Cross Accent* 6 (July 1995): 3–11; Quentin Schultze et al., *Dancing in the Dark: Youth, Popular Culture, and the Electronic Media* (Grand Rapids: William B. Eerdmans Publishing, 1991); Frank C. Senn, *Christian Worship in Its Cultural Setting* (Philadelphia: Fortress Press, 1983); Frank C. Senn, "'Worship Alive': An Analysis and Critique of 'Alternative Worship Services,'" *Worship* 69:3 (May 1995): 194–224; S. Anita Stauffer, ed., *Worship and Culture in Dialogue* (Geneva: Lutheran World Federation, 1994); Jon Michael Spencer, *Theological Music: Introduction to Theomusicology* (New York: Greenwood Press, 1991); Jon Michael Spencer, ed., *The Theology of American Popular Music, A Special Issue of Black Sacred Music: A Journal of Theomusicology* 3:2 (Fall 1989); James B. Twitchell, *Carnival Culture: The Trashing of Taste in America* (New York: Columbia University Press, 1992); and some contributions from me—"Beyond 'Alternative' and 'Traditional' Worship" *The Christian Century* 109:10 (March 18–25, 1992): 300–302; "Chant, Bach, and Popular Culture," *The American Organist* 27:11 (November 1993): 34–39; *The Church Musician* 2d rev. ed. (Minneapolis: Augsburg Fortress, 1997), Martin Marty's second Preface and the last two chapters; "The Future of Congregational Song," *The Hymn* 46:1 (January 1995): 4–9; "How Shall We Worship?" *Reformed Liturgy and Music* XXXI: 1 (1997): 3–10; "The Present State of Church Music," *Word and World* XII:3 (Summer 1992): 214–220; "Theology and Music in the Context of Popular Culture," *The American Organist* 28:11 (November 1994): 30–36; "Tradition, Liturgy, and the Visitor," *Word and World* XIII:1 (Winter 1993): 76–84.

of the church took their cue from the culture, assumed the bottom line should be the control, and sought to sell their product to the most people with music as the "tool." Many discussions of church groups sounded like the boardrooms or advertising agencies of corporate America. Instead of carpets, cars, and lipstick, however, the intention was to sell robed choirs, organs, praise choruses, musical styles, worship styles, "tradition" turned into its own narrow sectarian bias, or an equally sectarian "alternative" stance. Churches wrote mission statements and tried to "position" themselves where they would get the largest market share, then lined up against one another with power plays.

We are currently in the throes of this conflict,[25] different groups and people at different points in its trajectory. The world that overhears the clamor can only assume the partisans believe that truth is whatever will sell and that God, if there be such, has little or nothing to do with the deliberations. As usual, most of the church goes on singing its song to God as best it can in a wide variety of ways in spite of some of its leaders and their battles, thankful for whatever help it gets to sing and saddened by whatever stifles it.

"Intrinsicalness"

Part of the stifling relates to a lack of what Nicholas Wolterstorff has called "fittingness." Martin Marty calls it "intrinsicalness." He suggests that in our "postmodern utterly relativist market-oriented world," if Christians agree there is a God and that we are to bring our best gifts of response, then it follows that there are intrinsic "betters" and "worses" within "the standards and traditions of a culture."[26] The church at twentieth century's end has not sorted this out well and has tended to define everything, including its music, like the market-driven world around it rather than respond to its best instincts and treat people well. In place of the Te Deum and the long strand of the church's song which it represents, the temptation has been to substitute superficial praise choruses or poorly crafted attempts to tell God how we feel. That the church might have a message and a schooling responsibility has often escaped its recent gaze.

[25] As I was working on this chapter, the most recent issue of *The Christian Century* (May 14, 1997), arrived with these articles: David S. Luecke, "Is Willow Creek the Way of the Future," pp. 479–485; James L. Kidd, "Megachurch Methods," p. 483; and "Bill Hybels on a Megachurch Ministry," p. 484.

[26] Correspondence from Martin Marty, July 23, 1997.

As Marty notes, people get hooked on all sorts of things and work hard at them—"community college, bridge-playing, bowling, hair-styling, fishfly-tying, YMCA, fitness training, Tae kwon do, T'ai Chi, woodworking, barbershop-quarteting, bass-guitar playing, scouting, etc.,"[27] but the church at many points appears to have lost its nerve and the sense that its message is worth a comparable effort or that people deserve what is worth the effort, assuming that only what sells immediately has any value.

New catechumenal materials are being developed to counter this superficial trendiness. They point to a more substantive sense of the church and its song, a sense more aligned to essence. We are too close to see our legacy very well, but our children's children and those who follow will know whether we have bequeathed to them a spiritual wasteland on the trajectory Don Saliers points to when he quotes "William Inge's observation that the church that marries the spirit of an age becomes a widow in the next generation."[28] We can only look back across the church's history from our perspective.

Perspective

When we do that, on one view everything about church music is conflict, an indication of what I said in chapter 1—that music means much to Christian people because it is a primary place where the faith of a community takes flesh and comes to life. The stakes are high. A church that may be apathetic about many things is seldom apathetic about music—about a new hymnal, for example. In this view, though the conflicts point to how important music is to the Christian church, we in our moment are seen as one more conflict in the series and more connected to the previous ones than we dare to admit. We would like to believe that we inhabit a new "paradigm" or a world we describe with the prefix "post" (post-Christian, post-modern, post-Puritan, postdenominational, postpatriarchal, etc.). We are right when those designations suggest that our age, like every other age, faces new challenges that are not to be evaded. We are wrong when they deny our biblical roots and our common bond with and debt to the early church, the Middle Ages, the Reformation, and what followed right up to the present. We delude ourselves when we act as if the recent artificial bubble of church attendance

---

[27] Ibid.

[28] Don E. Saliers, "Contemporary/Traditional: The Dilemma of the Church Today," *The Covenant Companion*, LXXXV, 1 (January 1996). 19.

after World War II does not loom over us or when we shut out a broader historical vision that would free us from our myopia.

In another view the praise, prayer, story, and proclamation the church has continued to sing with the gift of music to bear them before God points to a reality in God that has sustained the singing in spite of our conflicts. The song itself is witness to Christ's promise to be with us to the end of time (Matthew 28:20). That we have been able to sing together at all is a mystery. The song points not to trying to save the church's life, which Jesus told us is a formula for losing it or to attempts by the church to gain the whole world (Luke 9:24–25), but to losing our life for Christ's sake and the world's, to a hearing and singing with one voice beyond our hearing and singing, which join us to our sisters and brothers in Christ before us and after us. That hearing beyond hearing is about Christian faith, life, and freedom, which the church voices in its ecumenical creeds and then parses in various ways. Here's one of them.

If God acted in Christ, if sin and death have been sent reeling, and if the very self of God is joined to our humanity in a new creation; if this new creation lives in an economy of grace called church where in word and sacrament God brings to pass what they promise for the life of the world; and if the church and its singing transcend our doing and understanding, then our sectarian self-interests and attempts to best one another with worship and music as the tools are seen for what they are—movements that bear the weight of their own religious destruction no matter how much we seek to fill them with our spirit and pretend that spirit to be of God. Then we see that God continues to be at work in church and world in spite of ourselves, that God calls us together in the Spirit around one font, pulpit, and table where Christ is the host and where with one voice we sing a new song. It is not the counterfeit song of our novelty, old or new, contrived to prop up our churches with our own ingrown struts. It is what its proleptic reality always has been, the new song of the psalms in Christ, the song of the church that pours itself out for the life of the world in praise to the Father, Son, and Holy Spirit from age to age and forever.

Chronology[*]

B. C.   c. 1750   Abraham and Sarah go from Ur to Canaan, stop
at Haran; Canaan is promised to Abraham

lineage: Abraham and Sarah
Isaac and Rebecca
Jacob
Joseph

1700   Israelites in Egypt

c. 1300   Exodus, Wilderness, Ten Commandments:
Moses, Miriam

c. 1200   Israelite Conquest of Canaan: Joshua

c. 1200   Judges: Deborah, Gideon,
Samson, Samuel ⎯⎯▶ *Prophets*[**]

c. 1000   Monarchy: Saul, David, Nathan, Solomon (Temple)

922   Death of Solomon; division of kingdom
into Judah (south) and Israel (north)

c. 850   *Elijah*

c. 750   *Amos*

c. 745   *Hosea*

721   Fall of Samaria (Israel, north) to Assyria

742–700   *Isaiah*

---

[*]This timeline, as the introduction indicates, is not tied to any plot of the book.
It is a skeletal grid to help set things in context, modeled somewhat on the one Martin Marty gives in *A Short History of Christianity* (New York: Meridian Books,
1971), pp. 361–369, though his is tied to the plot of his book.

[**]The prophets appear in italics in this timeline.

621	Deuteronomic Reform under Josiah
c. 626–587	*Jeremiah*
587	Fall of Jerusalem (Judah, south) to Babylon
c. 593–573	*Ezekiel*
c. 540	*Second Isaiah*
538	Edict of Cyrus, permitting exiles to return
520–515	Rebuilding of Temple: Haggai, Zechariah
450	Ezra, Nehemiah
167	Maccabean Revolt, Temple rededicated
63	Pompey (Roman) captures Jerusalem
c. 20	Herod rebuilds the Temple
c. 5	Birth of Jesus
A. D. 27	John the Baptist
30	Crucifixion of Jesus
c. 35	Conversion of Paul
c. 50	Council at Jerusalem
c. 45–50	Beginning of the writing of Paul's letters
63	Roman General Pompey captures Jerusalem
64	Death of Peter and Paul
	Rome burns, persecution of Christians
c. 65	Beginning of the writing of gospels, Mark
60 or 70	Liturgical portion of the *Didache*
70	Temple at Jerusalem destroyed by Titus (Roman)
c. 96	Writings of Clement of Rome
c. 35–c. 107	Ignatius, bishop of Antioch
112	Letter of Pliny to Trajan
c. 150	*Apology* of Justin Martyr, Christian apologist
c. 155	Polycarp, bishop of Smyrna, burned alive
	Rise of Montanism
c. 160	Valentinus comes to Rome from Alexandria and spreads Gnosticism
c. 163–167	Martyrdom of Justin Martyr
172	Condemnation of Montanism in Asia Minor
180	Writings of Irenaeus, bishop of Lyons
c. 130–c. 200	Irenaeus

c. 150–c. 215   Clement of Alexandria, teacher

215   Hippolytus, *Apostolic Tradition*

c. 170–c. 220   Tertullian, writer, Montanist

c. 170–c. 236   Hippolytus, theologian and writer

250–251   Decian persecution

c. 185–c. 254   Origen, theologian and writer

c. 258   Cyprian, bishop of Carthage

269   Council of Antioch: Paul of Samosata reproached for forbidding singing of psalms to Christ

c. 270   Papyrus from Oxyrhynchos (Egypt) includes a hymn, the only known example of music from this period

c. 305–306   Antony organizes groups of hermits

313   Edict of Milan; toleration for Christianity

314   Council at Arles: Donatists condemned

319   Arius fl. at Alexandria

325   Council of Niceae

c. 350   Latins by now have a poor knowledge of Greek Schools for singers appear in Rome

356   Antony, father of Egyptian monasticism

358–364   Rule of St. Basil, monastic rule of the east

c. 360ff.   Canons of Laodicea

366   Hilary of Poitiers brings hymns to West from Syria and Greece

367   Athanasius's Easter letter, first official document to prescribe 27 books of the New Testament as canonical

c. 296–373   Athanasius

374   Ambrose becomes bishop of Milan

386   Empress Justina wants to impose Arianism on Milan. Ambrose and the people occupy the basilica, surrounded by soldiers. Ambrose provides the besieged people in the basilica with hymns and psalms to sing.

387   Augustine baptized by Ambrose in Milan

397   Augustine becomes bishop of Hippo

c. 340–397   Ambrose, "father of hymnody," bishop of Milan

c. 400	The people are still singing the liturgy; in town churches and places of pilgrimage monks are beginning to form choirs
c. 400	Pelagius comes to Rome from Britain
–407	Chrysostom, preacher, bishop of Constantinople
410	Fall of Rome
c. 342–420	Jerome, *Vulgate*
429	Vandals take North Africa
354–430	Augustine, theologian, bishop of Hippo
431	Council of Ephesus
–461	Leo the Great, pope from 440, asserts primacy of Rome
–461	Patrick, missionary to Ireland
496	Baptism of Clovis; beginning of the conversion of the Franks
c. 500	Beginning of episcopal schools from which universities develop
c. 480–c. 524	Boethius, philosopher, *De Musica*
529	Second council of Orange
540	Rule of St. Benedict
c. 480–c. 550	St. Benedict of Nursia, founder of Western monasticism
483–565	Justinian, Byzantine emperor from 527
568	Lombard descent into Italy
596–97	Augustine's mission to Britain
c. 540–604	Gregory I, "the Great," pope from 590
622	Flight of Mohammed to Mecca
c. 570–629	Mohammed, Islam's founder
629	Burst of Islam into Syria, Egypt, Constantinople, North Africa
c. 560–636	Isidore of Seville
680	Council of Constantinople
726	Iconoclasm of Leo III, Byzantine emperor called "the Isaurian"
c. 673–735	"The Venerable" Bede, father of English history
753	Pepin seizes kingship

c. 675–c. 754	John of Damascus, hymnwriter, theologian, defender of icons
680–754	Boniface, "German" missionary
741–768	Pepin, Frankish King
774	Charlemagne, son of Pepin, becomes king of Lombards
800	Charlemagne crowned by Leo III
c. 735–804	Alcuin, "Carolingian Renaissance," at Charlemagne's court, 781–796
c. 742–814	Charlemagne, Holy Roman Emperor
–816	Leo III, pope from 795
778–840	Louis the Pious, son of Charlemagne, king of Acquitane
843	Treaty of Verdun
	Feast of Orthodoxy, end of Iconoclastic Controversy
776–856	Rabanus Maurus, German missionary, theologian opposed Radbertus's sacramental realism, *Veni Creator Spiritus* sometimes ascribed to him
c. 785–c. 860	Radbertus, Benedictine theologian, real presence of Christ in the Eucharist
801–865	Anskar, Apostle to Scandinavia
–868	Ratramnus, monk, theologian, opposed Radbertus's sacramental realism
910	Monastery at Cluny founded, reform of monasticism
879–942	Odo, abbot of Cluny from 927
962	Pope John XII crowns Otto I, "the Great" of Germany
872–984	"Iron age" of noblemen popes
c. 1000	Peace of God and Truce of God soften the warring of the period
1028	Guido d'Arezzo demonstrates staff notation in Rome
1031	Guido d'Arezzo agitates against simony
c. 962–1048	Odilo, fifth abbot of Cluny, from 994
1054	Eastern and Western parts of the church split
1059	Berengar, theologian, recants his opposition to sacramental realism

1066	Norman Conquest
1077	Henry IV humiliated by Pope Gregory VII at Canossa
1079	Second retraction of Berengar
c. 1021–1085	Gregory VII, Hildebrand, pope from 1073
1096	First Crusade
1096	Cistercian Order founded at Citeaux by Robert of Molesme
1098	Anselm, *Cur Deus Homo*, scholasticism
1050–1106	Henry IV, King of France
c. 1033–1109	Anselm, archbishop of Canterbury, theologian
1122	Council of Worms
1079–1142	Peter Abelard, theologian
936–1150	Romanesque architecture
1145–	Gothic architecture after St. Denis
1090–1153	Bernard, abbot of Clairvaux
c. 1118–1170	Thomas Beckett, archbishop of Canterbury
1098–1179	Hildegard of Bingen, abbess, mystic, poet, composer
1180–	Satires on corruption and avarice of the papacy
c. 1177 to 1192	Adam of St. Victor, sequence writer
1204	Fourth Crusade, sack of Constantinople
1215	Magna Carta
1215	Fourth Lateran Council Transubstantiation, Franciscans recognized
1160–1216	Innocent III, pope from 1198, height of papal power
1170–1221	Dominic, founder of the Dominicans
c. 1181–1226	Francis of Assisi, Canticle of the Sun, founder of the Franciscans
1232	Inquisition founded
1225–1274	Thomas Aquinas, height of scholasticism
c. 1322	Philippe de Vitry, *Ars Nova*
1265–1321	Dante, author of *The Divine Comedy*
c. 1300–c. 1349	William of Occam, nominalist
1347–1350	Great Plague (Black Death), one quarter of Europe's population dies
1300–1377	Guillaume Machaut, composer

1309–1377	"Babylonian Captivity of the Church," popes exiled at Avignon
c. 1325–1384	Wycliffe, English reformer, questioned transubstantiation
c. 1369–1415	Jan Hus, reformer in Bohemia
1378–1417	Great Schism
1414–1418	Council of Constance, Hus burned at stake
1412–1431	Joan of Arc, "Maid of Orleans"
1431	Council of Basel
1447	Construction on Vatican begins
1453	Fall of Constantinople
c. 1380–1471	Thomas à Kempis, writer, "Imitation of Christ"
1452–1498	Girolamo Savonarola, preacher in Florence
1431–1503	Alexander VI, immoral pope, supporter of the arts
1509	Henry VIII becomes King of England
1517	Luther's 95 Theses
c. 1440–1521	Josquin Desprez, composer
1529	Marburg Colloquy, split between Swiss "Reformed" and German "Lutherans"
	Diet of Speyer, "Protestant" first used
1530	Diet of Augsburg, "Lutheran" posture
1484–1531	Ulrich Zwingli, reformer in Zurich
1540	Jesuits established by Pope Paul III
1473–1543	Nicholas Copernicus, astronomer
1483–1546	Martin Luther, reformer in Wittenberg
1491–1547	Henry VIII, King of England
1511–1553	Michael Servetus, physician, denied the Trinity, denounced by Catholic Inquisition, put to death by Calvinists
1489–1556	Thomas Cranmer, archbishop of Canterbury, editor of the *Book of Common Prayer*
1491 or 95–1556	Ignatius Loyola, founder of the Jesuits
1559	Final edition of Calvin's *Institutes of the Christian Religion*
1510–1561	Louis Bourgeois, choirmaster in Geneva; editor, *Genevan Psalter*

1562	Genevan Psalter
	Sternhold and Hopkins Psalter ("Old Version")
1545–1563	Council of Trent
1475–1564	Michelangelo, sculptor, painter
1509–1564	John Calvin, reformer in Geneva
1565	Council in Milan, Archbishop Cardinal Carlo Borromeo. No instruments other than the organ admitted to the liturgy
c. 1513–1572	John Knox, Scottish Reformer
1573	Lobwasser's Psalter
1580	Formula of Concord
1582	Robert Browne's *Reformation Without Tarrying for Any*
1586	Lucas Osiander, *Fünffzig geistliche Lieder und Psalmen*, homophonic chorale settings, melody in the soprano
1452–1592	Leonardo da Vinci, painter, sculptor, Renaissance learning
1525–1594	Giovanni Pierluigi da Palestrina, composer
1532–1594	Orlandus Lassus, composer
1598	Edict of Nantes
c. 1564–1600	Richard Hooker, Anglican
1533–1603	Elizabeth I, Queen of England from 1558
1560–1609	Jacob Arminius, Dutch Reformed theologian, free will
1564–1616	William Shakespeare, poet
1543–1623	William Byrd, composer
1583–1625	Orlando Gibbons, English composer and organist at Westminster Abbey
c. 1560–1633	Robert Browne, Separatist Puritan
1636	Harvard College founded
1640	Bay Psalm Book
1644	Westminster Directory
1647	Johann Crüger, *Praxis Pietatis Melica*, chorale texts and melodies, with figured bass
1648	Peace of Westphalia, end Thirty Years' War
1596–1650	René Descartes, "I think, therefore I am"
1598–1662	Johann Crüger, hymn tune writer and editor

1606–1669	Rembrandt van Rijn, Dutch painter
1670	Philip Jacob Spener organizes first *collegia pietatis*
1608–1674	John Milton, poet
1675	Spener, *Pia Desideria*, pietism
1607–1676	Paul Gerhardt, hymnwriter
1604–1683	Roger Williams, champion of religious freedom
1684	Edict of Nantes revoked by Louis XIV
1615–1691	Richard Baxter, Puritan pastor
1624–1691	George Fox, founder of Quakers
1694	Halle University opened
1696	Tate and Brady Psalter ("New Version")
	John Toland, *Christianity not Mysterious*
1635–1705	Philipp Jakob Spener, pietism
1707	Isaac Watts, *Hymns*
1714	Second of Freylinghausen's massive *Gesangbuchs*
1638–1715	Louis XIV, "Sun King" of France from 1643
1644–1718	William Penn, Quaker, founder of Pennsylvania
1719	Isaac Watts, *Psalms of David*
1720–	American "Great Awakening"
1672–1725	Peter I, "the Great," czar of Russia from 1682
1642–1727	Isaac Newton, scientist, laws of universe
1727	Zinzendorf begins leadership of Moravians
1670–1739	J. A. Freylinghausen, pietist, hymn editor
1668–1733	François Couperin, "le Grand," harpsichordist, organist, composer
1738	Aldersgate experience of John Wesley
1741	Bethlehem, Pennsylvania, dedicated by Zinzendorf
1674–1748	Isaac Watts, hymn writer
1749	*Annus qui* of Pope Benedict XIV
1685–1750	J. S. Bach, church musician in Leipzig
1703–1758	Jonathan Edwards, American theologian, revivalist
1685–1759	G. F. Handel, oratorio composer in England
1700–1760	Count Nicholas Ludwig von Zinzendorf, Moravian leader
1769	Watt's steam engine patented

1770	Hargreave's spinning-jenny patented
1714–1770	George Whitefield, Calvinist preacher of evangelical revival
1776	U.S. Declaration of Independence, separation of church and state
1780	Sunday School movement of Robert Raikes
1775–1783	American Revolutionary War
1707–1788	Charles Wesley, hymnwriter
1776–1788	Edward Gibbon, *Decline and Fall of the Roman Empire*
1790	Height of slave trade
1703–1791	John Wesley, founder of Methodists
1795	John Paine, *Age of Reason*
1789–1799	French Revolution
1746–1800	William Billings, rugged American composer, "fuging tunes"
1801	Cane Ridge camp meeting, symbol of American "Second Great Awakening"
1724–1804	Immanuel Kant, German philosopher, reason
1814	Jesuits reestablished by Pope Pius VII
1769–1821	Napoleon Bonaparte, French general, emperor
1770–1831	G. W. F. Hegel, philosopher; thesis, antithesis, synthesis
1833	Disestablishment in Massachusetts, church and state now legally separated
	Prosper Louis Pascal Guéranger opens Solesmes abbey
	John Keble's Assize Sermon on National Apostasy
1768–1834	Friedrich Schleiermacher, theologian, religion as "feeling of absolute dependence"
1847	Karl Marx and Friedrich Engels, *Communist Manifesto*
1813–1855	Søren Kierkegaard, Danish existentialist theologian
1859	Charles Darwin, *Origin of Species*
1864	Pope Pius IX, *Syllabus of Errors*, against modernisms
1816–1866	John Mason Neale, hymnwriter and translator
1870	Vatican Council, pope "infallible"

1838–1876	Philip P. Bliss, gospel hymnist
1827–1878	Catherine Winkworth, translator of German chorales to English
1818–1883	Karl Marx, "dialectical materialism"
1801–1890	John Henry Newman, Tractarian and Cardinal
1809–1892	Charles Darwin, evolution
1819–1893	Philip Schaff, historian, ecumenist, hymnologist
1895	Sankey, Bliss, et al., *Gospel Hymns Nos. 1 to 6*
1896	Founding of the American Guild of Organists
	Peter Christian Lutkin becomes Dean of the School of Music at Northwestern University and starts a Department of Church Music
1837–1899	Dwight Moody, revivalist, founder of Moody Bible Institute
1844–1900	Friedrich William Nietzsche, philosopher, attacks on Christianity
1903	Pope Pius X, *Motu proprio, Tra le sollecitudini* on sacred music
1840–1908	Ira Sankey, gospel singer with Moody
1908	Federal Council of Churches in the United States
1858–1913	Rudolf Diesel, German engineer, "diesel" engine
1914	Austrian-Hungarian Archduke Francis and wife Sophie assassinated, World War I
1916	Pius X School of Liturgical Music opened at Manhattanville College of the Sacred Heart
1918	Karl Barth, Commentary on Romans
1922	Founding of the Hymn Society of America
1926	Westminster Choir College founded by John Finley Williamson
1928	Union Seminary, New York, School of Sacred Music founded by Clarence Dickinson, professor of music since 1912, and his wife Helen Snyder Dickinson
1929	Stock market crash
1932	Franklin Delano Roosevelt elected president of the United States
1933	Adolf Hitler becomes dictator of Germany
1934	Barmen Declaration, confessing church against Hitler

1856–1939	Sigmund Freud, psychoanalysis
1941	Pearl Harbor, World War II
1908–1942	Hugo Distler, German organist and composer
1943	[Episcopal] Hymnal 1940
1945	Bombing of Hiroshima
1948	World Council of Churches at Amsterdam
1950	National Council of Churches in the United States
1951	H. Richard Niebuhr, Christ and Culture
1955	Rosa Parks, Montgomery bus boycott
1894–1962	H. Richard Niebuhr, theologian
1963	Martin Luther King, Jr., Letter from a Birmingham Jail
1878–1965	Martin Buber, Jewish philosopher
1962–1965	Vatican Council II
1929–1968	Martin Luther King, Jr., civil rights leader
1892–1970	Reinhold Niebuhr, theologian
1882–1971	Igor Stravinsky, composer
1973	Union Seminary School of Sacred Music closes, becomes Yale University Institute of Sacred Music
1978	Lutheran Book of Worship begins spate of denominational hymnals
1917–1982	Erik Routley, hymnologist
1989	Fall of the Berlin Wall and communism
1990s	"Church growth" and "entertainment evangelism"

Bibliography

Abba, R. "Priests and Levites." *The Interpreter's Dictionary of the Bible* (New York: Abingdon Press, 1962): K–Q, 876–889.

Ainsworth, Henry. *A Defense of the Holy Scriptures, Worship, and Ministerie, used in the Christian Churches separated from Antichrist: Against the challenges, cavils and contradiction of M. Smyth: in his book intituled The Differences of the Churches of the Separation.* Amsterdam: Giles Thorp, 1609.

———. *The Book of Psalms, Englished, both in Prose and Metre.* Amsterdam: Giles Thorp, 1612.

Allen, Richard (comp.). *A Collection of Spiritual Hymns and Song, Selected from Various Authors.* Philadelphia: John Ormrod, 1810.

The Anchor Dictionary of the Bible. Ed. David Noel Freedman. New York: Doubleday, 1992.

Anderson, Bernhard W. *Out of the Depths.* Philadelphia: The Westminster Press, 1983.

The Ante-Nicene Fathers. Ed. Alexander Roberts and James Donaldson. Grand Rapids: Wm. B. Eerdmans Publishing Company, 1885ff.

Apel, Willi. *Gregorian Chant.* Bloomington: Indiana University Press, 1958.

Appleby, David P. *History of Church Music.* Chicago: Moody Press, 1965.

Armstrong, Anton Eugene. "Celebrating 75 Years of Musical Excellence: The Evolution of the St. Olaf Choir." Michigan State University Ph. D. diss., 1987.

Armstrong, William H. *Organs for America: The Life and Work of David Tannenberg.* Philadelphia: University of Pennsylvania Press, 1967.

Arnold, Denis. *Bach.* New York: Oxford University Press, 1984.

Augustine. *Confessions.*

———. "On Music (*De musica*)." Trans. Robert Catesby Taliaferro. *The Fathers of the Church* (New York: Cima Publishing Co., Inc., 1947): II, 153–379.

———. *St. Augustine's De Musica: A Synopsis* . Ed. and sum., W. F. Jackson Knight. London: The Orthological Institute, c. 1949.

Aulen, Gustaf. *Christus Victor.* Trans. A. G. Hebert. New York: The MacMillan Company, 1961.

Aune, D. E. "Worship, Early Christian." *The Anchor Dictionary of the Bible*, ed. David Noel Freedman (New York: Doubleday, 1992): 6: Si–Z, 973–989.

Bainton, Roland. *Here I Stand: A Life of Martin Luther*. New York: Abingdon Press, 1950.

Baker, Frank, and Williams George Walton, ed. *John Wesley's First Hymnbook*. Charleston: The Dalcho Historical Society, 1964.

Balado, J. L. Gonzalez. *The Story of Taizé*. London: A. R. Mowbray & Co. Ltd., 1994, first English edition, 1980.

Bangert, Mark. "Dynamics and New World Musics: A Methodology for Evaluation," *Worship and Culture in Dialogue*, ed. S. Anita Stauffer (Geneva: The Lutheran World Federation, 1994), pp. 183–203.

The Baptist Hymnal. Nashville: Convention Press, 1991.

Barclay, Robert. *An Apology for the True Christian Divinity Being an Explanation and Vindication of the Principles and Doctrines of the People Called Quakers*. Philadelphia: Friends' Book Store, 1908, dedication to Charles II, signed 1675.

Barlow, Joel. *Psalms Carefully Suited to the Christian Worship in the United States of America, Being Dr. Watts's Imitation of the Psalms of David as Improved by Mr. Barlow*. 1786.

Baroffio, Giacomo Bonifacio. "Ambrosian [Milanese] rite, music of the." *The New Grove Dictionary of Music and Musicians* (London: Macmillan Publishers Limited, 1980): 1, 314–320.

Barth, Karl. *Church Dogmatics*. Trans. G. W. Bromiley. Edinburgh: T. & T. Clark, 1956ff. (first half of volume I trans. by G. T. Thompson, 1936).

Barton, William. *The Book of Psalms in Metre*. 1644; 2d ed., 1645; 3RD ed., 1646; 4th ed., 1654.

The Bay Psalm Book: A facsimile reprint of the First Edition with a list of later editions. Ed. Wilberforce Eames. New York: Lenox Hill, n. d.

The Bay Psalm Book: A Facsimile Reprint of the First Edition of 1640. Ed. Zoltan Haraszti. Chicago: The University of Chicago Press, 1956.

Beckwith, John (ed.). *The Canadian Musical Heritage, 5, Hymn Tunes*. Ottawa: Canadian Musical Heritage Society, 1986.

Bell, John, and Graham Maule. *Heaven Shall Not Wait*. Chicago: GIA, 1987, rev. 1989.

———. *Enemy of Apathy*. Chicago: GIA, 1988, rev. 1990.

———. *Love from Below*. Chicago: GIA, 1989.

Benbow, William. "The Function of Music in the Service of the Church," *The Lutheran Church Review*, XVII (July 1989): 482–Complete.

Bender, Harold S. *Conrad Grebel, c. 1498–1526, the Founder of the Swiss Brethren Sometimes Called Anabaptists*. Goshen: The Mennonite Historical Society, 1950.

Benson, Louis F. *The English Hymn: Its Development and Use in Worship*. Richmond: John Knox Press, 1962, reprinted from 1915.

Bent, Ian D. "Hildegard of Bingen." *The New Grove Dictionary of Music and Musicians* (London: Macmillan Publishers Limited, 1980): 8, 553–556.

Berger, Teresa. Trans. Timothy E. Kimbrough. *Theology in Hymns? A Study of the Relationship of Doxology and Theology According to A Collection of Hymns for the Use of the People Called Methodists (1780)*. Nashville: Kingswood Books, 1995.

Bergsten, Torsten. Trans. Irwin J. Barnes. Ed. William R. Estep. *Balthasar Hubmaier: Anabaptist Theologian and Martyr*. Valley Forge: Judson Press, 1978.

Berry, Mary. "Cistercian monks." *The New Grove Dictionary of Music and Musicians* (London: Macmillan Publishers Limited, 1980): 4, 411–413.

Berthier, Jacques. *Music from Taizé*. Chicago: GIA. Publications, Inc., 1978.

Best, Harold M. *Music Through the Eyes of Faith*. New York: Harper SanFrancisco, 1993.

Billings, William. *The Continental Harmony, Containing A Number of Anthems, Fuges, and Chorusses, in Several Parts. Never Before Published*. Boston: Isaiah Thomas and Ebenezer T. Andrews. Reprinted, Hans Nathan (ed.). Cambridge: The Belknap Press of Harvard University Press, 1961.

———. *The Singing Master's Assistant*. Boston, 1778.

Bishop, Selma L. *Isaac Watts, Hymns and Spiritual Songs, 1707–1748: A Study in Early Eighteenth Century Language Changes*. London: The Faith Press, 1962.

———. *Isaac Watts's Hymns and Spiritual Songs (1707): A Publishing History and a Bibliography*. Ann Arbor: The Pierian Press, 1974.

Blizzard, Judith. "Merbecke, John." *The New Grove Dictionary of Music and Musicians* (London: Macmillan Publishers Limited, 1980): 12, 168–170.

Bloom, Allan. *The Closing of the American Mind*. New York: Simon & Schuster, 1987.

Blume, Friedrich et al. *Protestant Church Music*. New York: W. W. Norton & Company, Inc., 1974.

Bonhoeffer, Dietrich. *Life Together*. Trans. John W. Doberstein. New York: Harper & Brothers, 1954.

Bornkamm, Günther. *Paul*. Trans. D. M. G. Stalker. New York: Harper & Row, 1969.

Brauer, Jerald C. *Protestantism in America: A Narrative History*. Revised Edition. Philadelphia: The Westminster Press, 1965.

——— (ed.). *The Westminster Dictionary of Church History*. Philadelphia: The Westminster Press, 1971.

Breckbill, Anita. "The Hymns of the Anabaptists: An English-Language Bibliography." *The Hymn* 39:3 (July 1988): 21–23.

Brent, Ian D. "Léonin." *The New Grove Dictionary of Music and Musicians* (London: Macmillan Publishers Limited, 1980): 10, 676–677.

———. "Pérotin." *The New Grove Dictionary of Music and Musicians* (London: Macmillan Publishers Limited, 1980): 14, 540–543.

———. "Rhythmic modes." *The New Grove Dictionary of Music and Musicians* (London: Macmillan Publishers Limited, 1980): 15, 824–825.

Brinton, Howard Haines. *Friends for Three Hundred Years; the History and Beliefs of the Society of Friends Since George Fox Started the Quaker Movement.* New York: Harper and Row, 1952.

Brown, Peter. *Augustine of Hippo.* Berkeley: University of California Press, 1969.

Bruce, Dickson D., Jr. *And They All Sang Hallelujah: Plain-folk Camp-Meeting Religion, 1800–1845.* Knoxville: The University of Tennessee Press, 1974.

Brueggemann, Walter. *Israel's Praise: Doxology against Idolatry and Ideology.* Philadelphia: John Knox Press, 1988.

———. *The Message of the Psalms: A Theological Commentary.* Minneapolis: Augsburg Publishing House, 1984.

———. *Praying the Psalms.* Winona: Saint Mary's Press, 1982.

———. *The Psalms and the Life of Faith.* Ed. Patrick D. Miller. Minneapolis: Fortress Press, 1995.

Brumm, James L. H. "Coming to America: RCA Hymnals in the 18th and 19th Centuries," *The Hymn* 41:1 (January 1990): 27–33.

Bryden, John R., and David G. Hughes (comp.). *An Index of Gregorian Chant* (Volume I: Alphabetical Index; Volume II: Thematic Index). Cambridge: Harvard University Press, 1969.

Bukofzer, Manfred F. "Popular and Secular Music in England (to c. 1470)." *The New Oxford History of Music, Volume III, The Ars Nova and the Renaissance, 1300–1540.* Ed. Anselm Hughes and Gerald Abraham (Oxford: Oxford University Press, 1986, first published 1960): 107–133.

———. *Music in the Baroque Era from Monteverdi to Bach.* New York: W. W. Norton & Company, Inc., 1947.

Burch Brown, Frank. *Religious Aesthetics: A Theological Study of Making and Meaning.* Princeton: Princeton University Press, 1989.

Buszin, Walter E. *Luther on Music.* St. Paul: North Central Publishing Company, 1958, reprinted from the *Musical Quarterly*, XXXII (January 1964): 80–97.

Calvin, John. *Commentary on the Book of Psalms.* Grand Rapids: Wm. B. Eerdmans Publishing Company, 1949

———. "Institutes of the Christian Religion." Ed. John T, McNeill. *The Library of Christian Classics*, XX–XXI. Philadelphia: Westminster Press, 1960.

Carpenter, Marjorie. Trans. and Annot. *Kontakia of Romanos, Byzantine Melodist I: On the Person of Christ.* Columbia: University of Missouri Press, 1970.

———. Trans. and Annot. *Kontakia of Romanos, Byzantine Melodist II: On Christian Life.* Columbia: University of Missouri Press, 1973.

Carroll, J. Robert. "Cold Facts on the Congregational Singing of Gregorian Chant," *The Gregorian Review* III: 3 (May–June 1956): 11–19.

Cattin, Giulio. Trans. Steven Botterill. *Music of the Middle Ages I.* Cambridge University Press, 1984.

———. Trans. Karen Eales. *Music of the Middle Ages II.* Cambridge University Press, 1985.

Chase, Gilbert. *America's Music: From the Pilgrims to the Present*. Revised Second Edition. New York: McGraw-Hill Book Company, 1966.

Cherwien, David M. *Let the People Sing!* St. Louis: Concordia Publishing House, 1997.

Chitty, Derwas J. *The Desert City: An Introduction to the Study of Egyptian and Palestinian Monasticism under the Christian Empire*. Oxford: Basil Blackwell, 1966.

Claghorn, Charles Eugene. *Biographical Dictionary of American Music*. West Nyack: Parker Publishing Company, Inc., 1973.

Clark, Keith C. "A Selective Bibliography for the Study of Hymns." *The Papers of the Hymn Society of America*, XXXIII. Wittenberg: The Hymn Society of America, 1980.

Clifford, James. *The Divine Service and Anthems Usually Sung in the Cathedrals and Collegiate Choirs of the Church of England*. 1663, 2d ed., 1664.

Coffin, Henry Sloane, and Ambrose White Vernon (ed.), *Hymns for the Kingdom of God* (New York: A. S. Barnes, 1931, 1st ed., 1909 or 1910).

Common Service Book of the Lutheran Church. Philadelphia: The Board of Publication of the United Lutheran Church in America, 1917.

Costen, Melva. *African American Christian Worship*. Nashville: Abingdon Press, 1993.

Cotton, John. *Singing of Psalmes a Gospel Ordinance*. London, 1650.

Cowell, Henry and Sidney Cowell. *Charles Ives and His Music*. New York: Oxford University Press, 1955.

Cox, Howard H. (ed.). *The Calov Bible of J. S. Bach*. Ann Arbor: UMI Research Press, 1985.

Creech, Joe. "Visions of Glory: The Place of the Azusa Street Revival in Pentecostal History," *Church History* 65:3 (September 1996): 405–424.

Crocker, Richard L. and John Caldwell. "Sequence." *The New Grove Dictionary of Music and Musicians* (London: Macmillan Publishers Limited, 1980): 17, 141–156.

Cross, F. L. (ed.). *The Oxford Dictionary of the Christian Church*. London: Oxford University Press, 1957.

Cruger, Johann. *Newes vollkömliches Gesangbuch, Augspurgischer Confession*. 1640.

Curwen, J. Spencer. *Studies in Worship Music*. London: J. Curwen & Sons, 1880.

Davenson, Henri [pseudonym for Henri Iréneé Marrou]. *Traité de la Musique selon l'Esprit de Saint Augustin*. Neuchatel: Les Cahiers du Rhône, 1942.

David, Hans T., and Arthur Mendel. *The Bach Reader: A Life of Johann Sebastian Bach in Letters and Documents*. Rev., with Supp. New York: W. W. Norton & Company, Inc., 1966.

Davidson, James Robert. *A Dictionary of Protestant Church Music*. Metuchen: The Scarecrow Press, 1975.

Davies, Horton. *Worship and Theology in England*. Princeton: Princeton University Press, 1970.

———. *The Worship of the English Puritans*. Westminster: Dacre Press, 1948.

Davis, Arthur Paul. *Isaac Watts: His Life and Works*. New York: The Dryden Press, 1943.

Davisson, A. *Kentucky Harmony or A Choice Collection of Psalm Tunes, Hymns, and Anthems*. 1816. Facsimile edition with Introduction by Irving Lowens. Minneapolis: Augsburg Publishing House, 1976.

Davison, Archibald T. *Church Music: Illusion and Reality*. Cambridge: Harvard University Press, 1960.

Dawn, Marva J. *Reaching Out without Dumbing Down: A Theology of Worship for the Turn-of the-Century Culture*. Grand Rapids: Wm. B. Eerdmans Publishing Company, 1995.

Day, Thomas. *Why Catholics Can't Sing: The Culture of Catholicism and the Triumph of Bad Taste*. New York: Crossroad, 1991.

Dean-Smith, Margaret. *A Guide to English Folk Song Collections, 1822–1952: with an Index to Their Contents, Historical Annotations and an Introduction*. Liverpool: The University Press of Liverpool, 1954.

Dean, Talmage W. *A Survey of Twentieth Century Protestant Church Music in America*. Nashville: Broadman Press, 1988.

De Bruyne, Edgar. Trans. Eileen B. Hennessy. *The Esthetics of the Middle Ages*. New York: Frederick Ungar, Publishing Co., 1969.

Decker, Harold A., and Julius Herford (ed.). *Choral Conducting Symposium*, 2d ed. Englewood Cliffs: Prentice-Hall, Inc., 1988, 1st ed., 1973.

Dix, Gregory. *The Shape of the Liturgy*. London: Dacre Press, 1970, first published, 1945.

The Documents of Vatican II. New York: Guild Press, 1966.

Dolan, Jay P., and James P. Wind (ed.). *New Dimensions in American Religious History: Essays in Honor of Martin E. Marty*. Grand Rapids: Wm. B. Eerdmans Publishing Company, 1993.

Douglas, Winfred. Rev. Leonard Ellinwood. *Church Music in History and Practice: Studies in the Praise of God*. New York: Charles Scribner's Sons, 1961.

Downey, James C., and Paul Oliver. "Spiritual," *The New Grove Dictionary of American Music* (London: Macmillan Press Ltd., 1986): IV, 284–290.

Dr. Martin Luthers Sämmtliche Schriften. Ed. Johann Georg Walch. St. Louis: Concordia Publishing House, 1880ff.

Dr. Martin Luthers Sämmtliche Werke. Ed. Johann Konrad Irmischer. Erlangen: Verlag von Hender & Zimmer, 1854.

Dr. Martin Luthers Werke, Breifwechsel. Weimar: Herman Boehlaus Nachfolger, 1933.

Duchesne, L. Trans. M. L. McClure. *Christian Worship: Its Origin and Evolution*. London: Society for Promoting Christian Knowledge, 1927.

Dudley Smith, Timothy. "Charles Wesley—A Hymnwriter for Today," *The Hymn* 39:4 (October 1988): 7–15.

Duffy, Kathryn Ann Pohlman. *The Jena Choirbooks: Music and Liturgy at the Castle Church in Wittenberg under Frederick the Wise, Elector of Saxony*. Chicago: University of Chicago diss., 1995.

Dunblane Praises. Dunblane: Scottish Churches' House, 1965.

Durnbaugh, Donald F. *The Believers' Church: The History and Character of Radical Protestantism.* New York: The MacMillan Company, 1968.

———. *European Origins of the Brethren.* Elgin: The Brethren Press, 1958.

Durnbaugh, Hedwig T. *The German Hymnody of the Brethren, 1720–1903.* Philadelphia: Brethren Encyclopedia, 1986.

Dwight, Timothy. *The Psalms of David, & . . . By I. Watts, D. D. A New Edition in which the Psalms omitted by Dr. Watts are versified, local passages are altered, and a number of Psalms versified anew in proper metres By Timothy Dwight, D. D, & . . .To the Psalms is added a Selection of Hymns.* 1800.

Eernisse, Glenn Phillip. "The Views of Erik on Inclusive Language," *The Hymn* 47:1 (January 1996): 34–40.

Eaton, John H. *Kingship and the Psalms.* Sheffield: JSOT Press, 1986; first published SCM Press, 1976.

———. *The Psalms Come Alive: Capturing the Voice and Art of Israel's Songs.* Downers Grove: InterVarsity Press, 1984.

Ellard, Gerald (ed.). *On the Sacred Liturgy, Encyclical Letter, Mediator Dei (November 20, 1947) of Pope Pius XI.* New York: The American Press, 1954.

Ellinwood, Leonard. *The History of American Church Music.* New York: Morehouse-Gorham Company, 1953.

The English Hymnal with Tunes. London: Oxford University Press, 1933, 1st ed., 1906.

The [Episcopal] Hymnal 1982. New York: The Church Hymnal Corporation, 1985.

Escot, Harry. *Isaac Watts: Hymnographer.* London: Independent Press Ltd, 1962.

Eskew, Harry. "Shape-Note Hymnody in the Shenandoah Valley, 1816–1860," Tulane University Ph. D. diss., 1966.

———, and Hugh T. McElrath. *Sing with Understanding: An Introduction to Christian Hymnology.* Nashville: Church Street Press, 1995, 2d rev. ed.

———, Music, David W., and Paul A. Richardson. *Singing Baptists: Studies in Baptist Hymnody in America.* Nashville: Church Street Press, 1994.

Essays on Church Music, Series I. n. p.: New York and Buffalo, 1898, 1898.

Essays in Church Music, Series II. n. p.: New York and Buffalo, 1900, 1901.

Etherington, Charles L. *Protestant Worship Music: Its History and Practice.* New York: Holt, Rinehart and Winston, 1962.

Etlich Christliche Lyeder Lobgesang und Psalm ("Achtliederbuch"). It was republished in Canada in 1984 in a facsimile reprint for the Amish Historical Library, Aylmer, Ontario from the original in the Germanisches National Museum, Nuernberg with permission.

Etwas vom Liede Mosis des Knechts Gottes und dem Liede des Lammes, das ist: Alt- und neuer Brüder-Gesang von den Tagen Henochs bisher, für alle Kinder und Seelen Gottes gesammelt. London, vol. I, 1753; vol. II, 1754.

Ewen, David. *The World of Twentieth Century Music*. Englewood Cliffs: Prentice-Hall, Inc., 1968.

Fackre, Gabriel. "Ways of Inclusivity—the Language Debate," *Prism*, 9:1 (Spring 1994): 52–65.

Fassler, Margot, and Peter Jeffrey. "Christian Liturgical Music from the Bible to the Renaissance." *Sacred Sound and Social Change: Liturgical Music In Jewish and Christina Experience*. Ed. Lawrence A. Hoffman and Janet R. Walton (Notre Dame: University of Notre Dame Press, 1992): 84–123.

The Fathers of the Church. New York: Cima Publishing Co., Inc., 1947.

Faulkner, Quentin. *Wiser Than Despair: The Evolution of Ideas in the Relationship of Music and the Christian Church*. Westport: Greenwood Press, 1996.

Fellerer, Karl Gustav. Trans. Francis A. Brunner. *The History of Catholic Church Music*. Baltimore: Helicon Press, 1961.

Fellowes, Edmund H. *English Cathedral Music*. Revised Second Edition. London: Methuen & Co. Ltd., 1945.

Ferguson, John. "Hymnody and St. Olaf: I, The Hymn in the St. Olaf Christmas Festival," *The Hymn* 38:4 (October 1987): 30–33.

———. "Hymnody and St. Olaf: II, The Hymn and the St. Olaf Tradition," *The Hymn* 39:1 (January 1988): 31–32.

Ferm, Robert L. *Jonathan Edward the Younger: 1745–1801*. Grand Rapids: Wm. B. Eerdmans Publishing Company, 1976.

Fink, Peter E. (ed.). *The New Dictionary of Sacramental Worship*. Collegeville: The Liturgical Press, 1990.

Flusser, David. "Jewish Roots of the Liturgical Trisagion." *Immanuel* 3 (Winter 1973/74): 37–43.

Foley, Edward. "The Cantor in Historical Perspective." *Worship* 56:3 (May 1982): 194–213. (See *Ritual Music* for a revision.)

———. *Foundations of Christian Music: The Music of Pre-Constantinian Christianity*. Bramcote: Grove Books Limited, 1992.

———. *From Age to Age: How Christians Celebrated the Eucharist*. Chicago: Liturgy Training Publications, 1991.

———. *Ritual Music: Studies in Liturgical Musicology*. Beltsville: The Pastoral Press, 1995.

Foote, Henry Wilder. "An Account of the Bay Psalm Book." *The Papers of the Hymn Society*, VII. New York: The Hymn Society of America, 1940.

———. *Three Centuries of American Hymnody*. Cambridge: Harvard University Press, 1940.

Frazier, James E. "The Milwaukee Symposia for Church Composers," *Worship* 70:3 (May 1996): 274–279.

Friesen, Abraham. *Thomas Muentzer, a Destroyer of the Godless: The Making of a Sixteenth-Century Religious Revolutionary*. Berkeley: University of California Press, 1990.

Frost, Maurice (ed.). *Historical Companion to Hymns Ancient and Modern*. London: William Clowes & Sons, Limited, 1962.

Gajard, Joseph. *The Solesmes Method: Its Fundamental Principles and Practical Rules of Interpretation.* Collegeville: The Liturgical Press, 1960.

Gardner, J. H. "Hymn Story, Hymn Myth: The Case of Ina Ogden," *The Hymn* 37 (July 1986): 30–34.

Garside, Charles, Jr. "Calvin's Preface to the Psalter: A Re-Appraisal," *The Musical Quarterly*, XXXVII:4 (October 1951): 566–577.

———. "The Origins of Calvin's Theology of Music: 1536–1543" (*Transactions of the American Philosophical Society* 69:4 (Philadelphia: The American Philosophical Society, August 1979): 5–35.

———. *Zwingli and the Arts.* New Haven and London: Yale University Press, 1966.

Gatens, William J. *Victorian Cathedral Music in Theory and Practice.* Cambridge: Cambridge University Press, 1986.

Gaustad, Edwin Scott. *Historical Atlas of Religion in America.* New York: Harper & Row, 1976.

Gelin, Albert. *The Psalms Are Our Prayers.* Trans. Michael J. Bell. Collegeville: The Liturgical Press, 1964.

Gelineau, Joseph. "Music and Singing in the Liturgy." *The Study of Liturgy.* Ed. Cheslyn Jones, Geoffrey Wainwright, and Edward Yarnold (New York: Oxford University Press, 1978): 444–454.

———. Trans. Clifford Howell. *Voices and Instruments in Christian Worship: Principles, Laws, Applications.* Collegeville: The Liturgical Press, 1964.

George, Timothy. *Theology of the Reformers.* Nashville: Broadman Press, 1988.

Gerrish, B. A. (ed.). *Reformers in Profile: Advocates of Reform, 1300–1600.* Philadelphia: Fortress Press, 1967.

Gill, Frederick C. *Charles Wesley, the First Methodist.* New York: Abingdon Press, 1964.

Gillett, E. H. *History of the Presbyterian Church in the United States of America.* Philadelphia: Presbyterian Publication Committee, 1864.

Glatthorn, Allan. "The Stages of Worship." *The Friends Journal* (December 1, 1961), reprinted by the Friends General Conference, Philadelphia.

Glover, Raymond (ed.). *The Hymnal 1982 Companion.* New York: The Church Hymnal Corporation, 1990 and 1994. Four volumes.

Goertz, Hans-Jürgen. *Thomas Müntzer: Apocalyptic Mystic and Revolutionary.* Edinburgh: T&T Clark, 1993.

Goldron, Romain. *Byzantine and Medieval Music.* n. p.: H. S. Stuttman Company, Inc., 1968.

Graham, Fred. "Moravian Church Music in America: A Model for Living." *GIA Quarterly* 8:3 (Spring 1997): 16–17, 41–42.

Grant, Robert. *Augustus to Constantine: The Thrust of the Christian Movement into the Roman World.* New York: Harper & Row, 1970.

Green, D. B., Jr. "Music, Text and Meaning in Religious Music." New Haven: Yale University Ph. D. diss., 1967.

Greene, Richard Leighton. *The Early English Carols.* Oxford: Clarendon Press, 1977.

Grew, Eva Mary. "Martin Luther and Music," *Music and Letters* XIX (1938): 67–78.

Gritsch, Eric W. *Reformer Without a Church: The Life and Thought of Thomas Muentzer (1488 [?] – 1525)*. Philadelphia: Fortress Press, 1967.

———. *A Tragedy of Errors: Thomas Müntzer*. Minneapolis: Fortress Press, 1989.

Grout, Donald Jay, and Claude V. Palisca. *A History of Western Music*. Fifth Edition. New York: W. W. Norton & Company, 1996.

Guiness, Os. *Dining with the Devil: The Megachurch Movement Flirts with Modernity*. Grand Rapids: Baker Book House, 1993.

Gunkel, Hermann. *The Psalms: A Form-Critical Introduction*. Introduction by James Muilenberg, trans. Thomas M. Horner. Philadelphia: Fortress Press, 1967.

Gurlitt, Wilibard (ed.). *Documenta Musicologica*. Basel: Baerenreiter Kassel, 1959.

Guthrie, Harvey H., Jr. *Theology as Thanksgiving: From Israel's Psalms to the Church's Eucharist*. New York: The Seabury Press, 1981.

Gutmann, Joseph. *The Synagogue: Studies in Origins, Archaeology and Architecture*. New York: KTAV Publishing House, 1975.

Haas, Alfred Burton. "The Papers of the Hymn Society of America, XXII: Charles Wesley." Springfield: The Hymn Society of America, 1957.

Haeussler, Armin. *The Story of Our Hymns: The Handbook to the Hymnal of the Evangelical and Reformed Church*. Saint Louis: Eden Publishing House, 1952.

Haïk-Vantoura, Suzanne. Trans. Dennis Weber. *The Music of the Bible Revealed*. Berkeley: Bibal Press, 1991.

Halter, Carl, and Carl Schalk (ed.). *Handbook of Church Music*. St. Louis: Concordia Publishing House, 1978.

Hambrick-Stowe, Charles E. *Charles G. Finney and the Spirit of American Evangelicalism*. Grand Rapids: Wm. B. Eerdmans Publishing Company, 1996.

Hanbury, Benjamin. *Historical Memorials Relating to the Independents or Congregationalists*. London: Fisher, Son, & Co., 1839.

Hannick, C. "Christian Church, Music of the Early." *The New Grove Dictionary of Music and Musicians* (London: Macmillan Publishers Limited, 1980): 4, 363–371.

Haraszti, Zoltan. *The Enigma of the Bay Psalm Book*. Chicago: The University of Chicago Press, 1956.

Harris, Michael W. *The Rise of Gospel Blues: The Music of Thomas Andrew Dorsey in the Urban Church*. New York: Oxford University Press, 1992.

Harms, John K. "Music of the Radical Reformation," *Church Music* (1977/2): 48–57, and (1978/1): 19–41.

Harper, John. *The Forms and Orders of Western Liturgy from the Tenth to the eighteenth Century: A Historical Introduction and Guide for Students and Musicians*. Oxford: Clarendon Press, 1991.

Harris, Michael W. *The Rise of Gospel Blues: The Music of Thomas Andrew Dorsey in the Urban Church*. New York: Oxford University Press, 1992.

Hastings, Thomas. *Dissertation on Musical Taste or General Principles of Taste Applied to the Art of Music*. New York: Da Capo Press, 1974, republication of the 1st ed., 1922.

Hawn, C. Michael. "Vox Populi: Developing Global Song in the Northern World," *The Hymn* 46:4 (October 1995): 28–37.

Hayburn, Robert F. *Papal Legislation on Sacred Music, 95 A. D. to 1977 A. D.* Collegeville: The Liturgical Press, 1979.

Heaton, E. W. *Everyday Life in Old Testament Times*. New York: Charles Scribner's Sons, 1956.

Heinz, Andreas (ed.). *Die Psalmen als Stimme der Kirche*. Trier: Paulinus-Verlag, 1982.

Heitzenrater, Richard P. *Wesley and the People Called Methodists*. Nashville: Abingdon Press, 1995.

Heller, George N., and Carol A. Pemberton. "The Boston Handel and Haydn Society Collection of Church Music (1822): Its Context, Content, and Significance," *The Hymn* 47:4 (October 1996): 27.

Helmore, Thomas. "Ecclesiastical Music," *The Ecclesiologist* X, New Series VII (February 1850): 342–349.

———. "Ecclesiastical Music, The Cantus Collectarum," *The Ecclesiologist* X, New Series VII (April 1850): 378–386;

———. *The Ecclesiologist* XI, New Series VIII (August, 1850): 104–110.

———. "Lecture on Gregorian Music at Brighton," *The Ecclesiologist* XIV, New Series XI (February 1853): 54.

———. "On Hymnody," *The Ecclesiologist* XII, New Series IX (June 1851): 172–178.

———. "On the Music of the Hymnal Noted," *The Ecclesiologist* XII, New Series IX (August 1851): 250–253.

Henry, James. *Sketches of Moravian Life and Character*. Philadelphia: J. B. Lippincott & Co., 1859.

Heschel, Abraham J. *The Prophets*. New York: Harper & Row, Publishers, 1962.

Hicks, Michael. *Mormonism and Music: A History*. Urbana: University of Illinois Press, 1989.

Higginson, J. Vincent. "Hymnody in the American Indian Missions." *The Papers of the Hymn Society*, XVIII. Wittenberg: The Hymn Society of America, 1954.

Hiley, David. *Western Plainchant: A Handbook*. Oxford: Clarendon Press, 1993.

Hitchcock, H. Wiley. *Music in the United States: A Historical Introduction*. Englewood Cliffs: Prentice-Hall, Inc., 1969.

Hodgson, Marshall. *So We Enter*. Chicago: 57TH Street Meeting of Friends, 1966.

Høeg, Carsten. *The Oldest Tradition of Byzantine Music*. London: Geoffrey Cumberlege Amen House, 1953.

Hoffman, Lawrence A. *The Canonization of the Synagogue Service*. Notre Dame: University of Notre Dame Press, 1979.

Hofstadter, Douglas R. *Gödel, Escher, Bach: An Eternal Golden Braid*. New York: Basic Books, Inc., Publishers, 1979.

Holladay, William L. *The Psalms through Three Thousand Years: Prayer Book of a Cloud of Witnesses*. Minneapolis: Fortress Press, 1993.

Hope, Norman Victor. "Isaac Watts and His Contribution to English Hymnody." *The Papers of the Hymn Society*. New York: The Hymn Society of America, 1947.

Hopper, Vincent Foster. *Medieval Number Symbolism: Its Sources, Meaning, and Influence on Thought and Expression*. New York: Cooper Square Publishers, Inc., 1969.

[Hovda, Robert W. (Ed.).] *This Far By Faith: American Black Worship and Its African Roots*. Washington: The Liturgical Conference, 1977.

Hughes, Dom Anselm (ed.). *Earl Medieval Music up to 1300*. London: Oxford University Press, 1961.

Huglo, Michael. "Cluniac monks." *The New Grove Dictionary of Music and Musicians* London: Macmillan Publishers Limited, 1980): 4, 502–504.

———. "Odo." *The New Grove Dictionary of Music and Musicians* (London: Macmillan Publishers Limited, 1980): 13, 503.

Hultgren, Arland J. "Liturgy and Literature: The Liturgical Factor in Matthew's Literary and Communicative Art." *Texts and Contexts: Biblical Essays in Their Textual and Situational Contexts: Essays in Honor of Lars Hartman*. Ed. Tord Fornberg and David Hellholm (Oslo: Scandinavian University Press, 1995): 659–673.

Hume, Paul David. *Catholic Church Music*. New York: Dodd, Mead & Company, 1956.

Hunter, James Davison. *Culture Wars: The Struggle to Define America*. New York: BasicBooks, 1991.

Hustad, Donald P. *Jubilate! Church Music in the Evangelical Tradition*. Carol Stream: Hope Publishing Company, 1981.

———. *Jubilate II: Church Music in Worship and Renewal*. Carol Stream: Hope Publishing Company, 1993.

Hymnal for Young Christians. Chicago: Friends of the English Liturgy Church Publications, 1967.

Hymnal Noted. Part I, 1851, bound with Part II, 1854. London: Novello, Ewer and Co., 1871.

The Hymnal of the Protestant Episcopal Church in the United States of America 1940. New York: The Church Pension Fund, 1943.

Hymnal: A Worship Book Prepared by Churches in the Believers Church Tradition. Elgin: Brethren Press, 1992.

Hymns Ancient and Modern for Use in the Service of the Church. London: Novello, 1860–1861.

Hymns for Now: A Portfolio for Good, Bad, or Rotten Times. Chicago: Walther League, 1961.

Hymns of the Church of Jesus Christ of Latter Day Saints. Salt Lake City: The Church of Jesus Christ of Latter Day Saints, 1985.

Hymns on the Lord's Supper . . . With a Preface concerning the Christian Sacrament and Sacrifice, extracted from Doctor Brevint. Bristol: Farley, 1745. Republished in J. Ernest Rattenbury, *The Eucharistic Hymns of John and Charles Wesley.*

Hymns Selected and Original, for Public and Private Worship. Published by the General Synod for the Evangelical Lutheran Church. Gettysburg: General Synod of the Evangelical Lutheran Church, 1828.

Idelsohn, A. Z. *Jewish Liturgy and Its Development.* New York: Henry Holt and Company, 1932.

———. *Jewish Music in its Historical Development.* New York: Schocken Books, 1967, first published 1929.

Inge, W. R. *The Parting of the Roads: Studies in the Development of Judaism and Early Christianity.* London: Edward Arnold, 1912.

Ingle, Larry. *First Among Friends: George Fox and the Creation of Quakerism.* New York: Oxford University Press, 1994.

The Interpreter's Dictionary of the Bible. New York: Abingdon Press, 1962.

Irwin, Joyce. *Neither Voice nor Heart Alone: German Lutheran Theology of Music in the Age of the Baroque.* New York: Peter Lang, 1993.

Irwin, M. Eleanor. "Phos Hilaron: The Metamorphoses of a Greek Hymn." *The Hymn* 40:2 (April 1989): 7–12.

Jackson, Dave, and Neta Jackson. *On Fire for Christ: Stories of Anabaptist Martyrs Retold from Martyrs Mirror.* Scottdale: Herald Press, 1989.

Jackson, George Pullen. *White Spirituals in the Southern Uplands: The Story of the Fasola Folk, Their Songs, Singings, and "Buckwheat Notes."* New York: Dover Publications, Inc., 1965, republication of 1st ed., 1933.

Jackson, F. J. Foakes (ed.). *The Parting of the Roads: Studies in the Development of Judaism and Early Christianity.* London: Edward Arnold, 1912.

Jarboe, Betty M. *John and Charles Wesley: A Bibliography.* Metuchen: The American Theological Association and the Scarecrow Press, 1987.

The Journal of George Fox. Cambridge: University Press, 1952.

Johansson, Calvin M. *Discipling Music Ministry.* Peabody: Hendrickson Publishers, 1992.

———. *Music and Ministry: A Biblical Counterpoint.* Peabody: Hendrickson Publishers, 1984.

Johnson, Aubrey R. *The Cultic Prophet and Israel's Psalmody.* Cardiff: University of Wales Press, 1979.

Joncas, Jan Michael. "Forum: Continuing the Conversation: The Milwaukee Symposia for Church Composers," *Worship* 70:4 (July 1996): 328–335.

———. *From Sacred Song to Ritual Music: Twentieth-Century Understandings of Roman Catholic Worship Music.* Collegeville: The Liturgical Press, 1997.

Jones, Ivor H. "Music and Musical Instruments: Musical Instruments." *The Anchor Dictionary of the Bible* (New York: Doubleday, 1992): 4: K–N, 934–939.

Jones, Cheslyn, Geoffrey Wainwright, and Edward Yarnold, (ed.). *The Study of Liturgy*. New York: Oxford University Press, 1978.

Julian, John. *A Dictionary of Hymnology*. New York: Dover Publications, Inc., 1957, reprint of Second Revised Edition, 1907.

Katz, Jacob. *The Darker Side of Genius: Richard Wagner's Anti-Semitism*. Hanover: Brandeis University Press, 1986.

Kavanagh, Aidan. "Jewish Roots of Christian Worship." *The New Dictionary of Sacramental Worship* (Collegeville: The Liturgical Press, 1990): 618–619.

Keach, Benjamin. *An Answer to Mr. Marlowe's Appendix* (bound with *The Breach Repair'd* with separate pagination).

———. *The Breach Repair'd in God's Worship*. London, 1691.

———. *Spiritual Melody, Containing near Three Hundred Sacred Hymns*. London: John Hancock, 1691.

Keble, John. *The Christian Year: Thoughts in Verse for the Sundays and Holidays Throughout the Year*. London: Frederick and Warne and Co., [1827].

Kelly, Thomas R. *The Gathered Meeting*. Philadelphia: The Tract Association of Friends, n. d.

Kleinig, John W. *The Lord's Song: The Basis, Function and Significance of Choral Music in Chronicles*. Sheffield: JSOT Press, 1993.

Kraus, Hans-Joachim. *Theology of the Psalms*. Minneapolis: Augsburg Publishing House, 1986.

Krauss, Elmer F. "Psalmody." *Essays on Church Music*, Series I (n. p.: New York and Buffalo, 1898, 1898): 71–79.

Krehbiel, Henry Edward. *Afro-American Folksongs: A Study in Racial and National Music*. New York: G. Schirmer, 1914.

Lamb, John Alexander. *The Psalms in Christian Worship*. London: The Faith Press, 1962.

Lang, Paul Henry. *Music in Western Civilization*. New York: W. W. Norton & Company, 1941.

Laster, James. *Catalogue of Choral Music Arranged in Biblical Order*. Metuchen: The Scarecrow Press, 1983.

Lathrop, Gordon (ed.). *Open Questions in Worship*. Minneapolis: Augsburg Fortress, 1994).

Lawlor, Robert. "Geometry at the Service of Prayer: Reflections on Cistercian Mystic Architecture," *Parabola* 3:1 (1978): 12–19.

Lawrence, Joy E., and John A. Ferguson. *A Musician's Guide to Church Music*. New York: The Pilgrim Press, 1981.

[Lawson, Mary Sackville] (ed.)]. *Collected Hymns[,] Sequences[,] and Carols of John Mason Neale*. London: Hodder and Stoughton, 1914.

———. *Letters of John Mason Neale*. London: Longmans, Green, and Co., 1910.

Leaver, Robin. "British Hymnody from the Sixteenth Through the Eighteenth Centuries," *The Hymnal 1982 Companion* (New York: The Church Hymnal Corporation, 1990): I, 365–392.

———. *Catherine Winkworth: The Influence of Her Translations on English Hymnody*. St. Louis: Concordia Publishing House, 1978.

———. "English Metrical Psalmody," *The Hymnal 1982 Companion* (New York: The Church Hymnal Corporation, 1990): I, 321–348.

———, (ed.). *J. S. Bach and Scripture: Glosses from the Calov Bible Commentary*. St. Louis: Concordia Publishing House, 1985.

Leupold, Ulrich S., ed. *Luther's Works*, Volume 53, Liturgy and Hymns. Philadelphia: Fortress Press, 1965.

———. "Luther's Musical Education and Activities" *Lutheran Church Quarterly* XII (1939): 423–428.

Levy, Kenneth. "Byzantine rite, music of the." *The New Grove Dictionary of Music and Musicians* (London: Macmillan Publishers Limited, 1980): 3, 553–566.

Levy, Kenneth, and John A. Emerson. "Plainchant." *The New Grove Dictionary of Music and Musicians* London: Macmillan Publishers Limited, 1980): 14, 800–844.

Lewis, A. J. *Zinzendorf the Ecumenical Pioneer: A Study in the Moravian Contribution to Christian Mission and Unity*. Philadelphia: The Westminster Press, 1962.

Lewis, C. S. *Reflections on the Psalms*. New York: Harcourt, Brace and Company, 1958.

The Liber Usualis with Introduction and Rubrics in English. The Benedictines of Solesmes (ed.). Tournai: Desclee Company, 1958.

The Library of Christian Classics, Volume I, "Early Christian Fathers." Ed. Cyril C. Richardson. Philadelphia: The Westminster Press, 1953.

Liemohn, Edwin. *The Chorale Through Four Hundred Years of Musical Development as a Congregational Hymn*. Philadelphia: Muhlenberg Press, 1953.

Liesch, Barry. *The New Worship: Straight Talk on Music and the Church*. Grand Rapids: Baker Book House, 1996.

Lloyd, A. L. *Folk Song in England*. New York: International Publishers, 1967.

Lockwood, Lewis. "Missa brevis." *The New Grove Dictionary of Music and Musicians* (London: Macmillan Publishers Limited, 1980): 12, 364.

Lough, A. G. *The Influence of John Mason Neale*. London: S.P.C.K., 1962.

Lovelace, Austin C. and William C. Rice. *Music and Worship in the Church*. New York: Abingdon Press, 1960.

Lovell, John, Jr. *Black Song: The Forge and the Flame, The Story of How the Afro-American Spiritual Was Hammered Out*. New York: The Macmillan Company, 1972.

Lowe, Edward. *Short Directions for the Performance of Cathedral Service*. 1661, 2d ed., 1664.

Lowens, Irving. *Music and Musicians in Early America*. New York: W. W. Norton & Company, Inc., 1964.

Luff, Alan. *Welsh Hymns and Their Tunes*. Carol Stream: Hope Publishing Company, 1990.

Lungu, N., G. Costea, and I. Croitoru. Trans. Nicholas K. Apostola. *A Guide to the Music of the Eastern Orthodox Church*. Brookline: Holy Cross Orthodox Press, 1984.

Lutheran Book of Worship. Minneapolis: Augsburg Publishing House, 1978.

Luther, Martin. "Preface to the Psalter." *Luther's Works*, Volume 35. Philadelphia: Muhlenberg Press, 1960.

Luther's Works. Philadelphia: Muhlenberg Press, 1960ff.

Lyon, James. *Urania*. Philadelphia, 1761.

Machlis, Joseph. *The Enjoyment of Music*. Fourth Edition. New York: W. W. Norton & Company, Inc., 1977.

Maertens, Thierry. Trans. Kathryn Sullivan. *A Feast in Honor of Yahweh*. Notre Dame: Fides Publishers, Inc.

Marissen, Michael. *The Social and Religious Designs of J. S. Bach's Brandenburg Concertos*. Princeton: Princeton University Press, 1995.

Marshall, Madeleine Forell. " 'The Holy Ghost Is Amorous in His Metaphors:' The Divine Love Hymn Reclaimed," *Cross Accent* 5A: 9 (January 1997): 17–23.

Martin, Ralph. *Worship in the Early Church*. Westwood: Fleming H. Revell Company, 1964.

Marty, Martin. *A Short History of Christianity*. New York: The World Publishing Company, 1971, first published 1959.

[Mason, Lowell (comp.)]. *The Handel and Haydn Society Collection of Church Music Being a Selection of the Most Approved Psalm and Hymn Tunes Together with Many Beautiful Extracts from the Works of Haydn, Mozart, Beethoven, and Other Eminent Modern Composers. Never Before Published in This Country: The Whole Harmonized for Three and Four Voices, with a Figured Base for the Organ or Piano Forte Calculated for Public Worship or Private Devotion*. Boston: Richardson and Lord, 1822. Unabridged republication of the first edition, New York: Da Capo Press, 1973.

Mathesius, Johann. *Dr. Martin Luthers Leben*. St. Louis: Druckerei des Lutherischen Concordia-Verlags, 1883.

Matthews, Victor H. "Music in the Bible." *The Anchor Dictionary of the Bible* (New York: Doubleday, 1992): 4: K–N, 930–934.

Maultsby, Portia K. "Afro-American Religious Music: A Study in Diversity," *The Papers of the Hymn Society of America*, XXXV. Springfield: The Hymn Society of America, [c. 1979].

Maxwell, Jack Martin. *Worship and Reformed Theology: The Liturgical Lessons of Mercersburg*. Pittsburgh: The Pickwick Press, 1976.

Mays, James Luther. *The Lord Reigns: A Theological Handbook to the Psalms* (Louisville: Westminster John Knox Press, 1994).

———. *Psalms*. Louisville: John Knox Press, 1994.

McCann, J. Clinton, Jr. *A Theological Introduction to the Book of the Psalms: The Psalms as Torah*. Nashville: Abingdon Press, 1993.

McKay, David P., and Richard Crawford. *William Billings of Boston: Eighteenth-Century Composer*. Princeton: Princeton University Press, 1975.

McKim, LindaJo H. *The Presbyterian Hymnal Companion*. Louisville: Westminster/John Knox Press, 1993.

McKinnon, James W., and Robert Anderson. "Aulos." *The New Grove Dictionary of Musical Instruments* (New York: Macmillan Press, 1984): 1, A–F, 85–87. [Very close to McKinnon, James. "Aulos." *The New Grove Dictionary of Music and Musicians* (London: Macmillan Publishers Limited, 1980): 1, 699–702.]

McKinnon, James. "The Church Fathers and Musical Instruments." Columbia University Ph. D diss., 1965.

———. "The Meaning of the Patristic Polemic Against Musical Instruments," *Current Musicology*. 1 (1965): 69–82.

———. *Music in Early Christian Literature*. Cambridge: Cambridge University Press, 1987.

McCorkle, Donald M. "The Moravian Contributions to American Music." *Music Library Association Notes*, Second Series, XIII:4 (September 1956): 597–606.

McLynn, Neil B. *Ambrose of Milan*. Berkeley: University of California Press, 1994.

Mearns, James. *The Canticles of the Christian Church, Eastern and Western in Early and Medieval Times*. Cambridge: University Press, 1914.

Meeks, Wayne A. *The First Urban Christians: The Social World of the Apostle Paul*. New Haven: Yale University Press, 1983.

Mendelssohn, Jack. *Meet the Unitarians*. Boston: Unitarian Universalist Association, n. d.

Merton, Thomas. *Bread in the Wilderness*. Collegeville: The Liturgical Press, 1953.

Meyers, Eric M. "Synagogue." *The Anchor Dictionary of the Bible*. Ed., David Noel Freedman (New York: Doubleday, 1992): 6: Si–Z, 251–260.

Meyer, Leonard B. *Emotion and Meaning in Music*. Chicago: The University of Chicago Press, 1970; first published, 1956.

Migne, Jacques Paul (ed.). *Patrologiae cursus completus Series Graeca*. Paris, 1857ff.

———. *Patrologiae cursus completus, Series Latina*. Paris, 1841ff.

Miller, Patrick D., Jr. *Interpreting the Psalms*. Philadelphia: Fortress Press, 1986.

———. "The Psalms as Praise and Poetry." *The Hymn* 40: 4 (October 1989): 12–16.

———. *They Cried to the Lord: The Form and Theology of Biblical Prayer*. Minneapolis: Fortress Press, 1994.

Miller, Roland E. *Muslim Friends, Their Faith and Feeling, an Introduction to Islam*. St. Louis: Concordia Publishing House, 1995.

The Milwaukee Symposia for Church Composers: A Ten-Year Report. Washington: The National Association of Pastoral Musicians and Chicago: Liturgy Training Publications, 1992.

Montagu, Jeremy. "Halil." *The New Grove Dictionary of Musical Instruments* (New York: Macmillan Press, 1984): 2, G–O, 118–119.

———. "Kinnor." *The New Grove Dictionary of Musical Instruments* (New York: Macmillan Press, 1984): 2, G–O, 432–433.

———. "Ugav." *The New Grove Dictionary of Musical Instruments* (New York: Macmillan Press, 1984): 3, P–Z, 694–695.

Moravian Book of Worship. Bethlehem: Moravian Church in America, 1995.

Morley, Thomas. *A Plain and Easy Introduction to Practicall Music*. 1597.

Morris, John G. *Fifty Years in the Lutheran Ministry*. Baltimore: James Young, 1878.

Moule, C. F. D. "Worship in the New Testament." *Ecumenical Studies in Worship* 9. Richmond: John Knox Press, 1961.

Mowinckel, Sigmund. *The Psalms in Israel's Worship*. Trans. D. R. Ap-Thomas. New York: Abingdon Press, 1962.

Music, David W. *Hymnology: A Collection of Source Readings*. Lanham: The Scarecrow Press, Inc., 1996.

Mussay, Mabel Hay Barrows (ed.). *Social Hymns of Brotherhood and Aspiration*. Boston: Universalist Publishing House, 1914.

Mussulman, Joseph A. *Dear People . . . Robert Shaw: A Bibliography*. Bloomington: Indiana University Press, 1979.

Myrdal, Gunner. *An American Dilemma*. New York: McGraw-Hill Book Company, 1964.

Myers, Kenneth A. *All God's Children and Blue Suede Shoes: Christians and Popular Culture*. Wheaton: Crossway Books, 1989.

[Neale, John Mason], "English Hymnody: Its History and Prospects," *The Christian Remembrancer* XVIII (October 1849): 335ff.

———. *Hymns for Children*. 1842.

———. *Hymns for Children, Second Series*. 1846.

———. "Hymns for Public Worship," *The Christian Remembrancer* V (January 1843): 39–52.

———. *Hymns for the Young*. 1844.

Nef, Karl. Trans. Carl F. Pfatteicher. *An Outline History of Music*. New York: Columbia University Press, 1957.

Nettl, Paul. *Luther and Music*. Trans. Frida Best and Ralph Wood. New York: Russell & Russell, 1967.

Nettleton, Asahel. *Village Hymns for Social Worship, Selected and Original, Designed as a Supplement to the Psalms and Hymns of Doctor Watts*. Hartford: Brown and Parsons, 1848, 1st ed., 1824.

Nevin, John W. *The Anxious Bench*. Chambersburg: Publication Office of the German Reformed Church, 1844.

The New Century Hymnal. Cleveland: The Pilgrim Press, 1995.

The New Dictionary of Sacramental Worship. Ed. Peter E. Fink. Collegeville: The Liturgical Press, 1990

A New Eusebius, Documents Illustrative of the History of the Church to A. D. 337. Ed. J. Stevenson. London: S.P.C.K., 1960; first published, 1957.

The New Grove Dictionary of Musical Instruments. Ed. Stanley Sadie. New
York: Macmillan Press, 1984.

The New Grove Dictionary of Music and Musicians. Ed. Stanley Sadie.
London: Macmillan Publishers Limited, 1980.

The New Oxford Book of Carols. Ed. Hugh Keyte and Andrew Parrott.
Oxford: Oxford University Press, 1992.

The New Oxford History of Music. Oxford: Oxford University Press,
1957ff.

New Songs for the Church, vols. I and II. Norfolk: Galliard, Ltd., 1969.

The New Westminster Dictionary of Liturgy and Worship. Ed. J. G. Davies.
Philadelphia: The Westminster Press, 1986.

Nichols, James Hastings. *Romanticism in American Theology: Nevin and
Schaff at Mercersburg.* Chicago: The University of Chicago Press, 1961.

Niebuhr, H. Richard. *Christ and Culture.* New York: Harper Torchbooks,
1956.

Nordin, John P. "Breaking the Hymnal Logjam: a Second Edition of the
LBW," *Lutheran Partners* 13:3 (May/June 1997): 24–30.

Norris, Christopher (ed.). *Music and the Politics of Culture.* New York: St.
Martin's Press, 1989.

Nuttall, Geoffrey F. *Richard Baxter and Philip Doddridge: A Study in a Tradition.* London: Oxford University Press, 1951.

———. *Philip Doddridge, 1702–1751, His Contribution to English Religion.* London: Independent Press Ltd., 1951.

Nygren, Anders. Trans. Philip S. Watson. *Agape and Eros.* London:
S.P.C.K., 1953.

Ochse, Orpha. *The History of the Organ in the United States.* Bloomington:
Indiana University Press, 1975.

Oesterley, W. E. O. *A Fresh Approach to the Psalms.* New York: Charles
Scribner's Sons, 1937.

———. *The Jewish Background of the Christian Liturgy.* Oxford: Clarendon Press, 1925.

———. *The Psalms in the Jewish Church.* London: Skeffington & Son, 1910.

*Olney Hymns, in Three Books. Book I. On Select Texts of Scriptures. Book
II. On Occasional Subjects. Book III. On the Progress and Changes of
the Spiritual Life.* London: W. Oliver, 1779.

The Oxford Book of Carols. Ed. Percy Dearmer, R. Vaughan Williams,
Martin Shaw. London: Oxford University Press, 1964; first published
1928.

Palisca, Claude V. (ed.). *Norton Anthology of Western Music*; 2d ed., vol.
I. New York: W. W. Norton & Company, 1988.

Parrish, Carl. *A Treasury of Early Music.* New York: W. W. Norton &
Company, 1958.

Parrish, Carl, and John F. Ohl. *Masterpieces of Music Before 1750.* New
York: W. W. Norton & Company, 1951.

Pass, David B. *Music and the Church: A Theology of Church Music.*
Nashville: Broadman Press, 1989.

Patterson, Beverly Bush. *The Sound of the Dove: Singing in Appalachian Primitive Baptist Churches*. Urbana: University of Illinois Press, 1995.

Patterson, Daniel W. *The Shaker Spiritual*. Princeton: Princeton University Press, 1979.

Patrick, Millar. Rev. James Rawlings Sydnor. *The Story of the Church's Song*. Richmond: John Knox Press, 1962.

Payne, Wardell J. (Ed). *Directory of African American Religious Bodies: A Compendium by the Howard University School of Divinity*. Washington: Howard University Press, 1991.

Peel, Albert and Leland H. Carlson (ed.). *The Writings of Robert Harrison and Robert Browne*. London: George Allen and Unwin Ltd, 1953.

Pelikan, Jaroslav. *Bach Among the Theologians*. Philadelphia: Fortress Press, 1986.

———. *The Christian Tradition: A History of the Development of Doctrine*. Chicago: The University of Chicago Press, 1971.

———. *Imago Dei: The Byzantine Apologia for Icons*. Princeton: Princeton University Press, 1990.

Pemberton, Carol A. *Lowell Mason: His Life and Work*. Ann Arbor: U. M. I. Research Press, 1985.

Peters, Erskine (ed.). *Lyrics of the Afro-American Spiritual*. Westport: Greenwood Press, 1993.

Peters, Ted (ed.). "Worship Wars," *Dialogue* 33:3 (Summer 1994).

Pfatteicher, Philip H., and Carlos Messerli. (ed.). *Manual on the Liturgy, Lutheran Book of Worship*. Minneapolis: Augsburg Publishing House, 1979.

Phillips, C. Henry. *The Singing Church: An Outline History of the Music Sung by Choir and People*. London: Faber and Faber Ltd, 1945.

Pipkin, H. Wayne, and John H. Yoder, (trans.). *Balthasar Hubmaier; Theologian of Anabaptism*. Scottdale: Herald Press, 1989.

Plass, Ewald M. *What Luther Says*. St. Louis: Concordia Publishing House, 1959.

Playford, John. *Introduction to the Skill of Music*. 1673.

Pleasants, Henry. *The Agony of Modern Music*. New York: Simon and Schuster, 1955.

Polack, W. G. *The Handbook to the Lutheran Hymnal*. St. Louis: Concordia Publishing House, 1958.

Polman, Bert F. "Church Music and Liturgy in the Christian Reformed Church of North America." University of Minnesota diss., 1981.

Praetorius, Michael. *Syntagma Musicum*. Wittebergae, 1615.

Pratt, Waldo Selden. *The Music of the French Psalter of 1562: A Historical Survey and Analysis, with the Music in Modern Notation*. New York: Columbia University Press, 1939.

Praying Together: The English Language Consultation. Abingdon Press, 1988.

Preus, J. C. K. *The History of the Choral Union of the Evangelical Lutheran Church, 1847–1960*. Minneapolis: Augsburg Publishing House, 1960.

The Presbyterian Hymnal: Hymns, Psalms, and Spiritual Songs. Louisville: Westminster/John Knox Press, 1990.

Prothero, Rowland E. *The Psalms in Human Life.* New York: E. P. Dutton and Company, 1941.

Psalms and Hymns for the Use of the German Reformed Church in the United States of America. Chambersburg: Publication Office of the German Reformed Church, 1834.

Quasten, Johannes. *Music and Worship in Pagan and Christian Antiquity.* Trans. Boniface Ramsey. Washington: National Association of Pastoral Musicians, 1973.

Raboteau, Albert J. *A Fire in the Bones: Reflections on African-American Religious History.* Boston: Beacon Press, 1995.

———. *Slave Religion: The 'Invisible Institution' in the Antebellum South* (New York: Oxford University Press, 1978.

Rainbow, Bernarr. *The Choral Revival in the Anglican Church (1839–1872).* London: Barrie & Jenkins, 1970.

Ramshaw, Gail. *God Beyond Gender: Feminist Christian God-Language.* Minneapolis: Fortress Press, 1995.

Rankin, Susan, and David Hiley. Ed. *Music in the Medieval English Liturgy: Plainsong & Medieval Music Society Centennial Essays.* Oxford: Clarendon Press, 1993.

Rattenbury, J. Ernest. *The Eucharistic Hymns of John and Charles Wesley.* London: The Epworth Press, 1948.

———. *The Evangelical Doctrines of Charles Wesley's Hymns.* London: The Epworth Press, 1941.

Rauschenbusch, Walter, and Ira D. Sankey (ed.). *Evangeliums-Lieder, Gospel Hymns mit deutschen Kernliedern.* New York: The Biglow & Main Co., 1890.

Rauschenbusch, Walter, and Ira D. Sankey. (ed.). *Evangeliums-Lieder 1 und 2, (Gospel Hymns) mit deutschen Kernliedern.* New York: The Biglow & Main Co., 1897.

Reckow, Fritz, and Rudolf Flotzinger. "Organum." *The New Grove Dictionary of Music and Musicians* (London: Macmillan Publishers Limited, 1980): 13, 796–808.

Reese, Gustave. *Music in the Middle Ages.* New York: W. W. Norton & Company, 1940.

———. *Music in the Renaissance,* rev. ed. New York: W. W. Norton & Company, Inc., 1959.

Rehm, Merlin D. "Levites and Priests." *The Anchor Dictionary of the Bible* (New York: Doubleday, 1992): 4, K–N, 297–310.

Rejoice in the Lord: A Hymn Companion to the Scriptures. Grand Rapids: Wm. B. Eerdmans Publishing Company, 1985.

Ressler, Martin E. *An Annotated Bibliography of Mennonite Hymnals and Songbooks, 1742–1986.* Gordonville: PA Print Shop, 1987.

Reynolds, William J. *Companion to Baptist Hymnal.* Nashville: Broadman Press, 1976.

———. *Hymns of Our Faith*. Nashville: Broadman Press, 1964.

———, and Price, Milburn. *A Survey of Christian Hymnody*. Carol Stream: Hope Publishing Company, 1987.

Rice, William C. *A Concise History of Church Music*. Nashville: Abingdon Press, 1964.

Robinson, Hastings (ed.). *The Zurich Letters*. Cambridge: The University Press, 1842.

Rogal, Samuel J. *Sisters of Sacred Song: A Selected Listing of Women Hymnodists in Great Britain and America*. New York: Garland Publishing Company, 1981.

Rosewall, Richard Byron. "Singing Schools of Pennsylvania." University of Minnesota Ph.D. diss., 1969.

Rothmüller, Aron Marko. *The Music of the Jews: An Historical Appreciation*. New York: The Beechhurst Press, 1954.

Rous, Francis. *The Psalmes of David in English Meter*. 1643; 1st ed., 1641; rev. ed., 1646.

Routley, Erik. *The Church and Music: An Enquiry in the History, the Nature, and the Scope of Christian Judgment on Music*. London: Gerald Duckworth & Co. Ltd., 1950.

———. *Church Music and the Christian Faith*. Carol Stream: Agape, 1978.

———. *The English Carol*. New York: Oxford University Press, 1959.

———. *Hymns and Human Life*. Grand Rapids: Wm. B. Eerdmans Publishing Company, 1959.

———. *Isaac Watts*. London: Independent Press, 1961.

———. *The Music of Christian Hymns*. Chicago: GIA. Publications, 1981.

———. *The Musical Wesleys*. London: Herbert Jenkins, 1968.

———. *A Panorama of Christian Hymnody*. Collegeville: The Liturgical Press, 1979.

——— with Lionel Dakers. *A Short History of English Church Music*. Carol Stream: Hope Publishing Company, 1997

Rowntree, John S. *The Society of Friends: Its Faith and Practice*. London: Headley Brothers, 1901.

Rupp, Gordon. *Patterns of Reformation*. Philadelphia: Fortress Press, 1969.

Ruth, Lester. "Lex Agendi, Lex Orandi: Toward an Understanding of Seeker Services as a New Kind of Liturgy," *Worship* 71:5 (September 1996): 386–405.

Sachs, Curt. *The History of Musical Instruments*. New York: W. W. Norton & Company, Inc., 1940.

———. *Our Musical Heritage: A Short History of Music*. Englewood Cliffs: Prentice-Hall, 1955.

———. *The Rise of Music in the Ancient World East and West*. New York: W. W. Norton & Company, Inc., 1943.

———. *Rhythm and Tempo: A Study in Music History*. New York: W. W. Norton & Company, Inc., 1953.

Saliers, Don E. "Contemporary/Traditional: The Dilemma of the Church Today," *The Covenant Companion*, LXXXV, 1 (January 1996): 18–20;

————. *Worship and Spirituality.* Philadelphia: The Westminster Press, 1984.

————. *Worship Come to Its Senses.* Nashville: Abingdon Press, 1996.

Salitan, Lucille, and Perera, Eve Lewis (ed.). *Virtuous Lives: Four Quaker Sisters Remember Family Life, Abolitionism, and Women's Suffrage.* New York: Continuum, 1994.

Sankey, Ira, James McGranahan, George C. Stebbins, and Philip P. Bliss. *Gospel Hymns Nos. 1 to 6 Complete.* New York: Da Capo Press, 1972, unabridged reproduction of the "Excelsior Edition," 1895.

Savas, Savas I. *Byzantine Music in Theory and Practice.* Roslindale: Hercules Press, 1965.

Schaff, Philip. *Saint Chrysostom and Saint Augustin.* New York: Whittaker, 1891.

Schalk, Carl. *God's Song in a New Land: Lutheran Hymnals in America.* St. Louis: Concordia Publishing House, 1995.

————. "German Church Song." *The Hymnal 1982 Companion* (New York: The Church Hymnal Corporation, 1990): I, 288–309.

———— (ed.). *Key Words in Church Music.* St. Louis: Concordia Publishing House, 1978.

————. *Luther on Music, Paradigms of Praise.* St. Louis: Concordia Publishing House, 1988.

————. *The Roots of Hymnody in the Lutheran Church—Missouri Synod.* St. Louis: Concordia Publishing House, 1965.

————. *Source Documents in American Lutheran Hymnody.* St. Louis: Concordia Publishing House, 1996.

Schattauer, Thomas H. "Announcement, Confession, and Lord's Supper in the Pastoral-Liturgical Work of Wilhelm Löhe: A Study of Worship and Church Life in the Lutheran Parish at Neuendettelsau, Bavaria." Notre Dame University Ph.D. diss., 1990.

————. "A Clamor for the Contemporary: The Present Challenge for Baptismal Identity and Liturgical Tradition in American Culture," *Cross Accent* 6 (July 1995): 3–11.

Schisler, Charles Harvey. "A History of Westminster Choir College." Indian University Ph.D. diss., 1976.

Schleiermacher, Friedrich. *The Christian Faith.* Ed. H. R. Mackintosh and J. S. Stewart. New York: Harper & Row, Publishers, 1963; English trans. of the 2d German ed., 1830. Two vol.

————. *On Religion: Speeches to Its Cultured Despisers.* Trans. John Oman. New York: Harper & Brothers, 1958, trans. from the 3RD German ed., 1821; 1st ed., 1799.

Scholes, Percy A. *The Mirror of Music.* Freeport: Books for Libraries Press, 1970.

————. *The Puritans and Music.* New York: Russell & Russell, Inc., 1962.

Schreiner, Susan E. *The Theater of His Glory: Nature and the Natural Order in the Thought of John Calvin.* Durham: The Labyrinth Press, 1991.

Schultze, Quentin, et al. *Dancing in the Dark: Youth, Popular Culture, and the Electronic Media.* Grand Rapids: William B. Eerdmans Publishing Company, 1991.

Schwartz, Elliot and Barney Childs. (ed.). *Contemporary Composers on Contemporary Music*. New York: Holt, Rinehart and Winston, 1967.

Schweitzer, Albert. *J. S. Bach*. Trans. Ernest Newman. Boston: Bruce Humphries Publishers, 1962; first pub., 1905. Two vol.

A Select Library of the Nicene and Post-Nicene Fathers of the Christian Church. Ed. Philip Schaff. Second Series, 1890ff. Republished Grand Rapids: Wm. B. Eerdmans Publishing Company, 1952–1956.

Sendrey, Alfred. *Music in Ancient Israel*. New York: Philosophical Library, 1969.

Sendrey, Alfred and Mildred Norton. *David's Harp: The Story of Music in Biblical Times*. New York: The New American Library of World Literature, Inc., 1964.

Senn, Frank C. *Christian Liturgy: Catholic and Evangelical*. Minneapolis: Fortress Press, 1997.

———. *Christian Worship in Its Cultural Setting*. Philadelphia: Fortress Press, 1983.

———. "The Dialogue Between Liturgy and Music." *The Hymn* 38:2 (April 1987): 25–29.

———. " 'Worship Alive': An Analysis and Critique of 'Alternative Worship Services,' " *Worship* 69:3 (May 1995): 194–224.

Sharp, Cecil J. Rev. Karpeles, Maud. *English Folk Song: Some Conclusions*. London: Mercury Books, 1965.

Shepherd, Massey H., Jr. *The Psalms in Christian Worship*. Minneapolis: Augsburg Publishing House, 1976.

Shorney, George. *The Hymnal Explosion in North America*. Carol Stream: Hope Publishing Company, 1988.

Shriver, George. *Philip Schaff: Christian Scholar and Ecumenical Prophet*. Macon: Mercer University Press, 1987.

Sizer, Sandra S. *Gospel Hymns and Social Religion: The Rhetoric of Nineteenth-Century Revivalism*. Philadelphia: Temple University Press, 1978.

Skeris, Robert A. *Chroma Theou: On the Origins and Theological Interpretation of the Musical Imagery Used by the Ecclesiastical Writers of the First Three Centuries, with Special Reference to the Image of Orpheus*. Altötting: Alfred Coppenrath, 1976.

——— (ed.). *Crux et Cithara: Selected Essays on Liturgy and Sacred Music Translated and Edited on the Occasion of the Seventieth Birthday of Johannes Overath*. Altötting: Alfred Coppenrath, 1983.

——— (ed.). *Cum Angelis Canere: Essays on Sacred Music and Pastoral Liturgy in Honour of Richard J. Schuler*. St. Paul: Catholic Church Music Associates, 1990.

——— (ed.). *Divini Cultus Studium: Studies in the Theology of Worship and of its Music*. Altötting: Alfred Coppenrath, 1990.

Smallman, Basil. *The Background of Passion Music: J. S. Bach and his Predecessors*. New York: Dover Publications, Inc., 1970.

Smith, Norman E. "Organum and Discant: bibliography." *The New Grove Dictionary of Music and Musicians* (London: Macmillan Publishers Limited, 1980): 13, 808–819.

Smith, R. Morris. "Church Music as a Part of Our Educational System." *Essays in Church Music*, Series II (n. p.: New York and Buffalo, 1900, 1901): 29–42.

The Snowbird Statement on Catholic Liturgical Music. Salt Lake City: The Madeleine Institute, 1995.

Soehngen, Oskar. "Fundamental Considerations for a Theology of Music," *The Musical Heritage of the Church*, ed. Theodore Hoelty-Nickel, VI (St. Louis: Concordia Publishing House, 1963): 7–16.

Songs for Today. Ed. Ewald Bash and John Ylvisaker. Minneapolis: American Lutheran Church, 1964.

Southern, Eileen. "Afro-American Music," *The New Grove Dictionary of American Music* (London: Macmillan Press Limited, 1986): I, 13–21.

———. *The Music of Black Americans: A History,* 2d. ed. New York: W. W. Norton & Company, 1983.

Spencer, Jon Michael. *Black Hymnody: A Hymnological History of the African-American Church*. Knoxville: The University of Tennessee Press, 1992.

———. *Protest and Praise: Sacred Music of Black Religion*. Minneapolis: Fortress Press, 1990.

———. *Theological Music: Introduction to Theomusicology*. New York: Greenwood Press, 1991.

——— (ed.). *The Theology of American Popular Music, A Special Issue of Black Sacred Music: A Journal of Theomusicology* 3:2 (Fall 1989).

Spener, Philip Jacob. Trans., ed., and intro., Theodore Tappert. *Pia Desideria*. Philadelphia: Fortress Press, 1964.

Spitta, Philipp. *Johann Sebastian Bach: His Work and Influence on the Music of Germany, 1685–1750*. Trans. Clara Bell and J. A. Fuller-Maitland. New York: Dover Publications, Inc., 1951. Three vol. bound as two.

St. Athanasius on the Psalms. A religious of C.S.M.V. London: A. R. Mowbray & Co., Limited, 1949.

Starnhold, T. and I. Hopkins. *The Whole Book of Psalms, collected into English Metre* (1562).

Stauffer, S. Anita (ed.). *Worship and Culture in Dialogue*. Geneva: Lutheran World Federation, 1994.

Steiner, Ruth. "Trope." *The New Grove Dictionary of Music and Musicians* (London: Macmillan Publishers Limited, 1980): 19, 172–187.

Stevens, John (ed.). "Medieval Carols." *Musica Britannica: A National Collection of Music, IV*. London: Stainer and Bell Ltd, 1970, rev. 2d. ed.

Stevens, John, and Dennis Libby. "Carol." *The New Grove Dictionary of Music and Musicians* (London: Macmillan Publishers Limited, 1980): 3, 802–813.

Stevenson, Robert M. *Patterns of Protestant Church Music*. Durham: Duke University Press, 1953.

Stiller, Günther. *Johann Sebastian Bach and Liturgical Life in Leipzig*. Trans. Herbert J. A. Bouman, Daniel F. Poellot, Hilton C. Oswald. Ed. Robin A. Leaver. St. Louis: Concordia Publishing House, 1984; first pub., 1970.

Stowe, Harriet Beecher. *Poganuc People: Their Loves and Lives*. New York: AMS Press, 1967.

Strunk, Oliver. *Essays on Music in the Byzantine World*. New York: W. W. Norton & Company, Inc., 1977.

———. *Essays on Music in the Western World*. New York: W. W. Norton & Company, 1974.

Strunk, Oliver. *Source Readings in Music History: From Classical Antiquity through the Romantic Era*. New York: W. W. Norton & Company, Inc., 1950.

The Study of Liturgy. Ed. Cheslyn Jones, Geoffrey Wainwright, and Edward Yarnold. New York: Oxford University Press, 1978.

Stulken, Marilyn Kay. *Hymnal Companion to the Lutheran Book of Worship*. Philadelphia: Fortress Press, 1981.

Sutton, Katherine. *Christian Womans [sic] Experiences of the glorious working of Gods [sic] free grace*. Rotterdam: Henry Goddaeus, 1663.

Sweet, William Warren. *The Story of Religion in America*. New York: Harper & Brothers, Publishers, 1950.

Symmes, Thomas. *The Reasonableness of Regular Singing: or Singing by Note*. 1720.

Tate, N. and N. Brady. *A New Version of the Psalms of David, Fitted to the Tunes used in Churches* (1696).

Temperley, Nicholas. *The Music of the English Parish Church*. Two Volumes. Cambridge: Cambridge University Press, 1979.

———. "The Tunes of Congregational Song in Britain from the Reformation to 1750," *The Hymnal 1982 Companion* (New York: The Church Hymnal Corporation, 1990): I, 349–364.

Terrien, Samuel. *The Magnificat: Musicians as Biblical Interpreters*. New York: Paulist Press, 1995.

———. *The Psalms and Their Meaning for Today*. Indianapolis: The Bobbs-Merrill Company, Inc., 1952.

Terry, Richard R. (ed.). *A Medieval Carol Book*. London: Burns Oates & Washbourne Ltd., 1931.

Tertullian. *Apology, De Spectaculis*. Trans. T. R. Glover. New York: G. P. Putnam's Sons, 1931.

Thompson, Bard. *A Bibliography of Christian Worship*. Metuchen: The American Theological Library, 1989.

———. "The Catechism and the Mercersburg Theology." *Essays on the Heidelberg Catechism* (Philadelphia: United Church Press, 1963): 53–74.

———. *Liturgies of the Western Church*. Cleveland: Meridian Books, 1961.

Thompson, E. P. *The Making of the English Working Class*. New York: Vintage Books, 1963.

Thompson, Ernest Trice. *Presbyterians in the South, Volume One: 1607–1861*. Richmond: John Knox Press, 1963.

Thurman, Howard. *Deep River and the Negro Spiritual Speaks of Life and Death*. Richmond: Friends United Press, 1975.

Tillyard. H. J. W. *Byzantine Music and Hymnography*. Charing Cross: The Faith Press, 1923.

Towle, Eleanor A. *John Mason Neale, D.D.: A Memoir*. London: Longmans, Green, and Co., 1906.

Trueblood, Elton. *The People Called Quakers*. New York: Harper & Row, 1966.

———. *Robert Barclay*. New York: Harper & Row, 1968.

Tufts, [John]. *An Introduction to the Singing of Psalm-Tunes In a Plain and Easy Method. With a Collection of Tunes in Three Parts*, 5th ed. Boston: Samuel Gerrish, 1726. Reprinted with an Introduction by Irving Lowens, Philadelphia: Albert Saifer, 1954.

Twitchell, James B. *Carnival Culture: The Trashing of Taste in America*. New York: Columbia University Press, 1992.

The United Methodist Hymnal. Nashville: The United Methodist Publishing House, 1989.

Velimirovic, Milos (ed.). *Studies in Eastern Chant*. New York: Oxford University Press, 1966.

von Ende, Richard Chaffey. *Church Music: An International Biography*. Metuchen: The Scarecrow Press, 1980.

von Rad, Gerhard. Trans. D. M. G. Stalker. *Old Testament Theology*, vol. I. New York: Harper & Brothers, 1962.

Wainwright, Geoffrey. *Worship with One Accord: Where Liturgy & Ecumenism Embrace*. New York: Oxford University Press, 1997.

Walhout, Donald. "Augustine on the Transcendent in Music" *Philosophy and Theology* 3:3 (Spring 1989): 283–292.

Walker, William. *The Southern Harmony & Musical Companion; Containing a Choice Collection of Tunes, Hymns, Psalms, Odes, and Anthems; Selected from the Most Eminent Authors in the United States: together with Nearly One Hundred New Tunes, Which Have Never Before Been Published; Suited to Most of the Metres Contained in Watts's Hymns and Psalms, Mercer's Cluster, Dossey's Choice, Dover Selection, Methodist Hymn Book, and Baptist Harmony; and Well Adapted to Christian Churches of Every Denomination, Singing Schools, and Private Societies: Also, An Easy Introduction to the Grounds of Music, the Rudiments of Music, and Plain Rules for Beginners*. Philadelphia: E. W. Miller, [1854]; 1st ed., 1835. Reprinted, Glenn C. Wilcox, ed. Berea: The University of Kentucky Press, 1987.

Walker, Wyatt Tee. *"Somebody's Calling My Name," Black Sacred Music and Social Change*. Valley Forge: Judson Press, 1992; 1st printing, 1979.

Walter Thomas. *The Grounds and Rules of Music Explained: Or, An Introduction to the Art of Singing by Note. Fitted to the Meanest Capacities*. Boston: Benjamin Mecom, [1760]; 1st ed., 1721.

Watley, William D. *Singing the Lord's Song in a Strange Land: The African American Churches and Ecumenism*. Geneva: WCC Publications, 1993.

Webber, Robert E. (ed.). *The Complete Library of Christian Worship, Volume 3, The Renewal of Sunday Worship*. Nashville: Star Song Publishing Group, 1993.

Weber, W. A. "The Hymnody of the Dutch Reformed Church in America, 1628–1953," *The Hymn* 26: 2 (April 1975): 57–60.

Weinlick, John R. *Count Zinzendorf*. New York: Abingdon Press, 1956.

Weiser, Artur. *The Psalms: A Commentary*. Philadelphia: The Westminster Press, 1962.

Wellesz, Egon. *Eastern Elements in Western Chant: Studies in the Early History of Ecclesiastical Music*. Oxford: The University Press, 1947.

———. *A History of Byzantine Music and Hymnography*. Oxford: The Clarendon Press, 1961.

Wentz, Richard E. *John Williamson Nevin: American Theologian*. New York: Oxford University Press, 1997.

Werner, Eric. "Music," *The Interpreter's Dictionary of the Bible* (New York: Abingdon Press, 1962): K–Q, 457–469.

———. "Musical Instruments." *The Interpreter's Dictionary of the Bible* (New York: Abingdon Press, 1962): K–N, 469–476.

———. *The Sacred Bridge: The Interdependence of Liturgy and Music in Synagogue and Church during the First Millennium*. New York: Columbia University Press, 1959.

———. *The Sacred Bridge: The Interdependence of Liturgy and Music in Synagogue and Church during the First Millennium, Volume II*. New York: KTAV Publishing House, Inc., 1984.

———, and Gerson-Kiwi. "Jewish Music." *The New Grove Dictionary of Music and Musicians* (London: Macmillan Publishers Limited, 1980): 9, 614–645.

[Wesley, John]. *A Collection of Psalms and Hymns*. Charles-Town: Lewis Timothy, 1737. Reprinted Nashville: The United Methodist Publishing House, 1988.

———. *A Collection of Psalms and Hymns*. London: Strahan, 1741.

———. *A COLLECTION of TUNES Set to MUSIC, As they are commonly SUNG at the FOUNDERY*. London: A. Person, 1742. Reprinted with an Introduction and Notes on the Tunes by Bryan F. Spinney, 1981, n. p.

———. *Sacred Harmony: or a choice Collection of Psalms and Hymns set to Music in two or three parts for the Voice, Harpsichord and Organ*. London: Bennett, 1780.

———. *Select Hymns: with Tunes Annext; Designed chiefly for the Use of the People called Methodists*. London: n. p., 1761. The *Tunes Annext* had a separate title page: *Sacred Melody: or a choice Collection of Psalm and Hymn Tunes*.

———. "The Preface," *A Collection of Hymns for the Use of People Called Methodists*. London: J. Paramore, 1780. In *The Works of John Wesley*, vol. 7, pp. 73–75.

Westermann, Klaus. *Praise and Lament in the Psalms*. Trans. Keith R. Crim and Richard N. Soulen. Atlanta: John Knox Press, 1981.

Westermeyer, Paul. "Beyond 'Alternative' and 'Traditional' Worship" *The Christian Century* 109:10 (March 18–25, 1992): 300–302.

————. "Chant, Bach, and Popular Culture," *The American Organist* 27:11 (November 1993): 34–39.

————. "Church Music at the End of the Nineteenth Century." *Lutheran Quarterly* VIII:1 (Spring 1994): 29–51.

————. "Church Music at the End of the Twentieth Century," *Lutheran Quarterly* VIII:2 (Summer 1994): 197–211.

————. *The Church Musician*, rev. ed. Minneapolis: Augsburg Fortress, 1997.

————. "The Future of Congregational Song," *The Hymn* 46:1 (January 1995): 4–9.

————. "How Shall We Worship?" *Reformed Liturgy and Music* XXXI: 1 (1997): 3–10.

————. "The Hymnal Noted: Theological and Musical Intersections." *Church Music* 73:2: 1–9.

————. "Hymnody in the United States from the Civil War to World War I (1860–1916)." *The Hymnal 1982 Companion.* Raymond F. Glover (ed.). New York: Church Hymnal Corporation, 1990, I, pp. 447–473.

————. *Let Justice Sing: Hymnody and Justice.* Collegeville: The Liturgical Press, 1998.

————. "The Present State of Church Music." *Word and World* XII:3 (Summer 1992): 214–220.

————. "Religious Music and Hymnody." *Encyclopedia of the American Religious Experience.* Charles H. Lippy and Peter W. Williams (ed.). New York: Charles Scribner's Sons, 1988, III, pp. 1285–1305.

————. "Theology and Music in the Context of Popular Culture." *The American Organist* 28:11 (November 1994): 30–36.

————. "To Be Human Is to Sing." *The Luther Northwestern Story* (Winter 1990): 4–8.

————. "Tradition, Liturgy, and the Visitor," *Word and World* XIII:1 (Winter 1993): 76–84.

————. "Twentieth Century American Hymnody and Church Music." *New Dimensions in American Religious History: Essays in Honor of Martin E. Marty.* Jay P. Dolan and James P. Wind (ed.). Grand Rapids: Wm. B. Eerdmans Publishing Company, 1993, pp. 175–207.

————. "What Shall We Sing in a Foreign land? Theology and Cultic Song in the German Reformed and Lutheran Churches of Pennsylvania, 1830–1900." University of Chicago, Ph. D. diss., 1978.

————. *With Tongues of Fire: Profiles in 20th-Century Hymn Writing.* St. Louis: Concordia Publishing House, 1995.

Wetzel, Richard D. *Frontier Musicians on the Connoquenessing, Wabash, and Ohio: A History of the Music and Musicians of George Rapp's Harmony Society (1805–1906).* Athens: Ohio University Press, 1976.

Whitaker, E. C. "Bidding Prayer." *The New Westminster Dictionary of Liturgy and Worship*, ed. J. G. Davies (Philadelphia: The Westminster Press, 1986): 91–92.

White B. F., and King, E. J. *The Sacred Harp, New And Much Improved and Enlarged Edition. A Collection of Psalm and Hymn Tunes, Odes,*

Anthems, Selected from the Most Eminent Authors: Together with Nearly One Hundred Pieces Never Before Published; Suited to Most Meters, and Well Adapted to Churches of Every Denomination, Singing Schools, and Private Societies (Philadelphia: S. C. Collins, 1860, 1st ed., 1844). Unabridged republication of an 1860 imprint of the third edition of 1859. George Pullen Jackson, ed., with Introduction. Nashville: Broadman Press, 1968.

White, James, Intro. *The Sunday Service of the Methodists in North America.* The United Methodist Publishing House, 1984.

White, R. E. O. *A Christian Handbook to the Psalms.* Grand Rapids: Wm. B. Eerdmans Publishing Company, 1984.

Whitley, W. T. (ed.). *The Works of John Smyth.* Cambridge: University Press, 1915.

Wilhoit, Mel R. "Alexander the Great: Or, Just Plain Charlie," *The Hymn* 46:2 (April, 1995): 20–28.

The Whole Book of Psalmes Faithfully Translated into English Metre. 1640. See *The Bay Psalm Book.*

Williamson, Francis Hildt. *Ears to Hear, Tongues to Sing: Church Music as Pastoral Theology,* in progress.

———. "The Lord's Song and the Ministry of the Church." New York: Union Theological Seminary Th.D. Diss., 1967.

Willimon, William H. *Word, Water, Wine, and Bread.* Valley Forge: Judson Press, 1980.

Wilson-Dickson, Andrew. *The Story of Christian Music.* Minneapolis: Fortress Press, 1996. Republication of 1992 Lion Publishing imprint.

Winkworth, Catherine. *Chorale Book for England: A Complete Hymnbook for Public and Private Worship, in Accordance with the Services and Festivals of the Church of England.* London, 1863.

———. *Lyra Germanica: Hymns for the Sundays and Chief Festivals of the Christian Year. Translated from the German.* London, 1855.

———. *Lyra Germanica: Second Series. The Christian Life.* London, 1858.

Winter, Miriam Therese. *Why Sing? Toward a Theology of Catholic Church Music.* Washington: The Pastoral Press, 1984.

Witvliet, John. "Spirituality of the Psalter: Metrical Psalms in Liturgy and Life in Calvin's Geneva," to be published in the *Calvin Theological Journal.*

Wolff, Christoph, Walter Emery, Richard Jones, Eugene Helm, Ernest Warburton, Elwood S. Derr. "Bach." *The New Grove Dictionary of Music and Musicians* (London: Macmillan Publishers Limited, 1980): 774–877.

Worcester, Samuel. *The Psalms, Hymns, & Spiritual Songs of the Rev. Isaac Watts, D. D. To Which Are Added Select Hymns from Other Authors; and Directions for Musical Expression.* Boston: Samuel T. Armstrong, 1819.

The Works of the Rev. Watts, D. D. in Seven Volumes. London: Edward Baines, 1800.

The Works of John Wesley, vol. 7. Ed. Franz Hildebrandt, Oliver A. Beckerlegge, and James Dale. Oxford: Clarendon Press, 1983.

Worship Third Edition: A Hymnal and Service Book for Roman Catholics. Chicago: GIA Publications, Inc., 1986.

Wolterstorff, Nicholas. *Art in Action: Toward a Christian Aesthetic.* Grand Rapids: Wm. B. Eerdmans Publishing Company, 1980.

Wren, Brian. *Faith Looking Forward.* Carol Stream: Hope Publishing Company, 1983.

————. *What Language Shall I Borrow? God-Talk in Worship: A Male Response to Feminist Theology.* New York: Crossroad, 1989.

Wyeth, John. *Wyeth's Repository of Sacred Music Selected from the Most Eminent and Approved Authors in That Science for the Use of Christian Churches, of Every Denomination, Singing Schools & Private Societies Together with a Plain and Concise Introduction to the Grounds of Music and Rules for Learners,* 5th ed. (Harrisburg: John Wyeth, 1820). Republished New York: Da Capo Press, 1974.

————. *Wyeth's Repository of Sacred Music. Part Second—(2d Edition.) Original and Selected from the Most Eminent and Approved Authors in That Science for the Use of Christian Churches, Singing-Schools and Private Societies. Together with a Plain and Concise Introduction to the Grounds of Music, and Rules for Learners* (Harrisburgh: John Wyeth, 1820, 1st ed., 1813).

Wyeth's Repository of Sacred Music Part Second. New York: Da Capo Press, 1964.

Yrigoyen, Charles Jr., and George H. Bricker, (ed.). *Catholic and Reformed: Selected Theological Writings of John Williamson Nevin.* Pittsburgh: The Pickwick Press, 1978.

Yoder, Don. *Pennsylvania Spirituals.* Lancaster: Pennsylvania Folklife Society, 1961.

Yoder, Paul M, et al. *Four Hundred Years with the Ausbund.* Scottdale: Herald Press, 1964.

Young, Carlton R. *Music of the Heart: John and Charles Wesley on Church Music and Musicians.* Carol Stream: Hope Publishing Company, 1995.

————. "The New Century Hymnal, 1995," *The Hymn* 48:2 (April 1997): 25–38.

Young, Robert H. "The History of Baptist Hymnody in England from 1612 to 1800." Los Angeles: University of Southern California D.M.A. diss., 1959.

Zuiderfeld, Rudolf. "Some Musical Traditions in Dutch Reformed Churches in America," *The Hymn* 36:3 (July 1985): 23–25.

Zwingli, Ulrich. "Of Baptism." *The Library of Christian Classics,* XXIV. Ed. G. W. Bromiley. Philadelphia: The Westminster Press, 1953.

INDEXES

General Index

stress of, see rhythm
Weinlick, John R., 224-225
Weiser, Artur, 29
Weisse, Michael, 222-223
Well Tempered Clavier (Bach), 241
Wellesz, Egon, 60, 81
We'll Understand It Better By and
    By" (Tindley), 281
Welsh, see Wales
Welsh Hymns and Their Tunes
    (Luff), 217-220
Wentz, Richard E., 272
Wer ist wohl wie du (Francke), 228
Werner, Eric, 9, 12-14, 16-18, 21, 23,
    27, 40, 41, 42, 43, 44, 51, 67, 78, 94
WER NUR DEN LIEBEN GOTT , 212
Wesley, Charles (1707-1788), 205-
    220, 225, 231-232, 251, 253-
    254, 262, 288
Wesley, Charles (1757-1834), 205
Wesley, John (1703-1791), 205-
    220, 223, 225-226, 228-233,
    251, 253-254, 288, 315
Wesley, Samuel (1662-1735), 205
Wesley, Samuel (1691-1739), 205
Wesley, Samuel (1766-1837), 205
Wesley, Samuel Sebastian (1810-
    1876), 205
Wesley, Sarah Gwynne, See Gwynne
Wesley, Susanna Annesley (1669-
    1742), 205
Wesleyan, 274, 285, 314
West Africa, 261
West Indies, 191
Westermann, Claus, 26
Westermeyer, Paul, 12, 19, 124,
    148, 197, 203, 245, 273, 277,
    290, 302, 305-306, 317
Western churches, 24, 27, 162, 165
Western Plainchant (Hiley), xi, 42,
    93, 100, 270
Westminster Assembly, 181, 188, 190
Westminster Directory, 181-182
Westminster Choir College, 296, 299
Westminster Presbyterian Church,
    Dayton, 296
Westminster Shorter Catechism, 25
Westphalia, 176
What Language Shall I Borrow?
    (Wren), 245

What Luther Says (Plass), 143
"When I Survey the Wondrous
    Cross" (Watts), 202
Whitaker, E. C., 123
Whitby, 103
Whitby, Synod of, 103
white monks, 130
white spirituals, 282-285
*White Spirituals in the Southern
    Uplands* (Jackson), 282
White, Benjamin, 284
White, James, 207, 209, 292
White, R. E. O., 23-24
Whitefield, George, 216-218, 225,
    251-252
Whitley, W. T., 188
Why Catholics Can't Sing (Day),
    100
Why Sing? (Winter), xii
"Why should the devil have all the
    good tunes?", 288
"Wie schön leuchtet" (Nicolai),
    228
Wilcox, John C., 284, 297
Wilhoit, Mel, 269
Willan, Healey, 303
Williams, William (Pantycelyn),
    219
William Billings of Boston (McKay
    and Crawford), 142, 249, 255-
    256, 262
William III, duke of Aquitane, 130
Williams, George Walton, 210
Williams, Peter W., 245
Williams, Roger, 188
Williams, William, Pantycelyn, 219
Williamsburg, Virginia, 258
Williamson, Francis, xii, xiv, 31,
    33, 76, 99-100, 196, 215, 229,
    269, 285
Williamson, John Finley, 296-297
Willow Creek Community Church,
    South Barrington, 315-316
Wilson-Dixon, Andrew, xi
WINCHESTER NEW, 212, 228
WINCHESTER OLD, 172
wind instruments, 281, 288
WINDSOR, 247-248
Windsor, 168
Wind, James P., 245, 302

Biblical References